LILIES

Lilium cernuum

A third-generation seedling from crossing
a tetraploid form of *Lilium* 'Black Beauty'
with a tetraploid form of *L*. 'White Henryi'.
Bred by Robert Griesbach.

Lilies

A Guide for Growers and Collectors

EDWARD AUSTIN McRAE

with a foreword by
John Bryan

Timber Press
Portland, Oregon

To my children

Catherine Joy McRae & Andrew Edward McRae

Who have greatly enriched my life

All photos by author unless otherwise noted.

Mention of a trademark, proprietary product, or vendor does not constitute a guarantee or warranty of the product by the publisher or author and does not imply its approval to the exclusion of other products or vendors.

Timber Press, Inc.
The Haseltine Building
133 S.W. Second Avenue, Suite 450
Portland, Oregon 97204, U.S.A.

Printed in Hong Kong

Library of Congress Cataloging-in-Publication Data

McRae, Edward A.
    Lilies: a guide for growers and collectors/Edward Austin
McRae; with a foreword by John Bryan.
        p.   cm.
    Includes bibliographical references (p.   ) and indexes.
    ISBN 0-88192-410-5
    1. Lilies. I. Title.
SB413.L7M39 1998
635.9'343—dc21   97-22341
                                                          CIP

Contents

Foreword

I have known Eddie McRae for more than 40 years. We were students at the Royal Botanic Garden, Edinburgh, in the 1950s, and on the same team at Oregon Bulb Farms in the 1960s, and remain good friends. My children still refer to "Uncle Eddie." We frequently chat on the phone about various things, but mostly about bulbs.

Much has been achieved in the second half of the twentieth century in the world of lilies. Eddie has written an interesting and valuable chapter acknowledging those responsible for early development of lily hybrids. Compared with today's complex hybrids, the bloodlines of earlier introductions were simple—not far removed from their parents, which often were species or closely derived from them. Without this valuable pioneering work, undertaken without the techniques regarded as routine today, the present complex hybridizing programs would not be as advanced, or even possible. Those who appreciate lilies (and surely all gardeners must) are fortunate to have, in this book, a thorough account of lily hybridizing.

Eddie worked at Oregon Bulb Farms with Harold F. Comber and Earl N. Hornback in the exciting days of the 1960s and obtained a solid practical knowledge of lily hybridizing. No better teachers could be imagined. He took full advantage of the opportunity and, building on this knowledge, he has now reached far beyond the horizons, and no doubt the dreams, of these pioneers.

Few if any have a better understanding and more experience of the road hybridizers have traveled, the present status of various programs around the world, and the future developments to be expected with lilies, the aristocrats of the garden. I encouraged Eddie to write this book, and I am honored to write the foreword. Those who peruse its pages will be enriched.

Jan de Graaff brought Eddie and me to Oregon in 1961. Unfortunately Jan is not now with us; I am certain he would have been proud to have written this foreword, as would Harold or Earl. We who worked with these gentlemen owe them much, and all who enjoy lilies owe them thanks.

Today lilies are popular cut flowers, garden subjects, and pot plants. It was not always so. As sales manager for Oregon Bulb Farms in the 1960s, I met amateur and professional gardeners who were not at all familiar with lilies. The situation has changed, though, and today no garden worthy of the name is without these beauties. Gardeners do not deserve the title if they have not grown and fallen in love with these modern Aphrodites.

While the love of lilies is enduring, pitfalls can be encountered, but there will be fewer of the latter for those who read this book. Here is language at once authoritative, correct, and easy to understand. Photographic plates and paintings augment the fine color photos.

Growing lilies in the garden and commercially, pests and diseases, propagation techniques, and many other facets are discussed. All who grow or wish to grow lilies can obtain helpful information here. It is difficult to imagine any better source of information, or any set forth in a better way.

Eddie has been awarded honors for his achievements as the world's leading lily hybridizer. If lilies could talk, they would say, as I do, "Well done! You achieved that thought to be impossible: you have gilded the lily."

John E. Bryan
F. I. Hort.

Acknowledgments

I would like first to thank my good friend John E. Bryan, who encouraged me to write this book and was kind enough to contribute the foreword.

The line drawings were made by Bob Mitchell, whose professionalism and understanding are much appreciated. Many photographs are the outstanding work of Herman v. Wall, who for many years was responsible for illustrating the catalogs and brochures of Oregon Bulb Farms. The beautiful paintings that appear here were done by the noted botanical artist Mary Comber Miles.

Peter Schenk supplied much important information on the Dutch lily industry. Robyn Miller, secretary of the Australian Lilium Society, and Bill Doreen in New Zealand sent helpful descriptions of lily growing in their countries. Martin Meskers gave valuable help and advice on forcing lilies. Don Egger provided technical information on tissue culture. The botanical details in Chapter 2 are based in part on information from *Lilien* (Feldmaier and McRae 1982).

Others in the lily community who have contributed in many ways to this effort include Judith Freeman and Mary Hoffman. I especially appreciate Mary's able assistance in carefully reviewing the final manuscript. An uncounted number of other friends and associates have shared their knowledge and enthusiasm over the years.

I am deeply indebted to Jane McGary, without whose editorial assistance this book could not have been completed so quickly and professionally. Neal Maillet of Timber Press has also been very supportive.

Introduction

Lilies are native to the Northern Hemisphere, in Asia, Europe, and North America. Wild lily species grow as far north as the Arctic Circle and as far south as the Philippine Islands and southern India. The vast majority of species, however, grow in the temperate zone. This distribution of the genus *Lilium* is one reason for its great adaptability in gardens.

Another characteristic that has made lilies among the foremost garden flowers is the almost endless variety in this group of plants. Size and flower form, color and fragrance, habitat preference and season of bloom, all exhibit tremendous variation, offering some combination of these features to suit almost any garden niche.

The recorded history of lily cultivation is a long one. *Lilium candidum* (Madonna lily) of the eastern Mediterranean has been grown since the time of the Egyptian pharaohs, on whose tomb walls it is depicted flowering in pots, and is still a garden favorite today. During its long history it has also become a religious symbol; its English name reflects its association with the Virgin Mary in the art of the early Christian era. In Renaissance painting of the Annunciation, Madonna lilies, symbolizing purity, appear in vases or held in the Virgin's or the angel's hand. This beautiful plant was carried from the Near East to southern Europe, over the Alps to northern Europe, and from England and Holland to the New World. It was even used as food and medicine.

Not so widely grown, but even more cherished by early European gardeners was *Lilium chalcedonicum*. This dazzling red lily was described by John Parkinson in 1629 as "the red martagon of Constantinople." It, too, spread throughout the gardening world. On a visit of Christchurch, New Zealand, I found it growing strongly and profusely, still a delight.

The discovery of America soon led to the introduction of American plants into European gardens. The eastern American lilies *Lilium canadense* and *L. superbum* were among them. The grace and rich coloring of the nodding flowers of *L. canadense* drew much attention, and the species was well known in English and French gardens in the seventeenth century.

Asiatic lilies arrived in Europe as China and Japan were explored by the Dutch and English in the eighteenth and nineteenth centuries. *Lilium lancifolium,* tiger lily, and a few other species were grown by the early nineteenth century. The exquisite Oriental lilies, such as *L. auratum* and *L. speciosum,* arrived around 1850. At the end of the nineteenth century, the noble trumpet lilies of the Chinese mountains were brought back by intrepid plant explorers.

These early traders and explorers discovered an advanced craft of floriculture in Japan. Japanese growers had already bred the early flowering hybrids *Lilium ×elegans* and *L. ×thunbergianum,* and had apparently been growing certain hybrids since the sixteenth century. A beautiful color-illustrated eighteenth-century Japanese book, which I examined in a horticultural library in Boston, clearly shows hybrids among such species as *L. auratum, L. japonicum, L. rubellum,* and *L. speciosum.*

The earlier commercial distribution of lilies in the West was by the firm of W. A. Constable in England. Its hardcover catalogs from the years preceding World War II are still treasured by lily enthusiasts for their wealth of photographs and information. The Dutch expatriate Jan de Graaff launched lilies toward commercial acceptance in the United States in the mid-1950s.

For many decades gardeners tended to regard most lilies as difficult. This attitude may have been caused by the difficulty of shipping lily bulbs in good condition during the early days. Unlike other bulbs such as daffodils, crocuses, or tulips, lily bulbs have no protective skin, or tunic, so they are vulnerable to drying, bruising, and rooting during storage and shipment. A century ago, many species and some early hybrids were imported from Asia, spending weeks or even months in transit. It is small wonder that many of these failed to grow. Today, however, gardeners can obtain bulbs that have been stored under controlled conditions and shipped rapidly, protected by careful packing and modern materials to prevent dehydration and bruising.

This book describes the wild lily species and then tells the story of how hybridizers and growers have created the garden lilies of today. Almost all these thousands of new lilies possess hybrid vigor and are much less insistent than their temperamental wild ancestors on being provided with special conditions of soil, shade, drainage, and climate. The enormously varied modern hybrids are thus much easier to grow in gardens. They have been selected for strength and resistance to disease as well as sheer beauty. In addition, the variety of forms available —from 45-centimeter (18-inch) lilies suitable for smaller gardens and containers to towering 2-meter (7-foot) garden giants—has increased dramatically in the 1980s and 1990s.

It has been a rare privilege to watch this beloved plant family evolve into the colorful, beautifully shaped, and balanced lilies now available. We can put the lily in its rightful place as an easily grown but spectacular plant for all gardens of the temperate and near-temperate zones in both hemispheres. Most Asiatic and Oriental hybrids are hardy to USDA Zone 3, if given an organic mulch in the colder areas, and the trumpet lilies and their hybrids usually grow well down to Zone 6.

With careful selection, gardeners can enjoy flowering lilies in constant succession for three months or more. This immeasurably increases the beauty and interest of the garden landscape. Indeed, we have reached the point where any competent gardener can and should display a small collection chosen from the unparalleled variety offered by the lilies of today.

PART ONE

Lilium 'Sunray'

CHAPTER 1

The Lily Plant

The genus *Lilium* belongs to the family Liliaceae, which comprises more than 200 genera of plants, including the familiar *Asparagus, Agapanthus, Allium, Fritillaria, Hemerocallis,* and *Scilla.* The genera most closely related to *Lilium* are *Cardiocrinum, Fritillaria,* and *Nomocharis;* indeed, several species have shuttled among these names over the course of botanical history.

The genus *Lilium* is described by L. H. Bailey (1876) as follows:

> Perennial, erect, leafy-stemmed herbs with underground scaly bulbs; flowers pendulous, inclined, horizontal, or erect, solitary or clustered, with six separate segments which are scarcely differentiated as between sepal-like and petal-like organs, each bearing a nectar-groove or furrow at the base; stamens six, hygynous or slightly adherent to perianth, mostly shorter than the segments, the anthers versatile, filaments very slender; pistil one with long style and three-lobed stigma; fruit a dry, loculicidal, many-seeded capsule.

In terms more accessible to the nonbotanist, this means that all lily plants survive over several to many years, annually sending up a new stem from their underground storage organ, the bulb. The flowers may be poised at various angles on their stalks, with one or several on each stalk. The parts of the flower come in sets of three or six, a pattern common to the family Liliaceae.

The discussion below gives details about the various parts of the lily

17

plant and their functions. Figure 1-1 shows a typical lily plant with its bulb, roots, stem, leaves, and inflorescence.

Figure 1-1. A typical lily plant.
A: Inflorescence, a: open flower,
b: bud, c: pedicel. B: Stem and foliage,
a: stem, b: leaves. C: Underground
parts, a: bulblets, b: stem roots,
c: bulb, d: basal roots. Drawing by
Bob Mitchell.

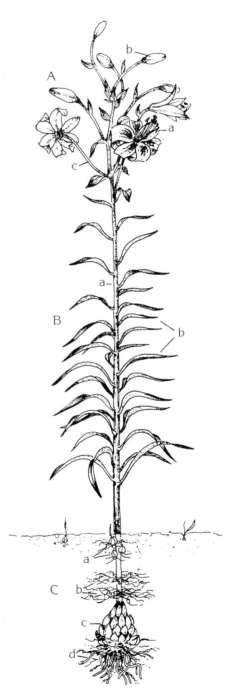

The Bulb

The lily bulb (Figure 1-2) is composed of firm, fleshy scales that store food for the following season's growth. The bulb consists of a short stem, or axis, to which the scales are attached. The axis, also called the basal plate, is the most important part of the bulb because it produces the roots, scales, and buds for new growth. The scales are modified leaves, much thickened and shortened; they provide nourishment for the developing plant until it has sufficient leaf area and root system to take up this task. The color of the scales is one feature by which a lily species may be identified; this color may change on exposure to light.

Lily bulbs are of two general types, concentric and rhizomatous. In the concentric type the axis retains the same shape and position each year. The bulb remains nearly concentric, with its scales arranged around a short vertical stem. The daughter bulb develops within the mother bulb and close to its axis. In some cases two or more daughter bulbs may develop around the axis and may even become separated, although they remain close together. Most European and Asiatic lilies have concentric bulbs. In species such as *Lilium lankongense, L. nepalense,* and *L. wilsonii,* the stem travels underground for some distance before emerging, bearing bulblets away from the mother bulb. This habit has been termed *stoloniferous.*

The rhizomatous type of bulb is best developed in the eastern American species *Lilium canadense, L. michiganense,* and *L. superbum.* The daughter bulb forms at the end of a horizontal, scaleless branch, which pushes out from the mother bulb. This daughter bulb flowers the following year and in turn produces its daughter bulb. Such lilies are usually found in wet meadow or marsh habitats where the soil is rarely disturbed; here their habit of growth allows them to seek fresh soil each year, eventually forming large colonies.

A modification of the rhizomatous type of bulb is exemplified in the western American species *Lilium pardalinum* and *L. parryi.* The stout perennial rhizome or rootstock is covered with scales. This rhizome may be as much as 2.5 centimeters (1 inch) in diameter and several years old in its oldest part. This growth habit is advantageous in the frequently disturbed soils of streambanks where these lilies usually grow, because if part of the rhizome is carried away by erosion, the remainder can still produce a plant.

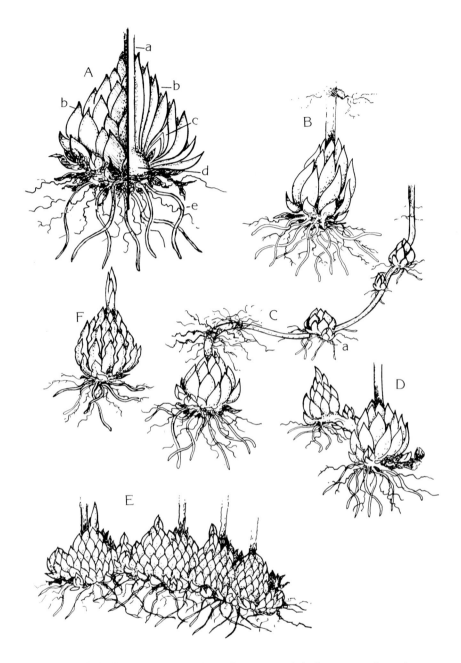

Figure 1-2. Lily bulbs. A: Cutaway view of a concentric bulb, a: stem, b: scales, c: daughter bulb, d: basal plate, e: basal root. B: Concentric bulb of a trumpet lily. C: Stoloniferous bulb of *Lilium nepalense,* a: bulblet. D: Rhizomatous bulb of *Lilium canadense.* E: Rhizomatous bulb of *Lilium pardalinum.* F: Concentric bulb of *Lilium dauricum,* showing jointed scales. Drawing by Bob Mitchell.

The roots of lilies serve two purposes: they absorb nutrients and moisture from the soil, and they anchor the plant. The basal roots, extending from the base of the bulb, serve as anchors; they also pull the bulb deeper into the soil. The stem roots just above the bulb are feeding roots, very important to the life of the plant. Bulbs must always be planted at a depth sufficient for the development of adequate stem roots.

The Stem and Leaves

A mature lily's flowering stem may be as short as a few inches in *Lilium nanum* or other high alpine species, or as tall as 250 centimeters (8 feet), as in *L. leucanthum* var. *centifolium* or *L. superbum.* Some stems rise straight from the bulb, as in *L. martagon* and *L. regale*; others travel horizontally underground before emerging, as in *L. lankongense* and *L. nepalense.* The color of lily stems varies from light green to dark purple; this feature may vary even within a single population of a given species.

The leaves range from the narrow, grasslike foliage of *Lilium pumilum* to the broad, lanceolate leaves of *L. auratum* var. *platyphyllum.* Some species, such as *L. taliense,* produce a naked, asparagus-like stem that rises 30 centimeters (12 inches) or more before the leaves expand.

Lilium martagon, L. hansonii, and their hybrids, as well as several North American lilies, bear their leaves in regular whorls around the stem, with gaps between the leaves. Occasionally some of the leaves are in whorls and others scattered along the stem. In most other lilies, such as the trumpet and Oriental species and hybrids, the leaves are arranged alternately. This is also the case in *L. candidum* and *L. ×testaceum,* but their leaves diminish in size from the base upward. Figure 1-3 shows the shapes and arrangements of leaves in several types of lilies.

The function of the leaves is to manufacture food, which is stored in the bulb for the following season's growth. The maintenance of this food-making part of the plant at its full efficiency for as long as possible is thus a major concern in growing lilies.

Several species and hybrids bear small purple bulbils in the axils of their leaves. If the flower buds are removed from the stem early in its development, more and larger bulbils will be produced, because this

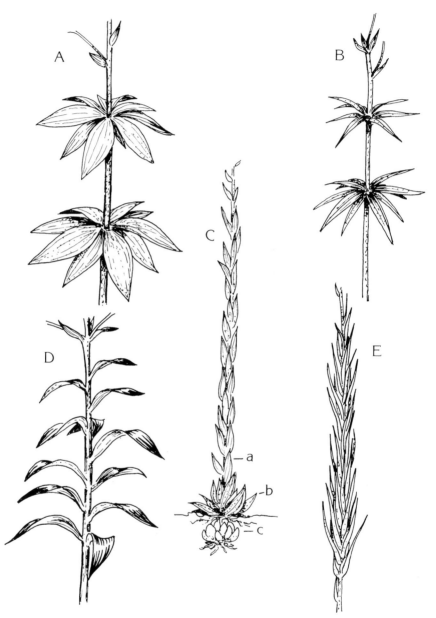

Figure 1-3. Lily leaves. A: Broad, whorled leaves of *Lilium martagon*. B: Narrow-lanceolate leaves in whorls. C: *Lilium candidum,* a: flowering stem, b: basal rosette with closely overlapping, fleshy stem leaves, c: shallowly growing bulb. D: Alternate leaves of an Asiatic hybrid. E: Lanceolate leaves of *Lilium ×testaceum.* Drawing by Bob Mitchell.

is an alternate reproductive strategy, useful when seeds are not present. The species *Lilium lancifolium* (synonym *L. tigrinum*) is well known for its bulbil production. The bulbils can produce new plants identical to the parent when they enter the soil (see Chapter 3).

The underground part of the stem may produce bulblets in certain species and hybrids. The stem roots, produced between bulb and soil surface, are feeding roots, and are very important to growth.

The Inflorescence

The term *inflorescence* refers to the entire part of the plant where the flowers are borne, or the flower head. The lily inflorescence may be a raceme, an umbel, or a single terminal flower. A raceme is a series of flower stalks along the stem, each bearing one or more flowers terminally. In an umbel, all the flower stalks originate from one point on the stem. Lily flower stalks, or pedicels, may be either branched or unbranched. Figure 1-4 shows types of inflorescences common to lilies.

The Flower

The flowers of lilies are quite diverse in form and color, and this diversity contributes enormously to the charm and beauty of the genus. The horticultural classification of lilies, outlined in Chapter 8, is based in part on the flower forms illustrated in Figure 1-5. The basic forms are turk's-cap, trumpet, and bowl shaped.

Turk's-cap flowers are pendent and have reflexed petals that curve backward toward the stalk. Some writers use the term *martagon form* for this type of flower, because the European *Lilium martagon* (turk's-cap lily) is a typical example.

Trumpet flowers have a variety of shapes, typically with a rather narrow conical throat that flares out toward the tips of the petals, which may reflex slightly. The well-known *Lilium longiflorum* (Easter lily) and *L. regale* (regal lily) are trumpet shaped.

Bowl-shaped flowers are more open than trumpet flowers, and the tips of the petals may reflex slightly, but not as much as turk's-cap. *Lilium auratum* (gold band lily) is a good example.

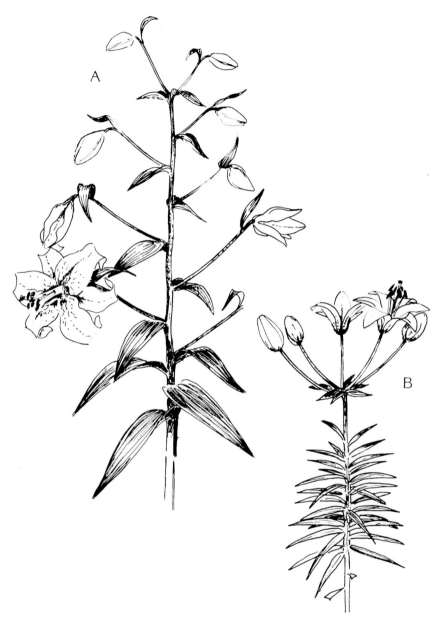

Figure 1-4. Lily inflorescences. A: Raceme of an Oriental lily. B: Umbel of a hybrid between *Lilium dauricum* and an Asiatic lily hybrid. Drawing by Bob Mitchell.

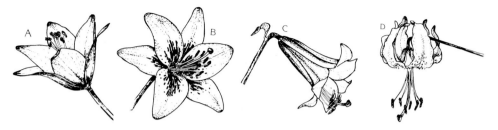

Figure 1-5. Lily flowers. A: Upright bowl-shaped Asiatic hybrid. B: Outfacing flat Asiatic hybrid. C: Semi-downfacing Chinese trumpet. D: Pendent turk's-cap. Drawing by Bob Mitchell.

The carriage of the flower is another feature used to differentiate lilies. Flowers may be upright or upfacing, outfacing, or pendent.

Figure 1-6 shows a diagrammatic view of a typical lily flower. The outer part of the flower, or perianth, consists of three petals and three sepals, which, because they are undifferentiated, or scarcely so, they are often termed *tepals*. All six tepals usually have the same color pattern.

Within the flower are six stamens, the male reproductive parts of the flower. These are composed of slender filaments, or stalks, with the anthers or pollen-bearing organs at their tips. The term *versatile* in Bailey's description of the genus means that the anthers can turn on the filaments. Lily pollen varies greatly in color from species to species and among hybrids, ranging from soft yellow to dark brown.

The center of the flower contains the pistil or female reproductive organs. It is composed of the ovary at the base (where the seeds form), a long style, and a three-lobed stigma at the tip (where the pollen settles).

At the base of each tepal there is a narrow groove, the nectary furrow. Nectar is secreted here to attract pollinating insects and birds. Some species and hybrids, however, lack nectaries.

The color of the lily flower is the feature most readily noticed by the casual observer. The color range includes various yellow and red pigments, but not blue. The biochemical and genetic aspects of lily pigmentation are beyond the scope of this book, but this topic has been studied by a few scientists, including Carl Feldmaier, Judith Freeman, and Charles Robinson.

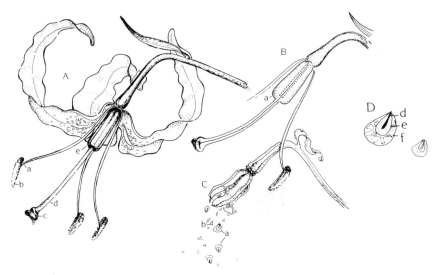

Figure 1-6. Lily reproduction organs. A: Cross section of lily flower, a: filament, b: anther, c: stigma, showing stigmatic fluid, d: style, e: ovary. B: Detail of reproductive organs, a: ovules. C: Seed capsule, a: fertile seed, b: chaff. D: Seed, d: embryo, e: endosperm, f: wing. Drawing by Bob Mitchell.

The Seed Capsule

The form of the lily seed capsule differs among species and hybrids, ranging from the relatively short capsule of *Lilium candidum* (Madonna lily) to the long, slender capsule of *L. formosanum*. All lily capsules are divided into three two-part sections with papery dividing walls, inside which the numerous flat seeds are stacked like coins in a wrapper.

All lily seeds are flat. Some, such as those of *Lilium auratum*, have large "wings"—the papery margin that aids in wind dispersal of the seeds. Others, such as those of *L. polyphyllum*, have very little wing tissue. In a fertile seed the embryo (future plant) appears as a line through the endosperm, the darker mass in the center of the seed.

CHAPTER 2

Lilies in the Garden

Lilies in the Border

Lilies can be used in several ways in the garden. They may be planted in mixed borders, or an entire section of the garden may be devoted to lilies alone. They are appropriate in formal plantings near the house or patio, or in naturalistic designs.

Lilies are most effectively displayed in groups of five or more. The spacing should be sufficient that each inflorescence can be seen as a separate entity, rather than crowded together in a mass with others. Lilies are stately, dignified plants with beauty of form as well as color, and this quality is most happily displayed when each stem has enough room to bend and sway naturally as the air moves, each flower exhibiting its own graceful lines.

Lilies are rarely used in formal bedding, although *Lilium candidum* (Madonna lily) and *L. ×testaceum* can be effective lining a path, perhaps in a medieval-style knot garden (where the Madonna lily was traditionally grown). In cottage-style gardens, however, clumps of *L. candidum, L. ×hollandicum, L. lancifolium* (tiger lily), or *L. regale* (regal lily) are very well suited near the house or close to a door. Paths of weathered brick or gray fieldstone make lovely backgrounds for white-flowered lilies.

Many specialists believe that the best way to grow lilies is in a garden of borders devoted primarily to these plants. A garden in which lilies predominate can be prepared with cultural conditions especially suited to them. Any other plants incorporated in such a garden are chosen solely to enhance the charm of the lilies. A few refined shrubs such as Japanese maples or small rhododendrons may be present, along with ferns or ornamental grasses. The low-growing ground covers act as mulch and background.

Lilies in the Woodland Garden

The ideal place to enjoy the beauty of lilies is a cool, sheltered, lightly shaded bay in the woodland, close to but not in the formal garden. Here their loveliness and perfection of form are better appreciated than when they are crowded among other flowers in the border. Moreover, in the woodland setting the supply of moisture is more uniform, because the canopy restricts evaporation, and the soil maintains a cooler, more constant temperature; all these factors benefit lilies enormously.

This woodland should be one of deciduous trees and shrubs, rather open, with shifting patterns of light and shade. The dark, sterile canopy of Douglas firs all too common in Pacific Northwest gardens is not hospitable to lilies. It is also important not to plant lilies within the root zones of greedy surface-rooting trees such as maples. Like most other ornamental plants, the lilies should be kept about 240 centimeters (8 feet) away from the base of any mature tree.

Trees absorb a tremendous amount of moisture from the soil. Thus it is imperative to provide the woodland garden with a good irrigation system if the ornamentals desired are those that grow during naturally dry times of the year, such as the summer of the western United States. Regular watering may be needed during the hottest periods.

Mingled with the lilies may be ferns, hostas, Solomon's-seal (*Polygonatum* spp.), and other plants with similar requirements. Small windflowers such as *Anemone blanda* and *A. nemorosa* offer bloom just as the lilies emerge from the ground. The larger *Meconopsis* species, such as *M. betonicifolia,* enjoy the same conditions as many lilies and grow with them in nature. The sun-dappled glades where the lilies obtain the sun they need can be carpeted with primroses, mat-forming campanulas, and other low-growing plants.

A path through light woodland may be lined with *Lilium auratum* var. *platyphyllum, L. japonicum, L. rubellum, L. speciosum* var. *rubrum,* and their many Oriental hybrids, using five or more bulbs of each variety in a group. In such a situation the lilies lean gracefully toward the path and its light, not assuming the rigid stance they have in the open garden.

Lilium hansonii, L. martagon, and their hybrids are exceptional in a woodland setting. Equally fine are other European species such as *L. monadelphum, L. pyrenaicum,* and *L. szovitsianum.* The North American species and their hybrids can also be viewed to perfection here, among them *L. humboldtii, L. pardalinum,* and *L. superbum.*

Where more sun falls, choose Asiatic and trumpet lilies that need more light. They will look all the better for the cool green shade in the background.

Selecting Lilies for the Garden

The types of lilies that can be grown easily depend on locality. Lilies that succeed without effort in one area may be difficult under different climatic and soil conditions. Nevertheless, a surprisingly large number of varieties are widely adapted and grow well in almost any temperate region.

The most adaptable species include *Lilium amabile, L. cernuum, L. concolor, L. davidii, L. hansonii, L. henryi, L. humboldtii, L. leucanthum* var. *centifolium, L. martagon, L. pardalinum, L. pumilum, L. regale, L. speciosum* var. *rubrum.* The list of modern hybrids that are easy to grow in a wide range of climates is now very long. It includes many of the common Asiatic hybrids, such as 'Connecticut King', 'Corina', 'Geneva', 'Gypsy', 'Jolanda', 'Matchless', 'Montreaux', 'Pollyanna', and 'Redsong'. Good garden strains of trumpet hybrids are Amethyst Temple, Golden Temple, Marble Temple (Plate 1), Moon Temple, and Silver Sunburst.

Oriental lilies are now available in a large range of colors and habits. They may still be somewhat temperamental in hot, humid climates, where mulching, shade, and careful irrigation can alleviate this problem to some extent. The clones 'Casa Blanca', 'Journey's End', and 'Stargazer', are readily available and easiest. Table 2-1 lists some of the finest garden lilies now available in commerce.

Plate 1. *Lilium* Marble Temple strain, one of the best trumpet hybrids for temperate-region gardens. Photo by Herman v. Wall.

Table 2-1. Hybrid lilies recommended for the garden.

Upright Asiatics
'Adelina', yellow
'Avignon' (tetra), red
'Brushstroke', white/cream
'Connecticut King', yellow
'Corina', red
'Daydream', pink
'Duet', white/cream
'Endeavor', orange
'Flirt', white/cream
'Foxtrot', orange
'Gran Paradiso' (tetra), red
'Gypsy', pink
'Hornpipe', orange
'Impact', orange
'Joanna', yellow
'Jolanda', orange
'Monte Negro', red
'Montreaux', pink
'Nepal', white/cream
'Nova Cento' (tetra), yellow
'Oreglow', orange
'Pollyanna', yellow
'Purple Reign', cream brushmark
'Redsong', red
'Selina', pink
'Sgt. Kelly', vibrant red
'Sorbet', pink
'Sunflight', white/cream
'Sunray', yellow
'Warhawk', red-orange bicolor
'White Ballerina', white
Yellow Blaze strain, yellow

Outfacing Asiatics
'Aloft', pure white
Chippendale strain, wine-rose
'Iowa Rose', soft pink
'Moonbaby,' cream brushmark
Rosepoint Lace strain, soft pink with speckles
'Summit', bright yellow

Pendent Asiatics
'Ariadne', dusty rose
'Classic', golden yellow
'Elf', lavender-pink, pollen-free
'Iona', peach with speckles
'Last Dance', bright yellow
'On Wisconsin', burgundy red
'Pal Mel', soft cream
'Red Velvet', burgundy-red
'Sally', peach
'Song of Kimberly', rich peach
'Tiger Babies', pastel peach
'Tinkerbelle', lavender-pink

Longiflorum × Asiatic hybrids
'Aladdin's Beauty', soft orange
'Aladdin's Glow', bright yellow
'Aladdin's Quest', soft pink
'Aladdin's Magic', peach-orange
'Aladdin's Sun', rich yellow
'Camelot', peach-pink
'Desert Song', peach-orange
'Easter Bonnet', bright yellow
'Hello Dolly', wine-pink
'Kiss Me Kate', rose-wine
'My Fair Lady', clear pink
'South Pacific', cream-white

Trumpets and Aurelians
Amethyst Temple strain, pink trumpets
Anaconda strain, copper trumpets
'Gold Eagle', rich yellow
Golden Sunburst strain, yellow bowls
Golden Temple strain, yellow trumpets
Herald Angels strain, white uprights
Marble Temple strain, white trumpets
Moon Temple strain, clear yellow
   trumpets
Silver Sunburst strain, pure white bowls
'White Henryi', white with orange
   center

Orientals
'Casablanca', pure unspotted white
Crimson Elegance strain, red shades

Golden Elegance strain, gold-banded
'Journey's End', rose-crimson
Rose Elegance strain, pink shades
Silver Elegance strain, pure white

Upright Orientals
'Acapulco', rose-pink
'Berlin', clear pink
'Le Rêve', clear pink
'Marco Polo', soft pink
'Siberia', pure white
'Stargazer', crimson
'White Stargazer', pure white
'Woodriff's Memory', clear pink

Orienpets
Anastasia', soft pink, cream margins
'Arabesque', glowing rose-red
'Black Beauty', intense red
'Catherine the Great', silky yellow
'Leslie Woodriff', crimson, cream
   margins
'Peter the Great', smoky red, gold
   margins
'Scarlet Delight', clear crimson
'Scheherazade', deep red with gold
   shading
'Starburst Sensation', crimson, white
   margins
'The Empress', crimson, cream-yellow
   margins

Lilies and Shrubs

Lilies are frequently grown in beds and borders otherwise devoted to shrubs. This can succeed very well if the plantings are properly prepared and managed. Shrubs form an excellent backdrop for the lilies and break the force of the wind. Tall lilies need a background of even taller shrubs or small trees; the more vigorous Chinese trumpets and the Oriental species and hybrids are displayed to perfection in such a setting.

Lilies rise out of low shrubs in a very effective manner. Some striking garden pictures can be composed by combining flowering shrubs with lilies that bloom at the same time, or the gardener can plan for several seasons of bloom. For example, deciduous azaleas flower in spring, then give the right kind of dappled shade to neighboring summer-blooming lilies.

The shrubs to be grown with lilies should not be so rampant that they compete with the lilies for nutrients; for example, lilacs or junipers would be unsuitable. Slow-growing shrubs are preferable for the front of the border; good choices include dwarf rhododendrons and heaths.

The shrubs should be spaced so that the lilies can be planted between them, far enough to prevent root competition but close enough that the shrubs shelter the lily stems and shade the ground over the bulbs. It may be necessary to prune older shrubs so that their branches do not interfere with the rising lily stems. A good rule is not to plant lily bulbs closer than 90 centimeters (3 feet) from a shrub's base.

Almost all lily species and varieties are suitable for planting among shrubs. Choose the sunniest spots for Asiatic and trumpet lilies and their hybrids. In spots that get some shade, plant martagons and Orientals.

Lilies in the Rock Garden

Most lilies are too tall for a rock garden setting. There are, however, a few shorter species and hybrids that can be charming here. The drainage is perfect, and the lily roots can be shaded by low-growing perennial plants and small ferns. The lilies may also grow in close association with dwarf shrubs such as species of *Cassiope, Daboecia, Vaccinium,* and the smallest rhododendrons.

A few small lilies that have performed well in rock gardens are *Lilium cernuum, L. concolor, L. pumilum,* and *L. rubellum.* Skilled growers succeed with *L. nanum* and *L. mackliniae.*

Some hybrids are short enough to provide spots of color in the rock garden. These include 'Buff Pixie', 'Butter Pixie', 'Orange Pixie', and the delightful 'Tinkerbelle', a hybrid derived from *Lilium cernuum.* These short Pixie Hybrids, however, tend to have flowers that are disproportionately large in a naturalistic garden setting. A degree of species-like refinement is preferred.

Lilies in Containers

Most lilies can be displayed effectively in containers in greenhouses, terraces, decks, or other settings in the formal garden. This method enables the gardener to grow them under controlled conditions and to program them to bloom at specific times.

Clay and plastic pots are available in many sizes and shapes. Those large enough for lilies include terra-cotta bowls, wooden tubs, boxes, and whiskey barrels. Any container used should have good drainage holes to allow for free water movement. Ideally, a container for lilies should be at least 45 centimeters (18 inches) deep, although short-growing lilies can succeed in a shallower pot.

Bulbs destined for container culture must be healthy and have a strong basal root system. It is best to plant only one variety in a container, with enough bulbs to give an effective display. They will fill the container with roots.

Besides excellent drainage, the container should be filled with a fertile, porous soil, watered carefully, and protected from winter and spring frosts. Many suitable commercial soil mixes are available. One used successfully in Oregon consists of two parts well-decayed bark-dust, two parts sphagnum peat, and two parts sharp pumice, with macro and micro nutrients added; its pH is about 6.0 to 6.5. The plants usually require additional feeding later in the growing season, which can be given by applying a slow-release fertilizer (e.g., Osmocote), or by using a liquid feed (e.g., Miracle-Gro) on a monthly basis.

The bulbs must be planted deep enough to allow stem roots to develop. They must be placed near the bottom of the container, firming the soil after planting. Planting is best done in early spring, after the bulbs have received sufficient vernalization (see Chapter 16).

The pots should be exposed to cool conditions initially to allow for good root development. Watering should be done sparingly at first, never saturating the soil; this will stimulate good root development as the roots reach out for moisture. If grown in a greenhouse, the plants need to be shaded later in the season, with 40 to 60 percent shade cloth being suitable in most climates. Mary Hoffman reports that her potted lilies do better if they have air circulation beneath the pots. This means displaying pots on small bits of rubble or even metal stakes (intended for training wires). An added benefit of elevating the pots an inch or more is that sour bugs do not invade pot holes.

Larger container planting of lilies can also feature companion plants. These are very effective in outdoor displays on a terrace or deck. Many annuals and perennials can be used, selecting colors that blend well with those of the lilies. Choose shallow-rooting companion plants with rather dense foliage to shade and cool the soil.

Many excellent drip irrigation systems are now available and do much to make the hobby more enjoyable. One or more emitters per container are used, depending on the size of the container. The system can be put on a timer to operate automatically. Maintaining a constant moisture level is crucial to success in container gardening.

A host of lily varieties is suitable for container culture. The standard Asiatic, trumpet, Oriental, and Orienpet cultivars are all excellent. The height and vigor of most trumpets, Orientals, and Orienpets naturally require much larger containers. Many species are also suitable. Species such as *Lilium lankongense* and *L. nepalense* that have a stoloniferous habit are restricted in containers, making them flower more readily. The martagon and Caucasian lilies (such as *L. monadelphum*) are not recommended, however; with little or no stem-root development, they generally do poorly in containers.

Some growers overwinter their pots under cover, with protection from rain, snow, and severe frost. Many, however, empty all the pots annually, storing the bulbs in a packing medium over winter and repotting in early spring. The health of the bulbs can be checked at this time, and they can be treated with fungicide if necessary.

Growing Forced Lilies Outdoors

Gardeners often wonder if gift lilies in pots can be planted out in the garden after they finish blooming. Typically these varieties are short Asiatics or Orientals, such as the Pixies and Little Rascals strains, often sold for Mother's Day. They can simply be planted out in the garden following flowering, while they are still in growth. As with any container plant, the soil ball should be carefully teased out so that the roots will enter the surrounding soil. If this is not done, the planting mix tends not to draw moisture from the different soil around it and becomes dangerously dry. At the same time, be careful not to damage the roots. The lilies should be placed in an area protected from full sun, particularly in the afternoon, because greenhouse and indoor culture produces tender foliage susceptible to sunburn. They will then follow a normal growth cycle.

The Easter lilies sold in pots are *Lilium longiflorum*, a tender species that cannot be grown outdoors in climates where winter temperatures dip below about –4°C (25°F). Moreover, it is usually not possible to keep them growing in their container, because they have been forced into bloom out of season. These plants are best discarded after flowering to avoid disappointment.

Public Gardens

Most botanic gardens maintain plantings of species lilies. Here these plants can be preserved and protected in proper settings, forming bold, attractive clumps. An interested and skilled staff is needed to keep a collection of lilies in good health over many years. Botanic gardens play an important part in preserving rare species that are threatened by the destruction of their habitats.

In public parks where carpet bedding and extensive container plantings are put in yearly, the uniformity of lily clones and strains is an advantage. The bulbs are available at reasonable cost from wholesalers and can be planted in fall or spring. The miniature Asiatic hybrids are good for large containers, and the brilliant upright flowers of many modern hybrids are tailor-made for formal designs. The short season of bloom is a disadvantage, however, and lilies in public gardens should be combined with late-flowering annuals.

Companion Plants

Large gardens offer many situations in which lilies can be grown, but since most hobbyists have limited space, it is fortunate that many lilies grow well in perennial borders with other flowers. Care must be taken in choosing companion plants to achieve effective combinations and avoid color clashes (Plate 2).

The viewer will enjoy lilies best when they are combined with other

Plate 2. *Lilium* 'Pirate' in the garden with companion plants

plants, and the lilies will be happier too. The foliage of lilies provides little shade to the ground; in the wild lilies grow among other plants that afford the necessary shade and protection against soil heating and evaporation. Associating lilies with other plants answers one of the main concerns of the grower. At the same time, the companion plants must not compete too keenly for moisture and nutrients, and they must provide a suitable visual foil for the beauty of the lilies.

It is very good to use low-growing perennials or dwarf shrubs around lilies. These plants cool the soil, answering the old rule for growing lilies: "Head in the sun, feet in the shade." There are many annuals and perennials suitable as ground covers for lilies. It is important, however, to avoid those with aggressive, overcompetitive root systems.

Low-growing annuals such as impatiens, petunias, or portulaca can be used. In formal settings, striking color combinations can be achieved —for instance, red lilies surrounded by blue or white petunias. Low-growing perennials are even more useful for this purpose. The clumping campanulas, dianthus, and penstemons do well in sun, while shadier situations may call for hostas or pulmonarias. Ferns are very graceful companions for lilies, their soft greens making a lovely background for the lily flowers.

Taller plants are also effective with lilies. White Madonna lilies in front of tall blue delphiniums is a classic planting. Another attractive planting sets a large group of white trumpet lilies against a background of scarlet climbing roses.

The adventurous gardener can invent many more interesting combinations. For example, a wide selection of ornamental grasses has become available, and lilies grow in the wild among grasses. Be sure, however, that the grasses are clump-forming, not running.

CHAPTER 3

Propagation

Few genera of plants are as amenable as *Lilium* to varied means of propagation. Besides the obvious means, seed, lilies can be increased from daughter bulbs that offset from the main bulb. In scaling, portions of the bulb are detached and induced to form new bulbs. Many kinds of lilies form underground bulblets on the stem just above the main bulb. Some produce stem bulbils in their leaf axils, and the production of bulbils on the stem can be induced in most lilies. Figure 3-1 shows the various parts of the lily plant that are useful in propagation.

The tissue culture laboratory has become an excellent tool for the propagation of new and desirable clones for the commercial market. A clone can be increased very rapidly by this method, with a single choice seedling yielding as many as 2 million tissue-culture bulblets in two years. Embryo culture is a form of tissue culture with the specific purpose of preventing the premature death of hybrids derived from unusual, incompatible crosses.

Propagation by Seed

There are several advantages to raising lilies from seed. First, virus diseases are not transmitted in seed tissue, so virus-free seedlings can be produced even from infected parents. Commercial growers use this fact to advantage, annually producing vigorous stocks of Asiatic, trumpet, and Oriental lilies that are free from disease. These stocks are grown on in isolation fields, protected from contact with virus carriers.

In fact, correctly grown lily seedlings are free from all diseases, including basal rot (*Fusarium*). Plantings of species that have become in-

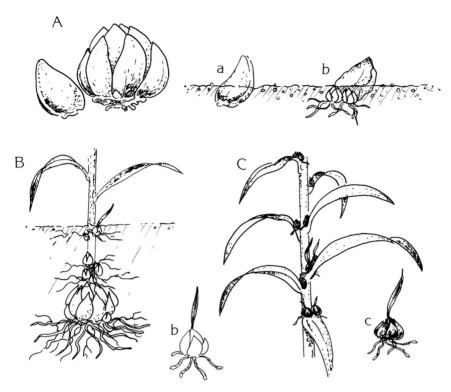

Figure 3-1. Lily propagation. A: Scaling of concentric bulb, with scales broken off at the basal plate, a: newly planted scale, b: scale with roots and bulblets after six to eight weeks of incubation. B: Lily plant producing stem bulblets underground above the bulb, b: detached stem bulblet producing new plant. C: Asiatic lily producing stem bulbils, c: detached stem bulbil producing new plant. Drawing by Bob Mitchell.

fected with fungal diseases can therefore be rescued by collecting their seed and growing it in a clean environment.

Seed production is the least costly method of raising large numbers of lilies. A single pod can contain 200 or more viable seeds. And, of course, this is the only road to adventure in hybridization.

Bulbs received from other regions may prove difficult to acclimatize, especially if they are shipped from the Southern Hemisphere to the Northern or vice versa. Seed, however, may be stored frozen until it can be sown to germinate at the proper time and assume a cycle of growth suitable for a given locale.

PRODUCING SEED

Lilies are self-sterile; that is, a plant will not set viable seed if pollinated with its pollen. Both species and hybrids must therefore be cross-pollinated, either by natural pollinators such as bees or by artificial means. The following steps are recommended for successful seed production in both species and hybrids.

Pollination may take place either under protection or outdoors. A greenhouse or protective structure is ideal because of the control over weather. Increased temperature during pollination and fertilization produces superior seed set. Excellent seed can, however, be obtained under various conditions.

The technique of deliberate artificial pollination is explained in Chapter 14. As the pods develop, they must be protected against *Botrytis* blight by regular spraying with a suitable fungicide. Inspect them regularly throughout the season, not only for disease but also for intruding pests.

The pods, or capsules, are collected just before they turn brown and start to split. If possible, they should be picked only in dry weather, although this may be impossible in some climates; it may also be next to impossible to ripen late-developing lily pods outdoors. If frost is forecast or the weather becomes persistently wet, the entire stem can be cut while the pods are still green. The cut stem is brought indoors and hung upside down in a warm, well-ventilated room to mature the pods.

After harvest, the pods are brought indoors and dried on newspaper-lined trays or paper plates in a well-ventilated room. They must be spread thinly. The room should not be too warm because the pods need to dry slowly; a temperature of 15° to 21°C (60° to 70°F) is ideal.

The seeds should be removed from the pods, or "shealed," when dry. If the pods are left until they become brittle, bits of capsule tissue can become mixed with the seed. During this process it is necessary to watch carefully for signs of disease, especially *Botrytis;* remove infected pods or seed and keep the remainder as clean as possible.

The seed should be left in the trays for a few days after shealing until it becomes completely dry, a process facilitated by daily stirring. Chaff can be removed from small quantities by placing the seed in a shallow pan and gently blowing on it while moving the pan around. The good seed, which is heavier, tends to remain in the pan while the chaff flies up over the side. For the larger quantities produced by commercial growers, there are excellent seed-cleaning machines.

Examine seed for the presence of embryos—a sign that the seed can produce a plant—by placing the seed on a white sheet of paper or frosted glass with strong light below it (an artist's light table is perfect for this). The embryo appears clearly as a dark line running lengthwise across the flat seed. Occasionally seeds are darkly pigmented, making it difficult to see the embryos; in this case, if the seed is plump and of regular shape, it is safe to assume that an embryo is present. If proper precautions have been taken in pollinating the flowers, species and closely related hybrids yield heavy, plump seed with well-formed embryos embedded in the endosperm.

Commercial growers determine percentage of germination by simply counting the number of embryos present in a given number of seeds. For large quantities, several lots of 100 seeds each are evaluated.

After drying and cleaning, small quantities of seed are placed in packets such as coin envelopes, and larger quantities in plastic sacks. All must be carefully labeled.

It is recommended that all seed be stored at a temperature below freezing following harvest. Under these conditions seed can remain viable for 35 years or more. Home growers who are going to plant the seed the same season can store it in a well-sealed container in the refrigerator.

GERMINATION PATTERNS

There are two types of germination in lilies, *epigeal,* meaning "above ground," and *hypogeal,* "below ground" (Figure 3-2). These two categories are again divided into immediate and delayed emergence; the vast majority of epigeal germinators are immediate, and the vast majority of hypogeal germinators are delayed. It is critical to know the germination category to which seed belongs before sowing it. Epigeal germinators are normally sown in early spring, and hypogeal germinators in late summer or fall. The descriptions of species in Chapter 7 include information about their germination patterns. Whether germination is epigeal or hypogeal, there are four basic principles in growing lilies from seed:

1. Plant in a well-drained soil mix.
2. Water sparingly at first, never allowing soil to become saturated.
3. Provide shade throughout the hot season; 60 percent shade cloth is ideal in most areas.
4. Spray regularly to control *Botrytis* and aphids.

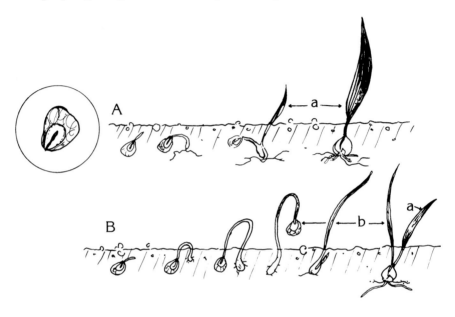

Figure 3-2. A: Hypogeal germination, a: development of true leaf after a cold period. B: Epigeal germination, a: true leaf, b: cotyledon. Drawing by Bob Mitchell.

EPIGEAL GERMINATION

In this pattern, the seed germinates quite rapidly after it is exposed to moisture and warm temperatures, producing growth above ground in a few weeks. The long, slender green cotyledon pushes up, frequently carrying the seed coat on its tip. This is followed by true leaves produced throughout the growing season. Most lilies with epigeal germination can flower in their second growing season if growing conditions have been favorable. Asiatic and trumpet hybrids belong to this group, as do many Asian species, including *Lilium amabile*, *L. concolor*, *L. longiflorum*, *L. pumilum*, and *L. wallichianum*.

Immediate epigeal germination in outdoor beds

Sowing seed in outdoor beds was very successful for many years in the northern Willamette Valley of Oregon. Millions of trumpet species and hybrids were raised from seed by this method, which was also used to a lesser extent for Asiatics. The keys to success are a good site with excellent drainage and land contours, and high soil fertility.

Seedbeds are usually established following a cover crop of rye. The area is plowed deeply in July and disked to produce good tilth. It is then professionally fumigated with methyl bromide, using a plastic cover after the chemical has been injected; the cover is removed after four weeks. This method effectively kills perennial weeds and weed seeds, essential in reducing the cost of seedling production. Diseases and pests such as nematodes are also controlled

Seed is planted in outdoor beds when the ground is workable in early spring; in the northern Willamette Valley this varied from late February to late April. The soil is disked and harrowed again before planting and the beds carefully leveled by raking. The seed is sown thinly by hand at a rate of one seed per 12 square centimeters (2 square inches), or 765 seeds per meter (700 seeds per yard) of a 120-centimeter (4-foot) wide bed. The seed is covered lightly, to a depth of approximately 1 centimeter (0.5 inch). An organic mulch is applied soon after planting to conserve moisture and prevent soil cracking. A thin application of well-decayed barkdust proved ideal in the Willamette Valley.

A good sprinkler system is essential; the seedbed must never be allowed to become dry during the germination stage. Fertilizer is applied according to specific recommendations based on soil analysis. A fertilizer low in nitrogen is recommended. My preference is to incorporate a general fertilizer in the soil before planting and later, in early July when there is a good flush of leaves, to apply a granular slow (three-month) release fertilizer.

A regular spraying program is essential to control *Botrytis* blight, using fungicides currently recommended for this disease. The beds must also remain free of weeds always; with fumigation this problem is minimized. Control of insects, particularly aphids, is also crucial on these small, vulnerable plants; a granular systemic insecticide is safest and is effective over a long period, whereas sprays may damage new foliage.

The seedbeds are dug and the young bulbs lifted in late fall or early winter after the tops senesce. The foliage of these young plants may persist later in the season than that of mature plants. The bulblets are graded by size and stored at a cold temperature until they are planted in field rows the following spring.

There is no reason why this method cannot be adapted to a much smaller scale by amateur growers. However, the home gardener may find it more difficult to sterilize the soil and may prefer to grow lily seedlings in containers.

Epigeal germinators can also be planted in greenhouses, either in beds at ground level or in trays of soil or raised benches. The procedure for the former is almost identical to that followed for outdoor beds: fumigation, early spring planting, sowing, mulching, and fungus and aphid control. The one exception is that the soil must be firmed before planting because the rototillers and spading machines used in greenhouse beds loosen and fluff it up excessively.

Special soil mixes are used to fill raised greenhouse benches, usually to a depth of 14 to 25 centimeters (6 to 10 inches). There are several soil mixes available; the essential requirement is good drainage. For many years I had success with a mix composed of equal parts of bark-dust, sphagnum peat, and crushed (horticultural) pumice. Lime was added to this to produce a pH of 5.5 to 6.0, along with a slow-release fertilizer (6–10–6) and micronutrients. Seed is sown thinly on the benches in February and covered lightly. Watering is carefully controlled, and plants are sprayed regularly to control *Botrytis* and aphids.

Immediate epigeal germination in containers

Epigeal germinators can be grown successfully in a wide variety of containers and media. The ideal method is to sow the seed in a soilless mix in February. The flats, trays, or pots can then be placed under protection in a greenhouse or coldframe. Many enthusiasts sow their seeds earlier under artificial lights. Such seedlings can be moved outdoors when the weather permits.

Care is critical for success in seed-sowing. Firm the mix thoroughly after filling the container. Distribute the seed evenly and cover it lightly with about 1 centimeter (0.5 inch) of soil, then firm it gently.

Watering must be done very sparingly at first. The soil must be moist always, but never saturated. It is always best to water in the early morning, so some surface drying can occur before evening. When seedlings are crowded, their leaves may form a thick cover later in the season, becoming matted together and making it difficult for them to dry out. It is very difficult to control *Botrytis* blight under these conditions. If a trickle irrigation system is installed, wetting the leaves can be avoided.

Delayed epigeal germination
Reports of delayed epigeal germination in some species and hybrids have not been substantiated in my experience. *Lilium candidum,* however, requires cool temperatures during germination and frequently fails to germinate immediately if the seed is sown late, when soil temperatures are high. Cold storage of the dry seed appears to be necessary for the seed of *L. sargentiae* and its closely related hybrids; if kept for at least two months in the freezer, the seed germinates perfectly.

HYPOGEAL GERMINATION
In this pattern the seed germinates slowly. The short cotyledon remains below the soil surface, within the seed coat, and its tissue nourishes a tiny bulb which forms at the side of the seed. After this it requires a period of cold storage (or, in natural conditions, a winter season) before above-ground leaves can develop.

In many lilies with this pattern, such as Oriental species and their hybrids, not all the viable seeds germinate the first year. This seems to be a natural protective strategy, holding some seeds in reserve in case weather or predation destroys the first batch of young bulbs. The home grower may wish to sow seeds in a large enough container to keep for two years to permit complete germination of a batch of seed, particularly if it is a rare species.

Seeds of Oriental lilies held for several years in freezer storage have consistently given 100 percent germination. Tests carried out by Ruth P. H. Clas in Albany, New York, demonstrated that exposure to light could also break natural dormancy; however, this is practical only with very small quantities of seed.

Immediate hypogeal germination
Lilium brownii var. *australe* and *L. dauricum* consistently show this type of germination, producing a large number of leaves in one season. They

can thus be sown successfully at the same time as epigeal germinators. *Lilium humboldtii* has also shown a tendency to this pattern.

Delayed hypogeal germination

The following observations apply primarily to Oriental species and hybrids. The seed is sown in late July or August in plastic bags containing a moist medium, which may consist of vermiculite, sphagnum peat, or a mixture of the two. The degree of moisture is critical. The medium must be moist but not saturated: no water should drip out when it is squeezed in the hand. This permits the aeration essential for good germination and satisfactory root development, which require oxygen.

The quantity of seed must be in proportion to the amount of medium. In commercial production, this works out to 50 grams of seed per 2 liters of medium, or 2 ounces of seed per 0.5 gallon of medium. The seed and medium are mixed in a bucket before being placed in plastic bags that have small holes for ventilation; the home gardener can now obtain the similar plastic vegetable storage bags, sold in supermarkets. The top of the bag must not be completely sealed, allowing further aeration. Each bag is clearly labeled.

The bags are placed in perforated trays or boxes and stored in the dark at a temperature of 15° to 21°C (60° to 70°F) for incubation. A period of three or four months is required for bulblets to form, depending on the variety.

Once sound, firm bulblets and roots have formed, the trays are moved to a cooler room (10°C/50°F) for approximately three weeks. They are then placed in cold storage (1°C/34°F) for a minimum of 12 weeks; this is known as the vernalization period.

The "pregerminated" seed is planted the following spring as described above for epigeal germinators, with one exception. Hypogeal bulblets are best sown in April, a month or two later than the seed of epigeal types, when soil temperatures and light conditions are ideal for immediate growth. In good conditions the tiny bulblets produce true leaves one week after sowing.

Western American lily species and hybrids, *Lilium martagon* and its hybrids, *L. monadelphum,* and other hypogeal-germinating species and hybrids from Europe can also be germinated in this way. In general, however, they require cooler temperatures; the recommended temperature for the initial stage is 10°C (50°F).

Alternatively, hypogeal germinators can be sown in beds, trays, flats, or pots in late July or August, using a reliable soil mix. The containers are placed in a cold greenhouse, frame, or other protected site. The seed germinates under natural conditions, overwinters, and emerges the following spring. Western American and European species and hybrids respond well to this method.

It is seldom advisable to plant the later-flowering Orientals in outdoor beds, some form of protection being recommended. Nonetheless, outdoor planting can succeed if the seedlings are allowed to remain down for two years.

Harvest the bulblets after the tops are completely senesced and pack them in dry sphagnum peat in cold storage (1°C/34°F) until the next spring planting.

Propagation by Bulb Division

Lily bulbs have a natural tendency to increase by offsets. These offsets can be separated from the bulbs in early fall when the bulbs are lifted. A sharp knife may be needed to divide bulbs of some varieties, particularly some western American hybrids with rhizomatous bulbs.

Propagation by Bulb Scales

Vegetative propagation by scaling is the most cost-efficient and rapid method to increase a clone. Commercial growers use this system extensively, believing that it rejuvenates their stocks. It also has a cleaning effect if carried out correctly, and diseases such as basal rot (*Fusarium*) can be controlled in the process. This technique is often used to increase a group of outstanding individuals selected from within a seed strain. Most lilies can be propagated readily from bulb scales (see Chapter 1 for a diagram and description).

One cannot overemphasize the principle that only sound, healthy bulbs with no traces of disease should be selected for multiplication by scaling. This method affords no protection against the transfer of virus disease, or any other disease for that matter. It is sheer folly to propagate material with serious disease symptoms of any kind.

The bulbs selected for scaling must be as clean as possible. Any excess soil adhering to the bulb should be washed off. The best results are obtained by selecting the largest bulbs from the stock; strength and vigor will then be optimally maintained.

For maximum bulblet formation, the scales must be broken off cleanly right at the basal plate. Because the scales are arranged spirally, they are removed around the bulb—as when dismembering an artichoke.

The time of year does not seem to be important for scaling; it depends on local conditions and individual preference. Bulblets can form on scales at any time if the correct stimulus is applied. It is well to remember, however, that lily scales decay rapidly if moisture and temperature levels are not satisfactory.

If the scales are to be planted outdoors, they are best taken very soon after flowering. This will give them enough time to form a callus and new bulblets before severely cold weather sets in. Growing climates vary greatly, but a good rule to follow is to allow at least two to three months of good growing weather to succeed with planting scales directly into the ground. Therefore, this method is never recommended for the later-flowering Orientals, although they can be grown similarly if the scale beds are covered with frames or other protective devices. It is very important to keep the soil evenly moist always after the scales are planted, a critical condition for bulblet development.

The direct planting method, although excellent for the amateur grower, is seldom used in commercial operations. *Lilium candidum* (Madonna lily) is an exception; because it forms leaves immediately after the bulblets develop, it lends itself only to this method of scaling. Excellent crops of this magnificent lily have been produced by scaling the bulbs in late June or early July and planting the scales in rows or beds. Adequate irrigation is essential after planting. With proper conditions (that is, moist soil with temperatures of 12° to 21°C/55° to 70°F), the scales produce large bulblets followed by overwintering leaves; these plants will flower beautifully the following June.

The older commercial method of scaling involves lifting the bulbs in late summer and fall. The scales are removed and subjected to an 8- to 12-week incubation period, followed by 8 to 12 weeks of cold storage (vernalization), then planted the following spring. This may still be the easiest method for the amateur grower. At present, commercial operations often scale bulbs after harvest, in late fall or early winter, in which case the following steps must be observed with special care.

Scale only clean, large, disease-free bulbs from stocks that are verified true to name. Break the scales off cleanly at the basal plate to permit good bulblet formation. Dust or dip the scales in a suitable fungicide; thiabendazole, also known as TBZ (e.g., Mertect), has been satisfactory as a dip for many years.

Pack the scales thinly in layers in a moist medium in trays or boxes; sphagnum peat and vermiculite are both excellent media and should completely cover the scales. The containers should be lined with a perforated plastic liner to conserve moisture, and vented to allow good aeration, a critical factor for satisfactory bulblet and root development.

Incubate the scales in a well-ventilated room at 15° to 21°C (60° to 70°F) until the bulblets and roots are fully formed. The duration of incubation depends on the variety; Asiatic hybrids require 6 to 8 weeks, trumpet species and hybrids 8 to 10 weeks, and Oriental species and hybrids 12 to 14 weeks. Trumpet hybrids do not require a cold period for shoots to develop; they must be watched closely, removing them from the incubator immediately when the bulblets are fully formed. Trumpet bulbs can also be scaled in early spring and the scales planted out directly into rows, where they will form bulblets when the soil becomes warm enough; leaves emerge following the development of the bulblet and excellent growth can be achieved the same season.

After removing the trays of scales with bulblets from the incubator, store them at an intermediate temperature (4° to 10°C/40° to 50°F) for three to four weeks, then place them in cold storage (1°C/34°F). The minimum vernalization period required to break dormancy varies; Asiatics generally require a minimum of 6 weeks and Orientals a minimum of 12 to 14. A longer period of cold storage is not harmful. Trumpets and their hybrids do not require cold to break dormancy and should be held at a slightly higher temperature (2°C/36°F), but one that is sufficiently low to deter sprouting, until planting time.

When soil conditions and temperatures are favorable, the scales are planted in outdoor rows or beds. The bulblets have now been conditioned to sprout readily, so it is important not to plant them too early and expose them to frost damage.

Scale plantings are usually allowed to remain in the ground for two growing seasons. Many Asiatic varieties can produce flowering stems the same season they are planted, an indication of superior vigor in the clone.

Propagation by Stem Bulblets

Small bulbs are produced on the underground part of the lily stem just above the bulb; Asiatic hybrids are particularly prolific in this respect. Stem bulblets saved when healthy stock is harvested should be replanted soon. This method was widely used in early commercial operations but has now been largely replaced by scaling.

Propagation by Stem Bulbils

Bulbils are usually dark purplish and about 1 to 2 centimeters (about 0.5 inch) in diameter. They are formed in the axils, where the leaves join the stem, in some species and hybrids, particularly *Lilium lancifolium* and its hybrids, *L. bulbiferum,* and *L. sulphureum.* The removal of buds before flowering frequently induces bulbil formation; other techniques have also been used, such as burying the stems. The number of hybrids that produce bulbils is quite small. Some authorities firmly believe that propagation from bulbils rejuvenates a clone, especially if it shows virus symptoms, since plants propagated by this method show increased health and vigor.

The bulbils are best collected a few weeks after flowering. In commercial fields, more bulbils are formed when bulbs are grown in low, moist sites. They can be planted in well-prepared outdoor beds in early fall, covering them lightly with 2.5 to 5 centimeters (1 to 2 inches) of soil, depending on their size. The bulbils immediately form roots and leaves, becoming well established before winter. Bulbils can also be planted in trays, flats, or pots, using a well-drained soil mix.

Propagation by Tissue Culture

Tissue culture is a method of propagating plants in the laboratory. Tiny amounts of plant tissue are placed in a sterile nutrient medium. Plant growth hormones are added to the medium to induce these cells to multiply and differentiate until they form tiny bulblets. This technique has revolutionized the horticultural industry by permitting the production of vast numbers of offspring from an individual plant. It is possible to select a seedling and within two years produce several hundred thousand bulblets, which can be marketed in another two years.

The cost of this technique is higher than that of scaling, so only the finest and most unusual clones should be selected for it. Initiation, the process of introducing the plant into sterile culture, costs from $50 to $150 per variety; after that, the cost of production ranges from about 23 to 75 cents per bulblet.

Tissue culture is commonly cited as a method of producing virus-free plants, but the method of doing this is much more complex than most people assume. When plant tissue is initiated into culture, it is tested with an ELISA (enzyme-linked immunosorbent assay) test for the presence of common lily viruses. If virus is present, it can be eliminated by "meristemming," a process in which tiny pieces of rapidly growing meristem tissue are removed, cultured, and repeatedly tested. Obtaining truly virus-free tissue in this way can take more than a year of repeated procedures. When the resulting plants leave the laboratory, of course, they can quickly become reinfected, so breeding virus-tolerant lilies remains a high priority.

The material used to initiate a lily tissue culture usually comes from bulb scales, but stem segments with an internode, or flower buds, can also be used. To avoid sacrificing a precious plant, the bulb may be carefully dug, leaving the stem intact in the ground, where it usually produces stem bulblets. Tissue cultures of endangered wild species have been produced from unopened flower buds.

The donor plant should be one that is unlikely to have been exposed to virus. The material to be cultured should be kept fresh and packed dry to prevent fungal growth.

Once the material reaches the laboratory, it is surface sterilized in a 10 percent solution of household bleach for 20 to 30 minutes. It is then rinsed and cut into segments (called "explants") approximately 5 millimeters (0.25 inch) square; the bottom half of the scale is used for this, the portion closest to the basal plate forming bulblets most readily. The explants are then placed in their culture vessels in a medium, wrapped in plastic, and stored at 21°C (70°F). Often a considerable percentage of the new cultures fails because of contamination by soil organisms. Those that survive produce visible bulblets within four to six weeks.

The medium in which the explants grow is a solution of basic fertilizer nutrients and a few complex vitamin-like compounds. Often, synthetic hormones are added; most lily media contain 0.03 milligrams per liter of naphthalene acetic acid (NAA), a synthetic auxin. Sucrose (table sugar) supplies the energy for growth. The medium is gelled with agar or a proprietary agent such as Gelrite. The most commonly used medium for lilies was developed by Toshio Murashige and Folke Skoog and is known as Murashige and Skoog, or MS, medium.

The most important factor in the medium is the concentration of sugar, which supplies all the energy that a normally growing plant would derive from photosynthesis. (Tissue culture takes place in the dark.) Lilies need higher levels of sugar than many other tissue-cultured plants. Sucrose is added at the rate of 45 to 60 grams per liter of medium; during the latter stages, when bulblets are being produced, this may be increased to as much as 90 grams per liter.

The cultures are grown in complete darkness at a temperature of 20° to 24°C (68° to 75°F). They produce few if any leaves, which maximize production of new bulblets as the energy is directed to that end.

After the culture has been initiated, it is repeatedly tested for virus until the technicians are reasonably sure it is virus-free. Then the multiplication stage starts, during which cultures are maintained in very active growth. Under optimal conditions, these cultures can be "subcultured" or divided into multiple new cultures every 8 to 10 weeks.

Subculturing takes place when the cultures have produced small clumps of bulbs 0.5 to 1 centimeter (0.25 to 0.5 inch) in diameter. These clumps are separated (a process called "singulation") and replated onto fresh medium. After 8 to 10 weeks, each forms a new clump.

Alternatively, the small bulbs may be dissected into their individual scales. This produces more bulblets but requires a longer cycle. Some varieties can also be subcultured by chopping the small clumps of bulbs into pieces about 1 millimeter square.

The last phase of tissue culture micropropagation of lilies is the rooting and bulbing stage, during which the subculture is made to produce as large a single bulblet as possible. The bulbing medium contains no growth hormones (because multiplication is not desired) and has an increased concentration of sucrose at 60 to 90 grams per liter. A period of 10 to 16 weeks is required to produce a high-quality bulblet.

Large single bulblets are the easiest to grow after they are removed from culture. Some laboratories produce small clumps of bulbs in the last stage, but the grower must invest extra labor in dividing these before planting, and losses in the first year are usually higher.

Bulblets originating in the sterile environment of the tissue culture laboratory must be scrupulously protected from infection, especially by fungi, in early stages of growth. Timing is also critical: varieties requiring a vernalization period before spring planting must not be delivered too late.

When the bulblets are removed from the culture vessels, they must be washed thoroughly in running water, removing all traces of agar. The bulblets are then dipped in a fungicide to protect against soil-borne diseases, such as *Fusarium* and *Cylindrocarpon.* A combination of TBZ (e.g., Mertect) and captan has been very effective.

The bulblets are then packed in plastic bags, using a well-aerated medium with a low moisture level; a mixture of dry sphagnum peat and moist vermiculite has proven ideal. The bulblets and their roots must be kept under optimal conditions, neither too wet nor too dry. Pack only a limited number in each bag, and ensure that there is good aeration. The bags are stored for a minimum of 8 weeks (for Asiatics) to 12 weeks (for Orientals) before planting. In the spring they are planted in sterilized greenhouse beds, or in trays of pasteurized soil that are also kept in the greenhouse.

It is imperative that *Botrytis* blight and aphids be controlled during the growing season. As for seedlings, aphid-proof greenhouses are very desirable.

A crop from tissue-culture bulblets must be harvested late, after the tops senesce. This ensures maximum bulb size.

TISSUE CULTURE AT HOME

The amateur grower who wishes to try this kind of propagation at home should refer to an excellent book on the subject, *Plants from Test Tubes* (Kyte and Kleyn 1996). The following notes summarize the process.

The most difficult aspect of tissue culture at home is the establishment of an aseptic environment. The nutrient solution in which the cultures grow readily supports fungi and bacteria that will ruin the plant material. A sterile transfer chamber can be used for tissue culture operations. Work should be done in an area with as little air movement and dust as possible, such as an uncarpeted, closed bathroom. Cutting tools and forceps can be wrapped in aluminum foil and cooked in a pressure cooker with the medium, or soaked in a 10 percent bleach solution for 15 minutes.

The minimal equipment needed includes distilled water, a laboratory scale, an autoclave or pressure cooker, a transfer chamber or laminar flow hood, an alcohol lamp and alcohol, various metric measuring containers, scalpels, forceps, culture vessels such as flasks or large test tubes, prepared culture medium, granulated sugar, and agar or Gelrite.

Prepared lily culture media and other necessary supplies can be purchased from the following suppliers:

Carolina Biological Supply
   Company
2700 York Road
Burlington, NC 27215
(800) 334-5551

Gibco
519 Aldo Avenue
Santa Clara, CA 95050
(408) 988-7611

Sigma Chemical Company
P.O. Box 14508
St. Louis, MO 63178
(800) 325-3010

VWR Scientific
P.O. Box 3551
Seattle, WA 98124
(206) 575-1500

A simple medium can be made with ordinary household ingredients, following this recipe:

Mix:
   ½ teaspoon (2 grams) Miracle-Gro soluble fertilizer
   3 tablespoons (45 grams) granulated sugar
   4 teaspoons (8 grams) agar
   33.8 ounces (1 liter) distilled water
Heat and stir to melt the agar.

Whether using a commercial or homemade medium, pour it into the culture vessels to a depth of approximately 3 centimeters (1.5 inches), cap loosely to allow steam to escape, and cook in a pressure cooker at 15 psi for 20 minutes to sterilize it. The best vessels to use are 30 × 120 millimeter test tubes.

Sterilize the chamber and all equipment. In the chamber, place cutting tools, forceps, prepared culture vessels with caps, a spray bottle of 10 percent bleach solution, and sterile rinse water. This water is prepared by pressure-cooking small jars of distilled water; half-pint containers will be sterile after 30 minutes at 15 psi. Nearby, have a sterile container filled with 5 percent bleach solution, another with alcohol, and an alcohol lamp.

Take scales from the bulb and clean them under running water. Immerse them in freshly prepared 10 percent bleach solution for 30 minutes, stirring every few minutes.

The rest of the procedure must be done in the transfer chamber. Pour off the bleach solution and rinse the scales a few times with the sterile water. Pick up a scale with the forceps and place it on a sterile glass plate. Wipe down this working surface frequently with bleach solution; many labs sterilize paper towels to place on the working surface, using a fresh towel for every few cultures. (You can also handle scales with gloved hands thoroughly washed with bleach solution.) Cut the scales into pieces about 0.5 centimeter (0.25 inch) square. Between cuts, sterilize the blade by dipping it into alcohol and holding it in the flame of the alcohol lamp; cool it by dipping it in a 5 percent bleach solution.

Place each piece of scale in a vessel; putting more than one into a container endangers the cultures, because some will surely be contaminated even with these precautions. Seal the container tightly and wrap the cap with plastic wrap so there is no air space between tube and cap. The culture does not need fresh air as long as sucrose is supplied in the medium; enough gases permeate the plastic wrap to support the culture.

Place the sealed cultures in an area with no direct sunlight and away from drafts and keep them at room temperature. Examine them often by holding them to the light; discard any that appear contaminated. Mold is obvious; bacterial contamination clouds the surface of the medium and forms a cloudy halo.

After 8 to 14 weeks the clean cultures should show obvious bulblet formation. Set up the transfer chamber and sterile instruments again, then remove the bulblets when they are large enough to handle. Carefully cut away all parent scale tissue and transfer each bulblet to new medium, submerging one-quarter of the bulblet in the medium. Again, put only one or a few bulblets in each vessel, because some contamination usually occurs at this stage.

From this point on, the cultures should be transferred every 8 to 12 weeks, when they have formed small clumps of bulbs. During each transfer, cut off any leaves that have formed, trim off the roots, and separate the clumps into single bulblets. It is even possible to scale the tiny bulblets.

When the desired number of bulblets has been produced, place the singulated bulblets on sucrose-enriched bulbing medium. Bulbing and cooling of the bulblets takes 20 to 24 weeks. Use a calendar to calculate the right time to initiate this last transfer so that the bulblets will be ready to plant at the appropriate season.

Small commercial growers and the most dedicated hobbyists may wish to conduct virus testing at home. Test kits for common lily viruses are available from Agdia, 30380 County Road 6, Elkhart, Indiana 46514. This company also tests samples sent to them.

EMBRYO CULTURE TECHNIQUES

Lily hybridizers know that it is difficult to raise viable seedlings from many promising crosses, particularly those between distantly related parents. When we see large seedpods that produce only puffy seeds with no visible embryos, or seeds that are wrinkled and hollow with small twisted structures in the center, we suspect that the embryos died before reaching maturity. The death of the embryo inevitably follows on abnormalities within the endosperm, the food supply that surrounds the embryo in the developing seed. In many crosses, the parents are too different genetically to produce normal seed with a good food supply, even though the embryos themselves may not be abnormal. In such crosses, there may be enough genetic similarity between the sets of parental chromosomes for a normal embryo to develop according to the specifications in its DNA; however, conflicting instructions from the maternal chromosomes of the endosperm predispose it to disintegration. That is, the embryo contains DNA from both parents, but the endosperm has only the seed or maternal parent's DNA, and the two may prove incompatible. After the endosperm disintegrates, the embryo dies for lack of nourishment.

If the embryo is removed from the ovule before this abortion takes place, however, it can be grown in a test tube on an artificial food source. Thus a new kind of hybrid plant can be raised. Embryo culture, the process of growing embryos *in vitro* (in glass) on a nutrient medium, is a form of tissue culture, with the specific purpose of preventing the premature death of hybrids derived from unusual, incompatible crosses.

The transfer of the embryos from the seedpod to the test tube takes place under conditions as nearly sterile as possible. The embryo is placed in a sterilized test tube filled with sterilized nutrient medium. Sterility is necessary because the "perfect food" that will sustain the embryo also serves as an excellent medium for fungi and bacteria, which would soon overrun the embryo. If the embryo is removed from the green pod, which is relatively clean inside, there is usually very little contamination.

The time at which abortion of the embryo occurs varies among crosses. In many crosses, such as pollinations on 'Easter Bunny' (Plate 3), it does not happen until shortly before the pod would open normally; the large embryos produced are easy to see and to remove with simple instruments. In other crosses, however, abortion may occur only a short time after fertilization. In these cases, a dissecting microscope or strong magnifying glass may be necessary to see the embryo, and a more complex nutrient medium may be necessary to sustain the embryo in culture. The longer the embryo has developed in the pod, the simpler the medium needed to sustain its growth.

The question most frequently asked about embryo culture concerns the condition of the green pod before the embryos are excised. In general, the pod should not be totally firm, but slightly soft to the touch; many pods turn a lighter color at this stage.

With suitable adaptations, lily embryo culture can be performed quite successfully in the home kitchen. The transfer is done inside a glass-topped box, which can be surface sterilized with alcohol or dilute laundry bleach. Some such boxes include a germicidal ultraviolet light that supposedly helps keep the space inside the box sterile without excessive use of chemicals. The test tubes full of medium are sterilized in a pressure cooker at 15 psi for 20 minutes.

Most embryos can be placed directly under artificial or natural light, and growth will soon be apparent. Lily embryos from crosses that normally would show delayed hypogeal germination are stimulated by this exposure to light. Smaller embryos, especially those that should show epigeal germination, benefit from a preliminary period of development in darkness.

When the embryo cultures develop several leaves and good roots, they are ready to transfer to soil. This usually occurs after 6 to 12 weeks. The embryos are gently removed from the gel, using some instrument such as a large crochet hook. Any medium clinging to the roots is gently but thoroughly removed under running water. The tiny plantlets are then dipped for five minutes in a fungicide solution (e.g., Mertect), using the lowest concentration. They are transferred to a pasteurized soil mix (two parts sphagnum peat, two parts well-decayed barkdust, and one part pumice, with added nutrients).

The plantlets must be kept uniformly moist, and misting of the leaves is highly beneficial until the seedlings adjust to life outside the test tube. They are allowed to remain in a warm area (such as a greenhouse with temperatures of 10° to 21°C/50° to 70°F) with good natural light for six to eight weeks to encourage root development. They are then ready for a cool period before beginning another cycle of growth.

Timing is very important in this technique. Embryo cultures are usually planted in November and given a rooting period through January and February, followed by a cool or cold period (3°C/38°F) until mid-May. They are then transferred to their growing site, preferably a small greenhouse with adequate shading. Most should flower the following year.

Some hopeful breeders mistakenly believe that through embryo culture absolutely any cross can be achieved. The truth is that there must be sufficient genetic compatibility between the parents to create a normal embryo. Astonishing crosses, however, have been achieved in this manner.

Many hybridizers have used embryo culture in their work. The magnificent *Lilium lankongense* hybrids of Chris North of Invergowrie, Scotland, are well known. Wilbert Ronald of Manitoba produced hybrids between *L. speciosum*, Asiatic hybrids, and the trumpet lily 'Damson'. The most experienced and accomplished practitioner by far is Judith

Freeman, to whom I owe appreciation for most of the information in this section. The number of hybrids she has produced through embryo culture is legion. They include the Tiger Babies, Chippendale (Plate 4), and Rosepoint Lace strains, derived from *L. lankongense,* as well as many hybrids in the Oriental and Orienpet groups. Embryo culture has opened many exciting doors in lily breeding and will continue to do so. An excellent article "Embryo Culture is Easy" by Arthur Evans appears in the 1993 yearbook of the North American Lily Society.

Plate 3. *Lilium* 'Easter Bunny', bred by amateur hybridizer Ruth Clas. Photo by Herman v. Wall.

Plate 4. *Lilium* Chippendale strain, raised by Judith Freeman via embryo culture. Photo by Judith L. Freeman.

CHAPTER 4

Cultivation

A common misapprehension about lily culture has been to a large part corrected in recent years. For a long time home gardeners believed that lilies were plants only for specialists and those with exceptional skill; the latter was a concession to the occasional gardener who succeeded where others had failed! Lily growers are now gradually convincing the gardening public that lilies can be grown by anyone, from the backyard gardener with a small plot of soil to the professional in charge of extensive grounds.

Most lily species and hybrids are easy to grow, provided a few fundamental facts are understood and some basic requirements met. The enormous strides made in lily breeding since the 1960s practically guarantee that hybrid lilies are plants for everyone. Increased hybrid vigor, greater disease resistance, and superior virus tolerance make many of these hybrids almost indestructible.

Purchasing Bulbs

The structure of their bulbs distinguishes true lilies from other bulbous plants (see Chapter 1). The bulb of a true lily consists of a bud surrounded by a rosette of scales that overlap but do not completely envelop one another (as the scales of tulips or onions do). The lily bulb has no membranous outer covering, or tunic, such as we find in many other bulbs, so it is essentially unprotected. Therefore, lily bulbs are termed *scaly,* whereas those of tulips, daffodils, or hyacinths are termed *tunicate.*

To the beginner, knowledge about the structure of the bulb may seem merely academic; however, it has direct application to practical culture. It explains why lily bulbs become desiccated so easily, and thus why they should not be kept out of the ground for long periods. If they must be dug up and immediate replanting is not feasible, they should be stored in such a way that the scales will not dry out.

A buyer choosing lily bulbs should look for fresh, plump, firm scales that are neither dry nor flaccid. To ensure freshness, commercial growers store bulbs that are harvested both early and late in cool storage (−1° to 4°C/30° to 40°F) quickly following digging. The bulbs are stored in trays or boxes lined with well-ventilated plastic liners, protected by a packing material such as sphagnum peat, wood shavings, or cedar tow.

The lily bulbs sold in garden centers and supermarkets in spring show the effects of cold storage before shipping. Sprouts can frequently be seen, winding their way out of the plastic bags! This problem could be avoided to some extent if retailers would keep the bulbs at outdoor temperatures, or purchase the bulbs from wholesalers only when they are sure to sell them quickly.

Lily bulbs purchased by the home gardener from a retail outlet may be packaged in several ways. The best is a system that preserves the moisture in the bulb and protects the roots: that is, a ventilated plastic bag with some packing medium such as sphagnum peat or cedar tow. Bulbs offered in cardboard boxes, paper bags, or in bulk in open bins rapidly dry out like figs. Moreover, those in bins become bruised and otherwise damaged.

The best way to obtain lilies for the garden is to purchase them from reputable mail-order suppliers. There are several growers who offer only or primarily lilies, and these should be the best available. The largest American specialists are B & D Lilies of Port Townsend, Washington, and The Lily Garden in La Center, Washington, who offer many of the rarer lily species and hybrids suitable for the sophisticated gardener. In addition, the better general plant suppliers often carry a good selection of lily bulbs purchased in bulk from reputable growers and kept in proper storage conditions. As in any other market, however, one gets what one pays for: buying from mass-market catalogues offering cheap lilies may bring undersized, poorly stored bulbs that are not even correctly identified.

Site and Soil

The single most important key to success in growing lilies is to provide a well-drained site. Lilies do not thrive for long where the soil is heavy and wet. Poor drainage is responsible for many of the losses frequently ascribed to other causes. If good underdrainage is provided, most lily species and hybrids will grow well in many different types of soil.

Probably the most satisfactory soil for lilies is a deep sandy loam that is well aerated and allows water to pass through freely. The presence of clay soil, however, should not deter anyone from growing lilies. Clay soils are rich in nutrients and can produce strong, healthy lilies if the physical qualities of the soil are handled correctly.

A sloping site for a lily bed is an asset that should not be ignored, especially if the water can drain freely. On flat land, tile or other drainage systems can be installed to carry away excess water. Remember that just digging a deep hole or trench in heavy soil and putting rocks at the bottom does not necessarily provide good drainage: the water must be able to move away freely, otherwise such a trench becomes a sump, and a graveyard for lily bulbs.

When preparing a special bed for lilies, it is advantageous to raise the level of the bed above that of the surrounding area. This prevents undesirably high moisture levels in the top 15 to 25 centimeters (6 to 10 inches) of the soil. This raised-bed method has been used very successfully by commercial growers, who typically build the beds 120 centimeters (4 feet) wide and 15 to 20 centimeters (6 to 8 inches) high, with a 30-centimeter (1-foot) path between beds.

The addition of sharp sand, washed gravel, or crushed pumice opens heavier soils and improves the flow of water; unwashed crushed rock, however, must not be added to clay or it will form a concretelike mass. A similar benefit is obtained by adding coarse organic matter such as commercial compost or barkdust. The addition of lime also affects soil structure, causing the flocculation of soil particles and allowing improved air and water movement.

Sandy soils that are low in humus should be amended with fine-textured organic matter. Well-rotted manures, compost, leafmold, or well-rotted fine barkdust are all excellent.

It is well known that lilies thrive better in reasonably fertile soil than in an impoverished substrate. The best plan is to improve the soil well before planting time by digging it thoroughly and loosening the subsoil, if necessary. Incorporating well-decayed organic matter before planting is highly recommended. Cow or horse manure is a good amendment, but it must be well aged. The finest lilies I have ever seen, both species and hybrids, were growing in soil amended with liberal quantities of horse or cow manure; however, care must be exercised in the use of manures, which can cause both nutritional and disease problems—in particular, they encourage high acidity, a condition ideal for the growth of the fungus *Fusarium*. This problem can be avoided if the manure is used as a mulch rather than mixed with the soil.

Light

Most lilies thrive best in sunny conditions. Where light is restricted, they have a strong tendency to lean toward the light. This is especially true of Chinese trumpet lilies and their hybrids, which must have abundant sunlight for good performance and maximum beauty.

There are a few kinds of lilies, such as *Lilium martagon, L. hansonii,* and their hybrids, that enjoy light shade. The later-flowering Oriental lilies also benefit from shade during the hottest part of the day, because their flowers tend to bleach out in strong sun. In choosing exposure, much depends on the local climate: in hot regions, most lilies do best with some afternoon shade. Nonetheless, very few lilies can survive where the shade is dense, such as on the north side of a house or under large conifers.

Planting Time

Most lilies do best when they are planted in early fall. The lily bulb naturally forms basal or contractile roots following fall planting; these anchor the bulb. Warm soil temperatures are critical for the development of these first roots, so late planting in cold soil does not produce the desired root growth.

A notable exception is *Lilium candidum* (Madonna lily), which must be replanted in late July or August, a few weeks after it flowers. At this time the bulbs are fully formed and dormant. After replanting, or if left in place, they naturally produce leaves in late summer or early fall and overwinter in this stage. This characteristic dictates shallow planting so that the leaves can reach the surface quickly and begin to photosynthesize; the bulbs of the Madonna lily should not be covered with more than 2.5 to 5 centimeters (1 to 2 inches) of soil. This is a Mediterranean plant adapted to dry summers and wet, mild winters, and its winter growth pattern is typical of many warm-climate bulbous plants.

Lily bulbs can also be planted in the spring when soil conditions permit it. Commercial growers store bulbs at temperatures just above freezing after the turn of the year. This conditions the bulbs to sprout quickly after they are removed from cold storage and exposed to warmer temperatures. It is therefore imperative that bulbs purchased in spring be kept as cool as possible before planting; if soil conditions are unfavorable, they can be stored in the vegetable bin of a household refrigerator until planting is possible. It is strongly advisable to postpone planting until the soil is warm and not waterlogged. An early spell of fine spring weather can be tempting, but it may be followed by a miserable cold period—hardly ideal conditions for bulbs conditioned to sprout and grow rapidly.

Planting Depth

The factors that determine how deep to plant a lily bulb include the habit of growth of the particular species or hybrid, the size of the bulb, the type of soil in which the bulbs are being planted, and the local climate. Most lilies produce roots from the stem directly above the bulb, along with the roots that emerge from the base of the bulb. The stem roots die annually with the stem at the end of the growing season. These roots are very important in feeding the plant during its active growth; therefore, the bulbs should be planted deep enough to allow ample development of the stem roots.

A good rule is to cover the bulbs with soil to a depth equal to three or four times their length (base to tip). Stem-rooting lilies with large bulbs, such as trumpet hybrids, may be covered with as much as 25 centimeters (10 inches) of soil.

Another reason for deep planting is that it keeps the bulbs cool during the heat of summer. The bulbs must be protected from the temperature fluctuations that occur in the top few inches of the soil. (High soil temperature is conducive to the development of disease.) Many lily enthusiasts plant bulbs too shallowly for optimal results.

The Madonna lily is an exception about planting depth as well as planting time. It produces roots only from the base of the bulb, not from the stem. Shallow planting is thus appropriate for it.

Some modification in planting depth may also be dictated by soil type and climate. Bulbs in heavy soil must be planted less deeply than those in lighter, warmer, sandy soils. In very warm regions, the bulbs benefit from deeper planting, which protects them from high temperatures in the soil near the surface.

Small seedling bulblets, or yearlings, should be covered with about 5 centimeters (2 inches) of soil, depending on their size. Their basal or contractile roots pull the young bulbs to a deeper level as they increase in size. This occurs with larger bulbs as well; if the soil structure permits it, they eventually draw the bulbs down to their preferred depth.

The gardener should be aware in placing lilies that in some groups, such as Orientals and hybrids of *Lilium wilsonii* and *L. lankongense,* the stem often does not rise straight up from the bulb but extends horizontally for a few inches before emerging. This is a strategy to allow the stem roots enough soil to develop adequately. The deeper a bulb is planted, the less likely this is to happen. This special attention must be given to the species and hybrids showing this stoloniferous habit.

Planting Techniques

There are several techniques that can be used in planting lily bulbs. Some require little physical effort, and others are more strenuous. The best method is to dig a single hole large enough to accommodate all the bulbs that are to be planted in a group; the depth depends on the size of the bulbs and the other considerations just mentioned. For example, to plant bulbs of the Asiatic clone 'Connecticut King' (Plate 5) that average 5 centimeters (2 inches) long, dig a hole 20 centimeters (8 inches) deep. Loosen the subsoil at the bottom of the hole to improve the drainage. Set the bulbs on their bases with enough space between them to allow full development during growth. A minimum spacing of 15 centimeters (6 inches) is best for Asiatic clones, with as much as 45 centimeters (18 inches) for taller lilies such as trumpets and Orientals. The

Plate 5. *Lilium* 'Connecticut King'

ultimate height and habit of the plants also affects the spacing chosen; for example, a variety that produces a broad, branching inflorescence will need more room to display its flowers than one with a tall, narrow habit. Overcrowding must be avoided, not only for aesthetic reasons but also because it restricts air circulation and thus promotes disease.

Fertilizers

The kind and amount of fertilizer needed depends on the fertility of the soil. No fertilizer may be necessary where a variety of other plants are growing well already. I recommend that the gardener submit a soil sample for analysis to determine nutrient levels and pH.

Most kinds of lilies prefer a slightly acid soil, with a pH of 6.0 to 6.5 being best. A complete, well-balanced fertilizer containing nitrogen, phosphorus, and potassium (typically in a ratio of 15–15–15) should be applied when necessary to ensure good growth. An application of garden lime maybe necessary if the soil is very acid. I believe that too much emphasis has been laid on soil pH in growing lilies, which are probably far more adaptable than has been widely suggested. As long as the pH is not extremely high (8.0 or above), most lilies will grow well enough.

In areas where the soil is very alkaline, lilies may be grown in raised beds made up of acidic compost, or in containers. There are also products on the market to acidify lime soils, but they are not as satisfactory as the former method. A few species of lilies are native to limestone areas and should tolerate alkaline soils well.

The point to emphasize about fertilizing lilies is that excessive application can be harmful because it promotes soft growth and makes the plants more susceptible to disease. This is true where the soil is heavy or rich in humus; such soils tend to be naturally high in nutrients, and artificial fertilizing should be done judiciously if at all.

Artificial fertilizer is best applied when the lily shoots are at the spear stage, just before the leaves unfurl. A handful of well-balanced granular fertilizer (12–12–12) should be gently worked into the soil around each plant. Especially suitable is a six-month slow-release product such as Osmocote, in a 20–20–20 formula. One application of this should keep the lilies happy for the entire season.

An old practice sometimes used to maintain lilies' health and vigor was to scrape away a couple of centimeters (an inch) of soil just as the lilies emerged and replace it with a mulch of well-decayed cow or horse manure. Well-decayed composts are also recommended.

Replanting Lilies

It is sometimes a problem to determine how long a clump of lilies should be retained in place before the plants are moved to a fresh location. When the bulbs have offset to produce several stems, it is usually desirable to separate the clump in fall and replant the bulbs.

Asiatic varieties tend to require lifting and replanting on a regular basis. Most of them form many bulblets along the underground parts of the stems; as a result, the clump becomes very crowded and flowering declines. Lifting and division should be done about every third year with stronger Asiatic varieties.

Sometimes it is obvious that a group of lilies is not thriving as it once did. In such cases, a move to a new location and fresh soil usually restores the plants to their former vigor. This replanting is best done three or four weeks after flowering. At this time, check the bulbs for disease, especially basal rot (*Fusarium*). Discard severely infected bulbs and treat the others with a suitable fungicide before replanting (see Chapter 5).

Pruning

Undeveloped seedpods should be removed after flowering if seed is not desired. This allows the bulbs to store as much food as possible. In the fall, after frost has been severe enough to end all leaf formation and after the tops senesce, the stems should be cut to the ground, removed, and if possible burned. This helps to remove disease organisms from the garden. Be sure to mark the site of the bulbs with a stake so they will not be damaged if work if done in the dormant bed.

Mulching

The moisture content of the soil can be conserved and moderated by covering the surface with a mulch. Mulch also smothers some annual weeds or prevents their seeds from germinating. It moderates soil temperature by preventing the exchange of heat with the air. Considering the needs of the lily bulb discussed above, we can see that a good mulch goes far toward meeting those requirements.

During winter, mulches protect the ground from deep freezing in very cold areas. Under a coarse mulch, such as straw, spring thawing proceeds gradually and root disruption is prevented. A layer of conifer branches laid down in fall helps to hold snow and increase insulation; the branches should be removed in spring just before the lilies emerge.

The material used for mulching depends on local availability. In most areas gardeners have several choices available to them. For the lily grower, well-rotted cow or horse manure, mushroom compost, leafmold, sphagnum peat, and well-rotted compost or barkdust are all excellent.

Weed Control

Lily hobbyists must be cautious in the use of herbicides to control weeds. These chemicals can act differently in response to climate and soil conditions. The one product highly recommended to control weeds before the lilies emerge is Round-up (main ingredient glyphosate). This excellent herbicide is effective against perennial weeds such as Canadian thistle, dock, bindweed, and crabgrass, killing them entirely if application is timed right. Round-up must be applied in spring for best results; this is best done when the weeds have enough foliage to absorb the chemical, but before nearby ornamentals (including lilies) emerge.

Irrigation

Lilies require adequate moisture during the growing season, before flowering, and for a few weeks after it. The moisture level can then be decreased gradually. The frequency of watering depends both on the local weather and on the moisture-retaining quality of the soil. The lily bed should never be saturated or waterlogged, nor should it dry out completely.

Soaker or "leaky" hoses are an excellent means of watering when groups of lilies are planted together. They can simply be laid on the ground around the planting, remaining as long as irrigation is required. Drip irrigation has become a sophisticated field, and a visit to a specialty garden store offers many ideas. Overhead watering may damage lilies, either physically when the sprinkler stream strikes the stems, or through promoting *Botrytis* and other fungal diseases; nevertheless, it is used in commercial plantings, which are in open, sunny fields where disease is carefully monitored.

Early blooming varieties, such as Asiatics, and late-blooming lilies, such as the August-flowering Orientals, have quite different moisture requirements. When the early flowering varieties should be on the dry side, the late ones are just approaching their flowering period and peak moisture requirement. Thus, it is best not to plant early and late bloomers in proximity.

In areas that are wet in summer, such as the mid-Atlantic region of North America, good drainage and cool soil are the keys to growing lilies. Recall that although many important species of lilies come from hot, humid Japan and eastern Asia, they tend to grow on steep slopes in volcanic soils. In North Carolina, for example, a hobby grower created a magnificent bed of lilies on a raised area, mulched very deeply with pine needles and in high shade afforded by nearby trees. Atmospheric humidity is another problem, because it promotes *Botrytis* and other fungal diseases; good air circulation mitigates this problem.

Air Circulation

Stagnant air, especially in humid summer climates, favors the development of the most prevalent lily disease, *Botrytis* blight; wet foliage also contributes to it. Constant air movement, however, speeds evaporation and drying of the foliage. This tells us to choose a site for lilies where we often feel a slight breeze—a slope or an area open at both ends to the prevailing winds.

Any hollow or pocket where air circulation is poor is also likely to act as a frost trap in spring. Frost damage may result in the loss of a season's flowering and in damage to the emerging foliage.

Lilies growing in their natural habitats are usually protected from high winds by the shelter of grasses, shrubs, and nearby trees. This should also be kept in mind when choosing a site. Lilies need not be planted in borders as flowering annuals and perennials often are; a clump of lilies can stand on its own as a landscape feature. The necessary wind protection can be provided by small trees, shrubs, or even a fence.

CHAPTER 5

Diseases

The susceptibility of lilies to several serious diseases has limited their popularity as garden plants. Their great beauty, however, has encouraged growers and gardeners to persist and eventually to overcome many of the problems encountered by the enthusiasts of earlier years. The great increase in the popularity of lilies has been possible only because new varieties have greater tolerance to virus and resistance to disease. These qualities have enabled modern lilies to be more persistent in gardens; they have also made possible the commercial cultivation of lilies as cut flowers and pot plants.

Natural, genetically determined resistance to disease, or tolerance of it, is very important in lilies. These abilities are controlled by many genetic factors, making some lilies virtually indestructible while others are extremely vulnerable. This range of susceptibility interacts with environmental factors.

It is important to understand that healthy plants, growing well in a medium and an environment that suit them, are strongly resistant to disease, just as healthy people are resistant to disease. This is a fact that many observant gardeners have used to advantage. Soils and climate affect the health of lilies; drainage, degree of acidity or alkalinity, soil texture and structure, and air circulation all influence disease control.

Growers must attempt to eliminate or reduce the environmental stresses that predispose lilies to infection. This is illustrated by several older varieties that are known to be infected with virus. When these plants are grown in unfavorable conditions—such as poor soils with inadequate drainage, seasonal reverses, rapid temperature shifts, or out-of-season forcing into flower—conspicuous virus symptoms such as mottling, streaking, or distortion soon appear. Yet given optimal conditions, even these infected plants may appear healthy for years.

Much research has been done on lily diseases, and excellent controls are available to commercial growers. Many of these chemicals, however, are neither safe nor legal for home garden use. Moreover, effective products are sometimes banned because dangerous toxicity is discovered; for example, the fungicide Benlate (benomyl) was banned after it was determined to be carcinogenic.

The best long-term approach to healthy lilies appears to lie in identifying and creating disease-resistant varieties and encouraging their use in gardens. This requires cooperation among hybridizers, commercial growers, retail outlets, and gardeners.

Hybridizing should be directed to producing stress-resistant varieties suited to as wide a range of environmental conditions as possible; furthermore, the new varieties should be selected for even greater resistance to disease and tolerance of virus. These healthy, strong-growing varieties should be selected not only for their floral beauty, but also for their ability to persist and perform well for many years. Commercial handlers must continue to improve methods of production, processing, packing, storage, and shipping to ensure that the customer receives healthy, disease-free bulbs in prime condition. Finally, the home grower must use good cultural methods: planting in an appropriate site in well-prepared soil at the proper time. Even the healthiest bulb cannot survive mishandling at this crucial stage.

The following discussion is designed to help the home gardener recognize, understand, and control lily diseases and pests. It is unwise to recommend specific chemical controls because they may be banned or superseded. It is better to seek recommendations from local extension or other advisory agents who are familiar with conditions in that area. Gardening periodicals are also helpful. The best source may be local members of lily societies and other growers.

An accurate diagnosis is essential before determining the best way to control a disease. This sometimes can be done only by isolating the pathogen using laboratory techniques; even then it may be difficult to distinguish the primary pathogen from secondary invaders. The gardener must also understand that the nature of an organism's life cycle may be relevant to its control. If disease symptoms are puzzling or unclear, request aid from an extension agent, lily hobbyist, or plant pathologist.

Virus Diseases

Lily viruses are tiny particles of DNA (genetic material) that reproduce within the plant's tissues by inducing the cells of the host plant to produce more and more virus particles; this process disrupts the normal activities of the cells, resulting in the outward symptoms of virus disease. Too small to be seen under the highest magnification of a conventional microscope, they are visible only with an electron microscope. In spite of their minute size, however, lily viruses always cause some damage. Specific viruses are identified by their characteristic shapes, sizes, and chemistry, generally by electron micrographs or by testing immunological reactions.

Virus infections produce several distinctive, damaging symptoms, including irregular mottling and flecking of the leaves, as contrasted with the uniform green color of healthy foliage; reduced plant size; distorted and twisted growth; color-breaking in the flowers and leaves; and concentric brown ring patterns on bulb scales. Lilies infected with virus are greatly weakened and become susceptible to other diseases. Many species and some hybrids are highly susceptible to viruses; others, however, tolerate virus infection and perform well despite it.

Because virus disease pervades almost all the tissues of an infected plant, any new plants naturally propagated from scales, bulblets, bulbils, or other tissues carry the infection. Only seeds and rapidly growing shoot tips remain uninvaded. Viruses do not persist in dead plant tissues; they require living cells in which to replicate.

There are several different virus diseases that infect lilies, and these produce a wide variety of symptoms. Three, which are transmitted from plant to plant by aphids, have been identified as lily symptomless virus, tulip-breaking virus, and cucumber mosaic virus.

Lily symptomless virus (LSV) is probably the most common lily virus. It occurs in many species and hybrids with no obvious virus symptoms, but it can cause stunting; it has also been called Lily Latent Virus. It is most serious in combination with other viruses, probably because of its general weakening effect.

Tulip-breaking virus (TBV) is the oldest known virus disease identified by science. Tulip flowers with the symptomatic color-streaked segments were painted by Dutch masters in the seventeenth century. TBV, the most deleterious of lily viruses, can be transmitted from infected tulips or other liliaceous plants to lilies; for this reason, "broken" or "Rembrandt" tulips, which carry the virus, should not be grown in the same area as susceptible lilies.

Cucumber mosaic virus (CMV) has a very wide range of hosts, including many commonly cultivated plants and weeds. Among the weeds are common chickweed (*Stellaria media*) and shepherd's purse (*Capsella bursa-pastoris*).

Other viruses that have been reported in lilies include Arabis Mosaic Virus (AMV), Tobacco Mosaic Virus (TMV), Tobacco Rattle Virus (TRV), Tobacco Ringspot Virus (TRSV), and Lily Virus X (LVX). None of these is a serious problem in lilies at present.

Soil-borne viruses—including AMV, TRV, and TRSV—are transmitted from plant to plant by nematodes, microscopic wormlike terrestrial organisms that feed on roots. Such viruses in lilies have been found only sporadically in the United States, the Netherlands, and Scotland. They usually occur in light sandy soils, or in cropland that has been used for years previously as pasture; both create a good environment for nematodes.

IDENTIFYING VIRUS DISEASE

Symptoms on a virus-infected lily may distinguish a particular virus. Examples include mottling or flecks on the leaves, stunted growth, distortion of leaves and growth tips, color-breaking in flowers, and brown concentric rings on bulb scales. Great care must be taken not to confuse virus symptoms with those of chlorosis caused by nutrient imbalance, improper soil pH, frost damage, chemical injury (especially herbicide damage), or root damage. The leaf mottling caused by nutrient excesses or deficiencies is usually a much more regular and uniform pattern than that caused by virus disease.

Growers check a suspected virus infection in the field by taking a leaf from the affected plant and using a solution prepared from it to inoculate a diagnostic assay plant kept in a greenhouse. LSV and TBV do not quickly produce reactions in diagnostic plants, but CMV can be transmitted through sap to several kinds of test plants, including cowpea, cucumber, and tobacco. All these react to infection with CMV by showing symptoms of mosaic after seven to ten days. *Lilium formosanum* rapidly develops symptoms if infected with any virus; it is thus an excellent indicator to plant among seedlings or clones to monitor the spread of virus.

All lily viruses can be seen with the aid of an electron microscope. An extract is taken from the infected plant. Rodlike virus particles can usually be identified by a five-minute procedure. The smaller, spherical particles of CMV closely resemble normal cell organelles and are much more difficult to identify.

A serological technique, the enzyme-linked immunosorbent assay (ELISA), is now being used extensively to identify lily viruses. It can be applied to crude extracts obtained from any part of the plant and is much more sensitive than electron microscopy. A commercial laboratory can perform thousands of tests in a week. An antiserum specific for each virus reacts with that virus alone to make diagnosis certain.

Serology and electron microscopy have also been combined to provide another sensitive means of identifying a virus. This is faster and more dependable than ELISA when dealing with low levels of virus.

VECTORS OF VIRUS DISEASE

Several species of aphids (plant lice or greenfly) can transmit virus disease. The heaviest populations of aphids usually occur from mid-May to early June, peaking again in August and September. Many gardeners say they have never seen aphids on a lily plant, but these insects are usually present. They may become most abundant after the lilies have finished flowering and the gardener's attention to insect control has waned. In Oregon's Willamette Valley, a major growing area, there is evidence of virus transmission throughout the season, especially when warm weather continues into late October. The aphids are so numerous that they even find older lily plants attractive. Aphid infestation can be monitored by aphid traps—shallow yellow pans filled with water or yellow "sticky strips" available from garden suppliers.

During warm periods, aphid populations increase and move around rapidly. Only a few virus-infected plants are needed to allow the disease to spread throughout a field or garden. At certain times aphids produce winged "migrants" that then fly afar to produce new colonies. The symptoms of virus spread may not be apparent until the following year; TBV, however, produces symptoms the same year from a spring infection.

The three common aphid-borne viruses—LSV, TBV, and CMV—are transmitted in the stylets (piercing mouth parts) of the insects. They may even be spread by aphids that do not colonize lilies. The aphid becomes viruliferous immediately upon running its stylet into the leaf, whether it sucks the sap or not.

There are many species of aphids, and growers may find some on their lilies that are not known to be virus carriers. Five main known vectors have been identified. The green peach aphid (*Mysus persicae*) has a dull, greasy appearance and increases rapidly in such crops as potatoes and spinach, reaching enormous numbers; it carries CMV. The melon aphid (*Aphis gossypii*) is lemon-yellow to very dark green; it carries LSV and CMV. The bean aphid (*Aphis fabae*) is black in color and abundant in late summer and fall; it carries TBV. The potato aphid (*Macrosiphium solani*) spreads virus by feeding on tender shoots. The purple spotted lily aphid (*Macrosiphium lilii*) is lemon-yellow with a purple spot on the basal half of the abdomen.

In colder northern climates, coastal areas, and windy locations, aphid populations and the viruses they carry are greatly reduced. The ability of certain growers to keep stocks healthy for many years in coastal areas underscores this fact. It is fascinating that these viruses are seldom found in lilies in the wild. For example, in one study LSV was not found in native populations of *Lilium columbianum*, even in plants growing adjacent to fields of infected Easter lilies. This suggests either that the species is immune, or that it is so susceptible that plants die almost immediately after they become infected.

GROWING VIRUS-TOLERANT AND VIRUS-FREE LILIES

There are many lilies that continue to grow and flower well despite being infected with viruses. They are never quite as strong as virus-free plants of the same clone; nevertheless, they may perform well for many years after infection. The hybridizer has an almost sacred obligation to breed for virus tolerance, whether for the garden or for cut-flower markets.

In the early years at Oregon Bulb Farms, it was noted that clones and strains with *Lilium davidii* ancestry were much more tolerant of virus. 'Paprika', 'Tabasco', and many others descended from the Stenographer and Patterson hybrids never showed serious virus symptoms and performed well long after known exposure to virus. Many of the Connecticut hybrids are also highly virus-tolerant, such as 'Connecticut King', 'Connecticut Lemonglow', 'Piedmont', and 'Sunray' (Plate 6). Their virus tolerance factors are inherited from a different source—probably *L. dauricum* or a form of *L. wilsonii*. Even more recently, an old clone of *L. leichtlinii* var. *maximowiczii* 'Unicolor' has produced remarkable virus tolerance in its progeny, which include the vigorous "brushmark" hybrids.

A high degree of virus tolerance is also found in many trumpet, Aurelian, and Oriental cultivars. Trumpet clones selected from Black Dragon, Golden Splendor, Pink Perfection, and *Lilium regale* have persisted for more than 30 years. This is also true of several Aurelian clones much closer to *L. henryi,* including 'Gold Eagle', 'Thunderbolt', and 'White Henryi'. Some forms of *Lilium speciosum* are highly tolerant, including the clones 'Shooting Star' and 'Uchida'. Several virus-tolerant

Plate 6. *Lilium* 'Sunray', a highly virus tolerant hybrid. Photo by Herman v. Wall.

clones of *L. auratum* var. *platyphyllum* were grown for many years. An increasing number of Oriental hybrid clones has been growing well for more than 40 years, including 'Allegra', 'Black Beauty', and 'Journey's End'. *Lilium martagon, L. hansonii,* and their varieties and hybrids seem to remain remarkably free of virus symptoms. Apparently they naturally repel aphids and never become infected.

Breeding for virus-tolerance factors is the only practical answer if lilies are to persist in the garden for many years. All hybridizers should be sure that at least one of the parents used has a high degree of virus tolerance. Hybridizers and growers also need to understand that crossing two highly tolerant clones does not produce an entire population with this characteristic; the inheritance factors are far too complex. Finally, all commercial clones should be tested thoroughly for this quality before they are introduced.

Even after a favorite lily clone has become infected with virus, there is a method of renewing its health and vigor. This fountain of youth is known as shoot-tip or meristem culture. It consists of removing the outer several layers from a rapidly growing shoot tip, under sterile conditions, and growing this "apex" on a nutrient medium in a laboratory vessel. If the shoot tips are very small (but still large enough to grow), a good proportion will consist of clusters of cells that have not yet been invaded by virus particles; these cultures will grow into normal, virus-free plants. Their freedom from virus must be verified by laboratory tests, and they must be kept carefully isolated from infected lilies and other plant hosts. They can be propagated rapidly by tissue culture from the originally cultured material.

This procedure was carried out by Oregon Bulb Farms and Oregon State University in the late 1960s on the clone 'Enchantment', with remarkable results. The virus-free stock was tested against infected stock five years later; the former were twice as tall, their foliage was much more lush, and the flowers were larger.

Virus-free lilies dramatically outperform material of the same clone that is infected. They are stronger-growing, taller, and healthier in appearance, and they have superior propagation qualities. This has been illustrated not only in field and garden studies, but also in vastly superior replication rates in the tissue culture laboratory. Thus we can see that the goal of commercial producers should be not just virus-tolerant but virus-free lilies.

CONTROL OF VIRUS DISEASES

Because the lily viruses important in the garden are all aphid-transmitted, they may be treated as a single problem. A multifaceted program of control involves removing or isolating infected plants, selecting virus-free stock, and controlling aphids.

Clumps of lilies that show severe signs of infection, such as mottled, distorted, or twisted leaves, stunted growth, or streaked flowers should be destroyed. Be sure that all bulbs and scales of these plants are removed and destroyed. This removal should be done early in the season; virus symptoms are most noticeable during cool spring weather, and plants are easiest to remove then, when the root system is small. Since viruses do not persist in dead tissue, affected lilies can also be killed with glyphosate (e.g., Round-up).

Certain virus-tolerant older varieties, such as *Lilium lancifolium* and *L. ×hollandicum*, are "Typhoid Marys" that carry infection without showing symptoms. If these must be grown, keep them in isolation, far from other lilies (especially seedlings). When acquiring new bulbs, keep them isolated until their status is known. Some tolerant plants may not betray infection with symptoms. Do not assume that just because the plants look healthy, they are virus-free.

Home gardeners should grow more lilies from seed. Lily viruses are not transmitted in seed tissue, so virus-free material can even be produced from two infected parents in this way. Seedling stocks can then be grown in isolation from known virus carriers to prevent infection. In larger gardens, lilies are best planted some distance apart from one another. In large, close plantings, the rate of disease spread is likely to be high. For the same reason, avoid planting lilies next to other host plants. For example, tulips (particularly those with broken-colored flowers) are hosts to TBV.

Insecticides sprayed on the plants or watered into the soil will not stop the spread of virus, because the aphids have time to transmit it before they are killed. This treatment does, however, reduce aphid populations, both decreasing the rate of disease spread and lessening the distortion of new growth caused by heavy aphid predation. For details of aphid control, see Chapter 6.

Many people believe that virus diseases can be transmitted by tools used to cut flowers, the sap of the infected plant being carried on the blade. This would seem plausible only if a healthy plant were cut im-

mediately after an infected one. We have no evidence of such transmission, but it is always wise to take precautions against even a remote
possibility.

Fungus Diseases

Fungi are organisms that live in or on plant tissues, deriving nutrients
from the host plant and destroying its cells. As in the case of viruses,
multiple fungal diseases affect lilies and tend to be more destructive in
combination than singly. The two most serious fungal diseases of lilies
are basal rot and *Botrytis* blight; the former is the more destructive because it attacks the bulb. Other fungal diseases, such as black scale disease, blue mold, *Cercosporella* blight of foliage, root rots, rust, *Sclerotium,* and stump rot, are rarely problems for the home gardener. The
best policy in the long term is to destroy ruthlessly any sick or suspect
plants, no matter what the cause of their symptoms. Attempts to revive
unhealthy lilies are usually futile.

BASAL ROT

The fungus *Fusarium oxysporum* var. *lilii* often occurs in combination
with another fungus, *Cylindrocarpon,* especially in the Netherlands.
Fusarium is more likely to damage Asiatic lilies, and *Cylindrocarpon* is
more serious in Orientals. Usually *Fusarium* is the primary pathogen
and *Cylindrocarpon* the secondary one. Cultures isolated from diseased
bulbs seldom indicate the presence of only one pathogen; usually there
are two or more. *Fusarium,* however, is the most serious soil-borne disease in North America and should be considered a primary pathogen.

Basal rot is recognized by a chocolate or dark brown rot that extends
into the scales from the basal plate. The scales may become detached
at the basal plate so that the bulb falls to pieces. The fungus invades
the bulb through the roots, the basal plate, and the basal end of the
scales. Many lily varieties are very susceptible, and the decay continues rapidly until the bulb disintegrates.

The pathogen is readily disseminated by spores, which can be carried in the soil or on the surfaces of bulbs, tools, agricultural equipment, or packing crates. Released from the debris of the decayed bulbs,
the fungus can remain viable in garden soil for at least three years without a host.

The usual symptoms of basal rot in growing plants are premature yellowing of the foliage, stunting, and premature senescence. All are typical reactions to ethylene, a gas produced by the decaying bulb tissues. Infected bulbs tend to produce many new scale bulblets, usually on the severed scales; however, such bulblets form at the infected end of the scale and are thus readily infected in turn. The main bulb is frequently destroyed, but masses of stem bulblets often form.

Fusarium is present in most soils and is most active and destructive when soil temperatures and moisture levels are high, during the summer months. It is prevalent where lilies have been grown for many years. In cool climates in northern areas the disease is less of a problem.

Many lily varieties are highly susceptible, but others show strong resistance, which can vary with climate and soil. The turgid, plump, soft bulbs of certain Asiatic hybrids, such as *Lilium cernuum* and its hybrids, seem prone to *Fusarium* bulb rot. There also appears to be a link between the red color in Asiatic hybrids and *Fusarium* susceptibility: 'Cinnabar', 'Pirate', and 'Scarlet Emperor' (Plate 7) are always among the first to suffer. 'Chinook' (Plate 8), 'Connecticut King', 'Enchantment', and 'Pollyanna' have shown some resistance. In my experience, trumpets, Aurelians, and Orientals have greater resistance. In soils with severe infection, however, especially where soil temperature and moisture level are high, basal rot can get the lot. There is some reason for optimism, though, and newer varieties have greater resistance.

Gardeners also need to understand more about cultural controls. They can begin by never planting bulbs that show signs of fungus disease. Growers and distributors of lily bulbs must make every effort to ensure that their bulbs are clean. This includes propagating them from clean scales, stem bulblets, bulbils, and seed. When basal rot is detected in a clump or bed of lilies, infected plants should be lifted and destroyed. In the more valuable varieties, some clean, healthy scales and stem bulblets may be identified and saved. In heavily infected sites, replace the soil to a depth of at least 45 centimeters (18 inches). Alternatively, chemical fumigation or sterilization of the soil can be undertaken before replanting. This should be done during a period of high soil temperature. Several products are available and great care is necessary in their application; only Vapam is currently approved for use by home gardeners.

Plate 7. *Lilium* 'Scarlet Emperor', an Asiatic hybrid somewhat susceptible to basal rot under certain conditions. Photo by Herman v. Wall.

Plate 8. *Lilium* 'Chinook', an Asiatic hybrid resistant to basal rot. Photo by Herman v. Wall.

The best weapon, of course, is preventing infection first, and there are several strategies for this. First, avoid fertilizers high in nitrogen, such as ammonium salts; these promote soft, rapid bulb growth and make bulbs very vulnerable to infection. Organic fertilizers such as manure and garden compost should be well decayed and should never be incorporated deeply into the soil where they will be close to the basal roots. Instead, use well-rotted manures and compost as a mulch; an added benefit is that mulch helps keep the soil cool, which discourages *Fusarium*.

Second, control soil moisture. *Fusarium* is always more active in low, wet sites, so lilies should be planted in well-drained positions. Avoid overwatering during the warm summer months. For several years the lilies at Columbia-Platte's fields received no irrigation, and in one year there was no rain for more than three months in the summer. The Asiatic lilies did not suffer and looked strong and healthy; the bulbs were simply smaller. *Fusarium* never appeared despite high soil temperatures.

Third, since acid soils may also aggravate the disease, an application of lime to increase pH may be advisable in some soils. Fourth, avoid mechanical damage during weeding, cleaning up, or transplanting the lilies, and control biting insects such as grubs and nematodes. Any lesion provides easy entry for basal rot organisms.

The disease was commercially controlled for many years by several fungicides, including benomyl (e.g., Benlate) and TBZ (e.g., Mertect). The bulbs are dipped in a solution or suspension; this can even eradicate the pathogen from infected bulbs. Since Benlate was taken off the market, home gardeners should consult local agencies for available fungicides effective against *Fusarium*.

In areas where *Fusarium* cannot be controlled in the open ground, lilies may have to be grown in containers, using a soilless mix or otherwise clean soil. Many kinds of lilies are perfectly content in large pots (see "Lilies in Containers" in Chapter 2).

The high temperatures necessary for scale propagation favor *Fusarium* infection, and bulbs can perish in infancy. It is therefore critical to scale only the healthiest bulbs, to wash them thoroughly before scaling, and to dip the scales in a fungicide before incubation.

Lily hybridizers in the commercial field must make greater efforts to breed varieties specifically for *Fusarium* resistance. This is even more crucial because key chemical controls are becoming unavailable.

BLACK SCALE DISEASE

Black scale is caused by the fungus *Colletotrichum lilii.* The symptoms are shallow, light brown or near-black, irregular lesions on the outer scales of the bulb. The infected tissues shrivel and die, making the bulb very unsightly. Black scale disease was a serious problem in the Easter lily industry in Louisiana many years ago but has not been reported recently.

BLUE MOLD

Blue mold is caused by *Penicillium* molds, with secondary infection by *Cylindrocarpon* and related fungal species. It occurs only on bulbs in storage and infects mostly their outer scales. It often resembles the blotches on a bruised apple. This problem is particularly prevalent in early dug bulbs that have suffered excessive mechanical injury.

The fungus grows well at low temperatures (its cousins affect fruits in the refrigerator). It can be recognized by chocolate-brown areas on the central or upper parts of the scales. If the rot is left unchecked, the bulbs can be destroyed. Some varieties are more susceptible than others. The disease can become rampant in severely damaged bulbs.

The best control is to avoid excessive bruising of the outer scales during harvesting and processing. If bulbs arrive with typical signs of decay and blue mold, the infected areas can be carefully removed if they are confined to small portions. Drying out and good aeration help. The bulb can then be dusted with a fungicide such as Captan. If the infection is severe, the bulbs should be returned or reported to the distributor.

BOTRYTIS BLIGHT OR FIRE

Botrytis blight is caused by two species of the fungus *Botrytis* that attack the above-ground parts of the plant. Both *B. elliptica* and *B. cinerea* can be present on the same plant, but the former is the more destructive. *Botrytis cinerea* flourishes in cool temperatures and is more apt to infect leaves, open flowers, and seedpods in cool summer weather and late fall. *Botrytis* is often considered the most important disease of lilies, especially in "Botrytis climates" such as the warm, moist coastal areas of the Pacific Northwest or the western coast of Britain. In drier, colder climates with low rainfall, it is seldom a problem.

The fungus overwinters as small black sclerotia that formed on the leaves in the previous season. These produce spores, which are blown about by the wind and splashed by rain onto the newly developing foliage in spring. The first signs of *Botrytis* can be white spots on the leaves; these become teardrop-shaped marks on the upper surface. They are lighter on the margin and darker in the center, so they are often called "pheasant eye" marks. In severe attacks during wet weather and warm, muggy conditions, the spots eventually coalesce, and the whole leaf collapses and decays.

Botrytis does not spread internally through a plant; instead, it continues to appear on new surfaces on the same and neighboring plants as more spores are produced and distributed. In severe cases it enters the stem and the plant collapses. The destruction of foliage can be very rapid. Brown spots appear on open flowers when *Botrytis* and moisture are present. These are believed to be caused by *B. cinerea* rather than *B. elliptica,* but this has not been conclusively demonstrated.

Botrytis is sometimes confused with other problems, including frost damage, sun scorch, hail damage, severe nutrient imbalance, or mechanical injury. To determine whether the problem is *Botrytis,* examine the spots early in the morning with a hand lens; if tiny, fuzzy strands of fungus are observed standing up like minuscule trees, get ready to spray. These visible signs of the fungus are the fruiting bodies that form conidia spores, the phase that spreads the disease to other parts of the plant and to its neighbors. Injury from hail, frost, or mechanical damage always makes it easier for *Botrytis* spores to enter the leaf. Spraying is strongly advised soon after an injury occurs.

The disease is not carried by the bulb, which may flower the following year if the infection was not too severe and did not occur early in the season.

There are many strains of *Botrytis* because both species mutate freely, making control difficult. The gardener must understand the life cycle of the fungus. The spores germinate and enter the leaves through the epidermal stomates. Moisture is essential for the spread of *Botrytis.* The formation of spores, liberation, and germination all take place within 12 hours; thus 24 hours of wet, moderately warm weather may lead to a considerable outbreak. Prolonged rains, frequent showers, fog, and heavy dew accompanied by warm temperatures, with moisture persisting on the foliage, produce perfect conditions for "fire."

With *Botrytis* disease, an ounce of prevention is worth a pound of cure. Therefore, early spraying is critical where environmental conditions tend to favor the disease. At the end of the growing season, remove all plant debris, pulling the old stems when they come away easily. Following a severe infection, remove the debris as soon as possible. Pull or cut the stems and rake off as many leaves as possible; all carry the resting sclerotia, which will rise up to bring new infection next spring. Burn the debris if possible; do not incorporate it in a compost pile. An application of fresh mulch is very beneficial at this time. Many growers spray the ground with a copper fungicide during the dormant season, but there is no proof that this kills resting or germinating spores.

Infection can occur at temperatures between 2° and 24°C (35° and 75°F) and is most likely in mild, moist, or foggy weather. It is advisable to remove spotted leaves when they are still wet in the morning; this can stop or at least inhibit further spread.

Spraying is essential for commercial growers and highly advisable to home gardeners in "fire" climates. Bordeaux mixture is an old remedy still used by Easter lily producers on the southern Oregon and northern California coast. The formula combines hydrated lime, bluestone (copper sulfate), water, and a spreader-sticker. It has the disadvantage of being awkward to mix, and it leaves an unattractive stain on foliage. Kocide, also copper-based, is inexpensive, effective, and easy and safe to use; it leaves a film on the leaf that kills the spore when it lands. A micronized copper spray (e.g., Kocide) is a good preventive, but it is not very effective once infection has occurred. Iprodione (e.g., Chipco 26019) and chlorothalonil (e.g., Daconil) have been effective and seem to stop infection after it has begun. There is, however, evidence that certain strains of the fungus are resistant to these products. It is wise to check with local agents about recent developments in chemical control.

Finally, spraying is only effective when the leaves are dry. Pay particular attention to covering the undersides of the leaves, for this is where infection takes place.

Lilies of the *Lilium candidum* group, which have overwintering foliage, must be watched very carefully. The fungus *Botrytis elliptica* was first described taxonomically from this lily. *Botrytis* infects the rosettes during fall and on warm winter days, providing a reservoir of infection for other lilies that emerge in spring.

Avoid planting lilies in areas with poor air circulation and poor air drainage. An open, breezy area is preferred. Low areas surrounded by shrubs, trees, or buildings can produce a *Botrytis* trap. Similarly, avoid planting in areas with too much shade where plant surfaces dry slowly. Warm, dry, sunny weather halts the infection. Planting lilies some distance apart also helps control the spread.

Many lilies are highly resistant to *Botrytis.* In Oregon, Orientals and Aurelians are much less susceptible than Asiatics. *Lilium lankongense* and its hybrids have shown remarkable resistance; however, *L. davidii* and some of its hybrids are particularly susceptible. The new tetraploid hybrids, with their thicker epidermis, seem more resistant to both *Botrytis* and leaf scorch.

There are many growers who never spray their lilies, and in some climates *Botrytis* may not be much of a problem. Be warned, however, that weather is unpredictable and severe infection can be sudden and amazingly destructive.

CERCOSPORELLA BLIGHT OF FOLIAGE

Cercosporella blight is practically unknown in North America, but in parts of Europe is it considered serious. Caused by the fungus *Cercosporella inconspicua,* it is reported to simulate a powdery mildew infection at its primary stage; in the secondary stage the lesions become brown; in the final stage, a blackened and burned appearance is characteristic.

ROOT ROTS

Root rots are associated with poor drainage, lack of soil aeration, and planting in soils that are too finely textured, such as heavy clays. The severity of the problem is related to soil temperature, local fungal flora, and geographical area.

There are several organisms associated with root rots. *Cylindrocarpon destructans, Pythium splendens* (in southern regions), and *Rhizoctonia solani* have all been implicated. Injury by root lesion nematodes

(*Pratylenchus penetrans*), also called meadow nematodes, opens up roots to infection by rots.

Rhizoctonia is a soil-borne fungus and a mild parasite of lily bulbs. The symptoms are dark yellow discolorations around the minute lesions caused by the fungal mycelia. The lesions are numerous and give the scales a yellow tint. Damage to the scales is slight, but the lesions can become entry points for other pathogens. If the bulbs are treated annually in a dip containing quintozene (e.g., Terraclor, PCNB), the *Rhizoctonia* is eliminated and the bulbs become white. *Rhizoctonia* is favored by warm temperatures, especially in greenhouses. There are many strains that can become pathogens in lilies.

The best control for root rots is to improve cultural practices, primarily drainage. Overwatering must be avoided at all costs.

RUST

Rust disease, caused by the fungus *Uromyces holwayi,* is more a novelty than a menace. It is recognized by elliptical rust-colored pustules on the upper surfaces of leaves and occasionally on stems. A rustlike condition in certain lilies, particularly the Oriental variety 'Journey's End', has been confused with rust disease. There is no fungal pathogen present; this is a symptom caused by virus infection. It is particularly noticeable when plants are growing under stress, as in forcing under low light conditions.

SOUTHERN WILT

Sclerotium disease can be very serious in many vegetable and flower crops, including onions, daffodils, and Dutch iris. It is caused by the fungus *Sclerotium delphinii* var. *rolfsii* and is most familiar as southern wilt of delphinium or crown rot of bulbous iris. The fungus produces characteristic round brown or reddish resting bodies, the sclerotia, which resemble turnip or cabbage seeds. The disease attacks the bulbs of actively growing plants during the warm summer months. The warm temperatures cause the sclerotia to germinate and attack plant tissues. Affected lily bulbs develop a white chalky or light brown rot, accompanied by conspicuous white strands (mycelia) of the invading fungus. The white, fanlike patches of coarse mycelia are a sure sign of the disease.

Affected rows of commercial plantings display tell-tale patches of brown plants. The disease spreads quickly under ideal conditions, and at harvest time all the bulbs will have turned to mush. The sclerotia are abundant in the soil around plants dying from the disease and can survive without a host for as much as 10 years.

This disease is seldom carried by commercially produced bulbs. Very few reports have been received of its occurrence in gardens. If sclerotium is detected, lift and wash the healthy bulbs surrounding the infection; remove and destroy infected bulbs and all surrounding soil to a depth of at least 30 centimeters (12 inches). Quintozene (e.g., Terraclor, PCNB) has been used as an effective control. A solution of this fungicide can be watered around infected areas to stop further spread. This is done when small pockets of infection occur in commercial plantings.

Southern wilt is native to the southern United States and could become a problem there if lilies are planted in sites previously used for such susceptible plants as delphinium, bulbous iris, or onions. The fungus does not thrive at low temperatures and thus is not much of a threat in northern regions.

STUMP ROT

Various species of water molds belonging to the genus *Phytophthora* occasionally invade the crowns of lilies as they emerge from the soil. The affected stems may remain as stumps. The bases of the leaves attached to the stems are destroyed, the leaves wither, and the remains of the crown lie flat on the ground. The browning of stem roots and decay of shoots are other symptoms. Affected lilies are a total loss for the current season, but they usually recover the following year. This condition occurs during cold, wet springs when the rate of growth is slow and mud can wash into the crowns. Planting lilies on ridges in commercial fields and on raised beds in gardens helps control the disease.

Other Disease Problems

PHYSIOLOGICAL BULB ROT

Physiological bulb rot is a general term for the rapid breakdown of bulbs that is not caused by a pathogen. Winter injury, damage by rodents, and total breakdown of the cells in bulbs harvested too early all fall into this category. The decay develops rapidly; the bulbs assume a wet, glazed appearance and soon become soft and mushy. No primary microorganisms are associated with this condition, but secondary organisms that live on dead tissue soon appear.

DAMPING-OFF DISEASES IN SEEDLINGS

Damping-off is caused by fungi that grow on the tissues of germinating lily (or other plant) seedlings. The cotyledons, or grasslike seed leaves, of epigeal germinators are more susceptible than are the first true leaves of hypogeal germinators. There are several fungi that cause damping-off, particularly species of *Pythium, Phytophthora,* and *Rhizoctonia.* The cotyledon or first true leaf simply topples over and decays because the fungus has attacked the tissues near the soil line, and the seedlings quickly die.

A series of strategies is employed to control damping-off. First, commercial and amateur growers should use pasteurized soil mixes or soil-less mixes when growing seedlings indoors. Since damping-off fungi are present in all natural soils, they must be destroyed by heating or chemical treatment before the soil is safe to use. Second, growers should use only clean, sterilized pots or other containers for growing seedlings. This can be accomplished by dipping containers in a 10 percent solution of household bleach (sodium hypochlorite). Third, growers should use freely draining soil mixes, and water very sparingly in the early stages of seedling growth. The surface of the soil should be allowed to become dry. Because high humidity and wet soil provide ideal conditions for damping-off, plants should be watered early in the day so that the soil can dry somewhat before nightfall. Fourth, growers should provide seedlings with good air circulation and as much light as possible. Sow the seedlings so that they will germinate in late March or April when conditions are most favorable for their development. (See Chapter 3 for specifics on timing germination.) Fifth, growers should grow seedlings outdoors in good, clean, well-prepared soil. Damping-off is seldom a problem under conditions of cool temperature and ample light. Finally, growers should use fungicides to control the fungi responsible for damping-off. These can be mixed in solution and watered into the soil. Thiophanate-methyl (e.g., Banrot) is widely available and combines several fungicides.

Soil Sterilization

In heavily contaminated soils where lilies have been grown for years, soil fumigation or sterilization may be the only recourse to eliminate pathogens. Soils are sterilized mainly to kill fungi, nematodes, perennial weeds, and weed seeds. The treatment is applied during the summer when soil temperatures are high and moisture levels relatively low; however, the soil must be moist for optimal results.

The chemicals can be either injected or watered into the soil. A tarp or plastic cover is usually necessary to prevent the chemicals from evaporating out of the soil. Most soil fumigants are highly toxic to humans and to living plants and must be used with the utmost care. Chemical-proof protective outer clothing must be worn to keep chemicals from contacting the skin, and a respirator mask to prevent inhaling the fumes. This is a job for professionals with industrial equipment; small growers or home gardeners contemplating this step should hire a contractor who specializes in such work.

The chemicals used include formalin (perhaps the most suitable for the home garden), methyl bromide, chloropicrin, and metam-sodium (e.g., Vapam). The last is diluted with water and applied with a watering can; it can be used safely on small areas by a gardener accustomed to handling industrial chemicals.

The soil must be well tilled before sterilization, free from clods and coarse organic matter. The tools used should also be clean. Time—usually about six weeks—must elapse before bulbs or other plants are set into sterilized soil; during this time the chemicals break down into harmless compounds.

Fasciation

Many lilies sometimes show irregular growth patterns known as fasciation. This has frequently been associated with disease-causing organisms. The condition is usually characterized by flattening of the stems and the production of countless small leaves. These fasciated plants often abort all their flowers, but in some cases (particularly in Oriental lilies) they may produce a multitude of flowers; a fasciated stem of Imperial Silver grown in Oregon produced 114 flowers. The stems of such lilies may twist into a spiral and sometimes split open. The condition is most frequently observed with older, larger bulbs, such as those of 'Edith Cecilia' and Pink Perfection. The tendency to fasciate is definitely genetic, and very warm temperatures in spring seem to trigger its expression. No disease is present, however, and the plants usually produce normal growth the following year.

Frost Injury

Late spring frosts can be devastating in northern regions. Frost damage can resemble the symptoms of certain diseases. Of the more widely grown lilies, Chinese trumpets are the most frost-susceptible, followed by Orientals; Asiatics appear to withstand a few degrees of frost more readily.

The emerging young shoots are frequently damaged. When severe frosts occur in late May and June, as may happen in northern or high-altitude gardens, many lilies may be in bud at this time, and the injuries can be quite serious.

In preventing frost damage, air drainage is of paramount importance. Plant lilies on slopes or other areas where the air is not stagnant. Avoid low-lying frost pockets.

In gardens subject to late frost, select late-emerging types of lilies to suit the climate. In severely cold areas, avoid planting trumpet lilies.

Sprinkler systems can be helpful in preventing frost damage. Watering has a tempering influence because heat is released as the water droplets freeze; moreover, a thin coating of ice on plants can protect tender foliage by preventing the freezing and rupturing of plant tissues. The smudge pots used in fruit orchards are also effective, if they are available and allowed in a given area.

When a frost is forecast, plants can be covered with tarps or other material such as row-cover fabric (Reemay is a popular brand). These may offer enough protection if the freeze is not too severe.

After a frost, the most severely damaged parts of the plants can be removed with a sharp knife. The affected plants should be sprayed immediately with a fungicide to forestall *Botrytis* infection.

A few years ago, the heating failed in a large greenhouse where we were conducting forcing trials on Asiatic and Oriental lilies. The outside temperature dropped to −4°C (24°F), and inside the greenhouse we recorded −3°C (27°F). When we entered the greenhouse very early on a clear morning, well before the sun was up, the plants were all crisply frozen, and we had little hope of their survival. We immediately sprayed them thoroughly with water and prayed for the best. All the Asiatic clones in the greenhouse survived, and all the Orientals perished. Their growth must have been extremely tender under these conditions in late February. Tough Asiatics growing outdoors would surely have endured much more cold.

CHAPTER 6

Pests

Lilies are prone to attack by several animal and insect predators, ranging in size from deer and elk to microscopic mites. The presence or absence of a specific predator depends on the region and climate zone in which the plants are grown. One can be assured, however, that predators are never as devastating as diseases such as *Botrytis, Fusarium,* or virus, which can destroy whole crops or garden plantings.

Aphids

The most important pests are aphids (see "Vectors of Virus Disease" in Chapter 5). These need to be controlled at all costs. Few insects breed more rapidly, so every measure should be taken to eradicate them on their first appearance. This is crucial if one is growing varieties or species known to be susceptible to virus. The several species of aphids that colonize lilies not only spread virus disease, but they also debilitate the plants physically, causing twisted leaves and distortion of flower buds.

Aphids produce their young viviparously in large numbers. On an infested plant one can often see large female aphids surrounded by scores of tiny offspring. These insects ordinarily move only by crawling, but at certain times they also produce winged migrant offspring that can fly for surprisingly long distances to colonize other plantings.

Systemic insecticides can be used to control aphids. When watered into the soil, the insecticide is taken up by the roots and absorbed through the conducting tissues of the plants. The aphids, being sucking insects, are then killed by the poisoned sap. This class of control is particularly effective in container plantings where the chemical remains concentrated longer. Systemic insecticide sprays should be applied to plantings on a regular basis. They can be combined with a fungicide. The insecticide acephate (e.g., Orthene) has been used quite successfully for aphid control, and marathon, which is sprinkled on the soil and watered in, can protect a plant from aphids for an entire growing season.

A variety of products are available for fumigating greenhouses. These must be used with caution under carefully controlled conditions. Aphids are particularly troublesome in greenhouses, where the environment is optimal for their increase and their natural predators tend to be excluded.

Insecticides available on the market change continually, but all must be used with the utmost care. Always consult the product label and brochure before using any garden chemical, and remember that the label's directions are legal requirements. Many states require an applicator's license for the use of certain chemicals. Always use rubber gloves and protective clothing; many insecticides can be absorbed through the skin and cause neurological damage.

Petroleum oil sprays or mineral oils reduce virus spread in many crops, including potatoes and lilies. The film of oil does not kill the aphids, but it prevents them from transmitting the disease through their stylets by clogging them. Oil sprays are considered to be 60 percent effective in controlling viruses in commercial plantings. The weekly sprays used by most commercial growers are hardly practical for home gardeners, but those with large lily plantings may find the effort worthwhile. Oil spraying should be avoided during the heat of the day, when it may produce leaf scorch and distortion; try to do it just before sundown. A light summer oil (e.g., Volck Supreme), used at about 1 percent dilution, is usually effective. Oils are quite safe to use and can be combined with most insecticides and fungicides.

Any spray can be dangerous to use on tender young seedlings. For this reason, it is better to control aphids, which are very attracted to seedlings, with a granular systemic insecticide such as marathon, which is sprinkled on the soil and watered in. Home gardeners can purchase similar products under such brand names as Dexol or Cole's systemic granules.

If aphids are continually moving into the planting from an outside source, efforts to control them are unlikely to be effective. Hybridizers and other enthusiasts may grow lilies in aphid-proof screen houses; however, aphids can be carried into such structures on clothing or tools, so a spray program should be maintained. Migrant aphids can be inhibited from moving between plants by barriers of other vegetation or gauze; the barrier must exceed the height of the lilies.

Finally, aphids overwinter by laying eggs, which are produced by the migrant phase. It is thus important to destroy any dead plant material that may harbor overwintering eggs.

Bulb Mites

The loose structure of lily bulbs makes them susceptible to infestation by pests that live between the scales. Bulb mites (*Rhizognyphus echinopus*) are troublesome but usually secondary pests; they attack many other bulbs along with lilies.

The adult mites are about the size of a pinhead, rounded, and yellowish white in color, often tinged with pink. In warm climates they are usually present in large numbers, particularly just above the basal plate and between the scales. They attack the roots and basal plate and eventually enter the center of the bulb. In Australia this pest has become devastating, capable of destroying whole crops if left unchecked.

The following methods of control may be used against mites:

- Treat bulbs with hot water at 44°C (111°F) for one hour.
- Fumigate dry bulbs with paradichlorobenzene (the active substance in mothballs) in an airtight container. Spread the fumigant over the bottom of the container, using 4 grams per liter of air space and exposing the bulbs for 12 hours.
- Dust the bulbs with flowers of sulfur (available in garden centers). This is probably the best method for the home gardener.
- Destroy badly infested bulbs by burning them.

Deer, Hares, and Rabbits

These herbivores often nibble on young growth, buds, seedpods, and other plant parts; however, they are seldom seriously destructive. In rural areas gardens can be protected by deer- and rabbit-proof fences, adequately maintained. The presence of a dog often deters deer from invading, and many cats will prey on rabbits.

Chemical controls and repellents (Ropel is often recommended), trapping, and shooting offer only temporary solutions, if indeed they are effective at all. Foul-smelling concoctions, both homemade and commercial, are sometimes effective against deer. The material is placed in muslin sacks and suspended around the plantings.

Leatherjackets, Wireworms, and Millipedes

These groups of underground pests can cause damage and losses in lilies and other crops. All are prevalent in grassland.

Leatherjackets are the larvae of the cranefly or daddy-long-legs (*Tipulidae*). They are sluggish, legless, dull-colored brownish creatures that may reach 3.75 centimeters (1.5 inches) in length.

Wireworms are the larvae of click beetles. They are slender, smooth, tough, and wiry creatures, measuring up to 2.5 centimeters (1 inch) in length. They are golden yellow and have six very short legs. These pests burrow into bulbs.

Millipedes are dull-colored, sluggish creatures with many legs. They curl up when disturbed.

All these underground pests can be controlled by dusting the ground with benzene hexachloride (BHC) or Bromophos. A nonchemical control involves baiting with slices of potato, carrot, or other root vegetable placed below the surface of the soil. These traps can be skewered on a stick to mark their position and lifted a few days later, when the attached pests can be destroyed.

Lily Beetle

Long prevalent in Europe, the lily beetle (*Lilioceris lilii*) has been reported in eastern North America. The larvae and adult beetles feed on the leaves of lilies and other liliaceous plants, including *Convallaria* (lily of the valley) and *Fritillaria.* Both life stages have voracious appetites and soon devour entire plants.

The larva is a humpbacked, dirty yellow grub with a dark head, repulsively covering itself in dark, slimy excrement. The adult is up to 8 millimeters (0.25 inch) long and bright scarlet with black legs and antennae. The eggs are laid on the underside of the foliage.

The following controls are effective:

- Spray plants with contact and systemic insecticides; both are effective.
- Drench soil with an insecticide such as acephate (e.g., Orthene) to kill the mature larvae that live just under the soil surface in winter. Also, avoid transporting infested soil to other sites.
- Beware of imported bulbs on which the beetles entered North America. Grateful recipients of gifts from overseas must be on their guard!
- Catch adult beetles between the fingers and smash them.

It is very important to report any new outbreaks in North America to the local agricultural extension agent and to the North American Lily Society. The lily beetle has only appeared in a few places on this continent, and with care, it should be possible to prevent any lasting infestation.

Lily Thrips

The adult lily thrip (*Liothrips vaneeckii*) is very tiny and black in color. The larva is salmon pink and minute. The adults and larvae live out their entire life cycle in the bulb. Feeding seems to be localized at the bases of the scales, where it seriously weakens the bulb, rendering it flabby. This allows the entry of bacteria and fungi, frequently resulting in the bulb rotting away.

The following controls can be used:

- Treat bulbs with hot water treatment at 44°C (111°F) for one hour to eradicate the pest.
- Dust bulbs with benzene hexachloride (BHC).
- Wash or dip bulbs in a solution of an insecticide such as acephate (e.g., Orthene) or malathion.

Lily Weevil

The lily weevil (*Agasphaerops nigra*) is a native of western North America from northern California to Vancouver Island. It has been reported both on native lilies of that region and on cultivated forms of *Lilium longiflorum* (Easter lily).

The larvae are minute, whitish, legless grubs with chestnut-brown heads. They burrow into the lily stem and bulb. Adult weevils emerge in March and April, feeding on the leaves of plants.

Systemic insecticides are highly effective in controlling weevils, with acephate (e.g., Orthene) being used most frequently.

Nematodes

Many species of nematodes or eelworms inhabit soils everywhere. Some are harmless or even beneficial to plants, but others are destructive. The most harmful to lilies are the root lesion or meadow nematode and the leaf-lesion nematode. These microscopic pests cause serious damage to lily crops in some regions if their populations are not under control.

Nematodes penetrate root tissues, killing cells as they go. They move inside the root, feeding, laying eggs, and destroying additional cells. The roots become soft and flabby, eventually succumbing to infection that moves into the basal plate, turning it into mush.

River water often carries nematodes, which can then enter croplands through irrigation. These pests also host bacteria; some species even carry virus diseases. Nematode infestation causes stunting of growth and can severely reduce commercial production. Crops parasitized by nematodes are seldom uniformly affected.

Foliar nematodes live in the soil. When a suitable host is present, they move through the stem in a surface film of moisture to invade the leaves and flowers.

The following controls are used for nematodes:

- Keep the foliage as dry as possible to control foliar nematodes by preventing movement of the organisms. Systemic insecticides are very effective.
- Treat bulbs with hot water at 44°C (111°F) for one hour.
- Fumigate soil with methyl bromide, chloropicrin, and metam-sodium (e.g., Vapam). This is a highly successful technique in commercial plantings. Steam sterilization of greenhouse soils is very important.
- Avoid planting lilies continuously in the same site; this prevents harmful nematode populations from building up in the home garden.
- Apply a granular nematicide such as fenamiphos (e.g., Nemacur) when planting bulbs.
- Try adding carnivorous nematodes to the soil. Organic gardening suppliers offer these to devour the plant-eating varieties.

Pheasant and Quail

These birds can develop the habit of pecking emerging shoots in very early spring. They may also peck down to destroy bulbs during cold periods when other food is scarce. Control should be restricted to trapping or shooting the birds only when damage is severe. Poison grains are strictly outlawed in most areas and must never be used to control pheasants and quail.

Rodents

Mice and voles often devour lily bulbs, especially when their populations are poorly controlled by animal and bird predators. If moles are active in an area, mice and voles often use the mole tunnels to get access to bulbs. Traps and poison baits are effective controls; in the home garden, a predatory cat or dog can be of great assistance.

Squirrels and chipmunks sometimes learn to prey on garden bulbs. The best control is to plant bulbs some distance from trees, since these pests do not like to venture far from the safety of their homes.

Several species of gophers are serious pests in lily plantings in western North America. They love lily bulbs and can devour great numbers in a season. Gophers in the Willamette Valley were controlled for many years by injecting cans of methyl bromide into their runs. On a small scale, trapping is also an effective way of controlling gophers.

Slugs and Snails

These hermaphroditic mollusks lay clusters of round, white, jelly-like eggs in little niches in the soil. These can be destroyed by frequent cultivation of the top few inches of soil, bringing the eggs to light and exposing them to frost and birds.

Slugs in particular can be a problem both above and below ground, depending on the species present. They find harbors in moist, shaded areas under dead leaves and other plant debris or among low-growing plants. They are particularly prevalent during rainy seasons.

Slugs and snails feed voraciously on lilies when the shoots emerge. Later in the season they can climb the stems, stripping the leaves completely.

To control slugs and snails:

- Limit habitat around lily plantings by controlling weeds and using mulch instead of ground cover planting.
- Place bait containing metaldehyde among plantings in the early evening hours. This is crucial at the time when lily shoots are emerging and during damp weather. Bait should be renewed after heavy rain. Liquid bait such as Deadline may be less attractive to pets than pelletized bait. Beer traps have been used successfully by some enthusiasts: simply pour the beer into a shallow dish and place it near the lily plantings in the early evening.

Symphylids

These tiny insects are prevalent in some soils and can be extremely difficult to eradicate. They can damage lily crops severely if their populations get out of control. The tiny creatures are barely visible to the naked eye; they are best diagnosed by submitting a soil sample to an agricultural laboratory. The usual control is soil fumigation.

PART TWO

Lilium 'Empress of India'

CHAPTER 7

Lily Species

The genus *Lilium* includes approximately 100 species distributed throughout the cold and temperate parts of the Northern Hemisphere. These wild species are the ancestors from which the garden lilies of today have been selected and hybridized. In addition, many of the true species remain popular in gardens today, including *Lilium auratum* var. *platyphyllum, L.candidum, L.henryi, L.leucanthum* var. *centifolium, L.pardalinum, L.pumilum, L.regale,* and *L.speciosum* var. *rubrum.* Other species are sought and grown by connoisseurs because they have a special grace and beauty that no modern hybrids possess.

The growing interest in ecology and conservation has stimulated many North American enthusiasts to grow lily species, especially those native to the growers' regions or otherwise environmentally well suited. The Lily Species Preservation Society was founded in 1995 in affiliation with the North American Lily Group, in recognition that many species in various parts of the world are endangered and must be preserved. The unique beauty of each species and its possible value for future hybridizing are both taken into account. Every effort must be made to preserve natural populations and to increase populations of species in cultivation, especially in botanic gardens and similar institutions.

It is commonly believed that species lilies are more difficult to grow than hybrids, but this is not necessarily true. It is important to remember that these plants have survived through millennia of climatic changes, natural disasters, diseases, and pests, during which natural selection has eliminated the weaker forms. Some species, such as *Lilium martagon* and *L. pumilum*, grow over vast areas in widely differing environments, so it is not surprising that they adapt well to gardens in many regions.

The best and safest way to build up a collection of lily species is by obtaining seed, either from natural populations or from cultivated populations known to be true. Species lily bulbs should be purchased only from specialists who are familiar with growing methods and disease control. Bulbs collected in the wild should never be sold or purchased.

Classification of the Species

Botanists over the years have published various classifications of the genus, giving different weights to plant form, flower form, or geographical distribution. Perhaps the most authoritative was that of Harold F. Comber, who published a revised subclassification of the genus *Lilium* in the 1949 *Lily Year Book* of the Royal Horticultural Society. Comber had profound knowledge of lily species and years of experience in growing most of them from seed. He followed this with extensive studies of their growth patterns. Besides the flowers, Comber considered other physical features, including seed, type of germination, arrangement of the leaves, and the form and growth habit of the bulb. He also gave importance to geographical distribution and speculated on the evolutionary relationships of the species and groups. This resulted in the seven-part categorization shown here:

1. Martagon Section: *L. distichum, L. hansonii, L. martagon, L. medeoloides, L. tsingtauense*
2. American Section
   2a. *L. bolanderi, L. columbianum, L. kelloggii, L. humboldtii, L. rubescens, L. washingtonianum*
   2b. *L. maritimum, L. nevadense, L. occidentale, L. pardalinum, L. parryi, L. parvum, L. roezlii*
   2c. *L. canadense, L. grayi, L. iridollae, L. michauxii, L. michiganense, L. superbum*
   2d. *L. catesbaei, L. philadelphicum*

3. Candidum Section: *L. bulbiferum, L. candidum, L. carniolicum,*
   L. chalcedonicum, L. monadelphum, L. polyphyllum, L. pomponium,
   L. pyrenaicum
4. Oriental Section: *L. auratum, L. brownii, L. japonicum, L. nobilissi-*
   mum, L. rubellum, L. speciosum
5. Asiatic Section
   5a. *L. davidii, L. duchartrei, L. henryi, L. lancifolium, L. lankongense,*
       L. leichtlinii, L. papilliferum
   5b. *L. amabile, L. callosum, L. cernuum, L. concolor, L. pumilum*
   5c. *L. bakerianum, L. mackliniae, L. nepalense, L. ochraceum, L. sem-*
       pervivoideum, L. taliense, L. wardii
6. Trumpet Section
   6a. *L. leucanthum, L. regale, L. sargentiae, L. sulphureum*
   6b. *L. formosanum, L. longiflorum, L. neilgherrense, L. philippinense,*
       L. wallichianum
7. Dauricum Section: *L. dauricum, L. maculatum.*

The more recent work of Victoria Matthews has resulted in the combining ("lumping") of many Eurasian entities formerly considered to be separate species; I believe this is very well advised. In section 3, Comber did not include *Lilium kesselringianum, L. kosa,* or *L. rhodopaeum.* He considered these Caucasian species so closely related to be varieties of one species, *L. monadelphum.*

Descriptions A to Z

The following descriptions of the species are intended for the interest and convenience of the hobbyist, hybridizer, and specialized grower. The present text is based in part on Carl Feldmaier's discussion in *Die Lilien* (1970). More technical details of identification and synonymy appear in earlier books (Feldmaier and McRae 1982; Fox 1985; Royal Horticultural Society 1992) and are omitted here. The closely related giant lily, *Cardiocrinum giganteum,* is described at the end of this chapter.

Lilium alexandrae (Wallace) Coutts 1934
This species is named for Princess Alexandra. Its Japanese name is *uke-yuri.* Native to the Ryukyus and a few other islands of southern Japan,

Plate 9. *Lilium alexandrae.* Photo by Herman v. Wall.

where the climate is very wet and frost-free, this lily grows in hollows where humus has collected on the coral-based substrate.

The stems are 30 to 100 centimeters (1 to 3 feet) tall; the leaves are broadly lanceolate. The flowers are pure white and trumpet shaped, carried horizontally or slightly raised, and have a delightful fragrance. Seed germination is delayed hypogeal.

Lilium alexandrae is one of the more difficult species to cultivate and should be treated like a rather tender *L. auratum.* Its low-latitude origin makes it want to grow slowly but steadily during winter. I grew plants successfully in pots in a cool, frost-free greenhouse for many years; smaller plantings were also successful outdoors in Oregon. In Albany, New York, seedlings of *L. alexandrae* survived two winters and a low temperature of −3°C (27°F) when mulched with 5 centimeters (2 inches) of pine needles.

Ruth Clas, an amateur hybridizer, raised a hybrid between *Lilium alexandrae* and *L. speciosum* that she named 'Easter Bunny'. The first embryo-cultured lily to flower at Oregon Bulb Farms in the early 1970s was a hybrid between *L. alexandreae* and *L. speciosum* 'Shooting Star', raised by Judith Freeman. Many hybrids were later raised from *L. alexandrae* and *L. speciosum* clones, all of great beauty. Judith Freeman continued this work, flowering the hybrids from crossing *L. alexandrae* with *L. rubellum, L. alexandrae* with *L. nobilissimum,* and *L. alexandrae* with 'Little Rascal'. The succeeding generations from these crosses proved quite fertile.

Lilium amabile Palibin 1901

The name *amabile* comes from the Latin word for "deserving of love, pleasing." Native to Korea and far-offshore Ullung-Do (Dagelet Island), this species grows in moist meadows in gritty soils derived from coarse volcanic material as well as on Paleozoic slates and limestones.

The stems are 30 to 100 centimeters (1 to 3 feet) tall; the soft, green lanceolate leaves are absent from the stem near the ground. The racemose inflorescence may have 5 to 15 unpleasantly scented turk's-cap flowers of gleaming orange-red, speckled with purple spots; they open in June and July. Seed germination is immediate epigeal. Seedlings are easy to grow, forming long, narrow bulbs with excellent root systems. They flower profusely in the second year. The plants are happy in a gritty, well-drained limy soil, with shade at the base as provided in the wild by grasses and shrubs.

There are three botanical varieties of the species including the type, variety *amabile*. Variety *luteum* Constable 1939 is a beautiful golden-yellow with black spots. Variety *unicolor* Comber 1935 has softer orange, unspotted flowers.

Hybrids derived from *Lilium amabile* include Frank L. Skinner's 'Duchess' (with *L. maculatum*); James Taylor's 'Cardinal' (with *L. lancifolium*); and Dr. Abel's Fiesta hybrids (with *L. davidii*). Columbia-Platte Lilies has bred free-flowering hybrids by crossing *L. amabile* with *L. callosum*, *L. maximowiczii*, and *L. pumilum*. Several Asiatic hybrids were also crossed with *L. amabile*, including 'Connecticut Lemonglow'. Hybridizers should work more with this strong species and its variants to produce dependable garden lilies.

Lilium amoenum Wilson 1920

The name *amoenum* means "pleasing." Native to Yunnan Province in China, this species grows in valleys and on slopes up to 2200 meters (7200 feet), in nearly frost-free conditions.

This delicate pink-flowered lily, only 15 to 30 centimeters (6 to 12 inches) tall, is closely allied to but distinct from the plant described by Augustin A. H. Léveillé under the name *Lilium sempervivoideum*. It resembles a small *L. rubellum*; the flowers are slightly nodding, bell shaped or bowl shaped, and deep rose in color.

Lilium arboricola W. T. Stearn 1954

The name *arboricola* means "tree-dweller." The species is native to forests of northern Myanmar (formerly Burma), where it grows as an epiphyte on trees.

One of the last discoveries made by the great plant-hunter Frank Kingdon-Ward, this lily is a curiosity in the genus for its epiphytic habit. Its seeds and bulbs were sent to England in 1953, where plants flowered in 1954. Bulbs propagated from this stock flowered in Liverpool and at Wisley for only two years, after which the species was apparently lost from cultivation.

The charming flowers are of martagon form, with a scent Kingdon-Ward described as being like nutmeg. The roundly reflexed tepals are tinted Nile green and have a silken surface texture, against which the cinnabar-orange stamens stand out in striking contrast. Fox (1985) further observed that the seed is extremely light, with an uncommonly broad wing. Seed germination is immediate epigeal. Bulbils are produced in the leaf axils.

Lilium auratum Lindley 1862

Gold band lily

The name *auratum* means "ornamented with gold." In Japan the species is named *yama-yuri,* meaning "mountain lily." Native to Japan, with indigenous wild populations only on Honshu, gold band lily grows among other vegetation on the margins of hillside woods, sometimes in a thin layer of humus, but usually in pure volcanic ash and lava debris.

Several varieties of this species have been brought into cultivation. In variety *pictum* Carrière 1867 (Plate 10) the central red "band" occurs as a flush of greater or lesser depth, rather than a band. The most important form is variety *platyphyllum* Baker 1880 (Plate 11), which has strong, purplish green stems from 90 to 200 centimeters (3 to 7 feet) tall, with dark green, broadly lanceolate leaves carried on short petioles; the leaves may be 22 to 25 centimeters (9 to 10 inches) long. The outfacing flowers are large, sweetly scented, and of flattened bowl shape. The tips of the petals recurve or roll back. The flowers, 25 to 30 centimeters (10 to 12 inches) in diameter, are ivory-white with a golden-yellow central band and carmine spots and papillae. They appear from August to September. Seed germination is delayed hypogeal, and excellent seedling populations can be raised. Grown in isolation from known virus carriers, such plants can remain strong and healthy for many years. Variety *praecox* Baker 1880 is a very early flowering form of the type. In variety *rubrovittatum* Duchartre 1870 the central band is deep crimson. Variety *virginale* Duchartre 1870, by contrast, is white with a gold band and yellow spots.

Several clones of varieties *pictum, platyphyllum,* and *rubrovittatum* that were very virus tolerant were used to breed superior forms of the species at Oregon Bulb Farms. Excellent selections from variety *virginale* also were used to produce the Melridge strain; similarly superior forms were later named the Kimono strain.

Lilium auratum has often been hybridized with *L. speciosum*. The original cross, made by Francis Parkmann in 1869, was introduced as *L. ×parkmannii* T. Moore 1875. Subsequently, similar crosses were made by Leslie Jury and J. S. Yeates in New Zealand; this material was the basis of the Imperial Crimson, Imperial Gold, and Imperial Silver strains raised at Oregon Bulb Farms. *Lilium auratum* forms were crossed with *L. japonicum* and *L. rubellum* by Norma Pfeiffer to pro-

Plate 10. *Lilium auratum* var. *pictum*

Plate 11. *Lilium auratum* var. *platyphyllum*. Photo by Herman v. Wall.

duce a series of beautiful hybrids also used. Similar work was done by Leslie Woodriff, who crossed *L. auratum* and hybrids of *L. auratum* × *L. speciosum* with *L. japonicum* and *L. rubellum* to produce his Atomic hybrids and Little Fairies. The Magic Pink strain resulted from crossing *L. auratum* var. *platyphyllum* with *L. rubellum*. Oregon Bulb Farms also raised hybrids between *L. auratum* var. *platyphyllum* and *L. alexandrae*. The dwarf *L. auratum* Tom Thumb strain from Yeates was used at Oregon Bulb Farms to breed the short-growing Little Rascals strain for pot culture.

In Japan, *Lilium auratum* was crossed with *L. longiflorum* to produce a series of hybrids. One clone, 'Yuri no Hakari', has been introduced in North America. The cross between *L. auratum* and *L. henryi,* also made in Japan, produced a hybrid numbered 82111. This fascinating plant produces a few fertile gametes and has been used extensively in Orienpet breeding on both sides of the Atlantic (see Chapter 12). A hybrid between *L. auratum* var. *platyphyllum* and the Chinese trumpet hybrid 'Copper King' was produced by Jaap Spaans in the Netherlands.

Lilium bakerianum Collett & Hemsley 1890

This species is named for English botanist John Gilbert Baker (1834–1920), director of the Royal Herbarium at Kew. The type was collected by Henry Collett in 1888 from the Shan Hills, northeastern Myanmar (formerly Burma). The species also occurs in Nepal in foothills of the eastern Himalayas, from 1200 to 3000 meters (3900 to 9800 feet), with more populations in western China. It grows in open, dry, stony country.

For the lily enthusiast, this is not so much a single species as a very complex group. The typical plant bears a tight raceme of up to 8 pendent, bell-shaped, sweetly scented flowers with a greenish base color, heavily overlain and spotted in reddish brown. The taller forms range from 30 to 100 centimeters (1 to 3 feet) in height; the shorter variety *delavayi* Wilson 1925 is only 20 centimeters (8 inches) tall. All varieties of the species have been found in different colors, including white, pink, yellow, and greenish, strongly marked in the throat and often heavily spotted with chestnut brown, purple, or carmine. Seed germination is immediate epigeal.

One problem with *Lilium bakerianum* in cultivation is the tenderness of many forms; nevertheless, it does not seem unlikely that plants from rocky, dry situations at 3500 meters (11,500 feet) in northwestern Yunnan might be found a small niche in someone's garden. The establishment of a fertile seeding group may be the answer.

At Oregon Bulb Farms we grew this lily in pots in a cool greenhouse for several years; it flowered on two occasions. There is no record of hybridization with it.

Lilium bolanderi S. Watson 1885

This species is named for American plant collector and botanist Henry Richardson Bolander. It is native to the Siskiyou Mountains of southern Oregon and northern California, at 900 to 1800 meters (3000 to 5900 feet). Inhabiting rocky soils and screes, it grows where the climate is moist in fall and spring, with snow cover in winter, and very hot and dry in summer.

This is a typical dryland bulb with loosely attached scales. The plants grow 30 to 120 centimeters (1 to 4 feet) tall and bear 3 to 8 whorls of waxy, blue-green lanceolate leaves. The sturdy stem carries up to 9 delicate flowers with a true bell shape. Color ranges from brick to wine-red, spotted faintly inside with crimson or pure red. The flowers open in July. Seed germination is hypogeal in late fall in cool conditions, and the first true leaf shows above ground with the coming of spring.

Lilium bolanderi is one of a group of western American lilies that require extreme drainage to survive, but the soil beneath them should not be allowed to dry out completely. Plants grown from seed typically flower in three years.

I observed the first hybrid from this species in the 1960s, in a population grown from mixed seed sent to us by Boyd Kline of Medford, Oregon. Several seedlings had the bell-shaped flowers of *Lilium bolanderi*; we believed they were hybrids with *L. pardalinum*. Derek Fox, in his book *Growing Lilies* (1985: 91), wrote the following:

> *Lilium bolanderi* has played an important role in the making of Pacific Coast hybrids initiated by Mayell with a cross using *L. pardalinum*. This was followed by bringing in *L. kelloggii* × *L. parryi*, putting the four species together. One of the resulting seedlings, pink in color, pollinated *L. pardalinum* var. *giganteum*

and produced my own Bullwood hybrids. Some of the Monterey hybrids also show the influence of *L. bolanderi*. The rich coloration, the bizarre spotting and the almost non-recurving tepals are all characteristics which have been captured in the hybrids, the last mentioned quality being most significant.

Plate 12. *Lilium bolanderi.* Photo by Billie Matthews.

Lilium brownii (F. E. Brown 1841) Miellez

This species is named for F. E. Brown, who first flowered the species in his nursery in England. It is native to southern China.

Three varieties of this beautiful trumpet lily are recorded. Variety *brownii* is the type, first sent to England from Guangzhou, China, in 1835. It grows 90 to 120 centimeters (3 to 4 feet) tall. The horizontally held trumpet, up to 15 centimeters (6 inches) long, is pure creamy white inside and rosy purple to chocolate-brown outside, sometimes overlain with green. The flowers open in July.

Harold F. Comber described this variety as a single clone that could be propagated only vegetatively; however, it sets seed when crossed with the other two varieties of the species. It is not very hardy in cold climates. It was grown by Edgar Kline of Lake Grove, Oregon, for many years. In the early 1970s we obtained it from a grower in Mossyrock, Washington; the bulbs were composed of an abundance of narrow scales, some of which were jointed. The clone proved remarkably hardy and persistent, usually producing two to three flowers. It was propagated by scaling and tissue culture.

Variety *australe* Stapf 1921, known as the Hong Kong lily, comes from the southern Chinese provinces of Fujian, Guangdong, Guangxi, and Yunnan, and from Hong Kong. This southern variety has narrow white bulbs, narrow lanceolate leaves, and a vigorous, nearly perennial growth habit. Populations were grown at Oregon Bulb Farms for many years; the plants varied in height from 150 to 180 centimeters (5 to 6 feet), and the leaves were broad to narrow lanceolate and quite sparse. The flowers were trumpet shaped and softly fragrant, with the coloring on the reverse varying from green to chocolate-brown. They appear in August and September. Seed sets readily, and germination is immediate hypogeal. The plants are not winter-hardy in cold climates.

Variety *viridulum* Baker 1885 (synonym var. *colchesteri* Wilson 1932) is found wild in nearly all parts of central China at elevations up to 1500 meters (4900 feet). The bulbs, which are gathered for food, are large and creamy white; the flower stems are 100 to 200 centimeters (3 to 7 feet) tall, with long lanceolate leaves. The strongly perfumed flowers are up to 15 centimeters (6 inches) long, pale yellow on opening but soon fading to white; the inner surface of the tepals has green shading, and the outer surface is marked with green and rosy purple. The flowers open in August and September, and seeds set readily.

None of the three varieties was used in hybridizing at Oregon Bulb Farms. *Lilium brownii* was reportedly crossed with *L. formosanum* (Zalivski 1938) and with *L. longiflorum* (Jaap van Tuyl 1980).

Lilium bukozanense Honda 1942
Hong Kong lily

This species is named for its only area of occurrence on Mount Buko, 60 kilometers (40 miles) northwest of Tokyo, Japan. There it grows at 600 meters (1950 feet) on near-vertical cliffs.

In the wild, this lily's stem hangs outward, holding upright a large, bowl-shaped orange-red flower with heavy spotting and narrow tepals.

The foliage is very narrowly lanceolate and glossy green. The slender stems grow up to 60 centimeters (2 feet) tall. The bulbs are firm and globose. Seed germination is immediate hypogeal, with the seedlings producing two or three flowers in the second year. The flowers appear in June.

The species was grown at Oregon Bulb Farms for several years quite successfully. The plant proved to be highly interfertile with several Asiatic hybrids, notably 'Connecticut King'. Its value as a parent is questionable, however, mainly because of its poor plant habit and narrow tepals.

Lilium bulbiferum Linnaeus 1758
Fire lily
This species is named for its tendency to produce bulbils on the stem. It is native to Europe, from the Pyrenees in the west to the western Czech Republic, Hungary, and Poland in the east, and from central and southern Germany in the north to southern Italy just below Naples.

Two forms are grown under the name *Lilium bulbiferum:* the typical form, which produces bulbils in the leaf axils, and variety *croceum,* which does not.

Subspecies *bulbiferum* is a rare plant in the wild, found occasionally in the Swiss regions of Oberbayern, Thuringen, and Erzgebirge. The bulbs are globose and white. The stem, 60 to 120 centimeters (2 to 4 feet) tall, with scattered lanceolate leaves, bears bulbils in the axils of the leaves during most summers. It flowers in a terminal umbel with up to 20 upfacing golden-orange bowl-shaped blossoms, marked with red-orange toward the tips, and with light spotting. The subspecies has been hybridized with *Lilium dauricum* to produce *L. ×hollandicum* Stearn 1950; with *L. davidii* var. *willmottiae* to produce *L. ×cromottiae;* with *L. pumilum* (Preston 1933; Kish 1942); and with *L. monadelphum* to produce *L. ×fialkovaja* (1914). It seems not to have been used in the last half of the twentieth century.

Variety *chaixii* Stoker 1939 is a dwarf form occurring in the Alpes-Maritimes of France, in the Vartal and the Val di Minera. The flowers are orange-gold with reddish tips.

Variety *croceum* (Chaix) Persoon 1805 is the orange-flowered form of the species and is the most common form in cultivation, plentiful in the cottage gardens of England, Ireland, and Scotland. Its distribution in the wild is said to cover central and southern Germany, Austria, Switzerland, the northern half of Italy, Corsica, southern France, and the Pyrenees. It is the only lily native to the Netherlands and was painted by the Dutch masters. It is distinguished from the typical form of the species by its flowers, which are more erect and shallowly cupped. The tepals are light orange to orange-red inside, deeper at the base and tip; externally they are orange to orange-red with a green keel.

Variety *giganteum* Terracciano 1906, a very large form growing 150 to 180 centimeters (5 to 6 feet) tall, occurs in the far southern end of the species' range, around Naples and Vesuvius and in the volcanic crater of Cigliano.

Seed germination for all forms of *Lilium bulbiferum* is delayed hypogeal. The species is one of the easiest lilies to establish in gardens, preferring full sun to light shade and taking kindly to most soils. Variety *chaixii* has proved the most difficult in cultivation, perhaps because of its more specialized ecological niche in nature.

Lilium callosum Siebold & Zuccarini 1839
Slimstem lily

The name *callosum* means "thick-skinned, thick, solid" and refers to the thickened (callose) tips of the bracts and upper leaves. The species is native to eastern Asia, from Taiwan north to the Amur River, extending in Siberia to the coast at Vladivostok and in the north to Khabarovsk, and reaching northern and central China, as well as Japan on Kyushu, Kaonsi, Shikoku, and the Ryukyus. It grows in meadows, among shrubs, on slopes, often in humus-rich soils.

Although possessing the widest distribution of any eastern Asian lily, implying that forms exist suitable to many climates, this small, elegant species is seldom seen in cultivation. It grows 30 to 90 centimeters (1 to 3 feet) tall and bears in July and August a slender stem of up to 12 small, lightly spotted turk's-cap flowers. The color is an unusual shade of brick-red finely sprinkled with black spots in the throat. Seed germination is immediate epigeal. The white bulb is small and round, with a flattened top.

Variety *flaviflorum* Makino 1913 is a yellow-flowered form indigenous to the island of Okinawa.

Both the type and the yellow form were grown successfully in Oregon for many years. Flowering was always in August, making seed-maturing difficult. The seed capsules were long, 2 to 6 centimeters (0.8 to 2.5 inches), and narrow. The species is lime-tolerant; garden soil with a reasonably high humus content and good drainage always proved adequate.

Lilium callosum has been hybridized with several other species and hybrids. Hiroshi Myodo's cross of variety *flaviflorum* with *L. concolor* var. *coridion* gave 'Sugekime'. Other reported crosses include *L. callosum* with *L. pumilum* (Sally Bucknell 1965) and *L. callosum* with *L. amabile* (Leonard Marshall 1983). The cross of variety *flaviflorum* with yellow Asiatic hybrids (Marshall 1980) produced unique and interesting bright yellow hybrids, some of short habit. 'Summit' is an excellent clone selected from this work.

Plate 13. *Lilium* 'Evening Star' ('Longistar' × 'Aristo'). Photo by Jaap Westland.

Lilium canadense Linnaeus 1753
Meadow lily

This species is named for Canada, from which its bulbs were first brought to Europe. It is native to eastern North America, from 35° to 50° north latitude, or roughly from North Carolina in the United States to southern Quebec and Ontario in Canada. It grows in moist meadows, ditches, and roadsides, on the edges of woodland or among shrubs that protect it from grazing and mowing.

The meadow lily's grace, poise, and fine proportions lend it special elegance. The fleshy rhizomes annually produce at their ends scaly bulbs, from which the following year a shiny green stem rises 60 to 150 centimeters (2 to 5 feet) tall, set with whorls of leaves. It bears an umbel of up to 20 flowers in June to July, usually yellow with dark purple spots. The flowers are of turk's-cap form, with the tepals only halfway reflexed to produce an exquisite bell shape. Seed germination is delayed hypogeal, with flowering plants produced in three to four years after germination.

In the garden, the bulbs should be planted in an acid, moist, very well drained bed with sand, loam, and peat. Along with good drainage, it is important to provide a constant source of water, readily accomplished with drip irrigation. As it is very susceptible to virus, this species should be planted in isolation from other lilies. Plantings in the Pacific Northwest have been short-lived, growing strongly for a few years before succumbing either to virus or to unfavorable climatic conditions.

Not surprisingly, given its great range, this species has given rise to many distinct varieties and forms. Variety *coccineum* Pursh 1814 has dark brick-red flowers with a yellow throat and is very heavily spotted. Variety *editorum* Fernald 1943 grows in drier sites in the Appalachian Mountains; it is distinguished from the typical form by its broader leaves and more delicate red flowers. Variety *flavum* Pursh 1814, with pure yellow flowers spotted in chocolate brown, is the most widely distributed form of the species. Variety *immaculatum* Jenkinson 1932 has pure cadmium-yellow flowers without spots; an entire series of this form was collected and grown by Mary Henry of Pennsylvania.

When I grew *Lilium canadense* in the western United States, it flowered beautifully for two or three years before gradually declining, probably owing to a combination of virus disease and unsuitable climate.

Many plants of eastern North America seem unable to adapt to the sparse rainfall and low atmospheric humidity of West Coast summers, even in irrigated gardens.

Many attempts have been made to cross *Lilium canadense* with other North American lilies, both eastern and western. There is little evidence of success, except with the closely related *L. grayi* and *L. michiganense*. The resulting hybrids may closely resemble variants already found in the wild. Hybrids have also been reported between *L. michauxii* and *L. canadense* (A. Showalter 1965) and *L. canadense* and *L. superbum*.

Lilium candidum Linnaeus 1753
Madonna lily

The name *candidum* means "dazzling white." The species is native to the eastern Mediterranean, specifically, Herat, Afghanistan; Lebanon; Haifa, Israel; Beirut; and Smyrna.

Known in Europe since ancient times, the white Madonna lily appeared in medieval art as an attribute of the Virgin Mary. It may have been brought into central Europe by returning Crusaders, or perhaps by travelers from Rome. It was cultivated millennia ago by the Egyptians, Cretans, Greeks, and Romans for medicinal use. Like some other important domesticated flowers, such as *Iris albicans,* it was distributed so widely that its original wild home is uncertain.

The bulb is broad and rounded, white or yellowish, with stout, perennial basal roots. The basal foliage emerges in September and overwinters as a rosette of glossy green, broadly lanceolate leaves. The flowering stalk grows in spring, usually 80 to 120 centimeters (2.5 to 4 feet) tall, bearing in June and July 5 to 20 pure white, widely trumpet-shaped, sweet-scented blooms. The pollen is pale yellow. Seed germination is immediate epigeal, requiring cool soil conditions for best results. If grown well, the seedlings can flower in their second year.

The bulbs must be divided and replanted in July, when they are solid and well formed and the leaves and stem have died down. They must be planted no more than 3 centimeters (1.5 inches) below the soil surface to allow the fall rosettes to develop adequately. The Madonna lily has a growth cycle appropriate to its southern homeland, where plants are typically dormant during the hot summers and revive with

Plate 14. *Lilium candidum*. Photo by Herman v. Wall.

the fall rains. It succeeds best in an alkaline soil, but it performs well in other loam or loess soils, as long as drainage is excellent. Plantings do best if infrequently disturbed. The planting site should be sunny and sheltered.

Several forms have been distinguished taxonomically. Variety *cernuum* Weston 1772 has small, pointed tepals and a black stem and is reported to set seed. Variety *plenum* Weston 1972 is a very rare double form. Variety *salonikae* Stoker 1935 is a fertile wild form with small, pointed tepals. During World War I an English soldier at the battlefront north of Salonika sent home this variety, a form with small tepals and smaller and more undulate basal leaves. It is found in Greece, in the Vardar Valley near Doiran, and near Demirkapu in scrub and on rocky slopes, ranging as far as the Albanian border.

The Cascade strain, grown for many years at Oregon Bulb Farms, arose from crosses made by George L. Slate between *Lilium candidum* and *L. candidum* var. *salonikae.* Slate selected mainly for flower placement, flower form and size, and *Botrytis* resistance during his 30 years of work. The strain was produced from seed using superior forms as parents, which ensured virus-free stock of great vigor.

The oldest and best-known hybrid of this species is *Lilium ×testaceum,* the Nankeen lily, a cross between *L. candidum* and *L. chalcedonicum* that originated in the Netherlands or Germany early in the nineteenth century. *Lilium ×testaceum* has been backcrossed to both its parents, producing some delicate and beautiful hybrids. In 1971 Charles Robinson of Ontario, Canada, crossed *L. candidum* var. *salonikae* with *L. monadelphum* to produce 'June Fragrance'.

A group of fascinating hybrids produced in the 1970s, including a deep rose-colored clone, was created by Judith Freeman, who crossed 'June Fragrance' with white and pink Asiatic hybrids. Embryo rescue was used to obtain these plants. Several equally unique hybrids were also obtained from Emerson Hickling, who crossed 'June Fragrance' with several Asiatic hybrids. Freeman again used embryo rescue to obtain hybrids from Hickling's crosses. She also crossed the Slate strain of *Lilium candidum* with *L. monadelphum* to produce a lovely hybrid similar to 'June Fragrance'.

Again with the help of embryo rescue, Wilbert Ronald has crossed

Lilium candidum with *L. cernuum* and various Asiatic hybrids. In the Netherlands, Jaap van Tuyl crossed *L. candidum* with both *L. longiflorum* and *L. henryi,* using advanced embryo culture techniques.

Lilium catesbaei Walter 1788
Pine lily

This species is named for the early American naturalist Mark Catesby, who explored the Virginia Tidewater area. The pine lily is native to southeastern United States, in Florida, Louisiana, Georgia, South Carolina, southern Virginia, and southern Illinois, growing in open pine woods and marshlands.

The bulbs are small, with tiny, loose, whitish scales. The persistent lower leaves are very small and narrowly lanceolate. The flower stalk is 30 to 50 centimeters (12 to 20 inches) tall with scattered, alternately or randomly placed, horizontally held linear-lanceolate leaves. The flower, usually borne singly, is an upfacing starry bowl, scarlet or yellow speckled with heavy brown spots. The long-petioled tepals are almost unique in the genus. The only species with which this one might be confused is *Lilium philadelphicum,* but *L. catesbaei* can be distinguished by its scattered rather than whorled leaves. Seed germination is immediate epigeal, with seedlings appearing above ground in 40 days.

This species' native habitat in acid soils and swamps suggests that this lily is demanding to grow. Feldmaier (1970) suggested planting the bulb in sandy, peaty mud on a substrate of sphagnum in a pot, then standing the pot in shallow water. Samuel L. Emsweller of the U.S. Department of Agriculture, Beltsville, Maryland, is reported to have cultivated it successfully by lifting each bulb in its ball of soil and potting it in sphagnum moss. The pots were plunged in a greenhouse bed of peat that was kept moist always. A grower in Florida sent some bulbs to Oregon Bulb Farms, which used a method identical to Emsweller's. Many of them flowered in 1978, but none attained sufficient size to allow us to maintain the planting.

There is no verified record of *Lilium catesbaei* being used in hybridization, although Emsweller obtained seed by crossing it with *L. grayi, L. philadelphicum,* and *L. superbum.*

Lilium cernuum Komarov 1901

Nodding lily

Named for its nodding flowers, this lily is native to Korea, Manchuria, and the Ussuri region of Russian Siberia.

The bulb of this small species is narrow, white, and set with rather thick scales. The stem grows 30 to 80 centimeters (12 to 32 inches) tall and bears narrow grasslike leaves. In June each stem holds up to 8 lilac-rose flowers (more in certain seedlings), stippled with carmine and with very fine scent. The pollen is orange. The seed is light to medium brown. Seed germination is immediate epigeal.

In the Diamond Mountains of Korea there is a white form, variety *candidum* Nakai 1917.

The species has been reported to be short-lived in cultivation in some areas. It should be restarted frequently from seed. *Lilium cernuum* was produced successfully from seed at Oregon Bulb Farms for several years. It is very cold-hardy. The bulbs must remain relatively dry following flowering; wet conditions in late summer are disastrous. In the wild these lilies grow in sandy loam, alluvial, or rocky soils among grasses and shrubs, usually in full sun but sometimes in light shade. I grew the species very successfully in a field of volcanic soil near Parkdale, Oregon, at 700 meters (2300 feet); the planting was breathtaking in its sheer beauty, with stems reaching 90 to 120 centimeters (3 to 4 feet) in height and an average of 8 flowers per stem.

Plate 15. *Lilium cernuum*. Photo by Judith L. Freeman.

The use of *Lilium cernuum* by Cecil Patterson at the University of Saskatchewan produced a second-generation seedling, numbered 37.538, from a cross with *L. davidii*. The most fertile hybrids from crossing 37.538 with *L. davidii* var. *willmot-*

tiae were 'Edith Cecilia' and 'Lemon Queen', which were used extensively at Oregon Bulb Farms to produce pastel colors in Asiatic lilies. 'Edith Cecilia' is the ancestor of almost all pink, peach, white, and cream Asiatics now in the trade.

Later Leonard Marshall crossed *Lilium cernuum* with *L. concolor, L. dauricum* var. *alpinum,* and *L. pumilum.* The beautiful clones 'Elf' and 'Tinkerbelle', offered by The Lily Garden, are derived from *L. cernuum* hybrids backcrossed to the species.

Lilium chalcedonicum Linnaeus 1753

Scarlet turk's-cap lily

This species is named for the ancient city of Chalcedon, known in modern Turkey as Kadiköpy, a suburb of Istanbul. It is native to Albania and Greece in the regions of Euboea, Mount Kandyli, and the Tirphys Range, at 1000 meters (3300 feet). It grows on dry hillsides on limestone, in grass, or under conifers.

From a broad yellowish white bulb rises a stem of 60 to 120 centimeters (2 to 4 feet) with many scattered, sessile leaves (the lower ones long and horizontal, the upper ones smaller and more upright and appressed to the stem). From July into August it bears up to 10 flowers of martagon form. The fleshy tepals are mandarin red, and the pollen is dark red-orange. Variety *maculatum* Constable 1930 has some dark spots. Seed germination is epigeal and often delayed and erratic.

The typical form has unspotted tepals. Variety *maculatum* has spotted tepals. The species formerly called *Lilium heldreichii* Freyn is now considered synonymous with *L. chalcedonicum.* Its populations occur in southern and southeastern Greece and in mountains on the border of eastern Albania. It differs from typical *L. chalcedonicum* in its more upright, clasping stem leaves.

This lily prefers warm, limy loam soil. It is very susceptible to *Botrytis.* Despite its warm homeland, it succeeds in Scotland and northern coastal Germany. My attempts to grow it in Oregon proved futile, despite repeated intense efforts; acid soil and moist spring weather may have been the culprits.

Lilium chalcedonicum hybridized (perhaps in the wild) with *L. candidum* to produce the well-known garden plant *L.* ×*testaceum.*

Lilium ciliatum P. H. Davis 1965

This species is named for the fine hairs (cilia) on the leaf margins. It is native to the southern and southeastern shores of the Black Sea in Turkey, growing at 1500 to 2400 meters (4900 to 7800 feet) in woodland and scrub or in meadows.

Many plants from this region of northern Turkey grow very well in the Pacific Northwest of North America, which has a similar climate. I have seen *Lilium ciliatum* growing profusely at the Van Dusen Botanic Garden in Vancouver, British Columbia, in 1996.

The bulbs are large, 5 to 10 centimeters (2 to 4 inches) in diameter, and the stem 60 to 150 centimeters (2 to 5 feet) in height. From June to July each stem bears 2 to 10 flowers of flattened globe shape, ivory or cream to sulfur-yellow in color with a purple-brown center and fine spotting. The leaves are linear-lanceolate, rough on both sides and furnished on the margins with long wavy hairs. The seed is rich brown, and germination is delayed hypogeal. This lily was for a while confused with *Lilium pyrenaicum* subsp. *ponticum,* from which it can be distinguished by its larger bulb, greater ciliation of the leaf margins, and paler flower color.

Scottish hybridizer Chris North crossed *Lilium ciliatum* (and several related species) with *L. pyrenaicum* and brought the hybrids to flowering using embryo culture. He judged that the resulting horticultural qualities could be found in selections of *L. pyrenaicum.*

Lilium columbianum Hanson ex Baker 1874
Columbia tiger lily

Named for the Columbia River, which flows through its native range, this species occurs in western North America from northern California through Oregon, Washington, and western Idaho in the United States, to southern British Columbia in Canada. It is found from sea level to 1800 meters (5900 feet), in moist meadows and open woodland that experience dry summers and wet weather the rest of the year.

The bulbs are small and white, around 4 centimeters (1.5 inches) in diameter, and the stalk is slender, 60 to 150 centimeters (2 to 5 feet) tall. The broadly lanceolate leaves are ranked in whorls along the stem. The inflorescence is a raceme of 2 to 10 small, pendent blooms, the tepals sharply reflexed about halfway. Flower color ranges from bright gold

Plate 16. *Lilium columbianum*. Painting by Mary Comber Miles.

to red-orange, with small purple spots scattered in the throat. Depending on elevation, the flowers appear in June, July, or August. Seed germination is hypogeal in fall in cool conditions; growth appears above ground the next spring.

Variety *ingramii* Anderson 1942 is a robust plant that may eventually prove to be a natural hybrid.

This is one of the easiest Pacific Coast lilies to grow in the garden. It requires an acid loam, not too heavy. Ideally it should have light shade and the protection of small shrubs such as rhododendrons. It needs plenty of moisture during the growing season but enjoys dry conditions after flowering.

Lilium columbianum hybridizes readily with *L. harrisianum, L. kelloggii, L. pardalinum, L. parryi,* and *L. washingtonianum.* Natural hybrids with *L. occidentale* are said to occur. Hybrids have been artificially obtained with *L. canadense* and *L. kelloggii.*

Lilium concolor Salisbury 1806
Morning star lily

Named for the unspotted nature of its flowers, this species is native to Hubei, Hunan, and Yunnan Provinces in central China; Honshu, Shikoku, and Kyushu Islands of Japan; Siberia from the middle Amur region to Vladivostok; and Korea. It is found at 300 to 1200 meters (1000 to 3900 feet), growing in sandy loam or humus over limestone, in meadows and scrub.

This small, delicate lily produces one or more upfacing, starry flowers in June or July, glistening scarlet-red without spots. The linear to lanceolate leaves are borne horizontally, on a stem from 30 to 90 centimeters (1 to 3 feet) tall. The bulb is small, round, and white, with usually broad scales, and not long-lived. The seed is small and germination is immediate epigeal.

The species is quite variable. Variety *coridion* Baker 1871 has citron-yellow flowers with small brown spots. Variety *partheneion* Baker 1871 has red flowers streaked in green and yellow and spotted in black. Variety *pulchellum* (Fischer) Regel 1876 from Korea, Manchuria, and Siberia has unspotted cinnabar-red to orange-red flowers. Variety *stictum* Hooker 1872 from Shantung has scarlet flowers with black spots.

Several superior clones have been selected. *Lilium concolor* 'Dropmore' is a selection from a cross made by Frank L. Skinner of the type form with variety *pulchellum*; this very hardy, robust plant has orange-red flowers. 'Okihime', with pure yellow, unspotted flowers, is larger than the type.

This species proved easy to grow in Oregon over a period of years. A stronger-growing form obtained from Japan by Oregon Bulb Farms flowered two months later than the type and had exceptional vigor, some stems carrying 30 flowers.

The status of *Lilium concolor* in lily breeding was early thought to be important because it was believed to be the parent of *L.* ×*maculatum* and thus the head of the family tree of the Mid-Century Hybrids produced at Oregon Bulb Farms in the late 1940s. This contention was correctly disputed by Moto'o Shimizu, who demonstrated that *L. concolor* could not have been involved in this breeding line.

Lilium concolor has been hybridized with *L. callosum, L. cernuum, L. dauricum,* and *L. pumilum.* Leonard Marshall's hybrid between *L. concolor* and *L. pumilum* was crossed successfully with the Asiatic clones 'Avalon', 'Enchantment', 'Matchless', and 'Pirate' to produce a host of charming small-flowered hybrids. The unique 'Fireworks' (Plate 17) is a strong clone with tiny, vibrant orange, outfacing flowers; its parents were 'Matchless' and (*L. concolor* × *L. pumilum*).

Lilium dauricum Ker-Gawler 1809

This species is named for the province of Dauria in southeastern Siberia. It is native to northeastern Asia, from the Altai Mountains into the Amur region and Kamchatka in the former Soviet Union, to Mongolia, northern Manchuria, North Korea, and Hokkaido, Japan.

The bulb of this long-cultivated lily is white and broadly spherical, from 3 to 8 centimeters (1.5 to 3 inches) in diameter, with stringlike, jointed scales; it grows quite large before the stem ascends. Rising 30 to 75 centimeters (12 to 30 inches), the typically ribbed stem has closely scattered, lanceolate, dark green leaves below 1 to 6 upfacing, cup-shaped flowers of orange-red to scarlet, variably spotted, carried in an umbel. The buds, leaves, and the surface of the stem are usually coated with downy hairs. Seed germination is immediate hypogeal.

Plate 17. *Lilium* 'Fireworks'

Variety *alpinum* Baker 1871 has stems only 10 to 20 centimeters (4 to 8 inches) tall. Variety *luteum* Wallace 1899 has pure yellow flowers with or without black spots.

This hardy lily grows best in rich, moist, lime-free soils. Flowering in May and June, it is the earliest Asiatic lily, which makes it a good parent in hybridizing earlier lilies for forcing.

Lilium dauricum hybridizes very readily. Isabella Preston used it in her Stenographer and Fighter Aircraft hybrids, and Jan de Graaff in his Golden Chalice strain. According to Moto'o Shimizu, this lily has been crossed for two centuries by Japanese gardeners with *L. maculatum* (synonym *L. wilsonii*), an orange-flowered Japanese species; the resulting hybrids are known as *L. ×elegans* (synonym *L. ×thunbergianum*).

The strong *Lilium ×hollandicum* clones that have survived in European and North American gardens for many decades were crosses between *L. bulbiferum* and *L. ×elegans*. The Rainbow hybrids from Oregon Bulb Farms were a cross between 'Tabasco' and an outstanding, virus-tolerant clone, *L. dauricum* var. *luteum* 'Golden Wonder'; the clone 'Aristo' was selected by Peter Schenk from the Rainbow hybrids. 'Connecticut King' was crossed with 'Golden Wonder' to produce the Sundrop strain and the clones 'Sinai', 'Salute', and 'Sahara'. The second generation of the cross between *L. maximowiczii* and 'Golden Wonder' produced the first dark brushmark Asiatic. Leonard Marshall crossed *L. dauricum* var. *alpinum* with *L. cernuum* to produce two fascinating seedlings with unusual large, irregular spots, almost blotches; this pattern has been termed "spreckles."

Lilium davidii Elwes 1877

This species is named for its discoverer, French missionary and naturalist Père Armand David (1826–1900). It is native to western Sichuan and northwestern Yunnan Provinces in China, at 1500 to 3000 meters (4900 to 9800 feet).

The erect, rigid stalk bears scattered, horizontally held leaves, their tips curving upward. It has a long, pyramidal inflorescence with stiffly horizontal stems bearing 6 to 20, but sometimes as many as 40 flowers. The fragrant flowers are cinnabar to scarlet, spotted finely inside with black; the pollen is scarlet. The narrow, 8- to 12-centimeter (3- to

5-inch) long leaves have ciliate margins, and the stem and buds are generally woolly. The bulb is white, tinged with red when exposed to light, typically 3 to 5 centimeters (1.5 to 2 inches) in diameter and wider than tall. Seed germination is immediate epigeal.

Lilium davidii presents no difficulties in cultivation and grows readily in ordinary garden conditions. Through selection and crosses with its varieties *unicolor* and *willmottiae* (Wilson) Raffill 1938 we have acquired several excellent flowering forms, with larger flowers or with secondary and tertiary flowers on the stems.

Variety *macranthum* Raffill 1938 reaches 180 centimeters (6 feet) in height and bears 2 or more orange flowers per stalk.

Variety *unicolor* Cotton 1938 was first named *Lilium biondii*; the Dutch propagated it under the name *L. willmottiae* var. *unicolor,* and the English as *L. sutchuenense.* This good garden variety is shorter than the type, growing no more than 90 centimeters (3 feet) tall; the stem bears 10 to 15 pale orange flowers with indistinct reddish spotting. Its seedlings may be either unspotted or faintly spotted.

Variety *willmottiae* Raffill 1938 resembles the type but has a more elegant form. Its wiry stem bears a better-supported and longer flower stalk, and the leaves are thicker, longer, and not hairy. The flower color is orange-red with fine chestnut-brown spots. The stem sometimes runs horizontally underground and produces bulblets at the internodes. This variety originates in the Chinese provinces of Hubei, Sichuan, and Shaanxi, where it grows on mountains at 1200 to 2400 meters (3900 to 7800 feet). Through selection, Dutch and English growers have obtained strong-growing, very free flowering forms, termed 'Improved'. Easy in cultivation and succeeding in any soil, this variety is readily propagated by bulblets or seed.

Lilium davidii 'Maxwill' was selected in 1928 by Frank L. Skinner from a cross of *L. davidii* var. *willmottiae* with

Plate 18. *Lilium davidii.* Photo by Judith L. Freeman.

what he thought was *L.leichtlinii* var. *maximowiczii* but was probably another variety of *L. davidii*. This is a robust lily with a stronger stem than *L. davidii* and a beautiful pyramidal inflorescence. Its strong, erect stem makes it a good parent of hybrids with strong constitutions and good flower carriage.

Lilium davidii and its variety *willmottiae* have produced hybrids with *L. amabile, L. bulbiferum* var. *croceum, L. cernuum, L. dauricum, L. lancifolium,* and *L. pumilum.* Many of these important breeding lines have been influential in the Asiatic lilies of today. The Preston hybrids (*L. davidii* × *L. dauricum* hybrid) produced the Stenographer hybrids. Others include the Patterson hybrids (*L. davidii* × *L. cernuum*); *L.* ×*scottiae* (*L. davidii* var. *willmottiae* × *L.* ×*elegans* 'Mahogany'); the Burgundy and Citronella strains (*L. davidii* × *L. amabile*); and Chris North's 'Ariadne' (*L. davidii* × *L. lankongense*). The blood of *L. davidii* is in almost every present-day Asiatic group, adding a higher degree of virus tolerance than any other Asiatic species.

Lilium distichum Nakai 1915
Kochang lily

The name *distichum* means "having two rows" and refers to the fan-shaped arrangement of the inflorescence. The species is native to the Amur and Vladivostok regions in Siberia, and to Manchuria and Korea.

This lily belongs to the Martagon section and is not unlike *Lilium medeoloides.* The 30- to 90-centimeter (1- to 3-foot) tall stem bears whorls of leaves and, in July, a crowded raceme of 3 to 8 fleshy-tepaled flowers of a pale orange-red color with dark spots. Seed germination is delayed hypogeal.

Lilium distichum prefers a moist, shady woodland habitat. It seems to be midway between *L. tsingtauense* and *L. medeoloides,* so its cultivation, if it follows the former species, should present few problems to the skilled grower. An acid soil with plenty of humus, some shade, and copious moisture with good drainage should be fine conditions for it.

Lilium duchartrei Franchet 1887
Marble martagon

This species is named for French botany professor and lily enthusiast Pierre Étienne Duchartre (1811–1894). Native to China in northwestern Yunnan, western Sichuan, and southwestern Gansu Provinces, it grows in forest margins and clearings, and on hillsides from 2400 to 3500 meters (7800 to 11,500 feet), in moist, even marshy places.

This species, introduced by Père David in 1869, was once known as "Farrer's marbled martagon." The bulb is white and oval, 2.5 to 4 centimeters (1 to 1.5 inches) across, forming offsets. The stem is 45 to 150 centimeters (1.5 to 5 feet) tall, with lanceolate leaves. The pendent flowers, marble-white with scattered wine-red spots, are borne in an inflorescence of 2 to 12 on long, strongly outward-held stalks arranged in an umbel. The flowers are beautifully scented; the anthers are orange and the pollen yellow. Seed germination is immediate epigeal.

In gardens this lily succeeds in fresh, moist humus in shade. Here the offset-producing stem can wander horizontally underground, possibly making a colony.

Chris North reported obtaining a hybrid by crossing this species with *Lilium lankongense* and growing the resulting seedlings with embryo culture techniques. Leonard Marshall achieved the same cross in the hot summer of Wyoming.

Lilium fargesii Franchet 1892
This species is named for French missionary Paul G. Farges (1844–1912). It is native to Hubei, Shaanxi, Sichuan, and Yunnan Provinces in central China.

Very rare in cultivation, this species is small and delicate, with grassy leaves and small, greenish white, pink-speckled martagon flowers. Seed germination is presumably immediate epigeal.

A photograph of the type specimen collected by Farges appears in Woodcock and Stearns's *Lilies of the World* (1950: Figure 40). Derek Fox (1985: 119) considered the species related to *Lilium callosum*; Haw (1986: 128) noted the even closer affinity with *L. xanthellum*.

Lilium formosanum Wallace 1891
This species is named for Formosa, an earlier name for Taiwan. It is native to Taiwan, primarily on the northern part of the island, in volcanic soils and on sandstone, from sea level to more than 3000 meters (9800 feet).

The bulb is white or yellowish, 3 to 4 centimeters (about 1.5 inches) in diameter. The dark purple stem is 120 to 150 centimeters (4 to 5 feet) tall, up to 3 meters (10 feet) in some selections, and set with long, grass-like leaves. The pendent flowers are narrow white trumpets, 12 to 15 centimeters (5 to 6 inches) long, widely flaring, generally with a pink tint along the midrib. The pollen is yellow. The flowers are usually borne 1 or 2 on a stem, but there are selections with 30 to 40 flowers. The seed capsule is an elongated cylinder, and the seeds very thin with a thickened margin. Seed germination is immediate epigeal. Each bulb constantly forms offsets, resulting in year-round flowering.

Several fine forms of this lily are in commerce. The most interesting is variety *pricei* Stoker 1935, a dwarf alpine that grows 30 to 60 centimeters (1 to 2 feet) tall and bears 1 or 6 long, narrowly tubular white trumpets, strongly tinged with pink on the reverse. It is winter-hardy and suitable for the rock garden, flowering in July or August. The low-elevation variety of this species may reach 200 centimeters (7 feet). A taller form of the species has been declared a noxious weed in western Australia.

In subtropical climates *Lilium formosanum* can grow from seed-sowing to flowering in as little as six to eight months, blooming in every season without going dormant. In northern climates it generally flowers in October in the open garden and then falls victim to frost. This exhausts it; the little bulb is not very winter-hardy and rarely survives.

Outside the subtropics, *Lilium formosanum* is best grown in a cool greenhouse. In the temperate garden it must be planted in a warm, sheltered site. Not surprisingly, it is short-lived, but it is easily renewed by offsets or seed. I once planted it in a sheltered garden west of Portland, Oregon, where it became well established; here there were apparently no virus carriers to infect it.

This species is very susceptible to virus, which makes it a useful test subject for virus infection. For this purpose the sap of plants suspected of harboring virus is transferred into plants of *Lilium formosanum*. If the test plants die of typical virus symptoms, the suspected infection is confirmed.

Lilium formosanum has been crossed with *L. longiflorum* (resulting in 'Formolongi'), *L. nepalense* (resulting in 'Formolense'), and *L. philippinense.* Variety *pricei* hybridized with *L. longiflorum* produces *L.* ×zaliv-

skii. In 1976 Hiroshi Myodo reported hybridizing *L. formosanum* with *L. speciosum.*

Lilium georgei (W. E. Evans) Sealy 1950

This species is named for botanist and plant explorer George Forrest (1873–1932), who found it in 1924. It is native to northeastern Myanmar (formerly Burma), at 2700 to 3400 meters (8,800 to 11,200 feet) in open, stony alpine meadows.

This alpine species (not to be confused with *Lilium georgicum,* a synonym of *L. pyrenaicum* subsp. *ponticum*) is close to *L. souliei,* from which it differs in the number of leaves and in flower color. The bulb is reported to be broadly ovoid, nearly 5 centimeters (2 inches) high, with fleshy, lanceolate scales. The stout stem grows from 15 to 45 centimeters (6 to 18 inches) tall. The terminal inflorescence is a large, solitary, broadly bell-shaped nodding flower of soft blue-purple, held just above the topmost leaf.

Lilium grayi Watson 1879

This species is named for American botanist Asa Gray (1810–1888), who first collected it. Native to North Carolina, Tennessee, and Virginia in the United States, it grows on slopes in the Allegheny Mountains at 900 to 1800 meters (3000 to 5900 feet).

This uncommon species is closely related to *Lilium canadense,* which it resembles in carriage but differs in its flowers, which are glossy trumpets with tepals that are not reflexed. Both species have been hybridized in cultivation.

The flowers, borne 1 to 12 on a stem, are usually dark carmine, orange inside, strongly spotted in red-purple. The pollen is orange-brown. The bulb is a rhizome with yellowish white scales, similar to that of *Lilium canadense.* Seed germination is delayed hypogeal.

This beautiful lily is no more difficult to grow than *Lilium canadense.* It has been grown well both in the cool summers of Edinburgh, Scotland, and in the hot ones of Massachusetts. Derek Fox (1985) noted that it seems to demand an acid soil with plenty of moisture during the growing season. Excellent stems were grown in Gresham, Oregon, in full sun; liberal quantities of well-decayed horse manure had been applied.

Lilium hansonii D. T. Moore 1871
This species is named for New York artist and amateur lily grower Peter Hanson (1824–1887). Native to Ullung-Do (Dagelet) and Takeshima (Tok-Do) Islands off the coast of Korea and the Diamond and Negita mountains in mainland Korea, it grows in humus deposits on rocky cliffs and in scrub. It is also reported from eastern Siberia and Japan.

The bulb is yellowish white, roughly spherical, and 5 to 6 centimeters (2 to 2.5 inches) in diameter. The hollow, green, stout stem grows 60 to 150 centimeters (2 to 5 feet) tall, with numerous whorls of leaves and some single leaves on the upper part. The leaves are broad and lanceolate. The strongly fragrant June flowers, of turk's-cap form, are pendent, with thick, fleshy, reflexed tepals of orange-red, spotted in brown. There are 4 to 12 flowers per stem. The anthers are purple-brown with yellow pollen. Seed germination is delayed hypogeal.

This lily is very easy to grow, lasting for decades in the garden. It should be planted in a lightly shaded, moist site with rich leafmold added to the soil. It is tolerant of lime and not very susceptible to disease.

The resistance of *Lilium hansonii* to virus disease led Samuel L. Emsweller to cross it with *L. martagon* and *L. martagon* f. *album* to produce his Hansonii hybrids. Some growers believe that *L. hansonii* and its hybrids are avoided by aphids and thus are not infected with virus.

Lilium hansonii crosses readily with *L. martagon*; the hybrids are known as *L. ×marhan*. These can then be crossed with *L. medeoloides* (producing, e.g., 'Redman'). Hybrids of beautiful colors have been obtained in the second generation of crosses with *L. martagon* var. *album*, particularly delicate yellows and pinks. In addition, the dark wine-red of *L. martagon* var. *cattaniae* combines well with the yellow of the above lilies. Some other descendants include *L. ×dalhansonii* Powell 1893, Jan de Graaff's Paisley hybrids, and Edgar Kline's Painted Lady hybrids. The second-generation cross to both colored and white *L. martagon* forms produces beautiful clear colors.

Lilium henrici Franchet 1898
This species is named for Prince Henri d'Orleans. Native to Yunnan Province, China, in the Mekong and Salween drainages at 2700 to 3300 meters (8800 to 10,800 feet), it grows on the edges of thickets.

Because of its flat, open, outfacing flowers, this lily has sometimes

Plate 19. *Lilium hansonii*. Painting by Mary Comber Miles.

been placed in the genus *Nomocharis*. It grows 90 to 120 centimeters (3 to 4 feet) tall. The flowers are white with crimson-purple spots in the throat and green nectaries; they open in July. The bulb, 10 to 12 centimeters (4 to 5 inches) in diameter, is tinted red. Seed germination is immediate epigeal.

Coming from a wet monsoon climate, this lily succeeds in moist, cool coastal regions, given careful cultivation. For more than 50 years it has been remarkably well cultivated in a few Scottish gardens. An acid compost with a high humus content seems essential. Plenty of moisture should be available throughout the spring, and light shade is quite beneficial.

Lilium henryi Baker 1888

This species is named for Irish plant explorer and forestry professor Augustine Henry (1859–1930), who discovered the species. It is native to the mountains of Hubei and Guizhou Provinces in central China.

This indestructible species has large orange pendent flowers. Although it bears only 1 to 3 flowers in the wild, in good garden conditions it may have as many as 30 flowers and attain a height of 140 to 240 centimeters (5 to 8 feet). The bulb is large and spherical, fist-sized or larger, with large, long scales that turn dark purple on exposure to light, and stout, deep-plunging roots. The slender stem is sometimes purple-brown, slightly curved, and set with many broad, dark-green leaves. The inflorescence is a raceme with the flower stalks held horizontally or slightly upward, often with secondary and ternary buds. The flowers, borne from late July to August, are of turk's-cap form, orange with many brown spots and papillae, with green or blackish green nectaries in the interior of the flower; the pollen is dark orange. Seed germination is immediate epigeal, and the large brown seeds are best sown fresh.

Variety *citrinum* Wallace 1936, which has arisen repeatedly in gardens, is citron yellow in color but otherwise like the type. *Lilium henryi* 'Improved' is a form with a stiff, erect stem, commercially grown from seed in the United States. Both plants are usually preferred for hybridizing, the former for its color and the latter for its stiff stems.

This lily is a stem-rooter and can be increased from the bulbs that form along the stem below ground. This tendency to produce bulbs can be stimulated by planting the parent bulb on its side. It is long-lived given deep planting in full sun, in good garden soil with some lime content.

Among the many lily hybrids derived from *Lilium henryi* are Tom Barry's 'T. A. Havemeyer' (with *L.sulphureum*), Edouard Debras's *L. ×aurelianense* (with *L.sargentiae*), and Leslie Woodriff's 'White Henry' (with *L. leucanthum* var. *centifolium*) and 'Black Beauty' (with *L. speciosum*). Chris North of Invergowrie, Scotland, successfully crossed *L.henryi* with an Asiatic lily to produce 'Eureka'. The finest Orienpet hybrids have been attained through chromosome doubling with crosses to 'Black Beauty' in its tetraploid form. 'Black Beauty' was sterile in its diploid form.

A cross between *Lilium auratum* var. *platyphyllum* and *L. henryi* was given the number 82111 in Japan. It is being used extensively in Orienpet hybridizing. In the Netherlands, Jaap van Tuyl raised hybrids of *L. henryi* with *L. candidum* and with *L. longiflorum* using embryo rescue.

Lilium humboldtii Duchartre 1870

This species is named for German naturalist Alexander von Humboldt (1769–1859), on whose 100th birthday Theodore Roezl collected this species. It is native to the United States in the Sierra Nevada of central California, at 600 to 1200 meters (1950 to 3900 feet), in open woodland, in loam soils.

The large bulb is subrhizomatous, with yellowish white scales, growing very deep. The stem is 120 to 180 centimeters (4 to 6 feet) tall. The leaves, set in whorls, are undulate, shiny, and oblanceolate. In June it bears 10 to 15 turk's-cap flowers in a pyramidal inflorescence. They are bright orange, spotted with chestnut brown or purple, and the pollen is dark orange. Seed germination is hypogeal in late fall in cool conditions; however, many forms of the species produce leaves without a cold period.

Two botanical varieties are distinguished from the type, both from California. In San Diego County, variety *bloomerianum* Purdy 1901 (synonyms *L. ocellatum* var. *bloomerianum, L. fairchildii*) has flowers like those of variety *ocellatum* (which see), but it is a shorter-growing plant with narrower leaves than the other varieties. Variety *ocellatum* Elwes 1877 (synonyms *Lilium bloomerianum* var. *ocellatum, L. ocellatum*) occurs in Santa Barbara County and is distinguished from the type by its maroon spots or blotches that are margined with red (hence *ocellatum*, "like a little eye").

Lilium humboldtii is quite variable in all respects, so that among a thousand seedlings there are hardly two identical ones. It belongs to a group of species that inhabits soils that become dry and rock-hard in summer. Of the American West Coast dryland bulbs, this species is probably the least fastidious and the easiest to manage in cultivation. Growers must understand that it wants virtually dry conditions from July to November, and that the drainage must be very good. The soil need not have the humus content required by wetland lilies, except as a mulch. *Lilium humboldtii* loves sun and heat, but very light shade is acceptable.

Lilium humboldtii crossed with *L. pardalinum* was one of those important marriages that have proved so beneficial to lily growers. The joining of the dryland bulb's genes to those of the wetlander produced the Bellingham hybrids, from which the magnificent and indestructible clones 'Shuksan' and 'Star of Oregon' were selected. Fine plantings of the Bellingham hybrids thrived at the Royal Horticultural Society gardens at Wisley, England, for many years. 'Buttercup' and the San Gabriel strain, grown at Oregon Bulb Farms for many years, were hybrids between *L. humboldtii* and *L. parryi*.

Lilium iridollae M. G. Henry 1947
Pot-of-gold lily

This species is named from *iris*, meaning "rainbow," and *olla*, meaning "pot," to signify "the pot of gold at the end of the rainbow." It is native to southern Alabama and northwestern Florida in the southeastern United States, growing in peaty soils and sphagnum bogs.

Related to *Lilium canadense* and *L. superbum*, this species has small white bulbs produced on short stolons. The stem is 90 to 150 centimeters (3 to 5 feet) tall, with lanceolate leaves usually arranged in whorls; the upper half of the stem often is leafless. The flowers are typically borne singly, but there may be as many as 8 on a stem. Of martagon form, and pendent, with the tepals rolled under, the flowers are a warm, golden-yellow color, heavily spotted in brown on the lower part, with green nectaries. They appear from June to July. Seed germination is hypogeal in one to two months.

Mary Henry seems to have raised this lily from seed to flowering in a frame at her garden in Gladwyne, Pennsylvania, during the 1940s, when it received little attention except for watering. The climate and conditions it enjoys should make it an easy plant for many gardeners who fail with lilies that demand drainage and cool conditions. It must be assumed that this species is very rare in the wild, where it is under great pressure from unregulated grazing.

Lilium japonicum Thunberg ex Houttuyn 1780
Bamboo lily
The name *japonicum* means "Japanese." In Japan the species is named *sasa-yuri*, meaning "bamboo lily." Native to southern Honshu, Japan, from sea level to 1050 meters (3400 feet), it grows typically on east- or north-facing slopes among bamboos and rhododendrons.

The bulb is creamy white and oval, 4 centimeters (1.5 inches) in diameter, with small, elongated scales in an imbricate arrangement. The slender stem is 30 to 90 centimeters (1 to 3 feet) tall. The scattered leaves are lanceolate and rough-margined. There are generally 1 to 3 flowers per stem, clear pink or sometimes white; in form they are short, bell-like trumpets. The pollen is reddish brown. Depending on altitude, the flowers open from May to August. Seed germination is delayed hypogeal.

This beautiful lily is easily grown in some gardens and has long been cultivated in its Japanese homeland. It is very susceptible to virus. To succeed, it must have cool soil, which may be ensured by planting the bulbs deeply in half shade among grasses and other low plants, on a northern exposure. The soil should be sandy loam with added organic matter. Ralph Warner (pers. comm.) reported succeeding with these lilies by planting them over a drainage area with cold water flowing beneath them, that is, an artificial moraine.

Cultivation of this species has never been thought easy, but in places where it has become established it has proved long-lived and has performed well. In its native habitat it experiences heavy summer rains followed by a dry fall; most gardeners have natural conditions that are exact opposite. The most important requirement is sufficient moisture up to and during flowering time. Light shade is also needed to moderate temperatures.

Lilium japonicum crosses with *L. auratum, L. rubellum,* and *L. speciosum.* Norma Pfeiffer crossed it with forms of *L. auratum* to produce many beautiful seedlings. Second- and third-generation crosses from her work were used to produce lovely pink strains, including Imperial Pink, Pink Glory, and Celebrity. Several of the second- and third-generation clones from this cross showed remarkable virus tolerance. Leslie Woodriff used *L. japonicum* quite extensively to produce his Atomic hybrids and Little Fairies, which are the ancestors of many of the upright pinks now abundant in the Netherlands. LeVern Freimann of Bellingham, Washington, was the first to cross *L. speciosum* with *L. japonicum. Lilium japonicum* has also shown an affinity with *L. nepalense;* Jaap Spaans created a unique hybrid by crossing a hybrid of *L. japonicum* with *L. nepalense.*

Lilium kelleyanum Lemmon 1903
This species is named for San Francisco naturalist Lynwood J. Kelley. Native to the United States in the Sierra Nevada of California from Tulare County in the south to Siskiyou and Trinity counties in the north, it grows in damp places in montane coniferous forest.

Lilium kelleyanum is related to *Lilium pardalinum* and has also been known as *L. nevadense, L. pardalinum* var. *nevadense,* and *L. parviflorum.* The plants known as *L. shastense* and *L. inyoense* are now subsumed in *L. kelleyanum.*

This lily grows up to 200 centimeters (7 feet) tall and produces as many as 70 sweet-scented flowers in a pyramidal inflorescence. The flowers are cadmium-yellow, lightly spotted in purple, with a greenish tint at the base. Opening from June to mid-August, they are similar to the turk's-cap type, except that the tepals are not completely rolled under, so that they have an open crown shape. Seed germination is delayed hypogeal. The bulb is rhizomatous with many small, close-set scales.

According to Derek Fox (1985: 134), *Lilium kelleyanum* is not difficult to grow but may be difficult to grow to perfection. It enjoys conditions similar to those favored by *L. parvum,* in that the bulbs must remain moist while the foliage is warm and dry; for most gardeners, this is not easy. It will take to a reasonably acid loam with plenty of humus. It should be placed in an open, exposed situation to prevent close atmospheric conditions. A little light shade can be provided.

This species hybridizes in the wild with *Lilium parvum,* and in cultivation it has crossed readily with *L. parryi* and *L. pardalinum.* Oliver Wyatt's Fair Maids strain is said to have this species as a parent.

Lilium kelloggii Purdy 1901

This species is named for California botanist and physician Dr. Albert Kellogg (1813–1887). It is native to the United States in the fog-affected "redwood belt" from northwestern California to southwestern Oregon.

This fragrant lily has a very narrow distribution similar to that of *Lilium rubescens.* Despite its limited range, the species exhibits enormous variation in flower color. It is not found close to the ocean but rather on high ridges some miles inland. It has been observed growing at an elevation of 900 meters (3000 feet) in heavy, yellow, gravelly clay soils and brownish red loose loams. The drainage was excellent in these dry, rocky places, and there was little humus in the soils.

The small bulbs are 5 to 10 centimeters (2 to 4 inches) across. The stem is 45 to 120 centimeters (1.5 to 4 feet) tall, or rarely as much as 240 centimeters (8 feet), and the light-green leaves are arranged in 4 to 8 whorls. There are as many as 30 flowers in the tall, pyramidal inflorescence. These pendent turk's-cap blooms have strongly inrolled tips. They are ivory-white with pink spots, turning pink to magenta as they age, with the spots turning brown or wine-red; there is usually a citron-yellow central stripe on each tepal. The flowers appear in July. Seed germination is hypogeal.

In cultivating this dryland bulb, excellent drainage is essential. Some shade is preferable, with sufficient moisture available to keep the plant from drying out until flowering. This species is accustomed to copious fogs and dews, so it should not be too shaded, nor too exposed in areas with a dry atmosphere.

Seed obtained from Boyd Kline of Medford, Oregon, in the early 1960s produced some beautiful hybrids assumed to be crosses between this species and *Lilium bolanderi, L. humboldtii,* and *L. pardalinum.* The lovely clones 'Bunting', 'Nightingale', 'Robin', and 'Snowgoose' were introduced from this population. The charming dwarf pink 'Hummingbird' was also from this group. The Del Norte hybrids were sold as a group from Kline's seedlings.

A considerable quantity of this species was grown at Oregon Bulb

Farms in the 1960s. It was crossed with several western American hybrids, including 'Afterglow', 'Buttercup', and 'Shuksan', and was exceptionally compatible with these. The first generations had rather muddy colors, but the second generation had an abundance of clear pastels, including pinks, cream, and (remarkably) white.

Derek Fox has produced some magnificent hybrids from this species. His 'Lake Tahoe' (Plate 20) growing at the Edinburgh Botanic Garden was 200 centimeters (7 feet) tall and carried a multitude of fine pink flowers. It was the finest western American hybrid lily I have ever seen.

Lilium kesselringianum Mischenko 1914

This species is named for Wilhelm Kesselring (1876–1966) of the Darmstadt Botanic Garden, Germany. It is native to western Transcaucasia around Sakhum and Batumi, at 1500 meters (4900 feet).

This species is distinguished from the similar *Lilium monadelphum*

Plate 20. *Lilium* 'Lake Tahoe'

by its smaller stature of 60 to 120 centimeters (2 to 4 feet), its paler, straw-yellow flowers with cinnamon-brown spots, and its shorter stamens. The bulbs are rather large. The stem produces stem roots and is thickly set with leaves. The loose pyramidal inflorescence bears 8 to 10 flowers, finely spotted with cinnamon; the scent can be unpleasant. The anthers are brown. The seed capsule is 4 to 5 centimeters (1.5 to 2 inches) long. Seed germination is delayed hypogeal.

The plant known in botanical literature of the former Soviet Union as *Lilium kosa* Orekhova & Eremin is now considered a form of *L. kesselringianum*. It occurs in the northern Caucasus around Nalchik. This robust lily was first introduced in 1957 by Yuri Kos. Its bulb is very large, weighing up to 2 kilograms (4 pounds); the stem grows 150 to 180 centimeters (5 to 6 feet) tall. The flower is pale yellow and in wild forms lightly flushed with pink; the anthers are bright yellow and the pollen rusty yellow. There are usually 2 to 5 (sometimes 7) flowers per stem, with a pleasant scent like that of *Hesperis* (sweet rocket).

Little precise information is available on the cultivation of this desirable lily. Its requirements, however, should be similar to those of the other Caucasian lilies, *Lilium monadelphum* and *L. szovitsianum*.

Seed of *Lilium kesselringianum* and of the plant identified as *L. kosa* were acquired by Oregon Bulb Farms on several occasions from sources in the former Soviet Union. The seedlings were so similar to the better-known Caucasian species mentioned above that it was difficult to distinguish them as a separate group.

There is no record of *Lilium kesselringianum* being used as a parent. It was, however, crossed successfully with both *L. monadelphum* and *L. szovitsianum* on several occasions.

Lilium lancifolium Thunberg 1794
Tiger lily
This species is named for its lance-shaped leaves. In Japan the species is named *oni-yuri*. It is native to Japan, Korea, eastern China, and Manchuria, in diverse sites.

The tiger lily, long known as *Lilium tigrinum* Ker-Gawler 1810, is used as a food plant in Asia; the bulbs are said to taste rather like potatoes. The bulb is white, with thick, broad, fleshy scales. The stiff flowering stem is 100 to 200 centimeters (3 to 7 feet) tall, thickly set with leaves.

In June, round, dark-purple bulbils form in the leaf axils, then loosen and fall in autumn. The flowers are arranged in a raceme, with strongly reflexed tepals of orange-cinnabar color heavily spotted in chocolate brown. The pollen is reddish brown. The flowers open from August to late September.

Many tiger lilies in cultivation are triploid, with three sets of chromosomes. The double-flowered variety *flore-pleno* Regel 1890 is unattractive in the eyes of most gardeners, indeed, almost grotesque. Variety *fortunei* Standish 1866 has salmon-orange flowers and is usually covered with woolly hairs on the stem and buds. Variety *splendens* Leichtlin 1870 is the most widely distributed of the triploid forms.

The diploid forms of *Lilium lancifolium* have a normal chromosome count (2n = 24) and hybridize readily with carotinoid-bearing lilies, such as *L. amabile*, *L. bulbiferum*, *L. davidii*, *L. leichtlinii* var. *maximowiczii*, *L. maculatum*, or *L. ×umbellatum*. Diploid forms have been found at seven sites on Tsushima Island and on the nearby coast of Kyushu. They are smaller-flowered and less vigorous than the triploids. Oregon Bulb Farms used diploid forms of *L. lancifolium* for many hybrids. Variety *flaviflorum* Makino 1933 a yellow-flowered diploid, played a large role in the development of the yellow-flowered tiger lily hybrids, especially in Connecticut, where Stone and Payne used it extensively.

Hybrids of *Lilium lancifolium* are known with the following: *L. amabile* ('Cardinal'); *L. bulbiferum* var. *croceum* (*L. ×manglesii* Masters 1881); *L. leichtlinii* var. *maximowiczii* ('Tigrimax'); *L. maculatum* ('Margaret Johnson'); 'Umtig'; and *L. wilsonii* var. *flavum*. Leslie Woodriff produced the unique hybrid 'Pink Tiger' by crossing diploid *L. lancifolium* with *L. regale*. 'Pink Tiger' was then crossed with upright pastel Asiatics by Judith Freeman, yielding the Tiger Babies strain (Plate 21); by Richard Lighty, for 'Sally'; by Ruth Clas, for 'Pussycat'; and by Joe Mattas, for 'Katinka'.

Lilium lankongense Franchet 1892

This species is named for Lankong, northwest of Tali Lake (Erh Hai), where French missionary Père Delavay found it in 1886. It is native to Yunnan Province in China, in alpine and subalpine areas at 3000 meters (9800 feet).

This species is rather similar to *Lilium duchartrei*. The bulb is white

Plate 21. *Lilium* Tiger Babies strain. Photo by Judith L. Freeman.

(turning pinkish on exposure) and oval, about 3 centimeters (1.5 inches) across; it has firmly imbricated, ovate-lanceolate scales. The stoloniferous stem runs underground, producing offsets, then rises 90 to 150 centimeters (3 to 5 feet), bearing up to 15 flowers in a raceme. The pendent flowers are of turk's-cap form, delicate rose-red becoming darker with age, with copious spots; they open in July. Seed germination is immediate epigeal.

Lilium lankongense is not difficult to grow in light, moist acid soil and offers an unusual color and fine fragrance in the lily garden, where it prefers full sun or light shade. It has grown strongly in Oregon in open fields for several years. It has been reported to degenerate in some areas, perhaps owing to virus infection; clean stock and isolation from possible virus carriers are essential.

This species is lime-tolerant. A loose, friable soil with adequate humus content is obviously to its liking. An open exposure is best, except where conditions are too hot; then light shade is preferable.

It was discovered by Chris North of the Scottish Horticultural Research Institute that this species crosses with *Lilium davidii* and various Asiatic hybrids. The embryos from the seeds were removed and

Plate 22. *Lilium lankongense*

cultured on agar plates; the resulting hybrids include 'Adonis', 'Ariadne', 'Eros', 'Iona', 'Rosemary North', and 'Theseus'. Another hybrid strain is Judith Freeman's Southern Belles, which resulted from crossing *L. lankongense* with selected upright pink and white Asiatic hybrids. The Southern Belles strain was later crossed with virus-tolerant pink and white clones in the Asiatic division, including 'Alpenglow' and 'Snowcap'. The resulting hybrids were spectacular and proved to be much more virus-tolerant than the Southern Belles. They were introduced as the Chippendale (wine-pink) and Rosepoint Lace (speckled white) strains. Freeman used embryo rescue in all this work.

Lilium ledebourii (Baker) Boissier 1882

This species is named for Estonian professor of botany Karl Friedrich Ledebour (1785–1851). It is native to Azerbaijan, where it grows in mountains and forest clearings from 1000 to 1500 meters (3300 to 4900 feet), and to Iran, where it grows among large shrubs and bracken on the eastern slopes of the Elburz Mountains at 1600 meters (5200 feet).

This species of restricted distribution may be a disjunct relict related to the European lilies, particularly *Lilium pyrenaicum*. The broadly oval bulb, 5 to 7 centimeters (2 to 3 inches) across, has white, lance-shaped scales. The stem, 50 to 80 centimeters (20 to 32 inches) tall, is set with spirally arranged lanceolate leaves, smaller on the upper portion of the stem, which have short hairs on their margins. It bears 1 to 6 turk's-cap flowers, 5 to 6 centimeters (2 to 2.5 inches) in diameter, pale green to yellowish white with brownish red spots on the lower half of the tepal, and scented of vanilla. The anthers are greenish orange with orange-red pollen, and the stigma white. The flowers appear from June to July, ripening seed in August. Seed germination is delayed hypogeal.

The Russian authority V. Eremin considered this one of the most beautiful lilies. He provided seed in 1971 to Oregon Bulb Farms, and it proved indeed beautiful and unique. The species was seldom used in hybridizing, but Feldmaier (1970) noted that a cross had been reported with *Lilium candidum*.

Lilium leichtlinii Hooker f. 1867

This species is named for German botanist Max Leichtlin (1881–1910). It is native to Japan, in mountains in moist, grassy areas in rich soils.

There are two forms of this lily: the orange-flowered variety *maximowiczii* Baker 1871, and a yellow variety, the type. The latter is now rarely found wild; its type station is Mt. Yatsugatake in central Honshu. By contrast, the orange-flowered variety is found almost all over Japan. Shozo Noda, after studying both distribution and chromosomes, suggested that *L. leichtlinii* should be considered the variety, and variety *maximowiczii* the true type.

This lily grows 60 to 120 centimeters (2 to 4 feet) tall, with pendent flowers of reflexed martagon form, pure citron yellow with reddish purple spots. The stem bears up to 12 flowers in July to August. Seed germination is immediate hypogeal.

Variety *maximowiczii* (Regel) Baker 1871 is widely distributed throughout Japan, occurring on all three of the main islands, and co-occurring with the previously mentioned yellow-flowered form. It is also reported from Korea, Manchuria, and Vladivostok. It grows in moist places among tall grasses. The bulb is white, and the stem often travels horizontally below the ground surface. The flower stem is 60 to 200 centimeters (2 to 7 feet) tall, with scattered linear-lanceolate leaves. The inflorescence is irregular with up to one dozen turk's-cap flowers, cinnabar-orange with scattered brown-purple spots. Seed germination is immediate hypogeal. This lily has frequently been confused with *Lilium lancifolium,* which it resembles in bloom. In cultivation it flowers rather late, usually in August, and prefers a moist humus soil. The buds are often coated in woolly hairs, a quality passed on to its hybrids. It is a good garden plant, and may be seen growing strongly around Vancouver, British Columbia, and in New Zealand.

Owing to its rarity, *Lilium leichtlinii* (the yellow variety) is barely in cultivation. It was grown successfully at Oregon Bulb Farms for several years, where strong plants reached 150 centimeters (5 feet) in height.

Variety *maximowiczii* has been crossed with hybrids of *Lilium* ×*hollandicum* and *L. maculatum.* Well known is Isabella Preston's hybrid 'Tigrimax' (*L. leichtlinii* var. *maximowiczii* × *L. lancifolium*). 'Maxwill' appears not to be a hybrid, but rather a select form of *L. davidii.* 'Hagoromo' (*L. leichtlinii* var. *maximowiczii* × *L.* ×*elegans*) is popular as a cut flower. The woolly white buds make an attractive contrast to the red flowers.

A highly virus-tolerant clone labeled *Lilium leichtlinii* var. *maximowiczii* 'Unicolor' was obtained by Oregon Bulb Farms from Edgar Kline of Lake Grove, Oregon. This clone was distinct in having broader and sparser leaves. It was crossed with *L. dauricum* var. *luteum* 'Golden Wonder' to give a strong population of vigorous, outfacing orange-flowered seedlings. The second generation produced the first dark brushmark lily. The "unicolor" clone was also crossed with other Asiatics, including 'Connecticut King'; the second generation produced several beautiful clones, including 'Last Dance' (Plate 23), now offered by The Lily Garden. The Viva strain was a cross of *L. leichtlinii* var. *maximowiczii* 'Unicolor' and *L. pumilum.* 'Maxiclas', produced by Ruth Clas, was from a cross between (*L. callosum* × *L. amabile*) and *L. leichtlinii* var. *maximowiczii.*

Lilium leucanthum Baker 1901

The name *leucanthum* means "white flowered." The species is native to Hubei and Gansu Provinces in southern China. The original lily of this name, sent in 1889 to England by Augustine Henry from Hubei, was lost to cultivation. The varieties *centifolium* and *chloraster* are now widely distributed.

Plate 23. *Lilium* 'Last Dance'. Photo by Judith L. Freeman.

Variety *centifolium* Stearn 1935 (synonym *Lilium centifolium* Stapf & Elwes 1921) was found in 1914 by the English plant-hunter Reginald Farrer as two individuals growing in a garden in southern Gansu, China (Plate 24). From two seed capsules he brought back descend most of but not all the plants now grown under this name. This variety grows up to 2 meters (7 feet) tall, with 10 to 17 large white trumpets in a raceme. The trumpets are sweet-scented, borne horizontally, with white tepals and pale gold throats, and are streaked with rose-purple or brownish outside. The anthers and pollen are red-brown. The pistil and filaments are divided into fluffy hairs. The stem is set with scattered, dark green, linear leaves. The bulb is round, about 7 centimeters (3 inches) in diameter, with red-brown scales. It flowers in July to August. Seed germination is immediate epigeal.

Variety *chloraster* Wilson 1925 originates from Hubei and was discovered by Augustine Henry. It grows about 1 meter (3 feet) tall. The flowers are broad white trumpets with a clearly marked green stripe on both the outer and inner surface of the tepals; the pollen is red-

Plate 24. *Lilium leucanthum* var. *centifolium*. Photo by Herman v. Wall.

brown. The flowers open from late July to August. Seed germination is immediate epigeal.

The cultivation of *Lilium leucanthum* is easy in warmer climates. An open, sunny site with rich, well-drained soil is ideal. The species is, however, not winter-hardy in colder regions.

Jan de Graaff of Oregon Bulb Farms obtained seed from gardens in Gansu, China, in the early 1950s. This seed produced the spectacular Black Dragon strain (originally known as Black Magic). Both varieties of *Lilium leucanthum* cross with *L. regale*. Variety *chloraster* crossed with *L. henryi* produced the now lost *L. ×kewense*. Leslie Woodriff crossed variety *centifolium* with *L. henryi* to produce the famous and indestructible 'White Henryi'.

Lilium longiflorum Thunberg 1794
Easter lily

The name *longiflorum* means "long flowered" and refers to the shape of the trumpet flowers. The species is native to Japan, on the islands of Ryukyu, Okinawa, Oshima, Takeshima, and Kawanabe, where it grows in humus deposits on coral rocks near shore.

This species is sold by the millions as a pot plant at Eastertime in North America. Having arrived in England in 1819, in the second half of the nineteenth century it was grown in great numbers on the island of Bermuda, where its cultivation was ended by virus disease. It was then grown primarily in Japan until World War II, with an annual production of 26 million bulbs. After the onset of the war, cultivation became centered in the United States, particularly in coastal southern Oregon and northern California.

The bulb is whitish yellow, round-spherical, 5 to 7 centimeters (2 to 3 inches) across. The stem is 30 to 90 centimeters (1 to 3 feet) tall with scattered, dark green, broadly lanceolate leaves of equal length. It bears one or more outfacing, pure white trumpet flowers, 13 to 18 centimeters (5 to 7 inches) long, in an umbel. The pollen is yellow. Seed germination is immediate epigeal, and under optimal conditions flowering plants can be raised from seed in as little as six months.

Lilium longiflorum can be grown in the open garden, but it is not happy outdoors in colder climates; it is best considered a greenhouse or indoor plant. It flowers (when not forced) from August to September. Clones may be increased from the stem bulblets, set in large numbers. Scaling is also an important means of propagating commercial stocks.

As might be expected, this lily so important in commerce has led to several selected forms, particularly those chosen for short stature. The clones 'Creole', 'Croft', and 'Estate', once important, have now been superseded. 'Slocum's Ace' (usually called 'Ace') was selected by Clark Slocum at Langlois in 1935. It and 'Nellie White', the best-known variety in the United States, are the most popular Easter lilies in commerce. 'Ace' excels other clones in the wide opening of its trumpets, which are broader than long. In the Netherlands, the tall-growing 'Arai', 'White America', 'White Fox', and 'White Queen' are grown for cutflower forcing. Lovely new cultivars developed at Oregon State University by A. N. Roberts, including the clones 'Chetco' and 'Harbor', were introduced in the 1970s but failed to replace the old standards. A tetraploid form of the species was produced with colchicine by Samuel L. Emsweller of the U.S. Department of Agriculture, Beltsville, Maryland.

Lilium longiflorum was crossed with the Chinese trumpet variety 'Damson' by Peter Ascher of the University of Minnesota, who used embryo culture in his work. Ascher's student Dan Clark produced a host of hybrids using embryo culture at Sun Valley Bulb Farms in California. The Asiatic clones successfully crossed with *L. longiflorum* 'Ace' included 'Connecticut King', 'Gypsy', 'Juliana', 'Pirate', and 'Red Carpet'. Many beautiful clones now growing in North America and the Netherlands are descended from this material.

Dan Clark also crossed *Lilium longiflorum* 'Ace' with *L. leucanthum* var. *centifolium* to produce 'Dragoon' (Plate 25), a pollen-free, exceptionally strong clone now sold by The Lily Garden. 'Golden Splendor' was crossed with 'Ace' to produce a soft cream-yellow hybrid. The identical cross was made by De Jong Lilies in the Netherlands; their clone is now available in the tetraploid form. Peter Schenk of Bischoff Tulleken in the Netherlands crossed *L. longiflorum* with 'Sterling Star' to produce the strong clone 'Longistar', also available in tetraploid form.

In Japan *Lilium longiflorum* was crossed with *L. auratum* var. *platyphyllum* to produce several beautiful hybrids; 'Yuri no Hakari' is now available in the United States. Jaap van Tuyl in the Netherlands has produced several hybrids from *L. longiflorum,* including crosses with *L. can-*

Plate 25. *Lilium* 'Dragoon'. Photo by Judith L. Freeman.

didum, L. concolor, L. dauricum, L. henryi, and 'Mont Blanc'. Similar crosses were made by Hiroshi Myodo in Japan between *L. longiflorum* and *L. cernuum* and between *L. longiflorum* and *L. henryi.* All these unusual crosses were accomplished with the aid of embryo rescue.

Lilium lophophorum Franchet 1898

The name *lophophorum* means "wearing a crest" and refers to the fringes along the nectaries. The species is native to western Sichuan, Gansu, and Yunnan Provinces in China, and to southeastern Tibet, at 4000 and 4600 meters (13,000 and 15,100 feet).

First described as a species of *Fritillaria,* then as *Lilium,* then as *Nomocharis,* this has now settled as a lily. E. H. Wilson would have preferred to place it in a separate genus. It was first collected by Prince Henri d'Orleans in 1890 in western Sichuan near Kanting, better known in horticultural history as Tatsien-Lu. It is related to *L. oxypetalum* from the central Himalayas.

The bulb is from 4 to 5 centimeters (1.5 to 2 inches) high, with oblong, fleshy scales. The stem measures from 10 to 45 centimeters (4 to 18 inches) high and is cloaked in scalelike leaves on the lower part; on the upper part 5 to 10 ovate to oblanceolate leaves, with long points, are clustered together. The terminal flower, usually borne singly, is bright yellow, creamy yellow, or greenish yellow, sometimes spotted with red; if fully open it would be about 10 centimeters (4 inches) across. The flower is often lantern shaped, as the tips of the long, slender, pointed tepals adhere together (this is an adaptation to protect the reproductive organs from heavy rain). The inner tepals are bearded at the base. Seed germination is immediate epigeal.

I saw this species flowering at the Edinburgh Botanic Garden in 1989 and at the University Botanic Garden, North Vancouver, British Columbia, in 1996. It has been reintroduced from China and the Himalayas by several collectors, and the seed has been rather widely distributed among alpine plant enthusiasts.

Lilium mackliniae Sealy 1949
Manipur lily

This species is named for Jean Kingdon-Ward (neé Macklin), wife of plant-hunter Frank Kingdon-Ward. It is native to northern Myanmar (formerly Burma), at high elevations in mountains.

The Manipur lily was treated as a species of *Nomocharis* when it was found by Frank Kingdon-Ward in 1946. Its bulb is cream-white, 2.5 to 5 centimeters (1 to 2 inches) in diameter; the stem is usually up to 40 centimeters (15 inches) but as much as 90 centimeters (3 feet) in favorable conditions. There are 1 or 2 flowers, occasionally as many as 8 per stem, pendent, bell shaped, widely open, white or flushed with pale pink, about 5 centimeters (2 inches) in diameter; they open from June to late July. Increase is by seed and bulb scales. Seed germination is immediate epigeal.

This lily is growable in the open in the Pacific Northwest and Britain, planted in acid soil with excellent drainage and half shade. In colder regions it is probably not hardy, and it would be wise to give it some protection. It was grown successfully at Oregon Bulb Farms for several years, producing plants with as many as 10 flowers. It must be grown from seed on a regular basis because of its high susceptibility to virus. A beautiful form was grown for many years by Jane Platt in her garden in Portland, Oregon. It also succeeded in fairly full exposure in the rock garden at the Berry Botanic Garden in Portland.

Lilium maculatum Thunberg 1794

The name *maculatum* means "spotted." Native to Honshu, Japan, this lily grows on the Pacific shore on sand, rocky cliffs, and open meadows, and on the eastern coast farther inland, to 1000 meters (3300 feet), in moist acid soil.

According to the Japanese botanist Moto'o Shimizu, this is the correct name of a species better known as *Lilium wilsonii* Woodcock & Stearn 1950, the name Harold F. Comber preferred. It flowers from July to August, with the east coastal form flowering earlier. The glossy green leaves are broadly lanceolate. The flowers are rather large, borne in an umbel of 3 to 12 on stems 30 to 100 centimeters (1 to 3 feet) tall. They have a lovely goblet shape, and the color is usually orange-red with scattered dark spots. When the flower stem grows on cliffs, it often hangs out horizontally and bears the flowers erect.

This lily is undoubtedly a genuine species, because it comes true from seed. A claim that it is a hybrid of *Lilium dauricum* and *L. concolor* may be discounted. Seed germination is definitely epigeal, which differentiates this species from *L. dauricum.* The form grown in Western gardens comes from a small population of late-blooming forms. It is the latest of the Asiatic lilies, flowering in late summer and bearing dark apricot blooms with a strong golden-yellow midrib, whereas *L. maculatum* var. *flavum* Comber 1939 (synonym *L. wilsonii* var. *flavum*) is dark gold with a gold midrib.

Bulbs of the yellow variety *flavum* were found among imported bulbs of *Lilium auratum* var. *platyphyllum* received at Oregon Bulb Farms. The yellow variety was also erroneously grown for some time as 'Marlynn Ross'. Both the type and variety *flavum* grew strongly in cultivation for many years.

The firm of Stone and Payne in Connecticut used this species extensively in its breeding program; the Yellow Blaze strain was derived from crossing 'Nutmegger' with *Lilium maculatum* var. *flavum.* The gold color contributed to 'Connecticut King' and 'Sunray'.

Lilium maculatum and its variety *flavum* are highly compatible with other Asiatic species and hybrids. Crossing 'Connecticut King' with variety *flavum* produced the outstanding clones 'Adelina', 'Cordelia', 'Joanna' (synonym 'Yellow Giant'), 'Pollyanna', and 'Vanessa'. Peter Schenk crossed *L. maculatum* with an Asiatic hybrid to produce 'Gran Sasso'.

A cross made at Oregon Bulb Farms between 'Schuetzenlisl' and *L. maculatum* resulted in beautiful orange uprights of strong growth habit.

Lilium maritimum Kellogg 1875
Coast lily

The name *maritimum* means "maritime." This lily is native to coastal California in the United States, from Marin to Mendocino Counties, "sometimes in sandy soil, usually on raised hummocks in bogs, also in brush and woods, at low elevations" (Munz 1959: 1343). A dwarf form grows in the dry, sandy barrens among ferns on the forest margin, in a soil rich in leafmold and peat.

This small-flowered species has little rhizome-forming bulbs that do not branch and therefore do not form clumps. The flower stem may be from 10 to 200 centimeters (4 inches to 6 feet) tall, depending on habitat. Scattered, narrow-lanceolate leaves are mainly from the base, but in taller, more vigorous plants some of the leaves may be carried in whorls. The flowers are small, bell shaped, and dark to soft orange-red, 1 to 8 per stem. Seed germination is hypogeal in late fall in cool conditions.

The plants require only light shade. Young bulbs should be placed 6 to 8 centimeters (2.5 to 3 inches) below the surface and mulched with peaty, leafy soil as they get older. Their demand for water is not as high as might be thought, given their habitat, but moist conditions with good drainage are essential. It is unlikely that this species can be cultivated in northern gardens owing to the short growing season.

An excellent population of this species was grown on a north-facing slope in an Oregon garden for many years. The plants were about 30 centimeters (1 foot) tall and produced 2 or 3 charming bell-shaped flowers.

Lilium martagon Linnaeus 1753
Turk's-cap lily

The name *martagon* is derived from a Turkish word denoting a type of turban worn by Sultan Muhammad I. The species is native to Eurasia, in limestone hills up to 2300 meters (7500 feet), in beechwoods on lime substrates, at the margins of woods and shrub thickets, and in waste places, always in well-drained but well-watered soils.

The turk's-cap lily is one of the best known and longest cultivated lilies in northern Europe, where the bulbs were once used medicinally. It ranges throughout Eurasia to 124° east longitude and 68° north latitude, beginning in the west in Portugal, extending across southern France, reaching the Po River in the south, through northern Germany, across Austria, Dalmatia, and Macedonia in northern Greece, the plains of Hungary, Russia, and Ukraine, and reaching its eastern limit in Siberia east of Lake Baikal.

The bulb is round and yellow with scattered, pointed scales. The stem has a dark tint and is erect with typically one whorl of oblong to oblanceolate leaves. It grows 60 to 120 centimeters (2 to 4 feet) tall, up to 180 centimeters (6 feet) in cultivation. There are 3 to 13 flowers (as many as 50 in cultivation) in a raceme. The buds are often heavily coated in white woolly hairs. The flower color is quite variable; in lowland populations it is pale or brownish pink, and at higher elevations a strong, dark, muddy carmine-pink. The brownish violet spotting is also quite variable. In the same stand one can find individuals that are unspotted, others with spots to the middle of the tepal, and others very heavily spotted. The flowers are pendent; the fleshy tepals are reflexed halfway and have nectaries at the base. The anthers spread as widely as the tepals and have brownish yellow pollen. The pistil is longer than the stamens, with a dark-red stigma. The seed capsule is round-elongate and angular. The seeds are pale brown without a raised margin. Seed germination is delayed hypogeal. By planting the seeds immediately after harvesting one can induce more rapid germination, with a leaf appearing after a few months of chilling. In fresh garden soil and light shade *Lilium martagon* is easy to grow and increases by offsets.

Ranging over a vast area, *Lilium martagon* includes several distinct taxa. Variety *albiflorum* Vukotinovi, frequent in the wild, has white flowers spotted in carmine-pink.

Variety *album* Weston 1772 has pure white flowers and is frequently larger and stronger than the type. It comes true from seed and is very pretty when placed against dark foliage or conifers.

Variety *cattaniae* Visiani 1865 (synonym var. *dalmaticum*) comes from Dalmatia. It is an extraordinarily stately lily with deep wine-colored unspotted flowers in a large inflorescence.

Variety *caucasicum* Mischenko 1928 (synonym *Lilium caucasicum*) is found around the northeastern coast of the Black Sea in Abkhazia, and in Transcaucasia, at 300 to 500 meters (1000 to 1550 feet), in woodlands of oak and beech and among ferns and grasses. Its stem is 80 to 150 centimeters (2.5 to 5 feet) tall but may reach 220 to 250 centimeters (7 to 8 feet) in cultivation; it is stout and set with short hairs, and produces stem roots. The flowers are widely opened in a short, broad trumpet form, rose-lilac in color. The buds are very hairy.

Variety *daugava* Malta 1934 (synonym var. *koknese* Malta) has been described from Latvia, where it occurs on the dolomite hills near the mouth of the river Daugava (or Duna). It is distinguished from the type by its greater height, to 2 meters (6 feet) and by the short hairs on the stem. The leaves are also wider, up to 5 centimeters (2 inches). The 3 to 10 flowers have strongly reflexed tepals of pale purple-red with dark spots and red hairs on the tepals.

Variety *hirsutum* Weston 1772 is a form from the southern Alps in which the stem, underside of the leaf, and flower are heavily coated with woolly hair.

Variety *pilosiusculum* Freyn 1890, a geographical race from the Urals and Siberia, from Angara and the Lena region to Mongolia, has smaller leaves and a stouter, woollier stem, flower stalk, bud, and flower.

Variety *sanguineo-purpureum* Beck 1890 is a dark maroon-flowered form from the Balkans.

Lilium martagon prefers a semishaded area with filtered light and cool conditions, in a moist woodland soil with adequate humus. It flowers early in the garden, receiving sun before the trees have leafed out fully, and is protected from heat later in the season.

This species, in both its white and wine-red forms, has been crossed with *Lilium hansonii* to produce *L.* ×*marhan* Van Tubergen 1886 and *L.* ×*dalhansonii*. In addition there are hybrids with *L. medeoloides* and (by C. Bonstedt) with *L.* ×*umbellatum*.

The second generation from the cross between *Lilium martagon* var. *album* and *L. hansonii* produced lovely clear pinks, peaches, creams, and soft yellows that were favorites at Oregon Bulb Farms for many years. The strains were sold under the name Paisley hybrids. Following the work of Ed Robinson in Manitoba, more use has been made of these hybrids by crossing them to the red, upright-flowering *L. tsingtauense*.

Plate 26. *Lilium martagon*. Painting by Mary Comber Miles.

Lilium medeoloides A. Gray 1859
Wheel lily
This species is named for its resemblance to *Medeola virginica,* a liliaceous plant with whorled leaves. In Japan the species is named *kurumayuri,* meaning "wheel lily." It is native to Honshu and Hokkaido in Japan, north to Sakhalin, the Kurile Islands off Kamchatka, Cheju (Quelpart) Island off southern Korea, and Zhejiang Province in China. It grows on volcanic soils at 200 to 2500 meters (650 to 8200 feet), in half-shade at lower elevations and in the open at higher elevations.

This lily, related to *Lilium martagon* and *L. distichum,* has a snow-white bulb. The stem in low-altitude forms reaches 70 centimeters (28 inches), but in high-altitude forms only 25 centimeters (10 inches). The leaves are arranged in up to 4 whorls along the green stem, each whorl containing 4 to 10 broad-lanceolate leaves. The small, pendent flowers have reflexed tepals, orange to apricot in color, spotted in dark red to black, and about 3.5 centimeters (1.5 inches) in diameter. They appear from July to August. Seed germination is delayed hypogeal.

The Russian botanist D. L. Vrishch, following a Soviet tendency toward "splitting," distinguished the populations of Kamchatka and the Kuriles and the lower Amur as a separate species, *Lilium debile.* There are several horticultural varieties, some with unspotted flowers.

Cultivation should not be difficult, given an underlayer of gravel and some leafmold. Plants should be well mulched in winter and given half shade.

Lilium medeoloides was crossed in England with *L. martagon* var. *cattaniae* to produce 'Marmed'. Canadian Frank L. Skinner crossed *L. medeoloides* with *L. hansonii,* and American Ruth Clas did the reverse cross of *L. medeoloides* and *L. hansonii.* Although *L. medeoloides* was grown at Oregon Bulb Farms for several years, it was not used in hybridizing.

Lilium michauxii Poiret 1813
Carolina lily
This species is named for French plant explorer André Michaux (1746–1803), who first collected it. Native to Virginia, the Carolinas, Georgia, Alabama, Louisiana, and Florida in the southeastern United States,

it grows in dry, well-drained soils, from sea level to 760 meters (2490 feet).

First described under the name *Lilium carolinianum,* this species has stoloniferous bulbs and a stem of 30 to 100 centimeters (1 to 3 feet); the leaves are broadly lanceolate, usually with undulate margins, and arranged in whorls. The inflorescence is an umbel of 1 to 5 strongly scented, pendent turk's-cap flowers, gleaming orange-red, yellowish white at the throat. The species is stem-rooting and prefers lime-free, sandy, peaty soil, in which it should be planted 12 centimeters (5 inches) deep. Seed germination is hypogeal; considering the southern range of the species, a well-defined cold period before growth commences may not be necessary.

This species is rarely seen in cultivation, but this has been due mainly to lack of availability rather than to any difficulty in growing it. An acid sandy loam would seem preferable, with sufficient moisture while growth is active. Winter hardiness is doubtful in very cold regions.

Mr. Showalter of Harrisburg, Pennsylvania, reported hybridizing *Lilium michauxii* with *L. canadense, L. harrisianum,* and *L. michiganense.*

Lilium michiganense Farwell 1915
This species is named for the state of Michigan. Native to the United States, from near the Great Lakes in Michigan and Wisconsin, and along the Mississippi drainage in Ohio and Kentucky, it grows in moist soils, often by roadsides.

Like *Lilium canadense, L. michiganense* has a stoloniferous bulb. The stem rises 60 to 150 centimeters (2 to 5 feet), with elliptical leaves in whorls. It bears 1 to 8 flowers on long, upright flower stalks in a loose inflorescence. The pendent flowers are of graceful turk's-cap form, broadly reflexed like those of *L. canadense,* red-orange with copious red-brown spotting at the base, and reddish yellow pollen. They open from June to July. This lily prefers a light soil (pH 5.5 to 7), usually in open places in full sun. Seed germination is delayed hypogeal.

Lilium michiganense hybridizes with *L. canadense* and *L. michauxii.* Its cultivation is very similar to that of *L. canadense,* but the soil must never be stagnant. It is possibly less shade-tolerant, enjoying full exposure in a continental climate as long as there is moisture available. Good plants have been grown in both humus-rich sand and stiff clay.

Lilium monadelphum Bieberstein 1808
Caucasian lily

The name *monadelphum* comes from the Greek words *monos,* meaning "one," and *adelphos,* meaning "brother," referring to the way the stamens are fused into a tube around the ovary. Native to the northern Caucasus, from Maikop to Kuban on mountain slopes up to 2100 meters (6800 feet), it grows in thickets in black humus.

This early flowering lily grows 60 to 80 centimeters (2 to 2.5 feet) tall in the wild and up to 120 centimeters (4 feet) in good garden conditions. The stem bears on short flower stalks 5 to 20 strongly scented, pendent, widely open trumpet-form flowers of pure yellow to soft cream with or without faint lilac spots. The pollen is yellow. The bulb is rather large, shaped like a pointed egg.

A plant first described as *Lilium szovitsianum* var. *armenum* and later called *L. armenum* has now been classified as *L. monadelphum* var. *armenum* Eremin 1966. It is native to the Caucasus, in Armenia around Kirovakan (north of Yerevan) and Lake Sevan. It does not have the fusion of the filaments into a single tube, but botanists have now decided that it is a geographical variant of *L. monadelphum,* with which it readily crosses, producing quite uniform seedlings.

Lilium monadelphum likes a loamy, very well drained soil rich in leafmold. It sulks for a while after transplanting and should be moved only in fall. It is worth growing this lily from seed, which is set in large quantities and gives delayed hypogeal germination.

The seedlings should be kept in the seed bed for two or three years, then in fall should be planted out in well-drained loamy soil, 10 to 15 centimeters (4 to 6 inches) deep. It is advisable to cover them in winter with a mulch of leaves or compost. This is a long-lived lily and cultivation is easy. It takes kindly to a wide range of soils, light or heavy, acid, neutral, or alkaline. In England and western Scotland it has naturalized in widely different gardens, producing spectacular flowering groups in late spring and early summer.

Lilium monadelphum can be crossed, though with difficulty, with *L. bulbiferum* and *L. maculatum.* It was grown at Oregon Bulb Farms for several years, where the flower color varied from cream to yellow.

Charles Robinson of Ontario successfully crossed *Lilium monadelphum* with *L. candidum* var. *salonikae* to produce 'June Fragrance'. An identical cross was made by Judith Freeman, obtaining a similar hybrid of great beauty. Chris North of Invergowrie, Scotland, flowered a cross between *L. monadelphum* and *L. pyrenaicum.*

Lilium monadelphum hybridizes with *L. bulbiferum;* the result, *L. ×fialkovaja* (Mitschurin 1914) is one of the first lilies to bloom in the spring. In 1979 Judith Freeman crossed *L. ×fialkovaja* with pastel-colored, upright Asiatic lilies by means of embryo culture, raising a population of fragrant pink-white and peach-yellow bicolors later introduced as the Faberge strain. The bulbs resembled *L. monadelphum* and resented transplanting. Once established, however, the Faberge strain produced a wealth of beauty for many years. Chris North also flowered a cross with *L. candidum* by embryo culture.

Lilium nanum Klotzsch & Garcke 1862

The name *nanum* means "dwarf." The species is native to the Himalayas, from Bashahr east through Garhwal, Kumaon, Nepal, Sikkim, southeastern Tibet, and Bhutan, into China's western Sichuan and northwestern Yunnan Provinces, at 2700 to 4500 meters (8,800 to 14,800 feet).

Like some other dwarf alpine lilies, this species has suffered at the hands of the taxonomists, who have placed it in the genera *Fritillaria* and *Nomocharis* at various times. I still see an occasional reference to *Nomocharis nana,* for only a short time ago there were those who found it difficult to believe that anything so diminutive could be called a lily!

This alpine lily grows only 15 to 40 centimeters (6 to 15 inches) tall. It has delicate, widely opened, outfacing flowers of pale pink or creamy yellow, spotted inside with purple. The whitish bulb is up to 4 centimeters (1.5 inches) high. The slender stem rises directly, attaining 8 to 42 centimeters (3 to 15 inches) in height. The scattered leaves are linear or narrowly linear and up to 15 centimeters (6 inches) long.

Haw (1986) discussed two botanical varieties from China and Tibet. Variety *flavidum* (Rendle) Sealy 1952 differs in having yellow flowers; it is also known as *Lilium euxanthum* and was introduced into cultivation under that name in the mid-1990s. Variety *brevistylum* has yellow flowers slightly tinged with purple and a style only about 1 millimeter long.

Seed germination is immediate epigeal. Although seed obtained from collectors has germinated well, the bulbs do not progress very quickly. The best practice is to get the seedlings outside at the earliest opportunity, in a safe, undisturbed corner where they will have little or no disturbance and can build up to maturity in five or six years.

Introduced in 1852, *Lilium nanum* is still rare in gardens. It is most likely to succeed in the hands of specialists in alpine plants, especially in cool regions such as Scotland and the Pacific Northwest. Those who wish to grow it may be best advised to move to Perthshire in Scotland, where it has been grown for many years in acid soil with light shade.

Lilium nepalense D. Don 1821

This species is named for Nepal. Native to the Himalayas of Nepal, Bhutan, and Kumaon, it grows on crystalline limestones at 2000 to 3000 meters (6600 to 9800 feet).

The flower of this magnificent trumpet lily is widely flared and strongly reflexed. It is pea-green or pale lemon-yellow in color; in some forms it is deep red inside with dark purple throats. The stout stems bear 1 to 5 pendent flowers. The lily grows up to 120 centimeters (4 feet) tall, with broadly lanceolate leaves. The bulb is a flattened globe with broad, overlapping, generally whitish pink to purple scales. The stoloniferous flowering stem may travel horizontally below ground for up to 50 centimeters (20 inches), forming stem bulblets as it goes. This lily emerges unusually late, often in May, and flowers in July. The flowers exude an exotic fragrance at night. The seed is narrowly winged and pale brown. Seed germination is immediate epigeal.

Coming from the Himalayan foothills, *Lilium nepalense* might be suspected to lack hardiness; however, it has survived outdoors in Oregon for many years. Outdoor plantings in some shade produced five to six flowers per stem. The species can be grown in a pot or other container given plenty of moisture during its growing period, but it must be kept dry during fall and winter. It is necessary to cover it against fall rains.

Plate 27. *Lilium nepalense*. Photo by Herman v. Wall.

Variety *concolor* Cotton 1937, from Assam, is an entirely yellow form without the purple throat. Several magnificent plantings of this strong growing variety were observed in Australia and New Zealand in 1997. Breeders have tried many times to cross this colorful variety with various trumpet lilies, with little success to date.

Variety *robustum* Elwes 1879 was introduced to commerce. The pendent, emerald-green flowers with strongly reflexed tepals are purple-violet in the center and pleasantly scented. It is believed that this form can bear no more than a degree or so of frost. It emerges early in May and flowers from July to August. It requires a very well drained, deep, constantly moist soil, in which the stem can wander horizontally.

Crosses with Chinese trumpet lilies have been claimed, but these plants are genetically distant, and I do not believe that any true hybrids have resulted from such attempts. A successful cross was made in the Netherlands by Jaap Spaans, who produced a beautiful hybrid from crossing *Lilium nepalense* with a hybrid of *L. japonicum*. Crosses between *L. nepalense* and *L. auratum* × *L. japonicum* hybrids were made at Oregon Bulb Farms in the early 1970s; hollow seed with large dead embryos indicated that hybrid plants could have been raised had embryo culture techniques been available to us then.

Lilium nobilissimum T. Makino 1914

The name comes from the Latin word for "most noble." In Japan the species is named *tamoto-yuri*. It is native to Kuchi-no-shima in the Ryukyu Islands, Japan, growing on steep cliffs.

This species is distinct in all respects from *Lilium alexandrae*, and it is hard to understand why the two were once confused. The habit of *L. nobilissimum* is upright, 90 to 120 centimeters (3 to 4 feet) in height, with a stout stem and broad leaves. The waxy-textured, pure white, scented trumpet flowers, as many as 6 in number, are borne on short upright stalks. The pistil is long with a broad stigma. The pollen is deep yellow. Seed germination is delayed hypogeal, with flowering plants produced in three or four years.

This species is very late flowering and has been difficult to establish in outdoor culture. It is not winter-hardy in cold climates, where it must be grown in the greenhouse, flowering in August to September. It

should succeed, could its requirement for extreme drainage be met, in
temperate coastal regions. It does
best in an alkaline, stony soil. It is
very susceptible to *Fusarium.*

In 1962 *Lilium nobilissimum* was
crossed with the Oregon Bulb Farms
hybrids 'Pink Glory' and the Imperial Silver strain. The progeny first
flowering in 1967. These combined
the upright inflorescence of *L. nobilissimum* with the pink color of the
Oriental hybrids. Chromosome studies disclose that all these robust hybrids, having been produced in a very
hot greenhouse, were triploid (see
Chapter 12). Through embryo cul-

Plate 28. *Lilium nobilissimum*

ture, crosses were raised between
L. nobilissimum and *L. alexandrae, L. auratum,* and *L. speciosum* (Schenk
1985). Later crosses with *L. nobilissimum* and Oriental hybrids at Oregon Bulb Farms produced diploid lilies in a wide range of colors.

Lilium occidentale Purdy 1897
Eureka lily
The name *occidentale* means "westernmost." Native to the Pacific Coast
of the United States, from northern California into southern Oregon,
this lily grows in the drier parts of sphagnum bogs. This species is very
rare and must be considered under great threat from human activities.

The bulb is a small short rhizome. The flower stem is 60 to 180 centimeters (2 to 6 feet) tall, with small elliptical leaves in whorls. It bears
1 to 15 small, pendent, turk's-cap flowers with a green base color and
orange throat with brown spots, the slightly recurved tips tinted carmine. The anthers are purple with red-orange pollen. The flowers open
in July. Seed germination is hypogeal in late fall.

Lilium occidentale should be planted in lime-free loam soil with leafmold and peat. Samuel L. Emsweller described how this lily and *L. co-*

Plate 29. *Lilium occidentale*

lumbianum grew on opposite sides of a road at one Oregon site, within 100 meters (330 feet) of each other. The latter was growing in dry ground that may have been wet in season, but *L. occidentale* was in a low, dried-out bog where the gullies indicated that the bulbs were under water during the wet months.

Lilium oxypetalum Baker 1874

The name *oxypetalum* means "sharp petaled." The species is native to the Himalayas of western Nepal, Kumaon, and Garhwal, from 2900 to 4000 meters (9500 to 13,000 feet). It occurs on rocky slopes and in open coniferous forest on limestone.

Growing 20 to 25 centimeters (8 to 10 inches) tall, *Lilium oxypetalum* has 1 or 2 bell-shaped, pendent, greenish yellow flowers. Seed germination is immediate hypogeal.

Variety *insigne* Sealy 1952 has flowers of purplish pink and green and is a stronger grower than the yellow form. It was introduced in 1939 by George Sherriff from Simla in the Hill States of India.

This species has been superbly cultivated in Scotland for many years.

It is justly appreciated, fitting happily into the northern environment as it does into the subalpine Himalayas. It grows best in leafy humus in light shade, with excellent drainage.

Lilium papilliferum Franchet 1892
Likiang lily

This species is named for the papillose-glandular surface of the stem. Habitat: China (northwestern Yunnan), in dry places around 3000 meters (9800 feet) among boulders and in rocky alpine meadows.

Although discovered in 1888 by French missionary Père Delavay, this species was not cultivated until 1946, when plant-hunter Joseph F. Rock reintroduced it to cultivation and it flowered in England and the United States. From a small lance-shaped bulb (white turning purple with age) around 3 centimeters (1.5 inches) high rises a stoloniferous flower stem of about 60 centimeters (2 feet), which travels horizontally in the soil before emerging. The bulb and stem are similar to those of *Lilium nepalense.* The linear leaves are numerous. The flowers, 1 to 3 in number, are borne late in the season. They are sweetly scented, gleaming dark purple to near black. The tepals are reflexed, with the inner segments usually so strongly bent back that the entire flower has a triangular appearance. The anthers are brown, the pollen orange. Seed germination is immediate epigeal.

This is a very interesting lily, but it is rarely seen in the garden. Grown at Oregon Bulb Farms for several years, it required a well-drained loam with adequate humus. It emerges late, as does *Lilium nepalense,* missing the frost. It should be hardy with a little protection in colder areas.

Lilium papilliferum is closely related to *L. davidii.* It is reported to have been crossed with *L. davidii, L. duchartrei, L. lankongense,* and other species, but plants were not raised from these crosses, even with the aid of embryo culture.

Lilium paradoxum Stearn 1956
The name *paradoxum* means "contrary to expectation" and refers to the fact that this species could be placed with equal justification in *Lilium* or *Nomocharis.* The species is native to southeastern Tibet at around 3600 meters (11,800 feet).

In 1947 the Ludlow, Sherriff, and Elliott expedition found this single-flowered lily. It grows 20 to 45 centimeters (8 to 18 inches) tall, with leaves in whorls and an upright, purple, wide-open bowl-shaped flower 5.5 to 7 centimeters (2 to 3 inches) in diameter. Fox (1985) noted that the whorled, relatively broad leaves are an interesting feature, not seen in any other Himalayan or western Chinese species, but only in the true martagons and most North American species. As far as I know, this species has not been introduced to cultivation.

Lilium pardalinum Kellogg 1859
Leopard lily

The name comes from the Latin word for "leopard," referring to the spotting on the flower. The species is native to the Pacific Coast of the United States, from southern Oregon to San Diego County, California, in woodland near streams.

The leopard lily is the hardiest and easiest to grow of the western American forest lilies, as well as one of the most desirable. On a stout, branching rhizome are several bulbs with many yellow, brittle, multiple-parted scales. The flower stem grows 120 to 200 centimeters (4 to 7 feet) tall. The lanceolate leaves are arranged in whorls along the stem. The flower is scentless, borne on an elegant out-arching stalk with strongly reflexed turk's-cap flowers around 5 centimeters (2 inches) in diameter. The flower color is gleaming orange-red, carmine-red at the tips, marked in the center with strong red-brown spots bordered in orange, with green nectaries and orange pollen. The flowers open in July. Seed germination is hypogeal in late fall in cool conditions.

Variety *fragrans* is a sweetly scented form found by Carl Purdy on riversides and seeps in the Cuyamaca Mountains of San Diego County. It may be a hybrid with the fragrant *Lilium parryi*.

'Red Giant', the sunset lily, was formerly known as *Lilium harrisianum* Beane & Vollmer. It has been treated either as a giant form of *L. pardalinum* or as a hybrid between that species and *L. humboldtii*. Beane and Vollmer described it from a wild population on the banks of Van Duzen Creek in northern California. The rainy climate and frequent flooding of the mountain stream results in the lily being frequently inundated, sometimes when in flower. The rhizome, growing in earth and gravel, is often washed out and deeply buried in gravel

Plate 30. *Lilium pardalinum*. Painting by Mary Comber Miles.

and sand. This extraordinarily magnificent lily, usually 150 to 200 centimeters (5 to 7 feet) tall, bears large flowers, 8 to 10 centimeters (3 to 4 inches) wide; they are gleaming carmine-red inside from the tip to the midpoint, and chrome yellow from the middle to the base, tinged in the throat with green, with large spots, typically gold ringed in chocolate-brown. The giant form of *L. pardalinum* is very amenable to cultivation. It prefers a cool, rather moist soil with shade at the base and full sun on the upper part of the plant. The rapidly multiplying bulb should be dug, divided, and replanted every three or four years.

Lilium pardalinum is the most important parent plant among the American species. With another important parent, *L. humboldtii,* it produced the famous Bellingham hybrids. 'Shuksan', the greatest of these, is now 60 years old and still going strong. *Lilium pardalinum* produces hybrids with a special stamina, so all gardeners can grow and enjoy them. The species and its hybrids have been crossed with *L. bolanderi* and *L. kelloggii* to produce beautiful clear colors in the second generation.

Lilium parryi S. Watson 1878
Lemon lily

This species is named for Charles Christopher Parry (1823–1890), a U.S. government botanist working in the West. It is native to the southwestern United States, in the San Gabriel Mountains of southern California, and in Arizona, at 1800 to 3000 meters (5900 to 9800 feet). It grows in granitic soils that experience some winter snowfall.

Lilium parryi has a straight, upright habit. The trumpet flowers are borne horizontally on flower stalks rising obliquely upward. Their exquisite fragrance is seduction itself. The flower color is pale to bright yellow, spotted in light brown. The lower half of the tepal is rolled and reflexed. The lily is 60 to 180 centimeters (2 to 6 feet) tall with 1 to 15 flowers, sometimes as many as 50 flowers on one stem. The leaves are arranged in several whorls along the stem. The rhizomatous bulb has numerous jointed scales, white and turning yellowish with age. Seed germination is hypogeal. This species is not restricted to germinating in the late fall to winter period as are many other western American species; this may be due to the lower latitude of its range.

Variety *kessleri* Davidson 1924 comes from the San Gabriel Mountains and is more robust than the type in all respects.

This species is difficult to grow in some areas. Perfect drainage is necessary, so the bulb should be planted in a mixture of 2 to 3 parts leafmold and peat well mixed with grit and charcoal. It should not be planted too deep, and the base of the plant should be shaded. It needs plenty of water during the growing season, but after flowering it should be protected against rain until frost.

Lilium parryi will hybridize with *L. humboldtii, L. kelloggii, L. ocellatum,* and *L. pardalinum.* It was involved in breeding the Bellingham hybrids. A group of beautiful hybrids derived from *L. parryi* and *L. humboldtii* was grown for some years at Oregon Bulb Farms as the San Gabriel strain.

Lilium parvum Kellogg 1862
Sierra lily

The name *parvum* means "small" and refers to the size of the flower. The species is native to the western United States, in the Sierra Nevada of California and the Cascade Range of southern Oregon, at 1500 to 3000 meters (4900 to 9800 feet), along riverbanks and in snowmelt areas.

This alpine lily has a small, flat bulb on a short rhizome. The stem grows 90 to 120 centimeters (3 to 4 feet) tall and bears small, outfacing, bell-shaped flowers of yellow, orange, or red (depending on the altitude of the population), with brown spots. It flowers in June and July. Seed germination is hypogeal in late fall in cool conditions.

Forma *crocatum* Stearn 1947 has pure orange-yellow, bell-shaped flowers, spotted in crimson, without any red. Variety *hollidayi* is a pink color form.

Lilium parvum is readily increased from seed or bulb scales. It requires a site with good drainage, a sandy humus soil, plenty of moisture (it is really a wetland bulb, inhabiting damp snowbed sites in an otherwise dry zone), and snow or other cover in winter. It hybridizes with *L. parryi* and *L. pardalinum.*

Lilium philadelphicum Linnaeus 1762
Wood lily

The name *philadelphicum* apparently refers not to the species' native range but to the place from which Carl Linnaeus was sent material by early botanists (i.e., the city of Philadelphia in Pennsylvania). The species is native to North America, the type from the eastern slopes of the Rocky Mountains to the juncture of the Ohio and Mississippi Rivers, and variety *andinum* Ker-Gawler 1822 from the Missouri River to British Columbia in Canada.

The bulbs are formed on short stolons. The lanceolate leaves usually are arranged in several whorls on a stem of 45 to 90 centimeters (1.5 to 3 feet).

Variety *andinum* is distinguished by its linear leaves that are scattered along the stem. The 1 to 5 widely opened, upfacing, bowl-shaped flowers are borne in an umbel and are a lively orange-scarlet in color and more orange within, where they are frequently spotted heavily in dark brown. The tepals are small and claw shaped at the base, much like those of *Lilium catesbaei*. Seed germination is rapid and epigeal, particularly when the seed is exposed to light.

Mary Henry selected and grew many color variants of this species, from pale lemon-yellow through orange and red shades to strong brown and deep bluish red, with or without spotting. The species should be planted in well-drained, sandy loam with leafmold and peat, and covered in winter for protection against excessive wet.

Crosses claimed to be between Asiatic lilies and *Lilium philadelphicum* such as Frank L. Skinner's *L. ×phildauricum* and James Taylor's 'Goldcrest' are very questionable. There is no evidence of *L. philadelphicum* being involved in these hybrids. Even more dubious are reports of crosses between this species and *L. martagon* and *L. pumilum*.

Lilium philippinense Baker 1873
This species is named for its native range, the Philippines. There it grows in Luzon Province, on mountain slopes from 1500 to 2000 meters (4900 to 6600 feet).

Lilium philippinense has the most southerly distribution of any lily species, close to the sixteenth parallel. In July and August it bears 1 to 30 pure white, long-tubular trumpet flowers with dark green or brown reverse on a stem as tall as 90 centimeters (3 feet). Seed germination is immediate epigeal.

This species can achieve flowering size within 8 months from seed-set, so it can be very useful for pot culture and cut-flower production. Not surprisingly, it is quite tender and needs greenhouse culture in northern regions. Experience with it at Oregon Bulb Farms showed that it closely resembles *Lilium formosanum* in many respects.

Lilium philippinense has been crossed with *L. formosanum* and *L. longiflorum*. Despite hybrid vigor, the crosses produced nothing superior to the species, which are so beautiful in themselves that they are difficult to improve.

Lilium pitkinense Beane & Vollmer 1955

This species is named for Sarah Ann Pitkin, on whose property it was discovered. It is native to Sonoma County, California, in marshland.

This species, which Munz considers closely related to *Lilium occidentale,* was first discovered in 1952 in what appears to be its sole wild station at Pitkin Marsh in Sonoma County, California. The site is a swamp and marsh that has often been subjected to grazing by cattle.

Lilium pitkinense may reach 180 centimeters (6 feet) in height. It resembles *L. pardalinum* in appearance. The flowers are reflexed in turk's-cap form, a strong cinnabar-red or scarlet red with a yellow throat. They appear in July. The stem grows from a large, stout stoloniferous rhizome. Seed germination is hypogeal in late fall in cool conditions.

Variety *fiski* is a pink-flowered form.

Seedling populations of this species grown at Oregon Bulb Farms showed enormous variation in height, flower size, color, and flowering season. They resembled a hybrid population more than a true species. This observation, coupled with the species' singular wild occurrence, suggests that *Lilium pitkinense* in fact represents a natural hybrid population. The plants were all strong and easy to grow, much like smaller forms of *L. pardalinum.*

Eric Mayell crossed this species with *Lilium kelloggii* to produce extraordinarily choice hybrids with delicate mauve tints, known as the Monterey hybrids. *Lilium ×burbankii* crosses with *L. pitkinense,* giving hybrids with gleaming cinnabar or scarlet flowers.

Lilium poilanei Gagnepain 1934

This species is named for French forest officer Eugène Poilane, who collected it. It is native to two sites, both at 2000 meters (6600 feet). One site is in northwestern Vietnam near Chapa and the other in northwestern Laos between Muong-het and Muong-seng.

This little-known species, which is not to my knowledge in cultivation at this time, is said to be closely allied to *Lilium primulinum* from Thailand. It has a reddish stem growing 100 to 150 centimeters (3 to 5 feet) tall, with scattered lanceolate leaves 10 centimeters (4 inches) long and up to 15 millimeters (0.5 inch) wide. The flowers are funnel shaped and slightly recurved, creamy white to pale yellow in color, unspotted but with a red median stripe. The anthers are green and the pollen yellow, with the style and trilobed capitate stigma protruding.

Lilium polyphyllum D. Don 1840
The name *polyphyllum* means "many-leaved." The species is native to the Himalayas, from Afghanistan through Kashmir to Kumaon, at 1800 to 3700 meters (5,900 to 12,100 feet).

This species has the most westerly distribution of lilies on the Indian subcontinent. The long, narrow white bulb grows 25 to 60 centimeters (10 to 24 inches) deep with very long roots. The stem is 40 to 120 centimeters (15 inches to 4 feet) tall, sometimes as tall as 240 centimeters (8 feet), with scattered linear or narrow-lanceolate leaves. It generally bears 1 to 10 flowers, but sometimes as many as 40. The fragrant, nodding flowers are bell shaped, with the lower half of the tepals strongly rolled under. The flower color is greenish yellow inside the trumpet, and cream on the outside, prettily spotted with lilac. The pollen is orangered. The seed is round and unwinged. Seed germination is hypogeal in warm conditions, and growth is then delayed through a cold season.

This lily has always proven difficult in cultivation, preferring deep planting and no late transplanting; the long roots should be shaded. Recommended conditions include a northern exposure, protection from wind, and half shade. Hardiness seems not to be a problem. Ruth Clas of Albany, New York, grew it successfully for several years. At Oregon Bulb Farms, where it was grown for a while, deep planting of the long, narrow bulbs and good drainage were essential.

Lilium pomponium Linnaeus 1753
The name comes from the medieval Latin *pomponius,* said to have denoted a red pear. The species is native to the Alpes-Maritimes of France between Nizza and Ventimiglia, growing on exposed, brushy,

south-facing slopes among limestone boulders in rather dry, rocky soils.

The bulb is a creamy-white, pointed globe about 4 to 5 centimeters (1.5 to 2 inches) in diameter. The stem is usually 40 to 50 centimeters (15 to 20 inches) tall, purple-tinted with close-set, narrowly linear, grasslike leaves with silvery margins. There are up to 10 nodding red turk's-cap flowers with small black spots; appearing in July, they have an unpleasant scent. The pollen is cinnabar-red.

Increase is by seed and bulb scales. Seed germination is epigeal in cool conditions following fall rains. Cultivation is not difficult. Although apparently confined to limestone areas in the wild, *Lilium pomponium* accepts acid soils in gardens. It should be planted in loamy soil with leafmold and limestone grit in full sun.

Little use has been made in hybridizing this lily with others to which it is closely related. What attempts have been made gave unexciting results.

Lilium primulinum Baker 1892
Ocher lily

The name is derived from *Primula,* referring to the typical primrose-yellow flower color. The species is native to upper Myanmar (formerly Burma), China (western Yunnan), and Thailand.

The ocher lily has three botanical varieties. Variety *burmanicum* Stearn 1948 is 120 to 240 centimeters (4 to 8 feet) tall with 2 to 7 medium-sized turk's-cap flowers of greenish yellow, spotted with purple in the throat. It is winter-hardy in England given a protected site.

Variety *ochraceum* grows up to 240 centimeters (8 feet) tall with small, strongly reflexed flowers, wine-purple within with greenish ocher tips.

Variety *primulinum* has turk's-cap flowers that are entirely primrose-yellow.

Lilium primulinum seems to be very rare in cultivation, although variety *burmanicum* survived for many years on the Isle of Aran off the Scottish coast. Robert Withers grew the same variety in Victoria in southwestern Australia, using acid loam with plenty of humus and excellent drainage. All the varieties are likely to require winter protection in regions experiencing frost.

Lilium pumilum de Candolle 1812
Coral lily

The name *pumilum* means "dwarf." The species is native to South and North Korea, Manchuria, eastern Siberia (near Lake Baikal, the upper Yenisei River, and Transbaikalia), Mongolia, and northern China.

This graceful lily was previously known as *Lilium tenuifolium*. The bulb is small, conical, and white. The stem is quite variable in height, from 45 to 120 centimeters (18 inches to 4 feet), with many small grassy leaves; in May or June it bears 1 to 30 scented, nodding turk's-cap flowers of gleaming sealing-wax red, occasionally with small black spots in the throat. The pollen is scarlet. Seed germination is immediate epigeal.

Marina Baranova noted that yellow and white forms were found in the southern part of the Krasnoyarsk region. E. H. Wilson (1925) mentioned variety *flore-albo,* a white form said to have been in cultivation in Germany.

A select cultivar, 'Golden Gleam', was grown at Oregon Bulb Farms for many years. Its flowers are soft orange rather than the bright scarlet of the type. This color form breeds true from seed.

Yellow Bunting strain (Plate 32), originally described as a hybrid by Frank L. Skinner, is a short, recessive yellow-gold form of the species. Very early flowering with golden-yellow blooms, this lovely plant also comes true from seed.

Lilium pumilum likes full sun and well-drained soil, and is lime-tolerant. It commonly degenerates after a few years in the garden, so one must constantly renew it from seed. Bulbs should be planted 10 centimeters (4 inches) deep. It is a good cut flower.

Lilium pumilum can be crossed under controlled conditions with *L. amabile, L. callosum, L. cernuum, L. concolor, L. dauricum,* and *L. davidii* var. *willmottiae.* It is best used as a pollen parent, since as a seed parent it tends to produce apomictic seed (viable seed produced without fertilization, and therefore genetically identical to the seed parent).

Among the many hybrids derived from this species are *Lilium* ×*intermedium* (*L. pumilum* × *L. concolor* var. *pulchellum*; Harold Comber 1940); 'Goldcrest' (Asiatic hybrid × *L. pumilum* 'Golden Gleam'; James Taylor); *L. pumilum* × *L. amabile* (Norma Pfeiffer 1976); *L. pumilum* × *L. bulbiferum* (Fritz Ewald 1975); and 'Scamp' (*L. pumilum* × *L. dauricum* 'Golden Chalice'; Ruth Clas).

Plate 31. *Lilium pumilum*. Photo by Herman v. Wall.

Plate 32. *Lilium pumilum* Yellow Bunting strain.

Charles Robinson did extensive work with this species, crossing it with *Lilium davidii* var. *unicolor* and several Stenographer hybrids. Leonard Marshall crossed selected Rainbow hybrids ('Tabasco' × *L. dauricum*) with *L. pumilum,* producing four distinct hybrids. These were crossed with upright, virus-tolerant clones in a wide variety of colors to produce succeeding generations of beautiful, fragrant hybrids. Marshall also crossed *L. pumilum* with *L. cernuum* in 1969. The cross of the hybrid *L. concolor* × *L. pumilum* (Marshall) with several upright Asiatic clones produced charming small-flowered hybrids, including 'Fireworks' ('Matchless' × (*L. concolor* × *L. pumilum*)) and 'Roman Candle' ('Pirate' × (*L. concolor* × *L. pumilum*)). The remarkable Viva strain bred by Judith Freeman was derived from crossing *L. pumilum* with *L. leichtlinii* var. *maximowiczii* 'Unicolor'.

Lilium pyrenaicum Gouan 1773

This species is named for its native range, the Pyrenees. Native to Europe, Turkey, and the Caucasus, it grows on forest margins, in meadows, and on slopes from 500 to 1500 meters (1500 to 4900 feet).

This lily was described by botanists as early as 1590. In recent years, other entities formerly considered to be separate species have been reinterpreted as subspecies and varieties of *Lilium pyrenaicum,* as discussed below.

The type is now known as subspecies *pyrenaicum.* In England and Scotland it has become naturalized in hedges and on roadsides, becoming a weed in some places. The bulb is broadly round, about 7 centimeters (3 inches) in diameter, with yellowish white scales. The flower stem is 30 to 120 centimeters (1 to 4 feet) tall, set with many linear-lanceolate leaves. The unpleasantly scented flowers are borne in a raceme in groups of 1 to 12; they are small, 3.5 centimeters (1.5 inches) wide, nodding, strongly reflexed turk's-caps of a greenish yellow color with faint black spotting. Compared to the lush foliage, the flowers are quite small. They open early, from late May to June. The pollen is dark orange. Seed germination is delayed epigeal.

Variety *albanicum* Hayek 1932 has smooth leaves and 1 to 4 amber-yellow flowers with cinnabar-red pollen, usually with low stature; it occurs in the mountains of Montenegro, Albania, northern Greece, and Macedonia.

Variety *bosniacum* Hayek 1932 has smooth leaf veins and orange-red flowers; it is found in Bosnia in the Trescavica range in alpine meadows at 1400 meters (4600 feet) altitude, its range overlapping those of varieties *jankae* and *albanicum*.

Subspecies *carniolicum* (Koch 1837) formerly known as *Lilium carniolicum,* occurs in the Balkan region from Ukraine across Istria, Dalmatia, Croatia, Albania, and Greece to Bulgaria and Romania. It shows great variation and has been separated into several varieties, most of which have at one time or another been designated as distinct species. It has many scattered lanceolate leaves, held horizontally with the tips slightly curled outward. The turk's-cap flowers are borne on comparatively short, thick petioles.

Variety *jankae* Hayek 1932 has hairy leaf veins and margins, a red flower stalk, and canary-yellow turk's-cap flowers with small black spots in the throat; it occurs on the border of Bosnia and southern Croatia at elevations of 600 to 1300 meters (1950 to 4300 feet), and elsewhere in the Rhodope Mountains of Bulgaria and the Sieben Mountains of Romania.

Subspecies *ponticum* Koch 1849 occurs on the southern coast of the Black Sea, in Turkey near Trabezon on the Zigana Pass, near Artvin, and near Batumi, Georgia, from 1800 to 2250 meters (5900 to 7300 feet), on rocky slopes and grassy meadows, extending to above the tree line. The bulb is small and conical, with few scales. The flower stem is 40 to 75 centimeters (15 to 30 inches) tall with 1 to 3 (rarely up to 12) flowers. The leaves are short and wide, lanceolate with short hairs along the margins so that they appear to be edged in silver; the veins on the underside of the leaf are also covered with short hairs. The turk's-cap flower is 3 to 4 centimeters (about 1.5 inches) in diameter, without hairs. The color varies from pale yellow to deep yellow and orange, spotted with blackish purple in the throat; the throat is often entirely purple. The tepals are flushed with purple on the outside. The flowers have a strange, unpleasant scent and orange pollen.

Two varieties of subspecies *ponticum* are distinguished. Variety *artvinense* Davis & Henderson 1969 has 1 to 3 deep orange flowers on a weakly and sparsely foliated plant; it blooms from May to July and occurs at Artvin and the Bayburt Pass of Turkey at 900 to 1500 meters (3000 to 4900 feet). Variety *ponticum* Koch 1849, formerly known as *Lilium georgicum*, has 1 to 5 butter-yellow flowers on a short plant. It occurs in the Caucasus, in Georgia north of Tiflis, near Gudaur and the Georgian Military Highway and near Trabezon on the Risa Pass and Of-Bayburt Pass, on hillsides in long grass at altitudes from 2200 to 2500 meters (7200 to 8200 feet). It usually bears 4 to 7 deep golden flowers with striking orange anthers. The malodorous flower is trumpet shaped to bell shaped; the tepals are 5.5 to 7 centimeters (2 to 3 inches) long and generally purple, with darker purple papillae or spots along the keel.

Variety *rubrum* Marshall 1929, prettier than subspecies *pyrenaicum*, has orange-red flowers spotted in brown. It should probably be treated as the typical form, with the yellow form merely a variety. It grows wild in Spain near Burgos.

Lilium pyrenaicum may be increased by division, scales, or seed. All its subspecies inhabit hilly regions, growing among rocks and shrubs in very well drained, stony loams and gravels, based on limestone, with a thin surface layer of humus. In the garden they succeed in light, humusy loam in full sun or half shade.

Chris North of the Scottish Horticultural Institute made various crosses with *Lilium pyrenaicum*, growing the embryos artificially in a nutrient solution in the laboratory. With *L. pyrenaicum* as the seed parent, he obtained hybrids from *L. chalcedonicum*, *L. ciliatum*, *L. monadelphum*, *L. pyrenaicum* subsp. *ponticum*, *L. pyrenaicum* subsp. *carniolicum* var. *jankae*, and *L. szovitsianum*. A hybrid of *L. pyrenaicum* and *L. pomponium* was named 'Europa' (North 1978/1979).

Lilium regale Wilson 1912
Regal lily

The name *regale* means "royal." This species is native to the Min River valley of western Sichuan Province in China, growing in narrow canyons with steep, rocky sides.

The regal lily is a most valuable introduction of E. H. Wilson, who found it in China in 1903. Its range is restricted to a 50-mile stretch of the bleak Min Valley, where the climate is very hot in summer and very cold in winter. In June, however, these canyons are transformed into a paradise when the regal lily blooms by the hundreds of thousands on cliffs 1600 meters (5200 feet) high. Here in 1910 Wilson selected about 6000 to 7000 small bulbs, which became the foundation stock of commercial production of this lily in the West.

The bulb is round, about 5 to 8 centimeters (2 to 3 inches) in diameter, with lance-shaped scales that are dark purple in color. The strong, slightly curving stem is 80 to 120 centimeters (2.5 to 4 feet) tall or taller, set with scattered, single-veined, linear leaves. It bears a wheel-like umbel of 1 to 8 or more trumpet-shaped flowers with a strong fragrance. The flowers open widely in June and early July, with the tepals more or less reflexed. Inside the flowers are gleaming white with a chrome-yellow throat; outside, all the ribs of the tepals are overlain with rose-purple. The anthers and pollen are chrome yellow, and the filaments and stigma green. Seed germination is immediate epigeal.

Lilium regale sets copious seed that tends be apomictic. As a pollen parent it crosses readily with *L. sargentiae* (producing *L. ×imperiale* Wilson 1920), *L. sulphureum* (producing *L. ×sulphurgale*), and *L. leucanthum* var. *centifolium* (producing *L. ×centigale*). The seeds germinate well and quickly.

These lilies should be planted in sun in good humus soil with a mulch, since late frosts may destroy the young shoots. The plant is stem-rooting. There is no lily more welcome in the garden, nor less expensive, considering that it increases well by offsets. It grew strongly and profusely at Oregon Bulb Farms for many years. It is an indestructible lily in many climates.

In the United States there arose a pure golden-yellow lily of great beauty, *Lilium regale* 'Royal Gold'. I made the cross of *L. regale* and

Plate 33. *Lilium regale*

'Bright Star', producing a very beautiful, early flowering bowl-shaped aurelian type. Other fine individuals were derived from this hybrid in succeeding generations.

George Slate recommended that this species be crossed with *Lilium henryi* to obtain early flowering hybrids. Leslie Woodriff's 'Pink Tiger' was reputed to be a cross between *L. regale* and *L. lancifolium.*

Lilium rhodopaeum Delipavlov 1952

This species is named for its native range, the Rhodope Mountains of Bulgaria, where it occurs in meadows at 1300 meters (4300 feet).

Rather similar to *Lilium monadelphum,* this lily has pendent flowers, 8 to 14 centimeters (3 to 6 inches) in diameter, with reflexed tepals. The color, golden-yellow without spots, is darker than that of related species. There are 1 or 2, more often 3 to 5 flowers in an umbel, and the open in June. The pollen is scarlet. The bulb is white with many small scales. The stem is 80 to 100 centimeters (2.5 to 3 feet) tall, set along its entire length with long-linear leaves. Seed germination is delayed hypogeal.

In cultivation this species should respond well to the conditions preferred by *Lilium monadelphum.*

Lilium rosthornii Diels 1901
The origin of this name is unknown. The species is native to Sichuan and Hubei Provinces in China, growing in ravines and woodlands at 350 to 900 meters (1150 to 3000 feet). Known from only a few collections, this species is described by Haw (1986) as very similar to *Lilium henryi,* differing in having longer, linear-lanceolate leaves, a long-oblong capsule, and flowers with heavier, redder spots.

Lilium rubellum Baker 1898
The name *rubellum* means "reddish" and refers to the color of the flowers. In Japan the species is named *otome-yuri,* meaning "maiden lily." It is native to northern Honshu, Japan, from 900 to 1800 meters (3000 to 5900 feet), and grows on slopes in grass and brush.

The very large, long-oval, yellow bulb has large oval scales. The stem in nature is only 30 centimeters (1 foot) tall, but in cultivation may reach 50 centimeters (20 inches). Long-oval, short-petioled leaves are arranged spirally on the stem, more thickly on the upper part. The flower is a horizontal, bell-shaped trumpet, 4.5 centimeters (1.5 inches) long and 6.5 centimeters (3 inches) wide, delicate pink, sweet-scented, turning purple-rose with age; the pollen is golden-yellow. There are usually 1 to 3 flowers per stem. The seed capsule is ball shaped with triangular, brown seeds. Seed germination is delayed hypogeal.

The special quality of this delicately colored lily is that it produces early flowering hybrid offspring when crossed with other Oriental lily species and hybrids. In some of the hybrids the flower is formed within the bulb, which can cause a problem with bolting under forcing conditions.

The species needs a very acid soil with plenty of moisture (Ralph Warner wrote that he has seen it growing on a streambank with its roots in the flowing water), protection from rain, and winter cover of snow or artificial shelter. Its culture is not yet well understood. According to Koichiro Wada (pers. comm.), the bulbs should be planted in pots or wooden flats in damp sphagnum moss with good drainage and kept very well watered. The pots can be stood in full sun until the flowers open. The flowers, however, last better in half shade.

Lilium rubellum hybridizes with *L. alexandrae, L. auratum, L. japon-icum,* and *L. speciosum.* The Magic Pink strain was obtained by cross-ing it with selected virus-tolerant, red-banded clones of *L. auratum* var. *platyphyllum.* The cross between *L. alexandrae* and *L. rubellum,* grown through embryo culture, resembles *L. alexandrae* but is deep pink.

Norma Pfeiffer raised beautiful hybrids by crossing *Lilium rubellum* with both *L. auratum* var. *platyphyllum,* and with *L. auratum* × *L. japonicum.*

Leslie Woodriff was probably the first to use this species in hybridi-zing in North America. He crossed it with *Lilium auratum, L. japoni-cum,* and their hybrids with *L. rubellum* to produce his Little Fairies strain. 'Rosario' is perhaps the finest and most disease-resistant hybrid of *L. rubellum* yet introduced.

Lilium rubescens Watson 1879
Chaparral lily

The name *rubescens* means "becoming red" and refers to the color change as the flowers age. The species is native to the Pacific Coast of the United States, from San Francisco Bay in California to Siskiyou County in Oregon. It grows on north-facing slopes, in redwood groves in rather dry soils at elevations up to 900 meters (3000 feet).

The bulb is white with broad scales. The slender stem grows 60 to 180 centimeters tall (2 to 6 feet), sometimes taller, bearing many whorls of broad-lanceolate leaves; the whorls become smaller toward the top of the stem. The raceme carries up to 50, but normally 3 to 30, upright trumpets, in which the tepals first form a tube and then, in the last third of their length, are strongly reflexed. The flower color is white on open-ing, lightly sprinkled with purple, and gradually changes to rose-purple or wine-red. The flowers, notable for their fine scent, open in June and July. Seed germination is delayed hypogeal.

The cultivation of this species remains a problem, like that of the other dryland Pacific Coast lilies such as *Lilium kelloggii* and *L. bolan-deri.* In its native region it experiences high rainfall from autumn into spring, giving way to a very dry period from flowering time through late fall; to this is added the subtle effect of Pacific fogs and mists. Such conditions are difficult if not impossible to duplicate in cultivation. Suc-cess has been obtained by planting seedlings in a bulb frame, with care-fully controlled watering and a stony, gritty clay loam soil.

This species is reported to hybridize with *Lilium columbianum* and *L. bolanderi*. It has obvious evolutionary affinities with the more northerly *L. washingtonianum*.

Lilium sargentiae Wilson 1912

This species is named for the wife of Charles Sprague Sargent, director of the Arnold Arboretum. It is native to Sichuan Province, China, at 1100 to 1500 meters (3600 to 4900 feet), growing in stony soils among grass and shrubs, in a climate with a very hot summer and long cold winter.

E. H. Wilson collected this fine species on an expedition in 1903 in the valley of the Tung River, a tributary of the Yangtse Kiang. The bulb is round, about 15 centimeters (6 inches) in diameter, with broad, reddish purple scales. The purplish stem is 120 to 150 centimeters (4 to 5 feet) tall and bears many dark green, closely set lanceolate leaves, wider than those in *Lilium regale,* with bulbils developing in the axils. The large, beautifully sculpted trumpet flowers are pure white inside with a yellow throat, and purple-rose or brown and green on the reverse. The pink tone of the reverse can spread over the tepal margin onto the inner surface; the prepotency of this pattern has contributed to the development of the pink trumpet lilies. When the flowers open, the tepals are elegantly reflexed. The anthers are purple, the pollen brown, the pistil and stigma also purple. The raceme-form inflorescence can bear as many as 18 strongly perfumed flowers. Flowering time is about 14 days later than that of *L. regale,* usually in the second half of July. Seed germination is immediate epigeal.

Increase is by axillary bulbils, offsets, and seed. This species requires good drainage and a warm site in humusy soil. Its cultivation presents no special problems, but certain points must be considered. Unlike *Lilium regale,* it does not tolerate lime. In summer it is likely to be attacked by *Botrytis* blight, especially in climates with high moisture levels in spring. If hardiness is in doubt (and Wilson mentioned the unsuitability of the New England climate), added protection must be given. Outdoors, full exposure with adequate companion plants to shade the roots should be provided.

Lilium sargentiae hybridizes with *L. regale* (producing *L. ×imperiale*) and with *L. henryi* (producing *L. ×aurelianense*), giving a wide range of early and late-flowering hybrids in various colors and flower forms in succeeding generations.

Lilium sempervivoideum Léveillé 1915

This species is named for a dry bulb in the herbarium that resembled a *Sempervivum*. Native to Yunnan Province, China, it occurs at 2500 to 2600 meters (8200 to 8500 feet), in rocky meadows. This lily grows only 15 centimeters (6 inches) tall, with fine grassy leaves and up to 3 small, pendent white flowers with fine purple spots. Seed germination is immediate epigeal. It seems never to have been in cultivation in the West and would probably present the same challenges as other dwarf alpine lilies. Derek Fox (1985:198) wrote of it: "All writers are together in criticizing the ridiculous name given to this lily by Léveillé. It could be a little beauty with its campanulate flower."

Lilium sherriffiae Stearn 1950

This species is named for English plant explorer Elizabeth Sherriff. It is native to the Himalayas in Bhutan, at 2700 to 3600 meters (8,800 to 11,800 feet), growing on steep grassy slopes.

This delicate lily, 90 centimeters (3 feet) tall, bears 1 to 3 trumpet-shaped flowers, chestnut-brown marked with gold checkering or tessellation inside. The bulb is white, 12 to 30 millimeters (0.5 to 1 inch) in diameter. It was found by George and Elizabeth Sherriff and brought into cultivation by Mr. Knox-Finlay from seed they collected. Seed germination is immediate epigeal, and propagation by this means is relatively easy.

Derek Fox (1985: 199) wrote the following:

> The lily is unique in being the only one known to have tessellated flowers, commonly found in colchicums and fritillarias, and indeed the ones growing locally with the species. At first glance, this flower actually looks like a fritillaria, but its discoverers were not taken in by its mimicry.

This is another plant from the eastern Himalayas that has turned out to be more at home in Scotland than in England. Its swift demise in England may be due to the greater incidence of viruses and their vectors in the warmer climate.

Lilium souliei Franchet 1898

This species is named for French missionary Père J. A. Soulié (d. 1905), who discovered it and was later killed by Tibetan monks in 1905. It is native to northwestern Yunnan in China, southeastern Tibet, northern Assam and Bhutan, and perhaps northern Myanmar (formerly Burma), in mountains at 3000 to 4500 meters (9,800 to 14,800 feet). This alpine species has been assigned to both *Fritillaria* and *Nomocharis,* but has now settled in the genus *Lilium.* It is 15 to 45 centimeters (6 to 18 inches) tall, with a bell-shaped, pendent, deep maroon flower. The bulb is small with lance-tipped scales. Like other alpine species from the Himalayas and farther east, *Lilium souliei* is not amenable to cultivation. Despite numerous collections, it has not yet become assured of a place in gardens.

Lilium speciosum Thunberg 1794

The name *speciosum* means "splendid, brilliant." The species is native to Shikoku and Kyushu in southern Japan, the island of Taiwan, and Anhui, Jiangxi, Zhejiang, Hunan, and Guangxi Provinces in China. It grows in moist woodland and on slopes up to 1000 meters (3300 feet).

The wonderful *Lilium speciosum* was introduced to Europe from Japan by Philipp Franz von Siebold in 1830. The bulb is round, yellowish to purple-brown; the stem is stout, 90 to 200 centimeters (3 to 7 feet) tall with large scattered, broad-lanceolate, leathery green leaves. On this stiff stem are borne large, fragrant flowers with strongly reflexed tepals. The flowers, usually 4 to 30, appear in August to September. They are delicate pink to crimson with very undulate margins, sprinkled with carmine spots and papillae. Both the filaments and the pistil extend well out from the flower; the pollen is chocolate to purple-brown. Seed germination is hypogeal, delayed in some forms and immediate in others.

There are many natural forms of this species, as well as many selected color forms. The following are the best known:

Varieties *album* Baker 1873 and *album-novum* Mallet 1925 are both white-flowered forms; the latter is the better shaped.

Variety *gloriosoides* Baker 1880 has strongly reflexed and undulate tepals, more scarlet in color, with the color concentrated in the lower quarter at the base of the tepal. It is a very fine, rare but desirable form from China. Leslie Woodriff used a selection of it, 'Twinkle', in his hybridizing program.

Variety *kraetzeri* Baker 1874, a form selected for forcing, is pure white with a green central stripe on the tepals.

Variety *rubrum* Baker 1873 has a dark purple stem and carmine flowers; it is grown in the Netherlands for cut flowers, with popular selections including 'Brabander', 'Favourite', 'Grand Commander', 'No. 10', 'Shooting Star', and 'Uchida'. Most of these selections possess a high degree of virus tolerance.

The late flowering period of *Lilium speciosum* means that gardeners in areas with short growing seasons cannot always enjoy this lily in the open, where fall rains and accompanying *Botrytis* may ruin the flowers. Its full beauty can, however, be attained in pots or in a cold greenhouse. There is no difficulty flowering it outdoors in the Pacific Northwest. In the garden it should be given a well-protected site with fresh soil well supplied with peat and leafmold, with a mulch. Increase is by the numerous stem bulbils.

This lily hybridizes with *Lilium auratum* to produce some of the greatest triumphs of lily breeding. It has also been crossed with *L. alexandrae, L. henryi, L. japonicum, L. nobilissimum,* and *L. rubellum.*

The cross between *Lilium speciosum* and *L. henryi,* made by Leslie Woodriff, produced 'Black Beauty', which was sterile in its original diploid form. Limited fertility was secured by converting 'Black Beauty' into a tetraploid by colchicine. A similar hybrid was later produced in Japan by crossing 'Shikayama' (a hybrid of *L. speciosum*) with *L. henryi.*

Peter Schenk produced a beautiful clone by crossing *Lilium speciosum* with *L. nobilissimum.* Wilbert Ronald's 'Starburst Sensation', a huge-flowered crimson with pure white margins, is an unusual cross of *L. speciosum* with the pink Chinese trumpet lily 'Damson'.

The unusual variety *gloriosoides* was crossed with several hybrids of *Lilium ×parkmannii* at Oregon Bulb Farms to produce a series of exotic-looking hybrids. They were, however, sold as a mixed group and never named.

Lilium stewartianum Balfour & W. W. Smith 1922

This species is named for Lawrence Baxter Stewart (d. 1934), curator of Edinburgh Botanical Garden. It is native to Yunnan Province, China, at 3300 to 3600 meters (10,800 to 11,800 feet), in stony alpine turf and limestone scree.

This lily was found in 1913 by George Forrest and refound in 1949 by Joseph Rock. It flowered from the latter collection in England in 1952 but has not been reported in cultivation since that time.

This is a delicate lily with grassy leaves and a small, cylindrical, nodding flower, with the lower third of the tepals reflexed. The perfumed flower is deep greenish or olive-yellow with many small chestnut-brown spots. According to Haw (1986: 112), it is closely related to *Lilium fargesii, L. nepalense,* and *L. taliense.*

Lilium sulphureum Baker 1892

This species is named for the light yellow color of its flowers. It is native to China, from Mengtse on the Red River in southern Yunnan Province across northern Yunnan's Tali Mountains to the Shan States of upper Myanmar (formerly Burma), growing at 90 to 1900 meters (300 to 6200 feet) in gravelly loams on roadsides, on grassy slopes, and in open woodland.

This lily was for some time known as *Lilium myriophyllum* Franchet 1892. It was discovered in 1888 by the French missionary Père Delavay. The bulb is round, reddish purple with fleshy scales, around 10 centimeters (4 inches) diameter. The stem is 100 to 180 centimeters (3 to 6 feet) tall, set with horizontally held linear-lanceolate leaves, in the axils of which numerous bulbils are produced. The plant bears as many as 15 nodding trumpet flowers 15 to 20 centimeters (6 to 8 inches) long, with a good scent, dark gold in the throat paling to ivory at the tips; the reverse of the tepals is more or less overlain with pink. The anthers are brown, and the pollen yellow. Germination is immediate epigeal.

This lily can be grown in the open garden, but it does not persist well in northern climates. LeVern Freimann grew it in Bellingham, Washington, for several years, where he considered it only marginally hardy and very susceptible to virus disease. Success is most likely with good drainage, with gravel and other drainage material below. An acid loam with plenty of leafmold and sand is best, with bone meal added at planting, which should be 25 to 30 centimeters (10 to 12 inches) deep, in a protected site with shelter from cold winds. In winter a mulch of leaves and conifer needles should be provided. This lily emerges very late, usually around mid to late May. Flowering is also late, at the end of August or the beginning of September.

Lilium sulphureum has been used often in hybridizing. Professor Scheubel of Oberlahnstein, Germany, crossed it with *L. regale* to produce *L. ×sulphurgale,* which flowered in 1915. The cross of *L. ×sulphurgale* with *L. ×imperiale* produced the Crows hybrids. 'T. A. Havemeyer' is a hybrid of *L. sulphureum* with *L. henryi.* In addition, there exist hybrids with the trumpet lilies *L. centifolium* and *L. sargentiae.* The species has been used extensively by Peter Smithers in Switzerland to produce the Vico Sulphureum hybrids, crosses being made with several Chinese trumpets, including the African Queen and Golden Splendor strains.

Lilium superbum Linnaeus 1762
Turk's-cap lily

The name *superbum* means "excellent, proud." The species is native to the eastern United States, from Massachusetts west to Indiana and south to Alabama and Florida. Most common on the Atlantic seaboard, it grows in rich humus on moist slopes and in acid bogs and marshes.

This lily was well known in London by 1738; it was described in 1762 by Carl Linnaeus in his *Species Plantarum.* The bulb is round, sharply pointed, whitish, and stolon-forming. The lanceolate leaves are arranged in whorls. The purplish flowering stalk can reach up to 3 meters (10 feet) in cultivation; it bears a pyramidal inflorescence of up to 40 long-petioled, large, pendent turk's-cap flowers of orange-yellow, tinted with carmine red at the tips. In the center of the flower is a green star, and the throat is spotted with brown. The flower color is quite variable, with forms known in various shades of yellow, and a true red that was collected by Mary Henry. The flowers open from July to August. Seed germination is delayed hypogeal.

Variety *mary-henryae* Henry 1947 was found in 1940 near Marianna, Florida, by Mary Henry, growing along riverbanks and in forested places. It was first described as a variety of *Lilium superbum* and separated for a while as *L. mary-henryae.* It bears as many as 15 pendent flowers with reflexed tepals, orange with wine-red spots and green nectaries.

In the garden *Lilium superbum* should have moist, lime-free soil. It should be planted 15 to 30 centimeters (6 to 12 inches) deep, among small shrubs such as rhododendrons, with the upper part in full sun. It is susceptible to virus disease. I once viewed an excellent planting of this species in a garden in Perth, Scotland; the plants were 200 centimeters (8 feet) tall, growing in light shade.

Lilium superbum hybridizes with *L. canadense* and *L. michauxii.*

Lilium taliense Franchet 1892

This species is named for its native range near Tali Lake, China. It is native to the mountains between the Mekong and Jianchuan Rivers of northwestern Yunnan Province, northwest into Sichuan Province, and east to Yao Shan in northeastern Yunnan. It occurs at 2500 to 3300 meters (8,200 to 10,800 feet), on well-drained limestone soils.

This species first flowered in the West in 1935 at Nymans, Sussex, the boyhood home of the great lily authority Harold F. Comber. It resembles *Lilium duchartrei* in form and in the color of its pendent white turk's-cap flowers. Like *L. duchartrei,* it is fragrant, but it differs from that species in its raceme-form inflorescence and the dark purple nectary in the middle of each tepal. It can be as tall as 3 meters (10 feet) and carries 10 or more flowers per stem; the leaves are dark green and quite crowded on the upper part of the stem, with the lower 30 to 45 centimeters (12 to 18 inches) bare, suggesting a strategy of growing up through low shrubs. The seed is very light with a large wing. Seed germination is epigeal, and best results are obtained from early sowing. The bulbs are firm and mottled and are not stoloniferous like those of the related *L. duchartrei* or *L. lankongense.*

When I arrived in Oregon in 1961 I found a beautiful planting of this species raised from seed by Comber, in full flower in late June. Although I flowered *Lilium taliense* in later years, it was never to surpass this early population in strength and beauty. In a few of these plants, the tepals were so heavily spotted as to appear almost black.

In 1989 conferees at the International Lily Conference visited the Edinburgh Botanic Garden in early August. An unusual lily was in full flower, labeled "*Lilium taliense,* a recent introduction from the province of Yunnan." The plants were shorter than Comber's population, the

Plate 34. *Lilium taliense*

leaves soft green, and the inflorescence much more open. The flowers were larger, with a distinct yellow flush, small purple spots, and a distinct central band; one plant had nearly golden flowers. I obtained seed from this population and grew both this form and the Nymans form in 1991 in beds of volcanic soil at Parkdale, Oregon, above 700 meters (2300 feet). The lilies flowered beautifully in 1992, showing their remarkable differences.

Bulbs of each form were harvested and grown in the greenhouse, where I crossed the two forms in 1993, finding them quite fertile both ways. The seedlings from this cross should flower in 1996. I have found no record of this lovely species being used in hybridizing.

Lilium tsingtauense Gilg 1904

This species is named for Tsingtau (now Qingdao), China, whence dried specimens were sent for the first description of the species. The species is native to Shandong and Anhui Provinces in China, and to the Diamond Mountains of Korea. It grows in low limestone hills in moist places among open woods or herbs.

This lily was introduced in 1863, but it was lumped with *Lilium medeoloides* until separated in 1903 based on the bulb, which is white, oval, 2.5 centimeters (1 inch) in diameter. The hollow stem is 40 to 90 centimeters (15 inches to 3 feet) tall, the leaves mostly arranged in whorls with occasional scattered leaves. The leaves appear slightly marbled. In late July it bears 1 to 6 flowers, upright, star-shaped pointed bowls, gleaming orange-red with reddish spots, which are usually not distributed on the entire tepal with radial symmetry. The flower has a slight, unpleasant scent. The pollen is orange. The short and slightly fluted seed capsule contains a large seed without a raised margin. Seed germination is delayed hypogeal.

Variety *flavum* Makino 1925 has yellow flowers. Variety *carneum* Nakai 1917 is unspotted and red.

This interesting lily, distinctive in many respects, is best increased by seed. Its growing site must be lightly shaded by other plants and have ordinary moisture. The first forms introduced to Britain in 1901 were not strong-growing, but later introductions, apparently from Korea, are now well established. The good form with broad tepals now in general cultivation appears relatively easy to grow. Although not fussy, it presumably prefers an acid soil with plenty of humus. This species seems highly tolerant to virus diseases.

Lilium tsingtauense crosses with (*L. martagon* × *L. hansonii*) hybrids. Crossing *L. ×dalhansonii* with *L. tsingtauense* produced 'Dalhense', 'Hantsing', 'Sontsing', and 'Tsingense' (Robinson 1964), as well as unnamed hybrids bred by Otto Beutnagel in Braunschweig, Germany.

Lilium vollmeri Eastwood 1948

This species is named for Albert M. Vollmer, an authority on California lilies. It is native to Del Norte County, California, and Josephine County, Oregon, growing along watercourses, where the soil is constantly moist but drainage is fast.

This swamp lily has a horizontally creeping rhizome covered with yellow, single-jointed scales, from which arises a flowering stalk of 75 to 90 centimeters (2.5 to 3 feet). The dark green leaves are arranged in whorls or singly. The flowers, usually 1 to 3 but sometimes more, are borne on long petioles. They are of reflexed turk's-cap form, orange with dark red or near-black spots on the inner part of the tepal. Seed germination is hypogeal in late fall in cool conditions.

The cultivation of this lily is likely to be no different from that of *Lilium pardalinum*. This is relatively simple, given a free-draining medium, plenty of moisture, and adequate humus.

Lilium wallichianum Schultes & Schultes 1830

This species is named for Nathaniel Wallich (1786–1854), a Danish botanist and superintendent of the Calcutta Botanic Gardens. Native to the southern slopes of the Himalayas from Kumaon through Nepal, Sikkim, and Bhutan as far as Assam, at 1000 to 1500 meters (3300 to 4900 feet), it grows on limestone-based slopes in coniferous woodland, in brush and grass.

The dark purple bulbs of this trumpet lily lie 20 to 25 centimeters (8 to 10 inches) deep in the soil. The flower stem is 90 to 180 centimeters (3 to 6 feet) tall and bears scattered, linear, grassy, dark green leaves and one or sometimes more flowers at its tip. The flowers are 18 to 22 centimeters (7 to 9 inches) long, with a narrow trumpet flaring broadly at the mouth. The flower is creamy white, tinted green within. The pollen is yellow. The stem when arising from the bulb first wanders underground, producing stem bulbils at stem internodes.

Variety *neilgherrense* Wight 1858 (formerly considered a separate species) grows in southern India near 10° north latitude in the Nilgiri, Pulney, and Cardamon hills, at 1830 to 2600 meters (5950 to 8500 feet). A shorter plant, reaching 90 centimeters (3 feet), it has lanceolate leaves.

This splendid lily is not winter-hardy in colder regions but can be grown in a cool greenhouse, increased by seed or bulbils. It is one of the earlier lilies to flower, generally in early July. It flowered under glass at Oregon Bulb Farms on several occasions, but it was never grown outdoors there.

Harold F. Comber crossed *Lilium wallichianum* with its variety *neilgherrense* in 1934; at that time the latter was considered a separate species, so the hybrid was called *L.* ×*burnhamense.*

Lilium wardii F. Stern 1932

This species is named for Frank Kingdon-Ward (1885–1958), who first collected it. Native to southeastern Tibet in the Tsangpo Gorge (an extension of the Brahmaputra Valley), in the Lohit Valley, northwest and northeast of Sadiya, and farther along the course of the Lohit near Rima, at 2000 to 3000 meters (6600 to 9800 feet), it occurs in grassy places, scrub, and among conifers on steep slopes in dry places.

The bulb is flattish or bell shaped, usually no more than 5 centimeters (2 inches) in diameter, and lightly spotted with red. The stem wanders underground and produces offset bulblets at the internodes. The flower stem may be up to 150 centimeters (5 feet) tall, purple-brown with scattered, dark-green, lanceolate to lanceolate-elliptic, with three-veined leaves around 7 centimeters (3 inches) long. As many as 40 strongly fragrant turk's-cap flowers of deep pink with carmine spots may be borne in a single raceme. Seed germination is immediate epigeal.

Plate 35. *Lilium wardii*. Photo by J. Robertson.

In England this lily succeeds in half shade in loam with leafmold. Lime and wood ash can be mixed into the soil. It has been said that it will succeed in the Transvaal of South Africa if planted under conifers, where the needles provide a mulch. Despite its adaptability, it has failed to become widespread in cultivation. On a visit of Victoria, Australia, I found this lily growing strongly and profusely in many gardens and nurseries. *Lilium wardii* grew strongly in Oregon for many years, where it seemed to be reasonably virus tolerant. Kingdon-Ward believed it was indifferent as to soil, and our experience verified this, excellent populations being grown in acid, humusy loam and in heavy clay.

No hybrids involving this lily have been reliably reported.

Lilium washingtonianum Kellogg 1859
Mt. Hood lily

This species is named for Martha Washington, wife of George Washington, first president of the United States. Native to the western American mountains from the Sierra Nevada around Yosemite National Park north to Mount Shasta in California and throughout the Cascade Range, it grows on steep slopes at high subalpine elevations, frequently among conifers, sometimes in fairly dense shade.

The subrhizomatous bulb is white. The flowering stem is 120 to 200 centimeters (4 to 7 feet) tall, with light green, broad-lanceolate leaves. In June and July it bears 2 to 30 horizontal, trumpet-form flowers with slightly reflexed tepals, pure white in color with purple spots in the throat, turning more purple with age, and with an extraordinary spicy fragrance. Seed germination is delayed hypogeal.

Variety *minus* Purdy 1919, smaller than the type, is found at the base of Mount Shasta and is commonly called the Shasta lily.

Variety *purpurascens* Stearn 1948, the Cascade lily, extends from far northern California to Mount Hood in Oregon; it often opens already tinged lavender and turns quite dark with age.

Like other dryland western American bulbs, this stately species has proved difficult in cultivation. In western Oregon and Washington, however, it can become established in gardens and grow beautifully for many years. It resents transplanting and, because the bulbs deteriorate quickly when exposed to air, is not readily available in commerce.

The species has been hybridized with *Lilium columbianum, L. humboldtii,* and *L. parryi.*

Lilium wigginsii Beane & Vollmer 1955
This species is named for botanist Ira L. Wiggins (1899–). It is native to the Siskiyou Mountains of southern Oregon and northern California in the United States.

Although long known, this very rare lily was not described until 1955. It was formerly known as *Lilium roezlii.* In place of a bulb, *L. wigginsii* has a thick rhizome covered with small scales. The stem is around 120 centimeters (4 feet) tall and forms stem roots. The leaves are arranged in 2 to 4 whorls. The flowers, horizontal or nodding in open turk's-cap form, are pure yellow with purple spotting, borne on petioles 15 to 30 centimeters (6 to 12 inches) long. The pollen is yellow. Seed germination is hypogeal in late fall in cool conditions.

Cultivation is similar to that of *Lilium pardalinum* and should be relatively easy in an acid soil with adequate humus.

Lilium wilsonii Leichtlin 1868
This species is named for G. F. Wilson (1822–1902), original owner of the Royal Horticultural Society garden at Wisley. It is native to Japan.

Botanists first became aware of this lily when Wilson found it at Wisley, where it had arrived from Japan mixed in with a shipment of *Lilium auratum.* There was at first some question whether it represented a true species, but it comes true from seed, and so it was granted specific status. The Japanese botanist Moto'o Shimizu considered it a form of *L. maculatum,* which in Japan displays a wider variation in flower color and flowering time than does *L. wilsonii* as it is seen in the West. This is not surprising, since the plants distributed in Europe all descend from a few late-flowering forms. In the Netherlands this species was grown under the erroneous name *L. dauricum* var. *pardinum;* this is hard to understand, given the rapid epigeal germination of *L. wilsonii* compared to the immediate hypogeal germination of *L. dauricum.* The two species are, however, closely related and can hybridize. Japanese botanists and cytologists have determined that *L. wilsonii* is one of the ancestors of the long-known *L. ×elegans* cultivars.

From the white, ball-shaped bulb arises a stem to 90 centimeters (3 feet), with lanceolate, scattered leaves, bearing bowl-shaped flowers around 12 centimeters (5 inches) in diameter. The tepals are narrow at the base and very elegantly rolled back. The color is reddish orange, apricot colored with a golden central stripe, heavily sprinkled with large brown spots. The flowers open in August.

Variety *flavum* Comber 1939 is a form having primula-yellow flowers with a golden-yellow zone in the middle of the tepal, spotted in reddish purple, with 6 to 12 flowers borne on a stem 60 to 75 centimeters (2 to 2.5 feet) long; it is in commerce under the name 'Marlynn Ross'. This form has often been used for hybridizing, with *Lilium bulbiferum, L. dauricum,* and *L. lancifolium* var. *flaviflorum;* the golden blush on the

Plate 36. *Lilium wilsonii*

tepal is now seen in numerous hybrids, such as 'Connecticut King', and the gleaming green leaf color is also apparent, as in 'Sunray'. Variety *flavum* was also crossed with 'Connecticut King' to produce an outstanding group of strong hybrids, including 'Adelina', 'Cordelia', 'Joanna' (synonym 'Yellow Giant'), 'Pollyanna', and 'Vanessa'.

Johann Mak in the Netherlands bred an interesting hybrid by crossing *Lilium pumilum* with *L. wilsonii*. Other crosses involving this species are discussed under *L. maculatum*.

Lilium xanthellum Want & Tang 1980
The name *xanthellum* means "little yellow." This species is native to Sichuan Province, China, on open slopes at 3200 to 3600 meters (10,500 to 11,800 feet). Chinese botanists have described this new alpine lily species. Haw (1986: 127–128) regarded it as close to *Lilium fargesii,* from which it is geographically isolated. It also has larger bulbs. Its flowers are yellowish green, unspotted in the type and purple-spotted in variety *luteum*.

Cardiocrinum giganteum (Wallich) Makino
Giant lily

Named *giganteum,* meaning "very large," this species is native to the Himalayas, Myanmar (formerly Burma), and China. No discussion of genus *Lilium* would be complete without mention of *Cardiocrinum giganteum,* its close relative. (There are two less widely grown species, *C. cathayanum* and *C. cordatum*.) The foliage of this huge bulbous species resembles that of a hosta, but in flower it is much like a stupendous trumpet lily. The bulb takes seven to ten years to flower from seed, but it is worth the wait because the typical flowering stem is 240 to 300 centimeters (8 to 10 feet) tall, with as many as 20 large white flowers. After flowering the main bulb dies, but under good conditions it will have produced a number of offsets that will flower in a few more years. This plant prefers light shade, a rich humus soil, and adequate moisture in summer.

Cardiocrinums have not been prominent in American gardens to date, but commercial production has now begun and we may see more of these impressive subjects. Robert Long of Salem, Oregon, is grow-

Plate 37. *Cardiocrinum giganteum,* a close relative of *Lilium* species, with grower Robert Long.

ing bulbs by the thousands from both seed and offsets. There is reason to believe that the seed has a short period of viability and should be sown soon after harvest; it can also be stored frozen for several years. On a visit to Victoria, Australia, I found *Cardiocrinum giganteum* growing profusely in the Dandenong Range. The plants were magnificent.

CHAPTER 8

Hybrid Lily Classification

Many hybrid lilies are available in the trade, and new ones appear each year. Because many of them are short-lived in the trade, only a few major clones and strains are described in this volume.

Hybrid lilies are presently categorized in eight divisions under the horticultural classification proposed by the Lily Committee of the Royal Horticultural Society in 1964. The classes, originally devised for organizing shows, are the following:

Division 1. Asiatic hybrids
Division 2. Martagon hybrids
Division 3. Candidum hybrids
Division 4. American hybrids
Division 5. Longiflorum hybrids
Division 6. Chinese trumpet hybrids
Division 7. Oriental hybrids
Division 8. Hybrids not provided for in any previous division.

The ancestral species within a division were assumed to be closely related to one another. Since the 1960s, however, sophisticated laboratory techniques such as embryo culture and amputated style pollination have produced dramatic new hybrids between distantly related species. The emergence of these test-tube babies and their offspring prompts us to reconsider the horticultural classification. All such unusual hybrids were once lumped in Division 8, but their burgeoning numbers in commerce make this no longer feasible.

Two groups have now emerged in sufficient numbers in commerce that they should be considered for divisional status. The first is new hybrids involving *Lilium longiflorum,* the Easter lily, and Asiatic hybrids. The second is the Orienpet hybrids, which link the Chinese trumpets and their hybrids with *L. henryi* to the Oriental lilies.

The new *Lilium longiflorum* hybrids, including those with Asiatic hybrids, could simply be incorporated in Division 5, as long as they show characteristic *L. longiflorum* traits. The many now available are first- and second-generation crosses with *L. longiflorum* and clearly show the characteristics of that parent; as they are continually backcrossed to Asiatic hybrids, however, these qualities may become diluted and disappear. When the *L. longiflorum* traits are no longer visible, it would be appropriate to place the hybrids that appear to be purely Asiatic in Division 1.

An increasing number of Orienpets (see Chapter 12) becomes available every year. An entirely new division should be allocated to these magnificent plants, as outlined in the proposed revision of the horticultural classification.

In 1995 the Classification Committee of the North American Lily Society proposed a revision to the 1964 horticultural classification. Further discussion is scheduled to take place at international lily conferences in 1997. Polyploid forms, such as triploids and tetraploids, are placed in a subclass within each division as appropriate. Several divisions are subdivided according to the carriage of the flowers. Finally, two new divisions are proposed: one for Orienpet hybrids and another for the species.

Division 1: Asiatic hybrids.
Hybrids derived from the following species and their varieties:
L. amabile, L. bulbiferum, L. callosum, L. cernuum, L. concolor, L. dauricum, L. davidii, L. lankongense, L. leichtlinii, L. pumilum, L. lancifolium, L. wilsonii.
   1A: Upright-facing flowers.
   1B: Outward-facing flowers.
   1C: Pendent flowers.

Division 2: Martagon hybrids.

Hybrids derived from the following species and their varieties: *L. hansonii, L. martagon, L. medeoloides, L. tsingtauense.*

Division 3: Candidum hybrids.

Hybrids derived from the following species and their varieties: *L. candidum, L. chalcedonicum, L. monadelphum.*

Division 4: American hybrids.

Hybrids derived from any North American species. Present-day hybrids in this division mostly originate from the western American species *L. bolanderi, L. humboldtii, L. kelloggii, L. pardalinum,* and *L. parryi.*

Division 5: Longiflorum hybrids.

Hybrids derived *L. longiflorum.* Most such lilies in the trade are *L. longiflorum* × Asiatic hybrids (Division 1).

    5A: Upright-facing flowers.

    5B: Outward-facing flowers.

    5C: Pendent or downward-facing flowers.

Division 6: Chinese trumpet and Aurelian hybrids.

Hybrids derived from the following Chinese species with purple bulbs: *L. leucanthum, L. regale, L. sargentiae, L. sulphureum, L. henryi.*

    6A: Upright-facing flowers.

    6B: Outward-facing flowers.

    6C: Downward-facing flowers.

Division 7: Oriental hybrids.

Hybrids derived from the following species and their varieties: *L. alexandrae, L. auratum, L. japonicum, L. nobilissimum, L. rubellum, L. speciosum.*

    7A: Upward-facing flowers.

    7B: Outward-facing flowers.

    7C: Downward-facing flowers.

Division 8: Orienpet hybrids.

Hybrids derived from the crossing of species and hybrids from Division 6 and Division 7.

    8A: Upward-facing flowers.

    8B: Outward-facing flowers.

    8C: Downward-facing flowers.

Division 9: Species.
  All true species and their botanical varieties.
Division 10: Miscellaneous hybrids.
  All hybrids not covered in the above divisions.

In this book, Asiatic hybrids, Chinese trumpet hybrids, and Oriental hybrids—the three groups most important in horticulture—have separate chapters devoted to them. The Orienpets are discussed among the polyploid lilies in Chapter 12. The true species are covered in Chapter 7, as are the lilies closely derived from particular species, such as Divisions 3 and 5. The martagon and western American hybrids are briefly covered here.

Plate 38. *Lilium martagon* var. *album*, with Paisley hybrids in the background. Photo by Herman v. Wall.

Martagon Hybrids

The growing of *Lilium martagon,* its white variety *album* (Plate 38), and their hybrids was discontinued at Oregon Bulb Farms in the early 1970s. Sadly, these beautiful lilies did not possess the qualities of ease of culture and rapid propagation demanded of modern hybrids.

The Paisley hybrids (*Lilium martagon* var. *album* × *L. hansonii*) were a group of strong and indestructible lilies that grew profusely then. All the flowers were gold to bronze and very uniform. The second-generation population produced from these seedlings included a host of clear and attractive colors, including pink, lilac, cream, pure white, and bright yellow. They were simply stunning. The clones 'Achievement' (Plate 39), 'Desdemona', 'GayLights', 'Juliet', 'Ophelia', and 'Romeo' were named and introduced.

Plate 39. *Lilium* 'Achievement'. Photo by Herman v. Wall.

Western American Hybrids

The fate of the beautiful western American hybrids at Oregon Bulb Farms was similar to that of the martagon hybrids. 'Afterglow', 'Buttercup', 'Shuksan', and *Lilium pardalinum* 'Sunset' were still grown in the early 1970s. A group of bright yellow *L. parryi* hybrids, named the San Gabriel strain (Plate 40), was also prominent then; the clones 'Herald', 'Mariana', and 'Miranda' were introduced from this group.

Many seedlings of western American hybrids flowered at Oregon Bulb Farms in the early 1960s from seed obtained from Boyd Kline of Medford, Oregon. The unusual colors and forms found among them indicated that *Lilium kelloggii* had been used in the crosses. A few seedlings even had bell-shaped flowers inherited from *L. bolanderi*. The finer clones selected were the soft salmon 'Bunting' (Plate 41), clear pink 'Bluebird', soft pink 'Nightingale' (Plate 42), wine-red 'Robin', and softest pink 'Snowgoose'. The miniature 'Hummingbird', a clear pink, was also selected from Kline's seedlings.

The seedlings obtained from Kline inspired us to cross *Lilium kelloggii* with the clones 'Afterglow', 'Buttercup', 'Shuksan', and *L. pardalinum* 'Sunset'. The quantity of seed obtained was surprising, indicating rather high interspecific fertility among western American species and their hybrids. The first-generation seedlings all had rather muddy coloring. They were intercrossed to produce a second generation in which clear colors emerged; these were breathtaking—soft pinks, peach tones, wine pinks, pastel bicolors, and pure white. The beauty and gardenworthiness of these lovely western American hybrids should inspire others to use them in breeding.

Plate 40. *Lilium* San Gabriel strain. Photo by Herman v. Wall.

Plate 41. *Lilium* 'Bunting'. Photo by Herman v. Wall.

Plate 42. *Lilium* 'Nightingale'. Photo by Herman v. Wall.

CHAPTER 9

Asiatic Lily Hybrids

The most widely grown type of hybrid lily in gardens worldwide is the Asiatic hybrids, bred largely from the earlier-flowering Asian species. So many species are involved in their ancestry that there is almost infinite variation among them, particularly in the colors, which may be brilliant or soft, in all the warm shades and white. There is also an extensive range of heights and flower forms. The following discussion covers the most important lines; some of these figure as ancestors of the garden lilies of today, and some are still available in commerce.

The reader will note that upright flowers have been a common goal in breeding. This is due to the popularity of this habit for the cut-flower industry: packing is easiest with upright flowers. The gardener, however, may prefer the more graceful habits presented by outfacing or pendent flowers.

Mid-Century Hybrids

This group of Asiatic hybrids was produced during the 1930s and early 1940s at Oregon Bulb Farms. The original material came from several sources, including perhaps every Asiatic hybrid available then. An enormous number of crosses was made and huge quantities of seedlings raised. It is unfortunate that no accurate records survive from that period, and we can only guess at what crosses were made. The Mid-Century hybrids were a great milestone in Asiatic hybridizing, so it is important to recognize the main groups of lilies involved in their ancestry.

Stenographer and Fighter Aircraft Series. This group of lilies was produced by Isabella Preston at the Central Experimental Farm in Ottawa, Canada, beginning with a cross made in 1929 between *Lilium davidii* var. *willmottiae* and a seedling of *L. dauricum* or *L. ×elegans*. The strong, prolific hybrids ranged in color from red through orange; all were tall with outward-facing to downfacing flowers. The best seedlings were selected and cloned, and the Stenographer hybrids were individually named to honor women employees of the station: 'Brenda Watts', 'Edna Kean', 'Grace Marshall', 'Lilian Cummings', 'Lyla McCann', 'Muriel Condie', and 'Phyllis Cox'. Several of these lilies survive today: in 1996 I saw 'Lyla McCann' and 'Brenda Watts' growing strongly and profusely at Van Dusen Botanical Garden in Vancouver, British Columbia, at the grand old age of 65. The Stenographer hybrids were open-pollinated to produce a second generation that featured clearer colors and upright flowers. These were named after World War II fighter aircraft: 'Corsair', 'Hurricane', 'Spitfire', and 'Typhoon'. All this material was used extensively in early hybridizing at Oregon Bulb Farms.

Slate Hybrids. Additional material for the Mid-Century hybrids was obtained from George L. Slate of Geneva, New York. It included a group of *Lilium ×elegans* clones, among them 'Alice Wilson', 'Leonard Joerg', 'Mahogany', and 'Orange Queen'. All these had originated in Japan.

McLean Hybrids. A very important group of lilies used in producing the Mid-Century hybrids came from Forman T. McLean of the Boyce Thompson Institute in Yonkers, New York. These plants resulted from crossing the diploid form of *Lilium lancifolium* with several clones of *L. ×elegans* and *L. ×hollandicum*. One plant, 'Umtig 8', was reported to be the most fertile and was thus used extensively in hybridizing; it was a hybrid between diploid *L. tigrinum* and *L. ×hollandicum* 'Sappho'. An article by Jan de Graaff and Earl Hornback in the *Yearbook of the North American Lily Society* indicated that many Mid-Century hybrids came from crosses between 'Umtig 8' and *L. ×elegans* 'Alice Wilson'.

Other Sources. The early material assembled for the Mid-Century hybrids also included lilies from Frank Leith Skinner in Manitoba and Samuel L. Emsweller of the U.S. Department of Agriculture in Beltsville, Maryland. The Emsweller clones 'Brandywine' and 'Mega' proved especially useful.

Mid-Century Clones of the 1960s. The Mid-Century clones still in cultivation in the early 1960s were quite varied, indicating a wide range of parents. They included 'Enchantment', 'Firecrown', 'Harmony', 'Joan Evans', and 'Valencia' in orange shades; 'Cinnabar', 'Paprika', 'Sunstar', and 'Tabasco' in red shades; and the gold or yellow 'Croesus', 'Destiny', and 'Prosperity'.

Earl N. Hornback told me an interesting story about virus tolerance from those early years. A field planted with hundreds of select clones was almost wiped out by severe virus infection. Earl regarded this as a blessing, reasoning that the clones that survived were very virus-tolerant. Nature had done the growers a favor, making it possible for them to continue hybridizing, selecting, and growing with renewed confidence that they were working with strong material. The two clones that showed no virus symptoms over the next 10 years were 'Paprika' and 'Tabasco'. They also displayed more influence of *Lilium davidii,* and therefore more inheritance from the Stenographer series. Later experience has proven that *L. davidii* carries genetic factors for virus tolerance.

'Enchantment' was introduced into the Netherlands in 1960 and eventually became the most popular Asiatic lily in the cut-flower trade (Plate 43). By the late 1970s, some 320 hectares (800 acres) of 'Enchantment' were being grown, the foundation of the Asiatic lily cut-flower industry of today. 'Destiny', 'Harmony', and 'Tabasco' were also important in this trade for a long time.

Plate 43. *Lilium* 'Enchantment'

Patterson Hybrids

The object of Cecil Patterson's work at the University of Saskatchewan in the early 1930s was to produce hardy lilies that could withstand the extreme weather of the Canadian prairies. His most important break-through resulted from a cross between *Lilium davidii* var. *willmottiae* and *L. cernuum*. Seedling No. 37.538 from this cross was completely sterile as a seed parent, but its pollen was very fertile and was used successfully on various seed parents, such as *L.davidii* 'Oriole' and several Stenographer clones. The clones eventually named and introduced included 'Edith Cecilia', 'Lemon Queen', 'Orchid Queen', 'Pink Charm', 'Rose Dawn', 'Rose Queen', 'White Gold', and 'White Princess'.

Most of these varieties were very infertile aneuploids. Two, however —'Edith Cecilia' and 'Lemon Queen'—were fertile and were used extensively in early hybridizing. 'Edith Cecilia' resulted from a cross of *Lilium davidii* 'Oriole' and No. 37.538, and 'Lemon Queen' from a cross of the Stenographer clone 'Grace Marshall' and No. 37.538.

In later years both 'Edith Cecilia' and 'Lemon Queen' were crossed with large-flowered upright Mid-Century type hybrids, including 'Cinnabar', 'Destiny', 'Harmony', 'Mega', and 'Uncle Sam'. The second generation from these crosses produced the first upright pinks, peaches, creams, and whites; one upright pink-and-white bicolor was named 'Prince Charming' (Plate 44).

The introduction of *Lilium cernuum* into the Asiatic hybrids was undoubtedly one of the most important breakthroughs in lily breeding in the twentieth century, opening up exciting prospects. There are now many upright lilies in the pink, peach, cream, and white ranges; most if not all of these can be traced back to 'Edith Cecilia'.

Plate 44. *Lilium* 'Prince Charming'. Photo by Herman v. Wall.

Harlequin Hybrids. The Harlequin hybrids (Plate 45) produced at Oregon Bulb Farms for many years originally resulted from crossing 'Edith Cecilia' with 'Lemon Queen'. The range of beautiful colors found in these seedlings has never been equaled; it included shades of orange, lemon and buttercup yellows, reds, pinks, peaches, creams, pure white, and a great variety of bicolors. The second generation (to everyone's amazement) produced an equally fascinating array.

Plate 45. *Lilium* Harlequin hybrids. Photo by Herman v. Wall.

Mercury and Hallmark Strains. Several pendent and outward-facing clones were also selected from the Harlequin strain, including the pink, pollen-free 'Corsage', pink 'Discovery', peach 'Salmon Trout', and pure white 'Buccaneer'. The pinks and pure whites were segregated and pollinated independently to produce the Mercury and Hallmark strains respectively.

Lighthouse Hybrids. A strong, stately orange Mid-Century clone was named 'Lighthouse' because it stood head and shoulders above all the others in the field. It was crossed with 'Edith Cecilia' in 1959, with only a small amount of seed being produced. The resulting seedlings were spectacular: taller, stronger, and superior in flower form and substance to other 'Edith Cecilia' seedlings. The Lighthouse hybrids were crossed with other 'Edith Cecilia' and 'Lemon Queen' lines but proved quite infertile. It was suspected, and later proved, that all the Lighthouse seedlings were triploids, and that the clone 'Lighthouse' was a naturally occurring tetraploid. The Lighthouse hybrid clones were introduced as the Musical series. The most outstanding were warm red 'Adagio', vivid orange 'Fuga' (also known as 'Bittersweet'), soft yellow 'Minuet', clear pink 'Sonata' (Plate 46), and peach-gold 'Tarantella'.

Golden Chalice Strain. The Golden Chalice strain sold during the early years of Oregon Bulb Farms was a group of very early flowering golden yellow lilies. Seed germination for all these plants was immediate hypogeal germination, indicating that the strain was simply composed of selections from *Lilium dauricum.* It was correctly produced from two select clones: 'Golden Wonder' was the seed parent, and an

unnamed clone, 0.40, was the pollen parent. The latter had huge, broad-petaled flowers with magnificent substance, and apparently these were dominant characteristics, for all the offspring had the same fine qualities.

Rainbow Hybrids. These lilies introduced in later years came from a cross between 'Tabasco' and 0.40. The colors included shades of red, orange, and gold. All the seedlings had the superb flower form and substance inherited from 0.40. Several clones were selected from this population, including many attractive bi-

Plate 46. *Lilium* 'Sonata'. Photo by Herman v. Wall.

colors. One was 'Aristo', selected by Bischoff Tulleken in the Nether-lands, where it has now been grown for many years.

Sundrop Strain. 'Connecticut King' was crossed with 0.40 and 'Golden Wonder' to produce the Sundrop strain, a group of seedlings remarkably uniform in vigor, color, and flowering time. Bischoff Tulleken introduced the clones 'Sahara', 'Salute', and 'Sinai' selected from the Sundrop strain.

Panamint and Sutter's Gold Strains. The fine Panamint and Sutter's Gold strains were popular for many years. Like the Harlequin and Lighthouse hybrids, they were outstanding garden subjects. Their seed parent was a selected cream to soft yellow clone derived from a second-generation cross between *Lilium lancifolium* var. *flaviflorum* and (*L. leichtlinii* var. *maximowiczii* × 'Harmony'). The pollen parent was a cream white Hallmark clone. This cross produced equal proportions of seedlings in two distinct colors, bright yellow and soft cream. Their strength was unparalleled; most striking, however, were their broad petals and superb flower form. The bright yellows were named the Sutter's Gold strain, and the soft creams the Panamint strain. A magnificent triploid clone of the latter strain was named 'Hornback's Gold' (Plate 47) in honor of Earl Hornback.

The garden world urgently needs pendent and outfacing lilies similar to those found in the Patterson hybrid lines. Their disease resistance and virus tolerance are impressive. They make spectacular garden subjects, breathtaking in the proper setting. 'Edith Cecilia' and 'Lemon Queen' are still with us, offering this special kind of beauty.

Plate 47. *Lilium* 'Hornback's Gold'. Photo by Herman v. Wall.

Mid-Century Hybrids Crossed with Upright Pastels

The first upright-flowering commercial lilies in the pastel color range were produced from crosses made in the early to mid-1960s between Mid-Century hybrids and second-generation upright pastels derived from 'Edith Cecilia' and 'Lemon Queen' crossed with upright Mid-Century types; that is, this group mostly resulted from a second-generation backcross. The following clones emerged as superior in the early to mid-1970s, after eight years of field testing: pure white 'Avalon' ('Hallmark' × 'Destiny') F2; bright red 'Armada' ('Paprika' × upright peach); wine pink 'Challenger' ('Cinnabar' × upright pink); salmon 'Chinook' ('Enchantment' × upright peach); bright yellow 'Dayspring' (upright peach × 'Croesus'); clear red 'Pepper' ('Paprika' × upright peach); cream to white 'Juliana' (upright white × 'Croesus'); soft pink 'Peach Blush' (upright pink × *Lilium dauricum* clone); fluorescent red 'Pirate' ('Paprika' × 'Prince Charming'; Plate 48); cream to white 'Sterling Star' ('Hallmark' × 'Croesus'); and salmon orange 'Sunkissed' (upright peach × 'Croesus').

Plate 48. *Lilium* 'Pirate'. Photo by Herman v. Wall.

Connecticut Hybrid Crosses

Connecticut Hybrids Crossed with Mid-Century Hybrids. The arrival of the Connecticut hybrids at Oregon Bulb Farms in the mid-1960s gave the breeding program an enormous boost, especially concerning yellows. The firm of Stone and Payne in Connecticut had been hybridizing for unspotted lilies, using an unspotted upright clone, 'Gold Urn', to produce this characteristic. Other parents used included *Lilium lancifolium* var. *flaviflorum* and *L. wilsonii* var. *flavum*.

The material arriving in Oregon contained two of the original introductions: 'Connecticut Yankee', bright unspotted orange and pendent (Plate 49); and 'Nutmegger', bright spotted yellow and pendent. The upright clones included 'Connecticut King', a bright spotted yellow with a gold blotch; 'Connecticut Glow', warm red; 'Connecticut Queen', soft unspotted cream; 'Connecticut Lemonglow', a shorter, outward-facing, unspotted bright yellow; and 'Sunray', a short yellow with traces of spots. The first crosses made combined these clones with Mid-Century types.

A cross between the two early gems 'Enchantment' and 'Connecticut King' produced alarming results. Perhaps 90 percent of the seedlings showed acute abnormalities; some flowers had no color at all in their deformed tepals. This was an invaluable lesson in the dangers of breeding clones carrying bad recessive genes. Both 'Connecticut King' and 'Enchantment' carried genetic abnormalities, but if they were bred to clones that did not have these recessive genes, the "bad" genes would not be expressed in the first generation and the seedlings would all be normal. The seedlings from this cross that did show color were all orange, indicating that 'Enchantment' was homozygous or true-breeding for that color. About 25 attractive seedlings were selected for testing, and three clones—'Halloween', 'House of Orange', and 'Picasso'—were eventually introduced.

A cross between 'Enchantment' and 'Connecticut Lemonglow' produced normal orange seedlings, with only a few worth keeping. They included both upright and outfacing forms. 'Matchless' (upright, bright orange, and unspotted) and 'Orange Glow' (outfacing, vivid orange, unspotted) were two outstanding clones introduced.

Also resulting from the very early hybridizing was 'Joan Evans', with very soft orange, lightly spotted upright flowers. It was originally listed as a "Hollywood hybrid" (it was felt that naming lilies after movie stars might have marketing appeal). 'Joan Evans' was then crossed with 'Connecticut King', producing a group of very attractive seedlings. The yellow shades were particularly fascinating, by far the brightest and most spectacular yellows we had seen then. They showed two distinct color patterns: bright, unspotted lemon yellow, and soft golden yellow with orange blotches and a few spots. The clones 'Prelude' and 'Promise' were introduced from the unspotted lemon yellows selected, and 'Goldrush' and 'Golddigger' from the golden yellows.

The clones 'Croesus' and 'Sunstar' had shown themselves to be superior for breeding to other Mid-Century clones, yielding a superior inflorescence and excellent flower form. Both were also crossed with 'Connecticut King'. Crossing 'Connecticut King' with 'Croesus' produced seedlings with soft melon-orange coloring, the majority unspotted; the clones 'Foxtrot', 'Hornpipe', 'Oreglow', and 'Quickstep' were named and introduced after years of testing. The seedling population from crossing 'Sunstar' with 'Connecticut King' again showed a wealth of interesting and beautiful individuals, with colors ranging from soft to dark

Plate 49. *Lilium* 'Connecticut Yankee'. Photo by Herman v. Wall.

melon-orange. The majority were unspotted, again showing superior flower form and inflorescence. After testing, the clones 'Forerunner', 'Multnomah', and 'Tribute' proved superior.

Hybridizers must always be on the alert for seedlings that show unique or unusual characteristics. One day a unique bright yellow seedling was found owing to a young woman's keen eye for beauty in a new form. It was a bright, unspotted buttercup yellow with pure white blotches on the tepals, a characteristic never before seen. The discoverer and I continued our walk through adjacent groups of seedlings, eventually finding a bright unspotted orange with the same white blotches, and we marked both with blue ribbons. These two seedlings came from 'Connecticut King' crosses—the bright yellow with 'Joan Evans' and the bright orange with 'Enchantment'. The bulbs were potted the following spring and brought into the greenhouse for hybridizing. The two varieties proved highly fertile when crossed with each other, producing large quantities of seed. Their seedlings flowered at maturity three years later, yielding an abundance of bright yellows and oranges with varying degrees of white blotches on the tepals. A few were close to pure white, with only minute areas of yellow or orange. The yellow clones 'Charleston' and 'Sunnyside' were named and introduced—far too few for a group of seedlings with such unique and attractive qualities.

Connecticut Hybrids Crossed with Upright Harlequins. Several beautiful, strong, persistent clones were produced by crossing the Connecticut hybrids with the upright pastels that originated from second-generation crosses between 'Edith Cecilia' and 'Lemon Queen' and upright Mid-Century types. The following 'Connecticut King' hybrids were outstanding. 'Gypsy', an upright mellow pink (upright pink Harlequin × 'Connecticut King'), is still perhaps the strongest clone of its color in existence, showing high tolerance to virus and remarkable resistance to basal rot. 'Impala', an upright, huge-flowered rich yellow (upright cream yellow × 'Connecticut King'), was superior in all respects—strong habit, attractive foliage, and a spectacular inflorescence. Equally impressive were 'Snowcap', a lovely cream to white (upright white Harlequin × 'Connecticut King'), and 'Sunflight', a mixture of cream-yellow, gold, and soft orange ('Sunrise' × 'Connecticut King').

'Connecticut Queen' did not possess the strength of the other Connecticut hybrids, but its unspotted flowers had a soft, attractive cream-yellow color that was unique among Asiatic lilies of the time. 'Daydream' and 'Daystar', offspring of 'Connecticut Queen' and 'Gypsy', had a unique color that drew gasps of admiration: the softest cream-yellow, unspotted flowers were suffused with a soft pink, creating an almost perfect blend.

The main criticism of the early pink Asiatics was that the color did not compare to the beautiful clear pinks found in the Oriental hybrids derived from *Lilium rubellum* and *L. japonicum*. The Asiatic clone 'Zephyr' (Plate 50) was an exception, with the clearest pink ever found in an Asiatic lily; vases of 'Zephyr' and *L. rubellum* displayed together at a show in the Netherlands proved the colors identical. 'Zephyr' resulted from intercrossing a group of the clearest pink Asiatic seedlings then available. It stood head and shoulders above the other seedlings in the population, where vigor had generally been lost owing to inbreeding.

The clone 'Uncle Sam' was produced at Oregon Bulb Farms in the late 1950s from the cross (*Lilium lancifolium* var. *flaviflorum* × 'Harmony') × ('Mega' × *L. wilsonii* var. *flavum*). A strong, upright yellow with copious black spots, it was outstanding among the yellow Asiatics of

the time. Later it was crossed with an upright white Harlequin to produce a series of upright creams. The best cream clone was crossed with 'Connecticut King', yielding a wide range of bright yellow and cream seedlings. Three outstanding clones were named and introduced: 'Edith', soft cream with light spotting; 'Gold Medal', a huge-flowered, lightly spotted intense yellow with gold blotches; and 'Utopia', an intense yellow with a ring of spots in the center of the flower.

The cross of 'Edith Cecilia' with 'Connecticut King' produced a magnificent group of seedlings with out-

Plate 50. *Lilium* 'Zephyr'

facing to downfacing flowers in a wide range of attractive colors, all excellent garden subjects.

A soft pink outfacing Harlequin clone ('Edith Cecilia' × 'Mega') was also crossed with 'Connecticut King' and yielded an equally exciting array of colors in outfacing forms. The seedlings of this cross were intercrossed, and in the second generation there emerged remarkable colors in both upright and outfacing forms, with tones and combinations we had never seen before. Hybridizers ought to return to these lines for real adventure and spectacular garden lilies.

***Lilium ×hollandicum* Crossed with 'Connecticut King'.** The "candlestick lily" has survived in European and North American gardens for generations; huge clumps can still be seen in many areas. These impressive plants are clones of *Lilium ×hollandicum,* hybrids of uncertain origin. It is supposed that they originated in the Netherlands and England from crosses between the European species *L. bulbiferum* (perhaps its variety *croceum*) and *L. ×elegans,* a group of Japanese garden lilies introduced into the Netherlands in the early nineteenth century. Several *L. ×hollandicum* clones were used in hybridizing at Oregon Bulb Farms, the most attractive of which was a tall dark red found growing profusely near Anchorage, Alaska.

'Connecticut King' was crossed with this handsome lily, producing seedlings that varied from atrocious to very beautiful. Named and introduced were two clones, 'Jetfire' and 'Rosefire' (Plate 51). 'Jetfire' was a unique and beautiful unspotted red-yellow bicolor, nearly perfect in every respect; however, it was highly susceptible to tulip-breaking virus, a sad situation since it tolerated other viruses well. 'Rosefire' was similar but darker in color, with a few spots; it was not so susceptible to tulip-breaking virus and survives today.

Plate 51. *Lilium* 'Rosefire'

'Connecticut King' Crossed with *Lilium wilsonii* var. *flavum*. An outstanding group of indestructible yellow lilies resulted from crossing 'Connecticut King' with *Lilium wilsonii* var. *flavum*. The seedlings were

so uniform that it was sometimes difficult to distinguish them. 'Adelina', 'Cordelia', 'Joanna' (synonym 'Yellow Giant'; Plate 52), 'Pollyanna', and 'Vanessa' were named and introduced. All are yellow with gold blotches and traces of spots; the intensity of color varies slightly. These varieties continue to be widely grown in the Netherlands, where considerable acreage is devoted to 'Pollyanna'.

Plate 52. *Lilium* 'Joanna'

'Byam's Ruby' and 'Red Carpet' Crosses

These two clones arrived from Toronto, Canada, in the mid-1960s and both proved instrumental in producing superior lilies, especially in the red range. 'Red Carpet' came from A. J. Porter in Parkside, Saskatchewan and, along with 'Connecticut King', was surely one of the most valuable varieties ever for hybridizing. 'Red Carpet' is a short, unspotted red originally listed as a seedling of *Lilium* ×*scottiae* (*L. davidii* var. *willmottiae* × *L.* ×*elegans* 'Mahogany'). It was used extensively to breed short lilies for pot culture, a program described at the end of this chapter.

'Byam's Ruby' from Percy Byam of Toronto was not used as much as 'Red Carpet', but it produced some excellent seedlings when crossed with the Mid-Century clone 'Harmony'; of these, the bright red 'Firecracker', burgundy-red 'Firebrand' (synonym 'Prominence'), and rich red 'Heritage' were introduced.

A cross between 'Connecticut King' and 'Red Carpet' yielded a magnificent population of seedlings evenly distributed among three main colors—bright orange, warm red, and golden yellow. Their vigor, habit, flower size, and form were all outstanding. Their flowers either had a few spots or were unspotted. This excellent population was sold for several years as a strain, and eventually the warm red 'Fireball', golden yellow 'Nimbus', and vibrant orange 'Orangewood' were introduced.

'Red Carpet' enriched the lily world with several other outstanding offspring in the orange and red ranges, all showing remarkable strength, disease resistance, and virus tolerance. Among them were 'Bravo', mellow unspotted orange-red ('Connecticut Lemonglow' × 'Red Carpet'); 'Charisma', an outstanding miniature lily with vibrant unspotted flowers featuring a gold band ('Cinnabar' × 'Red Carpet'); 'Harvest', a huge-flowered bright orange with limited spotting ('Harmony' × 'Red Carpet'); 'Lovesong', a rather short burgundy-red ('Byam's Ruby' × 'Red Carpet'); 'Matador', rich intense red of intermediate habit ('Tabasco' × 'Red Carpet'); 'Redsong', a magnificent, taller bright red ('Connecticut Red' × ('Byam's Ruby' × 'Red Carpet')); 'Scarlet Emperor', a clear red with outstanding foliage ('Paprika' × 'Red Carpet'); and 'Venture', a smaller-flowered deep burgundy-red ('Tabasco' × 'Red Carpet').

Brushmark Hybrids

Lily hybridizers always do well to visit others involved in the same pursuit on a regular basis, and those working at Oregon Bulb Farms were no exception. At the nursery of Edgar Kline in Lake Grove, Oregon, we found a remarkably strong, healthy clone of *Lilium maximowiczii* var. *unicolor*; it grew profusely and impressed us with its virus tolerance. Oregon Bulb Farms obtained bulbs of this clone in the early 1960s.

Several crosses were made the following year, using *Lilium maximowiczii* var. *unicolor* as both a seed and a pollen parent. The most significant cross was with an equally virus-tolerant clone *L. dauricum* 'Golden Wonder' (the seed parent of the Golden Chalice strain). Both parents had unspotted flowers. The quantity of seed that resulted was much more than we would have expected in crossing two species.

The seedlings attained flowering size three years later and were uniform in all respects, as frequently occurs when two species are crossed. Their hybrid vigor was impressive: they reached 150 centimeters (5 feet) in height. The flowers—all outfacing, medium orange, and spotted—were interpollinated to produce the second generation.

The second-generation seedlings flowered in 1968 in a wide range of orange and golden yellow tones with varying flower habits and spotting patterns. However, they did not display the same hybrid vigor as the first-generation population. One remarkable seedling was spotted immediately in this population: it had upright flowers, soft melon-orange in color, with large oxblood-red blotches on the tepals, a characteristic we had never before seen in Asiatic lilies. The pollen of this fascinating seedling was used on 'Connecticut King', since we felt that combining the oxblood blotches and the gold blush of 'Connecticut King' would be interesting.

A large population of the resulting seedlings flowered in 1970 in shades of melon to bright orange, all showing remarkable vigor and excellent flower size and form. About 50 percent of them had "brushmarks." These fell into two distinct patterns: some flowers had clear red brushmarks and soft yellow pollen, and others had dark oxblood brushmarks and dark pollen. This is an excellent example of gene linkage, in which two characters are usually expressed simultaneously.

The first brushmark lilies were tagged, harvested the following fall, and planted out for further study. The next summer, we were surprised to see that many of our selections showed hardly a trace of brushmarks. The characteristic was obviously not as stable as we had thought. The previous summer had been very cool and wet before the selection phase, and we correctly assumed that the expression of brushmarks was in many cases influenced by environmental conditions. Again, we marked the seedlings that continued to show brushmarks, and the characteristic remained stable in these during years of further testing. The clones 'Accent', 'Endeavor', 'Impact', and 'Vanguard' were named and introduced from the original selections.

Mixed pollen from the darkest brushmarks was used to pollinate upright Asiatic creams and whites, including 'Sterling Star' and several numbered clones. The seedlings showing the darkest brushmarks and lightest base coloring were intercrossed to produce the second generation, in which there was a high percentage of clear brushmarks in an exciting range of colors including bright yellow, soft yellow, cream, peach tones, buff, and salmon. The selected clones included an unusually large number of outstanding, strong, disease-resistant individuals. Following years of testing, 'Artistic' (Plate 53) and 'Sgt. Pepper' were early introductions.

The percentage of strong, indestructible, and beautiful lilies that emerged from the original brushmark breeding line has seldom if ever been equaled in Asiatic hybridizing. Without question, the key was the high degree of virus tolerance inherited from the original parents.

Lilium maximowiczii var. *unicolor* was also pollinated with a mixture of pollen from selected upright pastel Asiatics and 'Connecticut King'. The orange-flowered seedlings of the first generation were intercrossed to produce a wide range of colors and forms in the second generation. The best of these second-generation seedlings were again crossed with choice upright clones, including 'Dayspring', 'Gypsy', 'Matchless', and 'Juliana'. The

Plate 53. *Lilium* 'Artistic'

material produced included individuals of unique form, color, and habit; such lilies can be developed only by returning periodically to true species (see "Breeding Lines with Staying Power" in Chapter 14 for a detailed discussion of this principle).

Lilium pumilum Hybrids

My interest in hybridizing with the coral lily, *Lilium pumilum*, peaked when I visited Charles Robinson of Erin, Ontario, in the early 1970s. Robinson had bred for several years with *L. pumilum*, and the variety of strong, beautiful hybrids growing in his garden was impressive. He gave an account of his work in the 1977 *Yearbook of the North American Lily Society*.

Lilium pumilum possesses several outstanding characteristics that it passes on to its offspring:

- Hardiness. Its habitat extends into the northernmost latitudes of eastern Siberia and Mongolia.
- Fragrance. A characteristic of paramount importance in Asiatic breeding because this desirable quality is almost nonexistent in the Asiatic group; it seems to have been ignored by most hybridizers.
- Spotless, clear colors. The clearly colored, bright, unspotted flowers found in varieties of *L. pumilum* are a desirable attribute.

- Adaptability to a wide range of soil conditions. It grows in soils from calcareous loams to those with a high humus content.
- Early flowering. It flowers earlier than any other Asiatic species, a very useful quality in both garden and forcing lilies.
- Adaptability to greenhouse culture. It has been forced successfully under greenhouse conditions for many years.
- Dilute genes. It carries genes that dilute flower pigments, offering the possibility of a wider range of pale colors.

The assembling of *Lilium pumilum* hybrid material commenced in the early 1970s. It included some interesting clones from Charles Robinson, originating from crosses of *L. davidii* var. *unicolor* and *L. pumilum*; the Stenographer hybrid 'Edna Kean' and *L. pumilum*; ('Edith Cecilia' × *L. davidii* var. *unicolor*) and *L. pumilum*; 'Elfenreigen' ('Fairy Dance' × *L. pumilum*); *L. davidii* var. *willmottiae* × *L. pumilum*; Fritz Ewald's cross between *L.* ×*hollandicum* and *L. pumilum*; Ruth Clas's 'Scamp' (*L. pumilum* × *L. dauricum*); and James Taylor's cross of 'Goldcrest' Asiatic hybrid and *L. pumilum*.

We were acutely aware that the upright-flowering characteristic needed to be more richly represented for us to be commercially successful with our *Lilium pumilum* breeding lines. Leonard Marshall of Casper, Wyoming, was an ardent amateur lily hybridizer of the time and consented to assist us. The high summer temperatures in Wyoming proved very helpful in obtaining fertile seed from the more difficult crosses. The early flowering Rainbow hybrids ('Tabasco' × *L. dauricum*) with their large flowers and excellent habit were selected to cross with *L. pumilum*.

Marshall crossed the selected *Lilium pumilum* forms with the Rainbow hybrids both ways (known as "reciprocal crosses"). A cross between a select bicolored Rainbow hybrid and *L. pumilum* was the most successful, producing four very attractive bright orange seedlings. The interspecific cross between *L. pumilum* and *L. concolor* was also successful. Myriad fascinating lilies were bred in upright, outfacing, and pendent forms in succeeding years. 'Avalon', 'Dayspring', 'Enchantment', 'Gold Medal', 'Juliana', 'Parfait', 'Pirate', 'Red Carpet', and 'Sunkissed' were crossed with (bicolored Rainbow hybrid × *L. pumilum*) hybrids; 'Avalon', 'Halloween', 'Matchless', 'Parfait', and 'Pirate' with 'Goldcrest'; and 'Avalon', 'Enchantment', and 'Matchless' with (*L. pumilum* × *L. concolor*). The styles were cut to assist fertilization in all the above crosses (see "Aids to Hybridizing" in Chapter 14), and the results were compared with an identical number of control flowers with uncut styles. A larger quantity of fertile seed was usually obtained with the cut styles. Fertility barriers did not prove a problem in succeeding generations of *L. pumilum* hybrids, in general.

'Albipayne', a clone originating from the hybridizers of the Connecticut hybrids, was used by Leonard Marshall in his later work with Asiatics, including the *Lilium pumilum* lines. A strong plant habit was the only visible asset of 'Albipayne'; the small flowers were distorted and pollenless, and what color remained in them was pure white. A cross between 'Albipayne' and (a bicolored Rainbow hybrid × *L. pumilum*) produced one seedling of breathtaking beauty. This tall, stately lily had pure white pendent flowers carried on a perfect inflorescence, further enhanced by excellent substance and an attractive ring of spots in the flower's center. This was only one of many beautiful lilies produced from 'Albipayne'. A variety of outstanding pure white outfacing hybrids resulted from crossing the pure white pendent lily to upright white varieties; 'Aloft' (Plate 54) and White Butterflies were among them, perhaps the finest of all pure white outfacing Asiatic lilies.

The beautiful and unique clones derived from the *Lilium pumilum* breeding lines are legion. Most were introduced by Columbia-Platte Lilies, later The Lily Garden. The upright, vibrant unspotted orange 'Burnside' and 'Portlandia' were introduced by Oregon Bulb Farms in the late 1980s.

There is a wealth of beauty still awaiting those who would hybridize with *Lilium pumilum* varieties and their hybrids. The limited work to date with the very early, bright yellow *L. pumilum* 'Yellow Bunting' is an example. The strength, beauty, disease resistance, and virus tolerance found in the existing clones of *L. pumilum* ancestry must encourage further work. A detailed account of breeding with the coral lily, written by Edward A. McRae and Judith Freeman, appeared in the 1985 *Yearbook of the North American Lily Society*.

Plate 54. *Lilium* 'Aloft'. Photo by Judith L. Freeman.

Asiatic Strains of the 1960s and 1970s

Several pendent and outfacing Asiatic lilies were grown at Oregon Bulb Farms in the 1960s and early 1970s, including the Harlequin hybrids. They were unfortunately forced from the stage by the influx of the more popular upright Asiatic varieties.

Burgundy Strain. The Burgundy hybrid strain came originally from crosses between *Lilium davidii* var. *unicolor* and *L. amabile* var. *luteum*. It included excellent lilies for the garden. The Burgundy strain comprised pendent to outfacing lilies in shades of deep red. The crosses between 'Black Butterfly' and 'Tabasco' and between 'Black Butterfly' and 'Paprika' produced an excellent seedling population, all deep red. The clones 'Fury' and 'Garnet' came from this strain.

Citronella Strain. Like the Burgundy hybrids, the Citronella strain included excellent lilies for the garden and came originally from crosses between *Lilium davidii* var. *unicolor* and *L. amabile* var. *luteum*. The Citronella strain was a group of pendent to outfacing golden yellows of exceptional form and beauty (Plate 55). The clone 'Amber Gold' was selected and introduced. A cross between 'Amber Gold' and a Sutter's Gold clone later produced an outstanding group of seedlings.

Miniature Asiatic Lilies

The idea of developing shorter Asiatic lilies for pot culture was born during a journey to the Oregon coast in the mid-1960s. A group of Dutch and North American lily enthusiasts was on the way to join a salmon-fishing expedition, but lily hybridizing was very much in our thoughts. In fact, it was the main topic of our con-

Plate 55. *Lilium* Citronella strain. Photo by Herman v. Wall.

versation. Given the popularity of chrysanthemums as year-round pot subjects, we felt that Asiatic lilies of miniature stature could enjoy similar acceptance. We had tested dwarfing compounds (see Chapter 17) to shorten several Asiatic varieties physically for growing in pots. Our goal, however, would be to develop genetically short varieties that did not require these hormone treatments. The Asiatic lily breeding program at Oregon Bulb Farms suddenly acquired a third dimension. Besides hybridizing for garden subjects and cut-flower varieties for greenhouse forcing, we were now seeking miniature forms for pot culture.

There were few short Asiatic lilies available to us. Those in our collection fell into four groups. First, we had three clones—'Alice Wilson', 'Leonard Joerg', and 'Mahogany'—of the *Lilium* ×*elegans* (synonym *L.* ×*thunbergianum*) group, some of which had been used in breeding the Mid-Century hybrids. These old Japanese lilies were mostly hybrids between *L. dauricum* and *L. wilsonii*. Second was a group of shorter lilies originating from the Patterson hybrids and later introduced as the Pastel hybrids. The parents of this material were a short Hallmark clone, ('Edith Cecilia' × 'Lemon Queen') F2, and a *L. dauricum* hybrid crossed with a second miniature Hallmark clone of the same parentage. Third were two clones selected from *L. dauricum*; both were 25 to 30 centimeters (10 to 12 inches) tall, with a very attractive, stocky habit. Finally, we had 'Harmony' from the Mid-Century group and 'Byam's Ruby' from Canada, added because of their relatively short habit.

We made some crosses and selected several pretty clones. Unfortunately, the majority lacked strength and staying power and were discarded. There were two exceptions. The first was 'Sunrise' (miniature Hallmark × *Lilium dauricum*), an outfacing soft cream with clear pink tips. The second, 'True Grit' ('Byam's Ruby' × *L. dauricum*), was one of several early flowering, red-orange bicolors of short stature that resembled the popular forms of *L. ×hollandicum*. Neither clone performed well under forcing conditions; 'Sunrise' stretched to three times its normal height in winter forcing. Both were later introduced as garden lilies.

It was obvious to us that an influx of good new material was essential before we could make real progress in breeding pot plants. We were simply working with too narrow a genetic range, without the characteristics we considered essential. Our hope of finding the desired types were soon to be realized.

A. J. Porter of Parkside, Saskatchewan, visited us in the mid-1960s and showed us slides of his new varieties. One miniature red lily was particularly fascinating. Porter identified it as "*L. ×scottiae* seedling" (*L. ×scottiae*, produced by Frank Leith Skinner in Morden, Manitoba, was a cross between *L. davidii* var. *willmottiae* and *L. ×elegans* 'Mahogany'). Porter kindly agreed to an exchange of varieties and we obtained this plant, an excellent clone later named 'Red Carpet' and still available commercially. These new plants grew 25 to 30 centimeters (10 to 12 inches) tall under field conditions. The leaves were long and quite dense, and the upright, bright red flowers were unspotted. The propagation and disease-resistant qualities were outstanding. The bulbs were exceptionally solid with excellent roots. The clone seemed highly virus tolerant, and its overall habit was the closest we had seen to our ideal pot lily.

Our second stroke of good fortune was the purchase of a group of Connecticut hybrids from Stone and Payne in 1967. This strong, disease-resistant material included some clones of short and intermediate heights, such as 'Connecticut Lemonglow', 'Keystone', and 'Sunray'. The broad leaves and stocky habit of 'Sunray' were appealing and would later prove invaluable in our pot lily program.

We acquired the clones 'Honey Bear' and 'Polar Bear' from Edwin H. Doerr of New Ulm, Minnesota. 'Honey Bear' was the better parent, very pollen-fertile though quite infertile as a seed parent.

We defined our goals more clearly, outlining the qualities we considered essential in a lily for pot culture:

- Plants 20 to 39 centimeters (8 to 14 inches) in height, of sturdy habit.
- Foliage full and not sparse, with long broad leaves preferred, not too dense.
- Flowers of good size, form, and substance, with bright, clear, and attractive color.
- A high bud count, since smaller bulbs would be acceptable for forcing.

Selected clones were to undergo the same stringent tests as garden and cut-flower varieties, with emphasis on strong growth habit, good multiplication naturally and from scales, disease resistance, and virus tolerance. Plants were to be tested under forcing conditions early; poor forcers would be eliminated, including those that scorched or stretched in winter or late fall forcing conditions.

Because 'Red Carpet' came closest to our ideal, we decided to work with it extensively. It showed low fertility as a seed parent, so we used it as a pollen parent. It figured in the following combinations, given here with the clones that were later named and introduced from each cross.

Cross:	'Byam's Ruby' × 'Red Carpet'
Clone:	**'Lovesong'**, short, with warm red flowers; used extensively as a pot subject
Cross:	'Cinnabar' × 'Red Carpet'
Clones:	**'Charisma'**, 20–25 cm (8–10 in.) tall in the field; unspotted vivid orange flowers with an attractive gold band
	'Inferno', taller than 'Charisma', with unspotted vivid orange flowers

Cross: 'Connecticut King' × 'Red Carpet'
Clones: **'Butternut'**, golden yellow flowers
              'Fireball', rich bright red flowers
              'Nimbus', golden yellow flowers
              'Orangewood', vivid orange flowers
Comments: An outstanding group of upright, stocky plants with
              red, golden yellow and rich orange flowers that are
              unspotted or with a trace of spots in the center. The
              seedling population was sold for several years as an
              excellent Asiatic mixture for the garden; all the
              plants were too tall for pot subjects.

Cross: 'Harmony' × 'Red Carpet'
Clones: **'Cherub'**, 20–25 cm (8–10 in.) tall; early, soft
              orange, huge flowers; strong, vigorous habit; a poor
              forcer that tended to develop too rapidly and
              produce deformed buds
              'Harvest', intermediate height; bright orange
              flowers; a popular cut flower in the late 1970s and
              early 1980s

Cross: 'Paprika' × 'Red Carpet'
Clone: **'Scarlet Emperor'**, intermediate height; bright red
              flowers; a popular garden lily

Cross: Pastel hybrid clone OH 6 × 'Red Carpet'
Clone: **'Fire Pixie'**, 25–30 cm (10–12 in.) tall; red-gold
              bicolor flowers; exceptional in field and greenhouse
              tests

Cross: 'Sunkissed' × 'Red Carpet'
Clone: **'Pixie Flame'**, 25–30 cm (10–12 in.) tall, stocky;
              unspotted red-gold bicolor flowers

Cross: 'Sunray' × 'Red Carpet'
Clones: None named
Comments: These plants were of intermediate height, with
              leaves broader than those of other yellow
              Connecticut hybrids and flower color range similar

Cross:	'Sunrise' × 'Red Carpet'
Clones:	**'Debutante'**, intermediate height; huge, unspotted, rose-pink flowers; an exceptionally strong and excellent garden lily
	'Wine Pixie', 30–40 cm (12–15 in.) tall; wine-red flowers; still used as a pot subject

These crosses with 'Red Carpet' produced excellent clones of miniature habit, the best being 'Charisma', 'Cherub', 'Fire Pixie', 'Lovesong', 'Pixie Flame', and 'Wine Pixie'. We decided to use the word *pixie* in all future lilies we developed for pot culture.

The next series of crosses was made in 1970, incorporating the varieties that produced the finest clones and seedling populations. Several superior forms were selected from those seedling populations and used en masse. Pastel hybrid clone OH 6 proved invaluable. This excellent lily was 20 to 25 centimeters (8 to 10 inches) tall, with long leaves and soft cream flowers. The one undesirable trait was a low bud count. Its offspring included many miniature lilies in a wide spectrum of colors.

The following crosses constituted the third series in our program. The clones selected and introduced are listed following each cross.

Cross:	Pastel hybrid clone OH 6 × ('Connecticut Lemonglow' × 'Red Carpet')
Clones:	**'Buff Pixie'**, soft buff-peach flowers
	'Butter Pixie', bright yellow flowers
	'Lemon Pixie', bright lemon-yellow flowers with green shading
	'Rouge Pixie', warm orange-red flowers
	'Ruby Pixie', rich red flowers
	'Peach Pixie', peach to bronze flowers
Comments:	By far the most prolific cross in producing miniature clones in a large color range, all of which were 25 to 30 centimeters (10 to 12 inches) tall, except for 'Lemon Pixie', which was 30 to 39 centimeters (12 to 14 inches).

Cross:	'Charisma' × 'Sunray'
Clones:	**'Irish Pixie'**, 39 to 43 centimeters (14 to 16 inches) tall; large bright orange flowers

'**Star Pixie**', 30 to 40 centimeters (12 to 15 inches) tall, rich to mellow orange flowers

'**Summer Pixie**', 30 to 39 centimeters (12 to 14 inches) tall; vivid orange flowers

Comments: An excellent population of seedlings, all with rich orange coloring. Many clones were selected and tested, and almost without exception their performance was outstanding, making very difficult the decision about which clones to retain.

Cross: 'Charisma' × 'Honey Bear'

Clone: '**Orange Pixie**', 25 to 30 centimeters (10 to 12 inches) tall; golden-orange flowers of outstanding form

Cross: 'Sunray' × *Lilium dauricum* Clone (Z.1)

Clone: '**Golden Pixie**', 30 to 39 centimeters (12 to 14 inches) tall, huge bright yellow flowers with gold centers

Cross: ('Prince Charming' × 'Harmony') × 'Peachblush'

Clones: '**Coral Pixie**', rose pink flowers

'**Dawn Pixie**', rose-red, heavily spotted flowers

'**Pink Pixie**', pink-cream bicolor flowers

Comments: These clones were much taller than we desired, 39 to 43 centimeters (14 to 16 inches), but they had exceptionally good form and because we lacked clones in the pink and peach range, we decided to propagate them until we obtained shorter ones from later crosses.

Cross: 'Charisma' × (*Lilium dauricum* × *L. bulbiferum* var. *croceum*)

Clone: '**Crimson Pixie**', 39 to 43 centimeters (14 to 16 inches) tall; huge warm red flowers

We tested these clones thoroughly in both field and greenhouse trials, discarding hundreds of inferior individuals. The named clones, therefore, are strong growers with high disease resistance and virus tolerance. Based on observations since that time, I believe the following are the strongest and most desirable: 'Buff Pixie', 'Butter Pixie', 'Fire Pixie', 'Golden Pixie', 'Irish Pixie', 'Lemon Pixie', 'Orange Pixie', 'Peach Pixie', 'Star Pixie', and 'Sun Pixie'.

Populations of seedlings from further crosses were evaluated in the mid-1980s and a new series of clones selected. Those with pastel coloring and broader foliage were strongly favored. Superior material was selected from the following crosses:

('Charisma' × 'Sunray') F_2
('Connecticut Lemonglow' × 'Red Carpet') F_2
('Connecticut Lemonglow' × 'Charisma') F_2
('Charisma' × pure white miniature Hallmark) F_2
('Sunray' × Pastel hybrid clone OH 6) F_2
('Sunray' × pure white miniature Hallmark) F_2

Several crosses between second-generation *Lilium pumilum* hybrids and 'Orange Pixie' produced spectacularly vivid colors, opening up an entirely new avenue. The short forms of *L. wilsonii* and *L. wilsonii* var. *flavum* (obtained from Yoshito Asano in Japan) produced exceptional hybrids of perfect habit when crossed with our best and most virus-tolerant miniature clones.

Three fascinating short clones from the cross of *Lilium longiflorum* 'Ace' with short Asiatics were used extensively in the mid-1980s. We used embryo culture to produce several exciting seedlings, including some pure whites and clear pinks. The new colors and flower forms were intriguing. Indeed, the results of the pot lily program exceeded our dreams. Clones selected from the later crosses were superior in foliar characteristics to their forebears, and the promise for the future seems unlimited.

In the late 1980s we started a similar program at Van der Salm Bulb-farm, using only the most disease-resistant clones from previous work. Although this program lacked some of the more exciting genetic material used earlier, the results have been rewarding. Several fine clones have emerged and been thoroughly tested over six years. The colors include clear oranges, vivid yellows, yellows with brushmarks, soft creams, and pinks. All are on the verge of introduction as I write this in 1996. The color range of pot lilies has now been expanded to include peach pink, clear red, wine, and white.

Cebeco Lilies has also continued to work with pot lilies, introducing the delightful 'White Pixie' (Plate 56). A visit to this company was quite encouraging; I viewed many very promising pot-plant varieties there. Peter Schenk of Bischoff Tulleken in the Netherlands has also produced some outstanding pot lily varieties.

Miniature lilies for greenhouse forcing, and for smaller gardens and border planting, have an exciting future. The strong clones now available should lay the foundation for vastly superior forms to come. To ensure success, growers must strive for the highest bulb quality, propagating the plants skillfully and growing and harvesting them at the proper time under proper conditions. With consistent performance thus guaranteed, we will be able to compete with other florist's plants and further promote the popularity of lilies. I am confident that better varieties will continue to emerge and that growers and forcers will attain these goals.

Plate 56. *Lilium* 'White Pixie'. Photo by Donald Leap, Cebeco Lilies.

CHAPTER 10

Oriental Lily Hybrids

The exotic beauty of the magnificent Oriental lilies is unsurpassed, not only among lilies but in the whole world of flowers. After being involved in their breeding and production for more than 30 years, I must cast a sure vote in their favor, confident that they will attain even greater beauty, adaptability, and usefulness in the future.

The typical Oriental hybrid is a late-flowering plant with broad alternate leaves. The flowers are usually large and showy, bowl-shaped, flat, or reflexed. Most have a powerful, sweet fragrance.

Considerable progress was made at Oregon Bulb Farms over the years, and a wealth of superior breeding material is now available from many sources. The success of future breeding rests squarely on the hybridizers' use of the finest, most persistent forms in existence. Adherence to this rule and the introduction of new material into the gene pool will produce Oriental lilies suited to a wider range of climates and conditions than ever before. These lilies should represent greater diversity in form, stature, and flowering time than those we see today.

The preeminent characteristics sought in Oriental hybrids are identical to those required of other lilies: vigor, disease-resistance, and tolerance to virus—that is, the ability to grow well and show no serious symptoms even after being infected. These qualities must be present in lilies chosen as parents. Success is never achieved overnight; several generations were required to eliminate undesirable characteristics and produce today's superior forms.

The original material used at Oregon Bulb Farms in the late 1950s and early 1960s came mostly from New Zealand. The lovely 'Jillian

Wallace', introduced in 1938, was involved in more hybrids than any other lily of this type in the early years. This hybrid between *Lilium speciosum* 'Gilrey' and *L. auratum* 'Crimson Queen' produced offspring with exceptional flower form and color. The Empress clones were also very prominent in the early years. 'Empress of India' (Plate 57), a hybrid between 'Jillian Wallace' and 'Crimson Queen', was a favorite for many years. In the original hybridizers' notes we can detect the excitement this lily caused: "In sheer magnificence it surpasses all others." The winner of several awards, including an Award of Merit, 'Empress of India' more than lived up to expectations. It showed remarkable virus tolerance for the time, surviving for more than 25 years.

'Empress of China', a lavender-spotted white, was a sister seedling and was also grown in quantity at that period. It was not the strongest-growing lily, but its ability to tolerate virus was unequaled. The apparent linkage of virus tolerance with the white color in Oriental hybrids has been well verified over the years.

'Empress of Japan', a huge-flowered, red-spotted gold band lily derived from crossing *Lilium ×parkmannii* with 'Jillian Wallace', completed the Empress series. It lacked the virus tolerance of the other clones, however, and it rapidly succumbed to infection.

Plate 57. *Lilium* 'Empress of India'. Photo by Herman v. Wall.

The Potomac hybrids were also prominent. Produced by Samuel L. Emsweller at Beltsville, Maryland, they originated from the cross (*Lilium auratum* × *L. speciosum* var. *punctatum*) × *L. speciosum.* The Potomac hybrids grew at Oregon Bulb Farms for many years, transmitting their superior virus tolerance to many generations of lilies. The beautiful 'Allegra' also came from Emsweller; it was a cross of (*L. auratum* × *L. speciosum* var. *album*) × *L. speciosum* var. *album.* Its purity of form and unblemished white flowers have yet to be surpassed, as has its virus tolerance; it still survives today, approaching its fiftieth birthday.

Several clones from J. S. Yeates in New Zealand had arrived at Oregon Bulb Farms in the early 1960s, including 'Elizabeth', 'Journey's End', and 'Red Ruby'. All had red coloring and remarkable virus tolerance. Some hybrids between *Lilium japonicum* and *L. auratum,* in their second and third generations, came from Norma Pfeiffer and were also used in early hybridizing in Oregon.

The early crosses at Oregon Bulb Farms included 'Jillian Wallace' with 'Empress of India', 'Jillian Wallace' with 'Empress of China', Potomac hybrids with 'Empress of India', and Potomac hybrids with a second generation (*L. japonicum* × *L. auratum*). A clear picture of the lovely seedlings remains. Careful tagging was necessary to separate colors resulting from some crosses, but others were already true-breeding for color.

A wise decision was made to continue this work. Out of it would come strains of Oriental lilies that bred true to color, flower form, flower size, season, and stature. The existence of these strains makes it possible to produce large quantities of vigorous, disease-free material that is true to type. The quantities and good health eventually produced could never have been achieved by normal clonal propagation techniques. A look at the breeding behind the plants seems in order.

Gold Band Lilies

The Japanese *Lilium auratum* var. *platyphyllum,* known to gardeners as the gold band lily for the striking yellow stripe running down the middle of its petals, provided the basis for this strain when combined with several red band (var. *rubrovittatum*) and var. *pictum* clones. These lilies stood out because of their ability to survive with virus infection.

The retention of vigor was a quality possessed by few Oriental clones in the early years. Obvious virus symptoms such as mottling and distortion might not be pronounced, but a decline in vigor soon became evident in most of them. The few clones that persisted vigorously, therefore, were of inestimable value in breeding.

The red band and var. *pictum* clones of *Lilium auratum* var. *platyphyllum* were used in breeding superior forms of this species. One clone with a beautiful red band was introduced under the name 'Crimson Beauty'. A var. *pictum* clone, carrying just a touch of color rather than a distinct band, proved to be true-breeding for this type. Obtaining clearer red bands was a more elusive goal, and the characteristic proved impossible to breed true. It was assumed to be more than a simple recessive gene; perhaps linkage genes were responsible for the red bands.

The lovely *Lilium auratum* is quite a variable species in nature. The original introductions from Japan included both the type, *L. auratum*, with narrow leaves, and the broad-leaved variety *platyphyllum*. Growers selected the finest unspotted or gold-spotted forms of variety *platyphyllum*, and subsequent generations were produced from seed. Magnificent lilies of great beauty and remarkable vigor were derived after only one generation of selective breeding. The parents were chosen for their broad petals, wide yellow bands, outfacing flowers of unusually thick substance, strong pedicels, and well-spaced inflorescences. Plants of intermediate stature and sturdy habit were always preferred to those with a floppy habit. Attractive foliage and vigor were also prerequisites.

A virus-tolerant form of the unspotted gold band lily was obtained from LeVern Freimann of Bellingham, Washington. His *Lilium auratum* f. *tricolor* 'Indestructible' had persisted in his garden for more than 25 years and added valuable genes to the pool for virus tolerance. This beautiful group of unspotted gold band lilies was introduced as the Melridge strain; the beauty of their flowers has seldom if ever been surpassed.

In breeding *Lilium auratum* var. *platyphyllum*, as in any breeding, we must be constantly alert for superior forms among the seedlings. These are cloned and tested; they are used in subsequent breeding only if they can be shown to transmit to their offspring overall beauty of form, vigor, and virus tolerance. *Lilium auratum* var. *platyphyllum* 'Apollo', a red band lily from Yeates, was used constructively in later hybridizing.

The market for strong, healthy forms of *Lilium auratum* var. *platyphyllum* is unquestioned. Few lilies, whether species or hybrids, can match their beauty.

Lilium speciosum **Hybrids**

The popular *Lilium speciosum* var. *rubrum* is widely grown and its natural variations are more extensive than those of any other species. Several of its clones have persisted for close to 50 years. Outstanding is 'Shooting Star', a lily of great vigor, beautiful flowers, thick substance, and long-lasting color, selected from seedlings grown by George L. Slate. 'Uchida', a fine clone from Japan, is also distinguished by beauty, disease resistance, and virus tolerance.

An interesting article by Frank Wilson in the 1960 *Yearbook of the North American Lily Society* shows that the clone 'Lucie Wilson' dates back at least to 1940; such persistence demands admiration. 'Grand Commander', a very rich red, and 'Rosemede' also come from Frank Wilson. 'Early Reliance' from W. F. Doreen of Levin, New Zealand, was another excellent lily with exceptional vigor and virus tolerance. 'Gilrey' is an outstanding clone from Australia that has survived 60 years.

Several crosses between these early clones of *Lilium speciosum* produced outstanding populations of uniform seedlings with very little variation, which were introduced as the Supernova strain. Crossing 'Shooting Star' with 'Grand Commander' gave the darker colors, but crossing 'Shooting Star' with 'Uchida' gave the superior flower forms. The opportunity to raise good strains of disease-free, uniform plants of *L. speciosum* var. *rubrum* is still available to us.

The late-flowering white form of *Lilium speciosum,* variety *album,* can also be raised from seed. The white color is a simple recessive, so two white clones can be used to produce a true-breeding white strain.

The unusual *Lilium speciosum* var. *gloriosoides,* with its exotically twisted tepals, engendered many interesting seedlings when crossed with other forms of *L. speciosum.* These lilies were surprisingly heat-tolerant in the warm summers of Oregon's Willamette Valley, a valuable characteristic. Most *L. speciosum* forms seem to prefer a cool climate, tending to drop their lower leaves during periods of intense summer heat. This may be alleviated by an organic mulch and adequate moisture during hot days.

Lilium auratum × *L. speciosum* **Hybrids**

Lilium auratum crossed with *L. speciosum* produced strains in three color types: Imperial Crimson, Imperial Silver, and Imperial Gold. With the introduction of *L. japonicum* to the breeding lines, a fourth strain, Imperial Pink, was created.

Imperial Crimson Strain. The Imperial Crimson strain is a group of lilies with medium-sized, bowl-shaped flowers in varying shades of red. The original strain came from crossing 'Jillian Wallace' with 'Empress of India', which produced a few seedlings with white or gold bands among mostly red bands. The deepest, clearest red clones were selected and backcrossed to 'Empress of India'. A wide range of variation in vigor and flower form was noted among the resulting seedlings, and only five of the originally selected clones proved to be homozygous (and therefore true-breeding) for the red color. Decreased vigor due to inbreeding was evident, however, and we used the vigorous 'Red Ruby' from Yeates to cross with the two finest true-breeding reds. As expected, this produced vigorous seedlings of excellent quality, true in flower form and color.

A quantity of seed labeled 'Crimson Glory', received from Leslie Jury in New Zealand, produced some magnificent plants, characterized by medium-sized, broad-petaled flowers of intense red with pure white margins. The plants also had compact stature and attractive broad, dark foliage. The two finest clones from this group were also crossed with the true-breeding reds to enhance the 'Imperial Crimson' strain.

The arrival of 'Stargazer' from Leslie Woodriff in the early 1970s proved valuable in breeding lilies in crimson-red shades. 'Stargazer' is homozygous for the red color. The clones 'Haley', 'Journey's End', 'Laura Lee', 'Pink Virtuoso', and 'Red Ruby' all produced excellent populations of seedlings when crossed with 'Stargazer'. Populations of crimsons with medium-sized flowers are now being sold under the name Crimson Elegance strain.

Imperial Silver Strain. The Imperial Silver strain consists of medium-sized, bowl-shaped, white flowers with rose or magenta spots. The prototypic clone was 'Empress of China', which showed a high degree of virus tolerance. A second parent in the early years was 'American Eagle', which originated from crossing 'Jillian Wallace' with *Lilium auratum* var. *platyphyllum*. This clone was originally the most vigorous of its type in cultivation; we recorded some plants 200 centimeters (7 feet) tall, with 35 flowers.

'American Eagle' was crossed with 'Empress of China' and produced whites and gold bands at a 3:1 ratio, indicating that the gold band is a recessive characteristic and that both of these parents, although bandless themselves, carry the recessive gold band gene. Similar white clones were selected and backcrossed to 'American Eagle' (the more vigorous parent), and four proved to be homozygous for white coloring without the band. These were then used to produce subsequent generations of Imperial Silver. In later years, forms were selected for outfacing flowers with overlapping petals, thicker substance, strong pedicels, and sturdy stems. Two outstanding parental clones were used for many years to produce the strain. The introduction of 'Allegra' into the Imperial Silver strain produced excellent seedlings of greater vigor, flower quality, and overall uniformity. 'Ballet Girl' from New Zealand also enhanced this strain in later years. The name Silver Elegance strain has been used for this group of lilies.

Imperial Gold Strain. The Imperial Gold strain carries medium-sized, bowl-shaped white flowers with the rich gold bands of *Lilium auratum*. The original 'Empress of Japan' was a hybrid between *L.* ×*parkmannii* and 'Jillian Wallace' and dates back to 1954. It had exceptionally large flowers of dinner-plate dimensions, but it failed to retain the vigor of its early years and was finally destroyed.

The first Imperial Golds were derived from 'Empress of Japan' crossed with a similar clone. The seedlings that resulted were of superb quality, and all carried the gold band, as expected. Several seedlings in which the gold band suffused to the margins of the petals were selected and intercrossed in the hope of eventually obtaining pure yellow flowers. Their offspring, however, showed an alarming loss of vigor, and vigorous material of different ancestry was immediately introduced. The dream of a true yellow Oriental lily was never realized.

A particularly vigorous clone selected in 1963 proved an excellent breeder in every respect and was the parent of the Imperial Gold strain for many years. Its medium-sized flowers were of fine form and its gold

Plate 58. *Lilium* 'Yellow Ribbons'

band was unusually bright. A later cross of this clone with a superior form of *Lilium auratum* var. *platyphyllum* produced a strain with increased vigor and larger flowers of fine form and substance. The backcross, using a superior hybrid of Imperial Gold to a virus-tolerant clone of *L. auratum* var. *platyphyllum,* was used to produce the strain for many years.

Several excellent clones were used in later years further to enhance the strain. These included 'Solar Eclipse', a magnificent clone from W. F Doreen in New Zealand; and 'Yellow Ribbons' (Plate 58), a virus-tolerant clone from the Strahms' lilies in Brookings, Oregon. This strain has been sold under the name Golden Elegance.

Imperial Pink Strain. The Imperial Pink strain consists of lilies with bowl-shaped flowers in shades of pink; this coloring shows the additional influence of *Lilium japonicum*. The introduction of the lovely pink of *L. japonicum* into lily breeding was part of the work of several hybridizers, most notably Norma E. Pfeiffer (reported in the 1942 *Yearbook of the North American Lily Society*) and Leslie Woodriff. Woodriff introduced his *L. japonicum* hybrids under the names Atomic hybrids and Little Fairies.

The material used at Oregon Bulb Farms came from Pfeiffer, who had crossed *Lilium auratum* with *L. japonicum*; she certainly used *L. auratum* rather than its variety *platyphyllum* in her early work, as the leaves of the hybrids were quite narrow. The finest seedlings were intercrossed over several generations to produce both second and third generations. One unfortunate characteristic of these lilies was their tendency to fade from clear pink to a muddy mauve hue, and all clones that showed this trait were eliminated. The remainder were propagated and exposed to virus infection in our trial fields; after a period of five years, only two survived: C.10 and C.16.

The finest clone, C.10, was the pollen parent of the Imperial Pink strain and is homozygous for the pink color. This clone has lovely, large bowl-shaped flowers of a clear, uniform pink color, with only tiny traces of spots and with an underlying gold band. It showed remarkable virus tolerance and propagated readily. The clones crossed with C.10 to produce the populations of Imperial Pink seedlings were 'Journey's End', 'Red Baron', and 'Sprite'. The tones of pink found among the seedlings varied from clear pink to rich rose, and the size and form of the flowers were remarkably uniform. The use of a rich crimson clone (unlike the others, homozygous for red) to pollinate C.10 in later years produced a group of seedlings of uniform rich color. All were rich rose pink, the result of crossing a true-breeding red clone with a true-breeding pink one. A cross between the white clone 'American Eagle' and C.10 produced a uniform population of soft pink seedlings.

The second clone retained from the test population of the cross between *Lilium auratum* and *L. japonicum,* designated C.16, was similar to C.10 in color; however, it was shorter in stature, reaching 60 centimeters (2 feet) rather than the 120 centimeters (4 feet) of C.10. The population of seedlings produced by crossing C.16 on 'Journey's End' was notable in that half its members were short, like the pollen parent. These beautiful plants, in a wide range of pink tones, were excellent subjects for small gardens. A strain similar to Imperial Pink has been sold under the name Rose Elegance strain.

Jamboree Strain. The smaller, flatter, more reflexed flowers resulting from the dominance of *Lilium speciosum* enjoyed wide favor, especially in the forcing trade, before upright Orientals appeared on the scene. The oldest strain of these produced at Oregon Bulb Farms was the Jamboree strain (Plate 59), a group of medium-flowered, semireflexed lilies in shades of red and pink. The seedlings were unusually vigorous and persistent. The original Jamboree cross was made in the 1960s, and vast numbers of bulbs

Plate 59. *Lilium* Jamboree strain. Photo by Herman v. Wall.

were marketed under this name. The durable Potomac hybrids were the maternal parents, with the persistent clones 'Jillian Wallace' and 'Empress of India' being the pollen parents. Later a magnificent population of intense red seedlings was also sold as the Jamboree strain. These plants resulted from a cross between *L. speciosum* 'Shooting Star' and 'Stargazer'. Their vigor, poise, and beauty were breathtaking. The uniformity of color, size, flowering time, and plant habit was seldom if ever equaled in a seedling strain.

Everest Strain. The Everest strain was characterized by medium-sized, reflexed, pure white flowers without spots. An earlier strain of this type was sold as the Flying Cloud strain. These lovely lilies are distinguished by their vigor, exotic appearance, and remarkable flower substance. The fine clone 'Allegra' was the maternal parent of the strain from the beginning and continues to be used by several hybridizers of Orientals to this day. The best populations of Everest seedlings were produced by crossing 'Allegra' with two strong, persistent, unspotted white clones with medium-sized flowers. In later years, two excellent outfacing pure white clones—'Furore' from Sun Valley and 'White Ice' from Ruth Strahm—were used to produce outstanding populations of seedlings with pure white, medium-sized flowers. 'Allegra' has been crossed with 'Casa Blanca' to produce magnificent unspotted white seedlings. Their flower size is more varied, owing to the influence of the huge-flowered 'Casa Blanca'; nevertheless, all are fine plants of exotic beauty.

Plate 60. *Lilium* Pink Glory strain. Photo by Herman v. Wall.

Pink Glory Strain. Pink Glory was considered by many to be the most ethereally beautiful strain produced at Oregon Bulb Farms (Plate 60). A lily authority from New Zealand, W. F. Doreen, gave his greatest praise to this strain after a thorough study of all the Orientals grown in the late 1960s. The flowers of the Pink Glory strain are of medium size, with slightly reflexed tepals. The delicate pink tones range from soft to deep rose; spotting patterns vary within the population, and many of the flowers are completely unspotted. The Potomac hybrids were the maternal parents; C.10, the beautiful clear pink second-generation hybrid of *Lilium auratum* and *L. japonicum,* was the pollen parent.

Celebrity Strain. The Celebrity strain was notable for its strength, elegance, and exotic beauty; it was pure joy to walk through a field of these remarkable seedlings. A cross between 'Allegra' and two selected unspotted clones from the Pink Glory strain, the Celebrity strain featured medium-sized, slightly reflexed flowers. The unspotted, silky, soft pink blooms were carried on plants of great vigor. 'Allegra' has been crossed with 'Rosario' to produce a similar group of seedlings. 'Rosario' (Plate 61) is a beautiful, early flowering pink clone of *Lilium rubellum* ancestry. It originated in the work of Leslie Woodriff and was by far the strongest and most virus-resistant variety in a group of clones with similar pedigrees. 'Rosario' is homozygous for the pink color.

Plate 61. *Lilium* 'Rosario'

Miniature Auratums. Seed of the dwarf form of *Lilium auratum* was obtained from J. S. Yeates of Palmerston North, New Zealand, in the early 1960s. An excellent account of the origin of these miniature or dwarf lilies is given by Yeates in the 1954 *Lily Year Book* of the Royal Horticultural Society. The dwarf characteristic is caused by a true recessive gene that emerged during inbreeding of *L. auratum* forms.

The seed from Yeates produced seedlings that were fascinating beyond words, all being miniature in habit. Their heights varied from 25 to 30 centimeters (10 to 20 inches); the plants were very stocky, with robust stems and strong, broad leaves, ovate with an apical tip. The flowers were completely outfacing except in a few plants that had upright flowers. The petals were of superb substance, and the flowers measured 10 to 12 centimeters (4 to 5 inches) in diameter. There was wide variation in spotting and in the intensity of the gold bands.

The apparent value of these Oriental lilies of miniature habit as pot plants and for small gardens prompted us to pursue further breeding work. The superior forms were selected from the original population and were used as parents. The succeeding generations were introduced under the name *Lilium auratum* Tom Thumb strain.

We decided to cross the finest forms of Tom Thumb with our best and most virus-tolerant Oriental clones. The plants chosen represented the entire color range found in our Orientals—crimson, silver, gold, and pink. An Imperial Silver clone was included that had a relatively short habit, although it was not related to the miniature auratums.

The first generation flowered in 1967. All the seedlings were tall, with one exception: the short Imperial Silver clone had produced more than 30 percent miniatures, and these plants were identical in habit to Tom Thumb. Their flowers, however, were more attractive than those of Tom Thumb and displayed distinct silver and gold tones, with the color of the gold forms being much superior to that of its miniature parent. More than 700 miniature plants from this cross were carefully tagged and harvested separately. It was interesting that Yeates reported similar results when he crossed his *Lilium ×parkmannii* 'Excelsior' with the dwarf *L. auratum*: 50 percent of the seedlings were dwarf.

The tall plants from the first-generation crosses were selected for superior forms in each color. These selections were then used to produce a second generation within each color group, and they were also backcrossed to the miniature *Lilium auratum*. Crosses of the taller plants produced a small percentage of miniatures in the second generation, as expected; the backcrosses produced well over 50 percent miniatures.

A second shipment of seed received from Yeates was sown in the same year. The seedlings were miniature, in colors including crimson, silver, and gold. We assumed that these seedlings were second-generation hybrids and that Yeates had crossed his finer Oriental hybrids with miniature *Lilium auratum* as we had done. Later Yeates sent selected dwarf clones from his work, including 'Little Jane' (pure white), 'Little Lavender' (white with lavender spots), and 'Little Robin' (red). These clones were miniature selections from the second-generation cross between 'Journey's End' and miniature *L. auratum*.

Little Rascals Strain. Miniature Orientals were now commercially available in three main colors, under the names 'Little Rascal' (silver forms), 'Little Red Rascal', and 'Little Gold Rascal'. These strains continued to be grown with great enthusiasm, and the plants received wide acclaim. They make charming, delightful pot plants, with long-lasting flowers that had a very pleasing fragrance. The scent of the pure unspotted whites was particularly attractive, close to that of paperwhite narcissus. These strains also bred true, as did the taller strains; the only difference was that they carried the recessive gene for dwarfness.

It seemed highly desirable to incorporate early flowering and clear pink color into these miniature lilies. The influence of *Lilium rubellum* seemed ideal for this purpose, and the finest selections of Little Rascals were crossed with Magic Pink clones. We were surprised to find that most of the seedlings in the first generation were quite tall (the influence of *L. auratum* var. *platyphyllum* in the Magic Pink strain). The best forms from the first generation were intercrossed; some of the superior clear pink seedlings were also backcrossed to Little Rascal clones of all colors. The succeeding generations produced an abundance of early flowering Little Pink Rascals.

There are now several clones of miniature Orientals available in the trade, in a full range of colors. 'Red Nymph' is perhaps the finest because of its superior habit. Plant habit is very important when selecting in this group of lilies. We prefer miniature plants with longer, less heart-shaped leaves and fuller foliage. The superb form and substance found in the flowers of miniature Orientals can also be expressed by an entire population of seedlings resulting from crossing a tall clone with these dwarf ones.

Lilium rubellum Hybrids

Magic Pink Strain. The use of *Lilium rubellum* was reported on by Norma E. Pfeiffer in the 1942 *Yearbook of the North American Lily Society*. The first *Lilium rubellum* hybrids I observed were in a display of Leslie Woodriff's Atomic hybrids in Portland, Oregon, in 1962. The value of this dainty alpine species to future generations of Oriental lilies is unquestioned for breeding earlier-flowering, shorter lilies. The finest *L. rubellum* hybrids at Oregon Bulb Farms flowered in the early 1960s resulted from a cross between *L. auratum* var. *platyphyllum* and *L. rubellum*. The plants were short-growing, with large, soft pink flowers of a bowl-shaped form similar to that of *L. auratum*. A second cross, (*L. au-*

ratum × *L. japonicum* F2) × *L. rubellum,* flowered a year later. This cross produced short plants with deep rose-pink, trumpet-shaped flowers. These two groups of seedlings made up the first Magic Pink strain (Plate 62). It is interesting that the short habit of *L. rubellum* is dominant. An unnamed Magic Pink clone selected in those early years persisted and retained its vigor for many years. This enchanting June-flowering lily played a major role in breeding early flowering Oriental lilies in all colors.

Plate 62. *Lilium* Magic Pink strain. Photo by Herman v. Wall.

Lilium nobilissimum Hybrids

Several select clones from the Pink Glory and Imperial Silver strains were crossed with the beautiful upright-flowering species *Lilium nobilissimum* in the early 1960s. The crosses were made in a small greenhouse where daytime temperatures were allowed to soar during pollination. We believed that higher temperatures aided fertilization in difficult crosses. A small amount of normal seed was obtained from both crosses at this time. If embryo rescue techniques had been available, many more seedlings could have been raised.

The seedlings flowered in the mid-1960s, and we were thrilled with their unique beauty. The cross between Pink Glory selections and *Lilium nobilissimum* produced two distinct colors—clear pink and pure white—and all were unspotted except for one seedling, which had a few lavender spots in the center of the flower. The beauty of these *L. nobilissimum* hybrids was unsurpassed among Oriental hybrids of the time. The clear, pure colors, flower form and substance, and stately plant habit were all superlative. The *L. nobilissimum* hybrids were originally named and sold in color groups: the Maharajah strain comprised the pink shades, and Taj Mahal the pure whites.

The four best clones in each color group were later rendered virus-free through shoot tip culture in the laboratory. These clones were then increased to substantial numbers through tissue culture. The four pink clones were named 'Coppelia', 'Isadora', 'Pantomime' (Plate 63), and 'Sylvia'; the four whites were 'Markova', 'Snow King' (the one with a few lavender spots), 'Swansong', and 'Sylphide'.

A few pure white clones of equal beauty were also propagated from seedlings of the cross between the Imperial Silver strain and *Lilium nobilissimum*. These were somewhat taller lilies with slightly larger flowers that appeared a little later. The beautiful clone 'Giselle' was named from this group. Names derived from the world of ballet were chosen for the *L. nobilissimum* hybrids to reflect their grace, beauty, and dignity.

The early crosses with these lovely hybrids were quite unsuccessful, and it was later found that all of them were triploids. In later years, however, crosses between *Lilium nobilissimum* and several Oriental clones produced fertile diploids.

Plate 63. *Lilium* 'Pantomime'

Modern Oriental Hybrids

The difficulty of satisfactorily propagating most Oriental clones some-what stifled their availability in the trade in the early years. There were, however, some outstanding individuals that were propagated. 'Jour-ney's End' (Plate 64), introduced by Yeates in 1957, is a hybrid between *Lilium auratum* var. *rubrovittatum* 'Philippa' and *L. speciosum* 'Gilrey'; its great vigor and virus tolerance surpassed all others in its class. The lovely pure white 'Allegra' from Emsweller has already been men-tioned; this clone is still alive and well and continues to receive acclaim.

Several outstanding Jamboree clones (from Potomac hybrids crossed with 'Jillian Wallace') also stood the test of time. 'Sprite' was a tall, soft pink lily that rose head and shoulders above the rest, proving adapt-able to a wide range of growing conditions. I observed a large group of 'Sprite' grown to perfection by Virginia Finch of Dunn, North Carolina, in the summer of 1975. Surrounded by tall pines, the bed was heavily mulched with pine needles and kept uniformly moist, and plants were growing beautifully despite temperatures exceeding 32°C (90°F).

Another magnificent clone was 'Cover Girl' (Plate 65), a sister seed-ling of 'Sprite'. Its large, soft pink flowers set it apart, and its perfor-mance in cultivation was superb. It was a fine natural propagator and a lovely garden subject.

The vibrant red color of 'Red Baron' made it a unique and worth-

Plate 64. *Lilium* 'Journey's End'. Photo by Herman v. Wall.

Plate 65. *Lilium* 'Cover Girl'. Photo by Herman v. Wall.

while clone. Selected from Imperial Crimson crosses using 'Red Ruby', it continues to grow satisfactorily, showing vigor and virus tolerance.

Two more outstanding clones that persist today are 'Crimson Beauty', a clear red band selection from *Lilium auratum* var. *platyphyllum,* and 'Shooting Star', a magnificent selection from *L. speciosum* var. *rubrum.*

Visits to Sun Valley Bulb Farms in Arcata, California, in the 1970s and early 1980s presented opportunities to see a wide variety of Orientals in flower, all originating from the work of Leslie Woodriff. The upright forms were of special interest, particularly the crimson 'Stargazer', which eventually became the most widely grown lily of all time (Plate 66). Several other uprights left an indelible impression, including a clear pink later named 'Le Rêve' (synonym 'Joy').

Plate 66. *Lilium* 'Stargazer'. Photo by Judith L. Freeman.

A series of other upright pinks, gold bands, red bands, and crimsons were used in further hybridizing at Oregon Bulb Farms, which led to a series of uprights in the late 1970s and early 1980s. The crosses producing the finest forms involved 'Stargazer' as one parent, with 'Allegra', 'Celebrity', 'Journey's End', and 'Le Rêve' as the other. Uprights in other colors were also used extensively.

The popularity of upright Orientals for the cut-flower industry started an avalanche of breeding by many companies in the Netherlands. Both 'Stargazer' and 'Le Rêve' were used extensively in the early work. The number of clones now available is mind-boggling; the finest will emerge only after years of propagation, growing, testing, and forcing.

The best clones in the pink range at present are 'Acapulco', a deep rose pink and perhaps the finest upright Oriental so far; 'Marco Polo', a lovely clear pink that tends to flower almost white when forced in summer; and 'Woodriff's Memory', a deeper but still soft pink that seems remarkably strong.

'White Stargazer' is by far the most popular and dependable of the upright whites and is used widely for forcing. 'Siberia', produced by Mak Brothers in the Netherlands, is now considered by many Dutch authorities to be the foremost white upright in the trade. The pure white 'Jan de Graaff' may be a winner in the future.

Two unusual uprights that have caught the eye of enthusiasts are 'Muscadet', a huge-flowered white with pink blotches, and 'Tom Pouce', a startling, huge pink-and-gold lily of great beauty and superb habit that is named after a little Dutch cake with pink icing.

The upright Orientals will continue to dominate the Dutch scene, although the large-flowered, outfacing pure white 'Casa Blanca' (Plate 67) is still widely forced and is popular for wedding decoration. The garden trade, however, must have a greater variety of forms, colors, and blooming seasons in its Orientals. To be meaningful, such variety must be commercially available. The strains of Orientals offer this variety, and we are glad they are being grown by several companies.

Three concerns emerge when we contemplate the production of Oriental lilies. First, this group offers and must continue to offer a great variety of colors, forms, and seasons to gardeners. Second, strong, healthy, disease-free material grown from seed must be used to produce bulbs of the highest quality; this means annual seedling crops derived from virus-tolerant clones of the highest quality. Third, strains should be grown in isolation from known virus carriers to remain virus-free. We have confidence that the Oriental lilies and their hybrids will continue to be the aristocrats of lilydom.

Plate 67. *Lilium* 'Casa Blanca'

CHAPTER 11

Trumpet Lily Hybrids

The true-breeding strains of Chinese trumpet lilies and their hybrids have been sold commercially for many years. If raised from seed on a regular basis, they remain strong and free from disease. The species involved in their ancestry are almost all natives of China; the one characteristic they have in common is purple bulbs:

- *Lilium henryi,* frequently called "the orange *speciosum,*" is native to the mountains of central China. Its large, nodding orange flowers have numerous prominent papillae; the leaves are broad-lanceolate. There is also a yellow-flowered form, *L. henryi* var. *citrinum.*
- *Lilium leucanthum* var. *centifolium* is a variable plant whose exact wild habitat is a mystery. The first plants grown in the West came from seed gathered from cottage gardens in southern Gansu province of China by the English plantsman Reginald Farrer. The pure white to cream trumpet flowers have a rose-purple or brownish reverse. This is the most beautiful and spectacular of the Chinese trumpet species.
- *Lilium regale,* a lovely lily from western China, was discovered by E. H. Wilson, the famous plant-hunter, in the valley of the Min River in western Sichuan Province in 1903. It is the hardiest lily in the trumpet group.
- *Lilium sargentiae,* a handsome trumpet lily, is native to Sichuan Province, China. It, too, was introduced into cultivation by E. H. Wilson, who discovered it in 1903 in the Tung River valley,

growing at elevations between 1050 and 1500 meters (3500 and 5000 feet). This species produces bulbils in the leaf axils and is reputed to be the tenderest lily in the trumpet group.

• *Lilium sulphureum,* native to Yunnan Province, China, and to upper Myanmar (Burma), is known for its lack of persistence in cultivation; it shows high susceptibility to virus disease.

The material that laid the foundation for the true-breeding strains at Oregon Bulb Farms originated from a wide variety of sources. The true species *Lilium henryi, L. henryi* var. *citrinum, L. leucanthum* var. *centifolium,* and *Lilium regale* were grown for many years. Three hybrids of *L. regale* were used: *L.* ×*imperiale* (synonym *L.* ×*princeps*), from a cross between *L. regale* and *L. sargentiae*), especially the clone 'George C. Creelman'; *L.* ×*sulphurgale,* from a cross between *L. sulphureum* and *L. regale;* and *L.* ×*centigale,* from a cross between *L. leucanthum* var. *centifolium* and *L. regale.*

The hybrids produced from crossing the trumpet lily species with *Lilium henryi* were important in the early work. 'White Henryi' (*L. centifolium* × *L. henryi*) was bred by Leslie Woodriff of McKinleyville, California. 'T. A. Havemeyer' (*L. henryi* × *L. sulphureum*) was bred by Tom Barry. *Lilium* ×*aurelianense* (*L. henryi* × *L. sargentiae*) was bred by Edouard Debras in France.

The work of LeVern Freimann of Bellingham, Washington, and Carlton Yerex of Newberg, Oregon, was instrumental in the earlier efforts at Oregon Bulb Farms. Both men contributed considerable quantities of material to the gene pool. Freimann worked with a wide range of species and hybrids, including *Lilium sulphureum, L. sargentiae,* and *L.* ×*aurelianense.* The Yellow Regal or Royal Gold group originated from *L.* ×*sulphurgale* hybrids; the yellow color was intensified through succeeding generations. Freimann also worked with pink and darker yellow trumpets, using *L.* ×*aurelianense* to improve flower placement and vigor in his seedlings.

Carlton Yerex was the first to obtain *Lilium* ×*aurelianense* from E. Debras in France and worked extensively with it. He backcrossed it to both *L. sargentiae* and *L. henryi* and used *L.* ×*aurelianense* pollen on other trumpet species and hybrids on his farm. The wealth of beautiful lilies developed by Yerex included the Camelot Trumpet and Pagoda

Bells strains. The many fine clones he introduced include 'Goldspire', 'Ta Ming', and 'Whirlybird'. Yerex also coined the name Aurelian hybrids for the material originating from *L. ×aurelianense* that showed distinct *L. henryi* characteristics. This name is now universally used for all hybrids between Chinese trumpet species and hybrids and *L. henryi*, including those derived from hybrids other than *L. ×aurelianense*.

The truly meaningful work with the trumpets and their hybrids at Oregon Bulb Farms was done by Harold F. Comber during the 1950s and early 1960s. Comber selected the finest colors and forms within each color group. He determined the superior parental combinations by numbering and crossing the clones individually within each group, evaluating the seedling populations when they flowered. The two clones producing the finest seedling populations were then used as the parents of the strain. The vigor and strength of these seedling populations were unsurpassed. The important qualities sought in parents were flower color, form, and substance; well-formed inflorescence and flower placement; and as sturdy a plant habit as possible.

True-Breeding Trumpet Lily Strains

Lilium regale. The forms of *Lilium regale* that showed the purest white coloring, the darkest rose-purple reverse, and the richest canary-yellow throat were selected as parents. The inflorescence was important: those with the best flower placement were preferred over those with a "bunched" habit. An excellent clone of *L. regale* was obtained from a garden in Montana where it had persisted for nearly 50 years; this was used as a seed parent to transmit superior virus tolerance and disease resistance.

Black Dragon Strain. The original seed for this magnificent group was collected from cottage gardens in China and given the taxonomic designation *Lilium leucanthum* var. *centifolium*. The name Black Magic was first used for the strain derived from it, with 'Black Dragon' being the clone used as the seed parent. These tall trumpets have pure white flowers with pale yellow throats; the flowers are enhanced by rich rose-purple coloring on the outer surfaces of the tepals. There is little variation in the seedling population—all are very beautiful. Because no other species was involved in their breeding, members of the Black Dragon strain are to be regarded simply as superior forms of *L. leucanthum* var. *centifolium*.

Sentinel Strain. Before this strain was developed, a similar group was sold during the early years of Oregon Bulb Farms under the name Olympic Hybrids. The clone 'George C. Creelman' (*Lilium regale* × *L. sargentiae*) was one of the original parents of the Sentinel strain. Lilies of this strain are early flowering, pure white with golden yellow throats; the tepals are also pure white on the reverse. The clone 'Goliath' was selected from this strain; it was also used as a parent for the strain.

Green Magic Strain. The clone 'Green Dragon' was the original seed parent of this strain. The flowers are huge, cream to pure white, with the reverse of the tepals green to soft brown. They are very complex hybrids that breed remarkably true in flower size, form, color, and season. They are quite early blooming, indicating some influence from *Lilium sargentiae*.

Golden Splendor Strain. This is a magnificent group of trumpet lilies of great vigor and breathtaking beauty. The remarkable uniformity of the seedling populations suggests a clonal group, but subtle difference can be seen when individuals are examined closely. The flowers are rich golden yellow with deep wine on the reverse of the tepals. Golden yellow trumpet lilies do not exist in nature, so their breeding history is of special interest to the hybridizer. Earl Hornback (1962) wrote that the genes that release the yellow throat color to cover the entire flower are recessive, and that "released" genes have to come from both parents to produce a solid yellow trumpet. The elimination of the factors restricting yellow color to the throat was enhanced further with the introduction of *Lilium henryi* hybrids into the colored trumpet lines; in *L. henryi* these factors are either very weak or completely absent. Several clones were introduced from the Golden Splendor strain, including 'Golden Spur', 'Life', 'Patrician', and 'Pioneer'. Similar seedling groups have been marketed as the Golden Temple strain (Plate 68).

Plate 68. *Lilium* Golden Temple strain

Moonlight Strain. This is an impressive group of lime-green to bright yellow trumpets with lighter coloring on the reverse of the tepals. The original Moonlight strain had a distinctive lime-green reverse. The beautiful clones 'Helios' and 'Limelight' were the parents. In later years, shorter parents with larger, brighter yellow flowers showing no color on the outside of the tepals were used as parents. The clearer yellow shades without darker reverse distinguishes the Moonlight strain from the Golden Splendor strain, which has more richly colored flowers with darker reverses. A group of seedlings similar to Moonlight has been marketed as the Moon Temple strain (Plate 69).

Pink Perfection Strain. This is a population of very dark trumpet lilies; their intense color is closer to purple than to pink. They are, however, magnificent in form, and many of the flowers have attractive gold centers. This strain has considerable influence from *Lilium sargentiae,* although most pink trumpets seen today are undoubtedly rather complex hybrids. The clone 'Damson' was an outstanding selection and was also used as the parent of the seed strain for many years. The very richly colored clone 'Midnight' (Plate 70) was selected to counteract the ten-

Plate 69. *Lilium* Moon Temple strain. Photo by Herman v. Wall.

dency of pink trumpets to fade when grown in the warmer and more humid climate of eastern North America. 'Midnight' proved to be very strong and disease-resistant and was used as a parent for many years. Seedling populations similar to Pink Perfection have been sold as the Amethyst Temple strain.

It was considered very desirable to breed trumpet lilies with clearer colors in true pink shades. An equally desirable trait was a shorter habit, so that the lilies could be grown in small gardens. The parents selected to achieve these goals were four selections from *Lilium regale* that showed clear pink margins and some suffusion of the pink color to the outer part of the tepals. Also used were three shorter, softer pink selections from the early Peacock strain. The first seedling population from crossing the

Plate 70. *Lilium* 'Midnight'. Photo by Herman v. Wall.

L. regale selections with the short pinks did not produce superior individuals; little pink coloring was present. The forms with the best habit, inflorescence, and flower form were intercrossed to produce the second generation, and we were ecstatic to find a high percentage of clear pink flowers among these seedlings, with the color extending to the throat of the flower in almost every case. We assumed that the genes restricting color were true recessives, and this was confirmed by the fact that the percentage of clear pinks in the second generation plants was about 20 percent, close to the Mendelian ratio. Later crosses among the clear pinks proved that they bred remarkably true.

Copper King Strain. This very fine group of trumpet lilies comes in shades varying from rich orange to softer, almost salmon tints. The colors (inherited from *Lilium henryi*) were the only ones that were difficult to breed true in trumpet lilies: seedling populations invariably contained some of soft yellow coloring. A series of crosses made in later years produced populations that were remarkably true in color. The name African Queen was used in earlier years for part of this group. African Queen and Copper King are distinguished by the color on the reverse of the tepals: African Queen has a softly colored reverse, and Copper King a dark reverse. The clone 'Anaconda' was selected from the strain, and that name has also been applied to the strain as a whole (Plate 71).

First Love Strain. The hybridizing of trumpet lilies was not confined to the production of separate color groups; enthusiasts occasionally ventured into more daring and creative avenues. In the early 1960s a cross was made between a stately Golden Sunburst clone with rich yellow open flowers (distinctly different from the trumpet form) and a Pink Perfection clone. The first generation consisted of muddy, unattractive colors on flowers of intermediate form. The individuals with better habit and flower form were then intercrossed to produce a second generation of seedlings that was unique and beautiful; the perfect blend of the golden yellow and pink colors was very appealing. A new spicy fragrance had also been created, pure delight compared to the heavy scent of most trumpet lilies. The finest color blends were selected, propagated vegetatively by scaling, and introduced as the First Love strain (Plate 72). Several superior Copper King clones were crossed

Plate 71. *Lilium* Anaconda strain. Photo by Herman v. Wall.

with First Love selections to produce some of the finest color tones ever seen in trumpet lilies. The colors varied from softest salmon shades to richer copper tones. Attractive blends of colors, similar to the First Love strain, were also present.

Sunburst Strains. The Sunburst strains, of various colors, were trumpet hybrids characterized by flat to slightly bowl-shaped flowers. Closely related to *Lilium henryi*, they were bred from *L.* ×*aurelianense*, 'T. A. Havemeyer', and 'White Henryi'. The

Plate 72. *Lilium* First Love strain. Photo by Herman v. Wall.

Sunbursts are later-flowering and have broad lanceolate leaves rather than the narrow leaves of trumpet strains.

The Golden Sunburst strain (Plate 73) is a stately and magnificent group of lilies with rich golden yellow flowers of excellent form. This virtually indestructible group has shown remarkable persistence in gardens. The flowers exude an appealing fragrance. The fine clone 'Lightning' was selected from and then used as a seed parent for the Golden Sunburst strain.

The flowers of the Pink Sunburst strain have rich orange centers. Bred late in the history of Oregon Bulb Farms, they were without question among the most beautiful of the Sunburst group, with breathtaking color combinations.

A rich, vivid bowl-shaped flower of intense orange graced the clone that produced the seedlings of the Orange Sunburst strain. The color was nonfading even in the warmest summer; the flowers simply developed an attractive pale margin following hot weather. The taller, softer orange clone 'Thunderbolt' (Plate 74) has been a favorite for many years; it is an aneuploid and has been used extensively in polyploid breeding.

The Silver Sunburst strain, a group of pure white seedlings with open, slightly bowl-shaped flowers, is very closely related to *Lilium* ×*aurelianense*. They have a stronger fragrance than other Sunbursts, suggesting that the white color and strong fragrance inherited from the trumpet lilies may be genetically linked.

Plate 73. *Lilium* Golden Sunburst strain. Photo by Herman v. Wall.

Plate 74. *Lilium* 'Thunderbolt'. Photo by Herman v. Wall.

Heart's Desire Strain. An unusually attractive group of pure white to cream lilies, these have bowl-shaped flowers with rich orange centers. They are shorter in habit than the Sunbursts, with narrower foliage similar to that of their trumpet parents. Their strength, vigor, and disease resistance are superb. The clones 'Bright Star' and 'Stardust' were selected from this strain.

Miniature Trumpets and Aurelians. A group of shorter trumpet lilies was grown under the name Peacock hybrids in the early years at Oregon Bulb Farms. Reaching 60 to 90 centimeters (2 to 3 feet) high, they were considered very valuable for future hybridizing. There were also a few shorter clones in both the Heart's Desire strain and *Lilium regale*. The seedling populations produced by crossing the shorter Peacock clones with the short Heart's Desire and *L. regale* clones were encouraging; most had a short habit. It was the second generation, however, that contained some lilies of truly miniature habit. They resembled tiny Christmas trees, ranging from 30 to 45 centimeters (12 to 18 inches) in height. Their flowers included pink trumpets, open pink flowers with orange centers, open whites both plain and orange-centered, and finally, a pure white with a dark reverse. The best clones were propagated and showed good vigor and disease resistance over several years. This strain was first sold as Little Pink Ladies and Little White Ladies; the clones 'Pink Elf' and the pure white 'White Elf' were introduced later.

Upright Trumpet Hybrids. The first upright golden yellow trumpet at Oregon Bulb Farms came from LeVern Freimann. It was identical to Golden Splendor except for its upright habit. This lily was used to produce succeeding generations of upright-flowered forms, golden yellow with dark reverse. Later an upright pink came from McClaren in New Zealand. Its color was intense and its substance and flower form excellent. A few upright Aurelian hybrids with white, orange-centered flowers were also selected and used in hybridizing. A cross between one of the upright clones and the finest Golden Sunburst selection produced a surprisingly beautiful and uniform group of seedlings that were later named Creme de la Creme strain. This population had cream to white flowers with gold to soft orange centers, and excellent plant habit. The absence of the pollen parent's rich yellow color indicates that it is recessive. The choice upright cream with a rich orange center was also crossed with (*Lilium auratum* var. *platyphyllum* × *L. henryi*), and embryo culture was used with the resulting seeds to produce two fine Orienpet clones. Cebeco Lilies of Aurora, Oregon, now grow large stands of upright trumpet hybrids in a range of colors. These have been introduced as the Herald Angel strain (Plate 75).

Early-flowering Aurelians. Several of the original trumpet lilies used at Oregon Bulb Farms came from George Slate of Geneva, New York. Later Professor Slate suggested that early flowering Aurelian hybrids would be a welcome addition to the trumpet lines. Perhaps going back to *Lilium regale* crossed with a late-blooming Aurelian was the answer. *Lilium regale* was pollinated with an exceptional late-flowering Aurelian with bowl-shaped, orange-centered white flowers, and a reasonable quantity of seed was obtained. The seedlings flowered in mid-June; all looked like *L. regale* (the species' reputation for producing apomictic seed was well deserved) except for one beautiful individual with white, semi-bowl-shaped flowers with rich orange centers. That this seedling flowered with *L. regale* is fascinating, indicating that the early flowering pattern was dominant. This seedling was used extensively in following years to produce many early Aurelians of great beauty.

Outlook for the Future

Hybridizing with trumpet lily species and hybrids continues to offer a vast field of opportunity. The great beauty and many forms, colors, and habits of these plants must be tapped. There are four principal observations to be remembered in pursuing this line of breeding:

1. The high fertility of most trumpet species and hybrids is a distinct advantage.
2. The ability to grow strong, disease- and virus-free strains from seed using two select parents can be utilized by both large and small growers.
3. Pollinations must be protected at all times, since trumpet hybrids are very attractive to natural pollinators.
4. The seed and pollen parents of each strain must be propagated regularly by scaling to maintain their health and vigor.

Plate 75. *Lilium* Herald Angel strain

CHAPTER 12

Polyploid Lilies

Each cell of a lily plant naturally has 24 chromosomes, or 12 pairs. These plants with their paired chromosomes are termed *diploid,* from the Greek word for "double." The sole exception to this rule is the form of *Lilium lancifolium* (synonym *L. tigrinum*) that is widespread in cultivation; each of its cells contains 36 chromosomes. This triploid clone is probably of hybrid origin, but most lily hybrids now grown are diploids.

The sperm and egg cells of an organism (plant or animal) are formed through a process called *meiosis,* which results in the production of cells that have only half the parent organism's chromosomal material; these cells are termed *haploid,* from the Greek word for "half." The haploid sperm and egg join in fertilization to form the new diploid cell that eventually becomes the offspring organism.

Sometimes, however, the process of meiosis fails, and a sperm or egg is produced that has the full complement of parental chromosomes; this type of cell is called a *non-reduced gamete.* When such a reproductive cell participates in fertilization with a haploid cell, an event that does not occur as easily as normal fertilization, the resulting offspring has three sets of chromosomes instead of the normal two and is termed *triploid.* When both sperm and egg have the diploid chromosome number, the offspring has four sets and is termed *tetraploid.* All organisms with more than the normal number of chromosomes are collectively called *polyploid.*

The effort to create polyploid lilies artificially has been driven by the fact that these plants tend to be larger, stronger, more substantial, and more persistent in every respect. This has obvious advantages in any growing context.

The offspring of a tetraploid parent and a diploid parent is a triploid. Such a cross usually produces few or no normal seeds. With their 36 chromosomes, triploid lilies are difficult to cross with other lilies.

Triploid lilies can also occur rarely among the seedlings of crosses between diploids; this results from a failure of meiosis in one of the parents, often caused by high temperatures or irradiation. Triploid clones that occurred spontaneously among seedlings of diploid crosses include 'Anniversary', 'Compass', 'Hornback's Gold', 'Schellenbaum', and 'Seashell'.

Triploids may also arise in crosses of two distantly related lily species, or a cross between a species and a distantly related hybrid. This breeding of distantly related forms frequently produces triploids that are sterile or have greatly reduced fertility. Thus the process of embryo culture may be necessary to raise the resulting seedlings. These triploids arise because distant crosses are typically facilitated by high ambient temperature, which also induces the production of non-reduced gametes. Examples of this type of plant are found in a group of *Lilium nobilissimum* × Oriental hybrids produced at Oregon Bulb Farms in the 1960s, including the clones 'Coppelia', 'Giselle', 'Pantomime', 'Snow King', and 'Sylvia'. Several of Yoshito Asano's Japanese hybrids were also triploid, including 'Shikayama' × *L. henryi* and *L. auratum* × *L. henryi*. Many hybrids between *L. longiflorum* 'Ace' and Asiatic hybrids were also triploid, as well as lines between *L. lankongense* and Asiatic hybrids, first and second generations, including the Southern Belles, Chippendale, and Rosepoint Lace strains, and the clone 'Ariadne' (Plate 76).

Tetraploid lilies have 48 chromosomes; this is double the normal number of diploids. Tetraploids can occur naturally as the result of failure of meiosis, as described for triploids, if there are irregularities in the formation of both parents' reproductive cells. They can also be produced vegetatively by treating diploid plant cells with the chemical colchicine.

Colchicine is an alkaloid derived from the plant *Colchicum autumnale,* sometimes erroneously called "autumn crocus"; it is also a member of the lily family, in the broad sense. This very toxic substance, when applied in very dilute form, can block mitosis. The use of colchicine is

Plate 76. *Lilium* 'Ariadne'. Photo by Judith L. Freeman.

effective only in cells that are actively dividing; such cells are found in seedlings, scales, and shoot tips. It is also useful in tissue culture.

In lilies, scales have been most frequently used for this purpose. Robert Griesbach has developed a treatment that involves incubating the scales at a relative humidity near 100 percent for five to seven days at 20° to 24°C (68° to 75°F) before colchicine treatment. Mitotic activity at the cut surface should create a slight (barely discernible) ridge of callus tissue during this shoot incubation period. Following this treatment, the scales are refrigerated at 3° to 7°C (38° to 45°F) for one or two days. The scales are then submerged in a freshly prepared 0.01 percent colchicine solution for 24 hours. Next, they are incubated within a mixture of moist sphagnum peat and vermiculite at 21°C (70°F) until bul-

blets form. Those that do not break dormancy spontaneously while being incubated are cold-treated for two to three months depending on
the degree of dormancy exhibited.

In a widely used adaptation of Griesbach's method, the clean scales
are incubated at 21 °C (70 °F) for two to three weeks before treatment
with a 0.01 percent colchicine solution for 24 hours. At this time a tiny
nubbin of growth can be seen at the base of the scale, and the cells are
in very active division, thus more susceptible to colchicine. The chemical oryzalin has been used as an alternative to colchicine in chromosome doubling. Arthur Evans' excellent article "Cooking Up Tetraploids
in the Kitchen," published in the 1993 yearbook of the North American Lily Society, makes excellent reading for those seeking to become
more involved.

Griesbach also experimented with treating seedling lilies with colchicine. He created plants of *Lilium regale* by submerging diploid seedlings in a freshly prepared 0.05 percent solution of colchicine for 24
hours. These tetraploids proved to be quite fertile, producing 20 to 50
viable seeds per capsule when intercrossed.

Tetraploid forms of Asiatic lilies, produced from both seed and chemical treatments, have shown a high level of fertility in most cases. This
fertility is increasing as more seedling populations of tetraploids are
produced—that is, continued breeding is selecting for fertile forms. The
same is true of the tetraploid trumpet hybrids produced by Griesbach,
which have proved highly fertile.

The tetraploid forms of Orienpets have, however, shown a generally
low level of fertility, or the result of their descent from distantly related
species. Even their fertility, however, is gradually increasing, and meaningful populations of seedlings will soon be a reality.

It has been possible to cross triploid Asiatic hybrids with tetraploid
Asiatic hybrids, but seed is produced only when the triploids are used
as the seed parents. The varieties 'Compass', 'Parisienne', and 'Sirocco'
produced significant seedling populations in such crosses; no seedlings,
however, were worthy of introduction.

I am confident that the magnificent tetraploid lilies will continue to
evolve to take their rightful place in the lily world. Their spectacular
beauty, strength, and disease resistance guarantee that. In the remainder of this chapter, I discuss several important groups of polyploid lilies.

Crosses between *Lilium longiflorum* and Asiatic Hybrids

The pioneering work with hybrids between *Lilium longiflorum* (the Easter lily) and various Asiatics was done in the late 1970s at Sun Valley Bulb Farms in Arcata, California. It was made possible by the technique of embryo rescue, in which the embryos are excised from the seed and grown in test tubes on a nutrient solution. The original goal was to produce colored versions of the Easter lily. The hybrids originally produced at Sun Valley through embryo rescue displayed a wide range of colors, flower forms, plant habits, height, and vigor. *Lilium longiflorum* 'Ace' was used exclusively as a parent, producing hybrids when crossed with 'Chiefwood', 'Connecticut King', 'Earlibird', 'Glee', 'Gypsy', 'Juliana', 'Pineapple', 'Pirate', 'Red Carpet', 'Redding', 'Showboat', 'Stoplight', 'Sterling Star', 'Sunkissed', 'Sunstar', 'Yellow Jewel', and the Yellow Blaze strain.

This material was brought to Oregon Bulb Farms in 1984 and extensive hybridizing work commenced in 1985. A few of the clones had enormous upright flowers and were reported to be second-generation hybrids; unfortunately, the records of the second-generation crosses had been lost. The Sun Valley hybrids were crossed with Asiatic clones in the pastel color range, using only the strongest and most disease-resistant clones, and they were crossed with several clones of *Lilium longiflorum,* including 'Ace', 'Chetco', 'Harbor', and 'Nellie White'. Several outstanding seedlings from the work of A. N. Roberts at Oregon State University were also used to pollinate the wide range of hybrids.

The pollen of almost all the *Lilium longiflorum* 'Ace' × Asiatic hybrids was found to be completely infertile, but there were a few exceptions. A taller hybrid with soft pink, trumpet-shaped flowers (*L. longiflorum* 'Ace' × 'Gypsy') had pollen that produced a large number of pollen tubes when examined under the microscope. Five other hybrids had pollen grains that were mostly misshapen, but a few pollen grains produced an occasional pollen tube. The single fertile pollen and those of low fertility were used to pollinate the *L. longiflorum* clones as well as the other hybrid seedlings, to produce a second generation. The crosses with *L. longiflorum* clones were a total failure. None of the hybrids produced seed when pollinated with *L. longiflorum* pollen, and none of the *L. longiflorum* clones produced seed when pollinated with pollen from the hybrids. The hybrids produced a considerable number of seedpods after being pollinated with pollen from mixed pastel Asiatic hybrids. All the pods were sent to the laboratory for embryo rescue. Several pods also resulted when the pollen of *L. longiflorum* 'Ace' × 'Gypsy' was used on the other Asiatic hybrids with 'Ace' and these were also embryo cultured. The few pods produced from the pollen of low fertility resulted in no viable embryos.

We repeated this work on a larger scale the following year, with nearly identical results. There were far too many pods produced by the cross of the hybrids with pastel Asiatic selections to embryo-culture them all, and several were allowed to ripen normally. We obtained many small, wrinkled seeds in which it was nearly impossible to tell whether an embryo was present. These were sown the following spring, and we were amazed when a considerable number germinated and developed normally.

Because many of the original 'Ace' × Asiatic hybrids were suspected to be triploids, it would have been wise to use tetraploid forms of both the Asiatic hybrids and *Lilium longiflorum* to cross with them. Unfortunately, no such tetraploid forms were available then.

This work has continued in both North America and the Netherlands. Cebeco Lilies of Aurora, Oregon, has strong, beautiful clones in a wide color range, named the Aladdin series, two of which are the yellow 'Aladdin's Dazzle' (Plate 77) and pink 'Aladdin's Quest' (Plate 78). Several fine clones were introduced in fall 1994 by the Park Seed Company as the Showtime series; they include clear peach-pink 'Camelot', soft orange 'Desert Song' (Plate 79), intense yellow 'Easter Bonnet', short wine-pink 'Hello Dolly', rose-pink 'Kiss Me Kate' and 'My Fair Lady' (Plate 80), and cream-white 'South Pacific'. Peter Schenk of Bischoff Tulleken in the Netherlands has produced a wide range of outstanding material from his 'Longistar' (*Lilium longiflorum* × 'Sterling Star'), including salmon-orange 'Centurion', cream-white 'Lamonta', and rose-pink 'Moneymaker'. Another Dutch series is the Royal Series, including wine-pink 'Royal Paradise', cream 'Royal Highness', orange 'Royal Perfume', and yellow 'Royal Victory'.

The names L.A. or A.L. hybrids seem to have become universally accepted for this group of lilies derived from crossing *Lilium longiflorum* with various Asiatic hybrids. They all show strength, hybrid vigor, disease resistance, and virus tolerance that make them exceptional gar-

Plate 77. *Lilium* 'Aladdin's Dazzle'. Photo by Donald Leap, Cebeco Lilies.

Plate 78. *Lilium* 'Aladdin's Quest'. Photo by Donald Leap, Cebeco Lilies.

Plate 79. *Lilium* 'Desert Song'

Plate 80. *Lilium* 'My Fair Lady'. Photo by John E. Elsley.

den plants. Their large, showy, mostly outfacing, and often fragrant flowers are borne on sturdy plants. They can be grown in a wide range of climates; glowing reports have been received from as far north as Winnipeg, Manitoba, and as far south as Louisiana. They are also winning favor in the cut-flower industry and will surely become even more popular as their color range expands. The future seems bright for these remarkable hybrids.

Tetraploid Asiatic Hybrids

Tetraploid Asiatics can be produced by treating scales or other vegetative material with colchicine, or they may occur in natural crosses involving non-reduced gametes. In any case, they are far from recent innovations. Tetraploid forms of 'Brandywine', 'Mega', and 'Mountaineer' were produced in the first half of the twentieth century by Samuel L. Emsweller of the U.S. Department of Agriculture Research Station in Beltsville, Maryland. The method Emsweller finally adopted was to soak freshly removed bulb scales in a 0.2 percent colchicine solution for two to three hours. Subsequently, several tetraploid Asiatic hybrids were produced by crossing diploid second-generation *Lilium pumilum* hybrids; this yielded non-reduced gametes. One cross—['Goldmedal' × (Rainbow hybrid × *L. pumilum*)] × ('Goldmedal' × 'Goldcrest')—resulted in several tetraploid clones in the orange color range. Four other tetraploid Asiatic clones arose naturally from a cross between two diploids— 'Enchantment' × ('Enchantment' × *Lilium pumilum*)—carried out by Jaap van Zuyl in the Netherlands. They were introduced as 'Puchanta', 'Pumena', 'Pumenta', and 'Pumivetta'.

Renewed interest in tetraploids has emerged, especially in the Netherlands, where several commercial firms are involved in the production of these hybrids. The tetraploid clones 'Avignon', 'Gran Paradiso', and 'Nova Cento' are now well known and are grown in the Netherlands in large numbers.

LeVern Freimann of Bellingham, Washington, produced the bright orange, pendent-flowered 'Apricot Supreme' around 1980; it is a magnificent lily of stately habit. A few years later, Freimann showed several beautiful tetraploid seedlings of 'Apricot Supreme' in a range of orange and red shades.

Many diploid Asiatic clones have now been converted to their tetraploid forms by colchicine. They include 'Adelina', 'Capri', 'Connecticut King', 'Connecticut Yankee', 'Corsica', 'Crete', 'Enchantment', 'Gypsy', 'Impact', 'Joanna' (synonym 'Yellow Giant'), 'Malta', 'Matterhorn', 'Mont Blanc', 'Nutmegger', 'Rhodos', 'Sterling Star', and 'Unique' (Plate 81). Besides those already mentioned, we can add to this list the older clones 'Bold Knight' and 'Lumberjack' to form an impressive breeding pool.

Thousands of tetraploid Asiatic seedlings have now been raised, in a wide variety of colors. In the Netherlands, Peter Schenk has an enormous number of excellent plants, and there is indeed much to which we can look forward. Such crosses as 'Gran Paradiso' × 'Lumberjack', 'Apricot Supreme' × 'Connecticut King' tetraploid, and 'Connecticut King' tetraploid × 'Nova Cento' produced fine seedlings in all respects.

A collection of tetraploid Asiatics was introduced in fall 1995 by the Park Seed Company under the name Goliath series. This included three upright-flowered clones—intense orange 'Goliath', rich burgundy 'Samson' (Plate 82), and golden yellow 'Paul Bunyan'—and two pendent ones—bright orange 'Hercules' and warm orange-red 'Gulliver'.

The tetraploid Asiatic lilies have been impressive in all respects. Strong growers, they also display outstanding increase and disease resistance. They are simply bigger in all respects than the diploid forms. Those now available commercially are the forerunners of stunning new colors and forms soon to follow.

Plate 81. *Lilium* 'Unique' (tetraploid form)

Plate 82. *Lilium* 'Samson'

Tetraploid Trumpet Hybrids

We must thank Robert Griesbach of Wisconsin for years of hard, painstaking work with this magnificent group of lilies. He began his work with lilies in 1961, and his first attempts at doubling chromosome numbers involved the use of germinating seeds and seedlings. The seedlings were immersed in a freshly prepared 0.03 percent colchicine solution for 24 hours. Griesbach succeeded in converting the Chinese trumpet lily species *Lilium regale* and *L. leucanthum* var. *centifolium* to their tetraploid forms by this method. He treated bulb scales to convert several other trumpet hybrids, including 'Bright Star', 'White Henryi', and plants from the Golden Splendor strain. His scale treatment is described at the beginning of this chapter. He then crossed these plants to produce a variety of colors. Griesbach released his tetraploid material for commercial production in 1989 and 1990. These lilies were awe-inspiring: the flowers were huge, and the plants larger, stronger, and more stately than their diploid counterparts.

The habit of Griesbach's tetraploid trumpet lilies varied enormously. Some were tall and had the slender, leaning posture of 'Bright Star' and 'White Henryi'; others were of sturdier habit and were used extensively as parents. Long trumpet-shaped flowers occurred in white, golden yellow, pink picotee, and copper tones. The bowl-shaped to open flowers included white and cream with rich orange centers, white and cream with lime green centers, gold, clear yellow, and a few oranges. I decided to intercross each color group individually to produce strains in each color that were strong and virus-free. The finest clones in each color were selected for habit, inflorescence, and flower form and color; they were then scaled for use as superior parents.

We were amazed at the size of the seeds produced by the tetraploid trumpet hybrids. They were at least twice the size of diploid seed. Sown in a cool greenhouse in early spring, the seeds produced enormous cotyledons followed by huge true leaves. We were impressed by their exceptional growth rate and stamina. Several of them formed bulbs 14 to 16 centimeters (about 6 inches) in circumference after only one year in the greenhouse.

The first commercial tetraploid trumpet hybrid strains were introduced in 1995 by Park Seed Company under the name American Classics. Individual color strains were named after national parks. The Grand Canyon strain has white to cream bowl-shaped flowers with orange centers; the Grand Teton strain (Plate 83), bowl-shaped white to cream flowers with soft lime-green centers; the Shenandoah strain, white trumpets with rose-pink petal margins, termed "pink picotees"; the Yellowstone strain, golden yellow trumpet flowers, mostly with dark reverse; and the Yosemite strain, white and cream trumpets, some with green to soft brown reverse. All the flowers are huge. Other col-

Plate 83. *Lilium* Grand Teton strain. Photo by John E. Elsley.

ors, including apricot trumpets and yellow bowls, will be named and introduced when sufficient numbers are available.

These magnificent lilies will bring a spectacular beauty to American gardens, and indeed to gardens all over the world, once they become generally distributed. The propagation of superior clones for commercial sale must now be undertaken to supplement the strains produced annually from seed.

The Orienpets

The marriage of the purple-bulb lilies of China (all trumpet lily species, *Lilium henryi,* and their hybrids) with the Oriental lilies of Japan (*L.alexandrae, L.auratum, L.japonicum, L.nobilissimum, L.rubellum,* and *L.speciosum*) has resulted in a group of lilies of great size, vigor, and beauty. This group is known as the Orienpets (Plate 84).

The forerunner of this group was 'Black Beauty' (*Lilium speciosum* var. *rubrum* × *L. henryi*), hybridized by Leslie Woodriff in the 1950s.

Plate 84. Orienpet bulbs.

'Black Beauty', however, was a mule (totally sterile) in its original diploid form. It was not until 'Black Beauty' was converted to tetraploid form by colchicine that some fertility was realized in it. Tetraploid forms of this clone were produced by Samuel L. Emsweller, LeVern Freimann, Robert Griesbach, and other workers.

Griesbach crossed a tetraploid form of 'Black Beauty' with tetraploid forms of 'White Henryi' to produce several beautiful seedlings, including the well-known 'Leslie Woodriff'. He also bred second- and third-generation crosses (Plate 85) from the original crosses to create hybrids of various colors and color patterns, including clear reds with golden-yellow margins. Most of Griesbach's hybrids possessed some degree of fertility and produced some normal seeds. Griesbach outcrossed the 'Black Beauty' tetraploid hybrids to his tetraploid trumpet hybrids, resulting in many unique new lilies similar to Aurelian hybrids.

Plate 85. A third-generation seedling from crossing a tetraploid form of *Lilium* 'Black Beauty' and a tetraploid form of *L.* 'White Henryi'. Bred by Robert Griesbach.

LeVern Freimann crossed a tetraploid form of 'Black Beauty' with the tetraploid form of 'Journey's End' produced by J. S. Yeates in New Zealand. Freimann hybridized several magnificent clones in the crimson range, including 'Catherine Walton' and 'Scarlet Delight'. Peter Schenk in the Netherlands made the identical cross to produce the beautiful 'Arabesque'. Freimann also crossed a triploid form of 'Thunderbolt' with a tetraploid form of 'Black Beauty' to produce such clones as 'Scheherazade' and 'Vern's Beauty'.

A fascinating variety of Orienpets was produced at Sun Valley Bulb Farms, Arcada, California, in the 1970s. These hybrids displayed a wide variety of colors, seasons, and flower forms, a few of which were similar to those of 'Black Beauty' but with larger flowers. Many of these continue to be grown by Cebeco Lilies of Aurora, Oregon.

The introduction from Japan of *Lilium auratum* var. *platyphyllum* × *L. henryi* opened another door in Orienpet hybridizing (Plate 86). This clone has been used extensively in both North America and the Netherlands. It produces non-reduced gametes and can thus be crossed readily with tetraploids.

The work with Orienpets has been exciting. Most if not all of it is being done on the tetraploid level. Various generations of hybrids from tetraploid forms of 'Black Beauty' are being crossed with second- and third-generation hybrids from *Lilium auratum* × *L. henryi*; the influence of *L. auratum* results in larger flowers. Crossing the Orienpets with tetraploid forms of Oriental hybrids is another exciting venture. Embryo rescue has been used to raise plants from many of these crosses.

The following Orienpet hybrids have been offered commercially to date: 'Arabesque' ('Black Beauty' tetraploid × 'Journey's End' tetraploid), 'Anastasia', 'Catherine the Great', 'Peter the Great', 'Scheherazade', 'Silk Road', 'Spectacular', and 'Starburst Sensation' (Plate 87), a beautiful hybrid of *Lilium speciosum* × 'Damson', produced by Wilbert Ronald of Morden, Manitoba.

The work with Orienpets is being continued by many hybridizers all over the world. Spectacular lilies in this division may be expected to appear in ever-increasing numbers. For example, 'Golden Stargazer', a stocky semi-upright Orienpet with large unspotted flowers and a spicy fragrance, was bred at Van der Salm Bulbfarm and may be the forerunner of new colors especially useful for the forcing industry.

Plate 86. A second-generation hybrid from crossing *Lilium auratum* var. *platyphyllum* with *L. henryi*. Photo by John E. Elsley.

Plate 87. *Lilium* 'Starburst Sensation'

PART THREE

A hybrid with the "spreckles" pattern

CHAPTER 13

Exhibiting Lilies

Lily enthusiasts come together, usually during June and July, to display their finest blooms in organized shows sponsored by the North American Lily Society and regional societies throughout the United States and Canada. Similar shows are held in Europe, the United Kingdom, Australia, and New Zealand. Lily stems are also welcome at flower and general garden shows.

At North American shows, both standard varieties and new introductions are shown. Awards are given, including medals from the American Horticultural Society, and a wide array of trophies, both regional and national. The entries are judged by qualified judges accredited by the North American Lily Society. Complete information about showing lilies can be found in the judging handbook published by the North American Lily Society.

Getting Lilies to a Show

Stems of lilies to be entered in a show should be cut when the first buds show color. They are usually cut two or three days before the judging, so it is essential that they open well before the show begins. If the buds are not colored when cut, no amount of exposure to sunlight or hot showers will induce them to open.

Using a sharp knife or pruners, cut as much of the stem as possible while still leaving at least 14 centimeters (6 inches) of stem to grow on and nourish the bulb. This may not be necessary if the planting contains several stems of the same variety. Cutting should be done early in the morning or late in the evening, under as cool conditions as possible. The foliage should be dry.

If the stems are to be shipped or carried as luggage in boxes, allow them to wilt down until they are, in the words of one authority, "limp as a buggy whip." Placing them in water is a mistake if they are to be packed for shipment. Slightly wilted stems can be packed much more easily without suffering damage; if packed when still turgid, the buds tend to snap off. Opened flowers can be shipped only with special precautions to protect them, such as wrapping tissue paper around the anthers and filaments to prevent staining; this is only worthwhile in the case of truly unique or outstanding stems.

Lay the cut stems in cardboard florist's boxes that have been lined with waxed paper or newspaper. Prevent packed stems from pressing on one another by placing cushions of rolled newspaper between them. The buds can be protected by supporting them with smaller cushions. Florist's waxed paper is useful to separate the layers of stems.

It is very important that florist's boxes be completely filled so that the stems and buds cannot shift. Fasten the stems securely at the center of the box, using strong string.

It is best to store the boxed stems at least overnight at a cool temperature, preferably about 4°C (40°F). A local florist may be able to help in this respect. Lilies that are ready to flower a few days too soon for the show can also be held at cool temperatures in a container without damage for about a week; these too should be cut at the colored-bud stage. The first flowers may open even in cool storage, but this is not a problem if they have only been open for a few days before the show.

Lilies cut for local shows can be placed in water immediately. Five-gallon buckets make good containers; to prevent the stems from touching one another—especially important if open flowers are to be transported—fit a piece of chickenwire over the top of the bucket and insert the stems in the mesh. Place enough stems in a bucket that they support one another, and use sufficient water to weight the bucket and prevent it from tipping. Individual stems can also be carried in large bottles, properly supported. It is quite easy to transport the stems; lilies are tougher than one might imagine!

It is strongly advised that the stems arrive at the show site at least

24 hours before judging. Upon arrival, obtain containers of water and open the boxes immediately. Remove each stem individually, carefully untangling it from the others. Cut 2 to 3 centimeters (about 1 inch) from the bottom of each stem, cutting at a slant to provide a larger exposed surface to absorb water. A sharp knife is better for this than pruners, which tend to crush the stems somewhat.

Straighten out any disarranged buds right away. Once the stems are in water, they begin to absorb it immediately and become turgid in less than half an hour. At that point moving the buds might easily snap them off.

Special care must be taken as the flowers open to prevent pollen from staining the tepals, especially with pale shades such as white and yellow. During transportation of open flowers, the anthers can be carefully covered with soft tissue paper, kept in place with a rubber band. Wet pollen smears very badly, but dry pollen can be brushed off with a small camel's-hair brush.

Grooming Lilies for Exhibition

The exhibitor should make every effort to display his or her lilies at their best. To achieve this, a little grooming may be necessary. Enthusiasts provide themselves with a sharp knife, a pair of sharp scissors, a clean sponge or soft cloth, thin florist's wire, and a soft camel's-hair brush. The following grooming practices are acceptable, provided they do not alter in any way the natural features of the lily stems.

Remove dirt or spray residue from leaf surfaces with a soft sponge or cloth. A very dilute soap solution can safely be used and gives the leaf a slight sheen. Putting oil or wax on the surface is taboo, because it produces an unnatural appearance.

Dead leaves must be carefully removed at the base. Dead tips or even margins of leaves can be snipped delicately away with scissors; it takes a keen eye to spot this surgery, if it is done correctly.

Dead, broken, or diseased floral parts can be removed similarly. A magnificent stem may have one flower that is past, and it is best in such cases to remove the flower and its pedicel, cutting it off with a sharp knife at its junction with the stem. Judges may fail to notice this; if they do notice it, they may deduct points accordingly.

Plate 88. *Lilium* 'Passionate', an outstanding Asiatic hybrid from Columbia-Platte Lilies.

Dry pollen can easily be brushed off open flowers with the camel's-hair brush. Wet, staining pollen, however, must be carefully removed from both petals and leaves with a soft sponge, using slightly soapy water.

Exhibitors who have shipped stems from a distance are often confronted with broken tips, pedicels, or other parts. These can be repaired by inserting a piece of thin florist's wire through the damaged stem or pedicel, providing it is not completely detached. Some exhibitors look askance at this technique, thinking of it as fooling the judges; however, it is heartbreaking to discard a beautiful stem because of a mechanical injury that is not the exhibitor's fault.

The placing of entries differs from show to show. The basic principle is to stage the stem correctly and attractively. Containers consisting of tubes (often made from PVC pipe) set into wooden bases are generally used in American national and regional shows. Remove the lower foliage from the stem so that no leaves are under water. The stem must be firmly set into the container; use a small wedge of florist's foam or wood to keep it in place, if necessary.

Criteria for Judging Lilies

All entries of a single class, such as upright Asiatics (class 1a), are judged against one another. They may be subdivided by color or by clone (if there are many entries of a single clone). Lilies are generally judged by a point system. The primary criterion is condition: stems should be free of any blemish from disease, healthy in appearance, with all open flowers in good condition. Another is vigor, expressed in size and general strong appearance of the entire stem. The flower placement also receives considerable attention: the flowers must not be crowded and should be attractively displayed. The form of the flowers is also very important, with narrow petals generally regarded as inferior. The flower color is given high value: it must be attractive and appealing. The substance of the flowers must also be considered.

Lily shows throughout North America are greatly enriched by several talented amateur hybridizers who show their creations on a regular basis. Ruth and Hugh Cocker from Minnesota, Hod Hoepner from Wisconsin, Vicki Bowen from Maryland, and Arthur Evans from Arkansas are just a few that have made outstanding contributions to the world of lilies.

CHAPTER 14

Hybridizing

In the simplest sense, a hybrid is the offspring of two species. Many genera of plants are capable of producing natural hybrids where the wild ranges of two species intersect. Such natural or wild hybrids are infrequent in the genus *Lilium*; one likely example is *L. pitkinense*. Where lilies from different regions have been brought together in gardens, however, hybrids have always been readily produced, whether by the action of pollinating insects or by the deliberate hand of the hybridizer.

Certain stable groups of lilies resulting from the crosses of true species are distinguished by botanical names with the symbol × between the genus name *Lilium* and the epithet assigned to the particular hybrid group. All members of such a hybrid group are similar to one another within a narrow range of variation; in most cases, they can be crossed with one another and produce offspring similar to themselves. In these senses, they are intermediate between the wild species. *Lilium ×aurelianense* (*L. henryi × L. sargentiae*), *L. ×hollandicum* (*L. maculatum × L. bulbiferum*), and *L. ×testaceum* (*L. candidum × L. chalcedonicum*) are important as garden plants and as the foundations for further hybridizing.

A second category of hybrids is the strain (also called a *group*, although this term is not used much by lily growers). Conventionally, the name of a strain is capitalized but not set off in single quotation marks (as are the names of cultivars). Amethyst Temple and Golden Temple are two examples of strains of Chinese trumpet hybrid lilies. Individual plants in a strain share a common ancestry and are similar in appearance and growth pattern, but they also display minor variations in color, foliage form, and size. When intercrossed, these plants are not likely to produce uniform offspring; therefore, the strain must continually be renewed by recrossing its original parents. The strain is a very important concept in lily breeding because the most economical and efficient way to grow large numbers of virus-free plants is to raise them from seed. The creation of uniform strains is a primary goal of commercial hybridizers.

The final category of hybrids is the clone. A clone is an individual organism with unique genetic material that can be reproduced exactly only by asexual means. In the case of lilies, clones are propagated by such means as scaling and tissue culture. Because lilies are self-sterile, two plants of the same clone cannot cross and produce fertile seed. (In genera that are self-fertile, however, when two individuals of the same clone cross, they produce offspring that are not genetically identical either to the parents or among themselves, because of the manner in which the chromosomes divide and rejoin during the reproductive process; see Chapter 12.) Clones grown as garden plants are also called *cultivars* (from "cultivated variety"). They are distinguished by names that are capitalized and enclosed in single quotations, such as 'Black Beauty' or 'Stargazer'. Most lily clones are hybrids, but clones can also be selected from true species; for example, 'Uchida' is a selected form of *Lilium speciosum*.

Most of the lily strains and cultivars offered in today's catalogs result from many generations of complex crosses. Their ancestry may involve not merely two species but many, with intervening generations featuring unnamed seedlings or named hybrid cultivars.

The enormous growth in the worldwide lily industry—from about 200 hectares (500 acres) in 1974 to more than 2800 hectares (7000 acres) in 1994—was due almost entirely to the early work of Jan de Graaff and his associates at Oregon Bulb Farms in Sandy, Oregon. Their assembling of a wealth of genetic material from many different sources laid the foundation for the commercial lily trade of today. We need to pay tribute to those who were instrumental in bringing hybrid lilies to the exciting stage we now recognize; they included hybridizers from all over the world and from many backgrounds. It is also imperative that others continue their pioneering work, introducing new species and hybrids into breeding lines.

There are more than 90 species of lilies from around the Northern Hemisphere, but only about 22 species have been used to produce the hybrid lilies sold today. Some of these, moreover, have been introduced only recently, and much work has yet to be done in perfecting their hybrids. This means that even the grower interested primarily in garden hybrids has a crucial stake in the conservation of wild species. Many of them are already listed as endangered, and every effort must be made to preserve genetically viable populations in the wild and to establish them in cultivation. This will ensure that both the unique beauty of each species and the qualities it can impart to hybrids survive for the future.

The best lily varieties grown today are not the end; they are the foundation on which the varieties of tomorrow will rise. One of the most difficult problems in hybridizing is the selection of the right parents. Careful judgment can be applied in selecting seedlings or prizewinners on the show bench; it is, however, the parental selections that lay the foundation for success in lily hybridizing.

When a hybridizer chooses parents, he or she must be something of an artist, able to visualize in advance the seedlings that will flower in the future. The hybridizer must weigh the qualities of the two parents along with the peculiarities of their forebears to understand the possibilities offered by a particular combination.

An amateur lily grower working in a home environment has a few advantages not enjoyed by the commercial grower. He or she can choose a group of lilies of special personal interest, while the commercial hybridizer usually has to work in a narrow range dictated by the demands of the market—for example, producing upright Asiatics and Orientals for the cut-flower trade. Lilies hybridized by the amateur, however, need not have great commercial potential.

The mechanics of hybridizing are simple, and nowhere simpler than in lilies. The reproductive parts of the lily flower, the stigma and anthers, are relatively easy to see and handle.

A knowledge of genetics is helpful but not essential to amateur hybridizing. A good hybridizer soon learns from shrewd observation how certain characteristics are inherited. For example, certain lily genes are obviously dominant and others recessive. Thus, if we cross an orange Asiatic lily such as 'Enchantment' with a bright yellow one, such as 'Connecticut King', the seedlings will all be orange-flowered: the orange color is dominant over the recessive yellow. (If the seedlings are hybridized among themselves, about one-quarter of the resulting second-generation seedlings will have yellow flowers as the recessive gene reemerges.) If a genetic factor is *homozygous,* it occurs on both chromosomes of a pair and thus passes to every gamete. The well-known crimson Oriental lily 'Stargazer', for example, carries a homozygous dominant gene for the red color, and when crossed with white and gold Orientals, it produces only red seedlings.

Mendel's Law, which expresses the operation of simple dominance and recessivity, is apparent in the true dwarf Oriental lilies. When a tall Oriental lily is crossed with a dwarf, all the resulting first-generation seedlings are tall, because the tall, or normal, gene is dominant and the dwarf recessive. If we then intercross the first-generation seedlings, the dwarf characteristic will appear in a small number (statistically, about 25 percent) of the second-generation seedlings.

These examples show that second-generation populations are very important in establishing hybrid groups. Most amateur hybridizers fail to explore further than the first-generation seedlings, selecting only the best individuals from a given cross. Recessive characteristics, however, emerge only in the second generation, and many of the most beautiful and unusual features of lilies can be manifested only by this strategy.

Selecting Parent Plants

Hybridizing plants is a complex and sophisticated science, but the few general rules and suggestions outlined here should help the beginner embarking on the adventure of creating new lilies.

The parents should be closely related. The more closely related they are, the greater the chance that viable seed will be produced. Pollen from one lily species is certain to fertilize the seed of another member of the same species, so garden plants of, for example, *Lilium candidum* can be easily crossed, provided they do not result from vegetative increase of a single clone.

Crosses within certain groups wider than the species are also likely to succeed. Asiatic hybrids, martagon hybrids, western American hybrids, trumpet hybrids, and Oriental hybrids are all fertile within their groups to some degree.

Lilies are self-sterile: pollen from one flower on a plant will not fertilize the egg of the same flower, or another flower on the same plant. If two plants are the same clone, they may as well be the same plant: pollen from one will not fertilize the eggs of the other. Hybridizers express this by saying that lilies cannot be "selfed." (Some other kinds of plants are self-fertile and are often selfed by hybridizers.)

The number of chromosomes in the cells of the parents must be the same. A lily cell normally contains 24 chromosomes, which occur in 12 similar (but not identical) pairs; this state is known as *diploid,* because there are two of each type of chromosome. Another state, called *tetraploid* from the word for "four," can occur when chromosome pairs fail to separate during the formation of the normally *haploid* ("half") reproductive cells. Tetraploidy occurs rarely in nature, but it can be induced by the application of certain chemicals, notably colchicine, a very toxic substance derived from *Colchicum* species (another member of the lily family). This state is desired by growers because tetraploid lilies tend to be larger, stronger, and of heavier substance than diploid ones. For a discussion of how this affects hybridizing, see Chapter 12.

Most lilies can be used as either seed or pollen parents—in hybridizer's jargon, they are "fertile both ways"—but some clones are more likely to produce fertile pollen, and others more likely to produce fertile seed. A *reciprocal cross* involves using the pollen of plant "A" on the stigmas of plant "B", and the pollen of "B" on the stigmas of "A". Hybridizers often ask, "Will reciprocal crosses of plants that are fertile both ways produce identical or very similar populations of seedlings?" After many years of conducting reciprocal crosses, I must answer negatively: the inheritance of certain characters is much influenced by whether a given plant is used as the seed or pollen parent. I have never heard a satisfactory explanation for this, but all my experience bears it out.

Mechanics of Hybridizing

We must first distinguish between *pollination* and *fertilization.* It is easy to cross-pollinate two flowers, but fertilization—the fusion of the genetic material from both parent plants—can take place only when several other conditions are fulfilled. After being deposited on the stigma, the pollen grains produce pollen tubes that grow through the style, finally entering the ovules in the ovary and depositing the genetic material carried in the pollen grains. The fertilized egg then develops into a seed that contains the embryo plant.

Pollen is best collected by removing the anthers early in the morning before they *dehisce,* that is, before the surface of the anther opens up, exposing the pollen. The anthers may also be removed by opening the bud when it becomes well colored, ensuring a perfectly clean operation. If the pollen has already dehisced and appears fluffy, the anther should be carefully removed with tweezers; the implements used should be sterilized between each operation by dipping them in a small bottle of alcohol carried for that purpose. The alcohol kills the leftover pollen and prevents contamination.

If you are crossing lilies that do not bloom at the same time, as happens, place the collected anthers in carefully labeled paper or plastic cups and dry them for a few days at room temperature. The duration of this treatment depends on temperature; usually three to four days are sufficient. The room should be insect-proof, because flies and other insects can easily mix the pollens.

Store the dried pollen in small bottles or jars with airtight caps. Pollen stored in a household refrigerator at approximately 4°C (40°F) remains viable for several months. Many hybridizers, however, keep pollen at room temperature, maintaining that it remains viable for months. Pollen can also be kept frozen for an indefinite period after drying. Reports of successful use of four-year-old frozen pollen suggest that much longer frozen storage may be possible.

Remove the anthers from the seed parent before they dehisce, if possible. This helps keep the entire operation as clean and efficient as possible and further prevents cross-contamination. In commercial work the anthers are removed when the buds are well colored, before they open naturally.

The pollen can be applied to the stigma in several ways. A 5-centimeter (2-inch) length of pipe-cleaner is an excellent tool and can be discarded following each pollination. Cotton Q-tips are also useful.

Cover the stigma thoroughly with pollen, preferably immediately after the flower opens. The pollen usually remains in good condition until the stigma becomes receptive. Many hybridizers, however, prefer to wait until the stigma becomes covered with stigmatic fluid, because the stigmatic fluid assists in inducing the formation of pollen tubes. The lifespan of pollens may vary, but I have experienced few problems in pollinating flowers immediately after they opened, obtaining satisfactory seed from both fertile and partially fertile crosses.

Immediately after pollination, cover the stigma with a cap made by wrapping a small square of aluminum foil around the end of a pencil or similar object. Press the open end of the cap gently around the style to secure it. The cap not only prevents other pollen from reaching the stigma, it also protects against the possibility of chemical spray residues reaching the stigma and killing the pollen.

Label the cross clearly by affixing a tag to the stem of the flower. List the seed parent first and the pollen parent second, for example, 'Connecticut King' × 'Red Carpet' (a cross, by the way, that produces beautiful lilies in shades of bright orange, golden yellow, and burgundy red). Every cross must also be recorded in a notebook, listing the cross and the date of pollination. Many hybridizers now transfer this information into a computer database.

Remove faded petals from the pollinated flowers as soon as possible to avoid fungus attack. The style, with cap attached, can remain until a natural abscission layer forms and it drops off. The procedures for harvesting and storing seed are described in Chapter 3.

Aids to Hybridizing

Mixed Pollens

Some lily hybridizers state that they have achieved greater success by applying a mixture of pollens from several plants. The theory is that the more compatible pollen (from closely related plants) induces receptivity in the stigma, which then allows the penetration of the less compatible (more distantly related) pollen; the latter is then able to reach and fertilize a proportion of the eggs. There is a strong possibility that certain mixtures of pollen may facilitate fertilization by normally incompatible pollen. The famous hybridizer Leslie Woodriff and his family used large quantities of mixed pollen for many years in their program. Perhaps the many unique combinations they produced will encourage others to experiment with this method. Obviously, there are drawbacks to this technique, primarily the inability to record and repeat crosses with confidence. A list of the pollens used will also be help-ful in identifying "unusual" seedlings when they flower.

Warm Temperatures

There is no question that warm or even hot ambient temperature is highly beneficial in stimulating pollen-tube growth and fertilization. For example, the clone 'Edith Cecilia' was for many years pollinated out-doors at Oregon Bulb Farms to produce the Harlequin hybrids. Many flowers had to be pollinated to obtain a sufficient quantity of seed. Then one year, temperatures near 38°C (100°F) occurred during the pollina-tion period, and the seed yield was almost tripled.

Over many years we used a small greenhouse to assist in unusual and difficult crosses. The temperature was allowed to soar during polli-nation. Among the many unusual crosses achieved here were between *Lilium longiflorum* and Asiatic lilies, *L. lankongense* and Asiatics, and *L. nobilissimum* and Oriental hybrids. Workers pollinating lilies at very high temperatures have a distinct advantage over those working at cooler temperatures. The high temperatures may, however, induce the formation of non-reduced gametes (see Chapter 12), introducing a new set of polyploid hybrids.

Amputated Styles

Sometimes pollen tubes penetrate the style for only a short distance and fail to reach the ovules. This can be true when the seed parent has a longer style than the pollen parent. A method has therefore been de-veloped to achieve results in crosses that are difficult because of this kind of incompatibility. The style is simply cut at an angle just above the ovary. Clean stigmatic fluid, or a sugar solution, is smeared on the cut surface before the pollen is applied. Stigmatic fluid is easy to col-lect from many lilies, including Chinese trumpet lilies and *Lilium longi-florum.*

Hot Water Treatment. In a method developed by Peter Archer at the University of Minnesota, the style is dipped in water at 49°C (120°F) for 5 to 6 minutes just before the pollen is applied. This apparently has the same advantage as high ambient temperature in stimulating the growth of pollen tubes.

Chemical Treatment. It has been suggested that the application of the growth-stimulating compound naphthalene acetic acid (NAA) to the base of the ovary may facilitate fertilization. There is limited information at present regarding the success or failure of this method.

Mentor or Recognition Pollens. To accomplish fertilization between incompatible plants, a compatible "mentor" or "recognition" pollen is first killed by freezing and thawing, gamma radiation, or treatment with methanol or ether. The killed pollen is then mixed with fresh incompatible pollen, and the mixture is liberally dusted on the stigma. If the procedure is correctly carried out, all the progeny will be sired by the normally incompatible parent.

Testing Pollen. When attempting crosses using unusual hybrids as parents, such as *Lilium longiflorum* × Asiatic clones or Orienpets, it is wise to test the pollen before using it. In many cases infertile pollen can be detected by the naked eye: it is crumbly rather than fluffy. To test questionable pollen, place it on a glass slide in a drop of clean stigmatic fluid, or in a solution made up by using one milliliter of a stock concentrate (200 milligrams of boric acid in 100 milliliters of water) with 9 milliliters of water and 1 gram of sugar. Cover the pollen and fluid with a smaller slide. Viable pollen will form pollen tubes in a few hours at room temperature, and these can be seen with a microscope at low magnification (40× to 100×). The normal pollen grains appear like footballs, with a thick pollen tube growing from one end. Pollen of low fertility consists mostly of shriveled, empty grains, with a few normal grains mixed in; the appearance of a few pollen tubes can be quite exciting in such cases.

Breeding Lilies with Staying Power

Are the hybridizers of today producing lilies with staying power equal to those of yesteryear? How many of the beautiful colors in the Asiatic and Oriental lilies of today will still be seen in gardens 50 years from now? Are the newer clones and strains true perennial jewels that will return year after year? These questions should be of concern to all lily enthusiasts.

Lily hybridizing has without question come a long way since the 1970s. More lilies are being sold than ever before, and the public has been induced to look beyond the Easter lily and tiger lily. Many of the newer clones, however, have been bred with the cut-flower and forcing industries in mind; examples are 'Acapulco', 'Berlin', 'Marco Polo', 'Stargazer', 'White Stargazer', and 'Woodriff's Memory'. It is too early to evaluate the disease resistance or tolerance, or the garden usefulness of such plants, bred as they were for mass production under carefully controlled conditions. I am confident that some fine garden lilies will emerge from the host of varieties (particularly upright Asiatic clones) now being grown in the Netherlands, but it will take time to find out which ones are dependable in the home garden. Of those introduced in the 1970s, 'Connecticut Beauty' (synonym 'Medallion'), 'Flaming Giant' (synonym 'Moulin Rouge'), 'Gold Lode' (synonym 'Golden Melody'), and 'King Pete' have successfully made the transition.

When pondering the problem of breeding peers to the long-lived lilies of earlier times, I am reminded of the wise counsel I received from two friends. Harold F. Comber advised, "Go back to a true line, either crossing two separate species, or crossing a species with a related hybrid of proven disease-resistant and staying-power qualities." I received almost identical advice from the late Donald Egolf of the Washington Arboretum, who was quite instrumental in my decision to become a plant hybridizer. I followed this advice on several occasions and usually obtained strong, disease-resistant hybrids. A brief account of early lily hybrids and these results shows how hybrid vigor, staying power, and disease resistance can be established.

In the 1960s we worked with the remarkable Russian lily *Lilium ×fialkovaja*, listed as a hybrid between *L. monadelphum* and *L. bulbiferum*. Its carmine-lilac flowers with yellow centers emit a delicate fragrance similar to violets. It propagates readily. Judith Freeman crossed it with pastel Asiatic hybrids to produce the Faberge strain, magnificent Mayflowering lilies. Although slow to propagate and establish after transplanting, once settled the Faberge strain persists for many years, and second-generation hybrids are equally rewarding.

I remember huge clumps of *Lilium ×testaceum* (*L. candidum* × *L. chalcedonicum*) growing in gardens on the west coast of Scotland many years ago. There was also a large planting near Sandy, Oregon. The first lilies from this cross were probably raised in Germany or the Netherlands about 1810. *Lilium ×testaceum* has been backcrossed to both of its parents to produce some charming though frail hybrids.

The robust Bellingham hybrids dating back to 1918 originated from complex crosses of *Lilium humboldtii, L.pardalinum,* and *L.parryi.* I have seen spectacular clumps of them at Wisley in Surrey, England, growing 200 to 240 centimeters (7 to 8 feet) tall. The clones 'Buttercup', 'Shuksan', and 'Star of Oregon' were excellent.

The Backhouse hybrids, well remembered at Edinburgh, go back as far as 1890; they were hybrids of *Lilium hansonii* with *L.martagon,* and jewels of persistence in most gardens. A similar cross between *L.martagon* var. *album* and *L. hansonii* produced the Paisley hybrids at Oregon Bulb Farms in 1950; the clear colors in the second generation were memorable.

At a hotel in Vernon, British Columbia, about 1963, I saw a planting of immensely strong lilies. These were one of the *Lilium ×hollandicum* or candlestick lilies originating in Europe in 1922 that persist in good health for many years. Probably hybrids between *L. ×elegans* and *L.bulbiferum,* they can be seen in gardens throughout Europe and North America and have produced many excellent descendants.

Returning again to Edinburgh, I remember the huge plantings of Stenographer hybrids, produced early in the twentieth century by Isabella Preston in Canada. These lilies, hybrids of *Lilium davidii* var. *willmottiae* with *L. dauricum,* were used extensively in early breeding at Oregon Bulb Farms. I am assured that several of the named clones from this group still flourish in Canada.

Among the early trumpet hybrids, I note 'George C. Creelman', a cross of *Lilium regale* with *L. sargentiae.* The stable hybrid group from this cross is known as *L. ×imperiale;* the Sentinel hybrids at Oregon Bulb Farms were descendants of these strong, noble lilies. The fine clone 'T. A. Havemeyer' (*L. sulphureum* × *L. henryi*) from Tom Barry still persists in gardens. Finally, all lily enthusiasts are familiar with 'White Henryi' (*L. henryi* × *L. leucanthum* var. *centifolium*), a member of the North American Lily Society's Hall of Fame (Plate 89). All these gems can produce strong, beautiful hybrids as well.

Lilium pumilum is involved in some Asiatic hybrids of great staying

Plate 89. *Lilium* 'White Henryi', a fragrant trumpet hybrid selected by Leslie Woodriff in the 1940s

power. I found J. C. Taylor's 'Goldcrest' (Asiatic hybrid × *L. pumilum* 'Golden Gleam') to be excellent in trials of persistence, as was Charles Robinson's 'Scarlet Robe' ('Edna Kean' × *L. pumilum*).

It may be too soon to tell which Oriental lilies are champions in persistence. 'Black Beauty' (*Lilium speciosum* × *L. henryi*) was the first clone elevated to the North American Lily Society Hall of Fame; 'Journey's End' (*L. speciosum* 'Gilrey' × 'Philippa') also persists for years. Two other older Orientals that survive include 'Allegra' (a backcross of [*L. auratum* × *L. speciosum*] to *L. speciosum* var. *album*) and 'American Eagle' (*L. auratum* var. *platyphyllum* × 'Imperial Silver').

Some more strong, persistent hybrids derived closely from species are the following: 'Aristo' ('Tabasco' × *Lilium dauricum*); 'Sinai', 'Salute', and 'Sahara' ('Connecticut King' × *L. dauricum*); 'Adelina', 'Cordelia', 'Joanna' (synonym 'Yellow Giant'), 'Pollyanna', and 'Vanessa' (*L. wilsonii* var. *flavum* × 'Connecticut King'; the Yellow Blaze strain ('Nutmegger' × *L. wilsonii* var. *flavum*); and Peter Schenk's strong 'Gran Sasso' (*L. wilsonii* × Rainbow type seedling). A race of very strong seedlings was also developed from crossing 'Schuetzenlisl' with *L. wilsonii*.

Judith Freeman and Leonard Marshall used species quite extensively in their work, and the list of good garden lilies they developed is impressive. 'Callie' (*Lilium callosum* var. *flaviflorum* × *L. amabile*) is a graceful lily with small, pendent orange flowers. 'Viva' (*L. pumilum* × *L. leichtlinii* var. *maximowiczii* 'Unicolor'), with glossy red-orange pendent flowers, can attain a height of 200 centimeters (7 feet). 'Big Max' and 'Last Dance' derived from complex crosses between *L. leichtlinii* var. *maximowiczii* 'Unicolor' and 'Connecticut King'. 'Smiley' (*L. amabile* × 'Connecticut Lemonglow') has soft golden flowers with a ring of spots and is slightly fragrant. 'Tinkerbelle' ([['Hartford' × 'Connecticut Lass'] × *L. cernuum*] × *L. cernuum*) is a delightful miniature with small, pendent pink flowers and graceful foliage; the taller 'Elf', from the same breeding, has myriad pollen-free pink flowers. The Summit strain (*L. callosum* var. *flaviflorum* × several complex Asiatic hybrids) comprises unusual late-flowering hybrids with small upright, outfacing, or pendent bright yellow flowers. 'Tiger Babies' ('Pink Tiger' × pastel Asiatics) has heavily spotted flowers of a unique peach-salmon shade; 'Pink Tiger', the seed parent, came from Leslie Woodriff, who listed it as a hybrid of *L. tigrinum* with *L. regale*.

Of special interest is a cross between *Lilium leichtlinii* var. *maximowiczii* 'Unicolor' and *L. dauricum*. The former (the seed parent) was a highly virus-tolerant clone that had persisted in Edgar Kline's garden in Lake Grove, Oregon, for many years. The first-generation seedlings had bright orange, spotted flowers, even though both parents were unspotted; the seedlings showed great hybrid vigor, reaching 200 centimeters (7 feet) in height. They were interpollinated to produce an interesting second generation. The most fascinating second-generation selection was a soft orange, upright-flowered clone with a dark brushmark, something quite different then. It was crossed with 'Connecticut King', and the clones 'Accent', 'Endeavor', 'Impact', and 'Vanguard' were selected from the resulting population. A host of other fine clones has been developed from this line by other hybridizers.

A similar line of fine material arose from crosses with *Lilium pumilum*. Four fertile seedlings resulted from Leonard Marshall's cross ('Tabasco' × *L. dauricum*) × *L. pumilum* in the late 1960s; they became the ancestors of a wealth of beautiful material produced at Columbia-Platte Lilies and Oregon Bulb Farms, notably 'Aloft', 'Musette', and

'Neon Lights'. Charles Robinson of Erin, Ontario, also bred some excellent hybrids from *L. pumilum*; his 'Wowee' and 'Cabriole' were introduced by Columbia-Platte.

The hybrids between *Lilium cernuum* and *L. davidii* produced by Cecil Patterson are fundamental to the present pink and white Asiatic lilies. 'Edith Cecilia', one of the Cernuum Hybrid clones, still survives and should be brought back into breeding programs.

Chris North's *Lilium lankongense* hybrids are truly spectacular; the influence of *L. davidii* is also pronounced in them. The Chippendale and Rosepoint Lace strains from Judith Freeman have a unique, refined beauty and are more virus-tolerant than their parental Southern Belles strain. North's cultivars have more *L. davidii* ancestry and appear to be more virus-tolerant still.

Many enthusiasts remember Charles Robinson's 'June Fragrance', a hybrid between *Lilium candidum* var. *salonikae* and *L. monadelphum*, similar to the long-ago cross that produced *L. ×testaceum*. Leonard Marshall and Judith Freeman raised plants from the reciprocal cross (*L. monadelphum* × *L. candidum*) via embryo culture. Two offspring of 'June Fragrance'—'Limerick' and 'Uprising'—are still grown commercially.

Several Asiatic clones have been crossed with *Lilium longiflorum*, the Easter lily. The resulting hybrids include Peter Schenk's 'Longistar' (*L. longiflorum* × 'Sterling Star'); Columbia-Platte's strong, healthy 'Red Ace' (*L. longiflorum* × 'Red Carpet'); and 'Casa Rosa', bred by Yoshito Asano in Japan and introduced in the Netherlands. 'Yuri no Hakari' (*L. auratum* var. *platyphyllum* × *L. longiflorum*) shows great promise (Plate 90).

The trumpet species hold treasures yet to be discovered. A cross made in 1970 between 'Bright Star' and *Lilium regale* underscores this: the few seedlings had bowl-shaped flowers with orange centers and proved quite fertile. This material still survives and holds out the hope of obtaining the much-desired early flowering Aure-

Plate 90. *Lilium* 'Yuri no Hakari', a Japanese introduction. Photo by John E. Elsley.

lian lilies. Also in this division, 'Thunderbolt' (*L. henryi* × *L.* ×*aurelianense*) has stood the test of time despite some susceptibility to virus, inherited from its grandparent *L. sargentiae.*

Many exceptional crosses have been made with Oriental lilies, using superior forms selected from the species, especially *Lilium auratum* var. *platyphyllum, L.japonicum, L.rubellum,* and *L.speciosum.* Three that produced outstanding seedlings were (*L. speciosum* 'Shooting Star' × 'Stargazer'); (*L. speciosum* 'Shooting Star' × *L. alexandrae*); and (*L. nobilissimum* × 'Pink Glory'). A fourth, (*L.nobilissimum* × 'Imperial Silver'), gave pure whites such as 'Giselle'. Peter Schenk bred a fine clear pink clone from (*L. speciosum* 'Uchida' × *L. nobilissimum*).

The great promise of returning to true lines is apparent when we realize that many species have yet to add their beauty to the hybrid gene pool. *Lilium nepalense, L. taliense, L. wardii,* and many North American species must have enormous potential.

None of this promise can ever be realized, however, unless we direct research efforts toward the preservation of species. We must establish connections worldwide and work diligently to promote the preservation of wild populations. We must also establish in cultivation populations of pure species, grown from sufficient quantities of wild-collected seed that the genetic diversity of each species is well represented. Such stocks will ensure both the preservation of species threatened in the wild, and the availability of material for the hybrids of tomorrow.

Principles of Commercial Hybridization

Many years of experience in hybridizing, selecting, testing, and growing hundreds of thousands of seedlings have made me aware of the necessity for clear rules and guidelines in a commercial breeding program. These allow growers to benefit from the lessons of the past and to avoid repeating unfruitful breeding lines. Amateur lily hybridizers also need to understand and use similar guidelines in their efforts.The following principles are distilled from the lessons learned in years of patient work.

1. A thorough knowledge of lilies, both species and hybrids, is essential if the work is to be meaningful and productive.

Plate 91. *Lilium* 'Willowwood'

2. A well-planned program must be outlined, with expected goals
   clearly established. We can hybridize not only to produce
   outstanding clones but also to develop uniform strains (groups)
   in species and certain kinds of hybrids. For example, excellent
   uniform strains of trumpet and Oriental hybrids have been
   produced commercially for many years.
3. Lilies selected from seedling populations for clonal propagation
   must have color, form, and habit with high commercial appeal.
   Important elements for success include tepal substance, good

flower form, attractive inflorescence with the flowers well spaced and not crowded, appealing foliage, strong stems, and good bulb form.

4. The clones or strains selected must be strong-growing (a result of hybrid vigor). In the case of clones, they must exhibit rapid natural multiplication and perform well in asexual propagation, whether by scaling or by tissue culture.

5. Tolerance of virus disease is critical for all clones. In the production of seedling strains, it is preferable that both parents be highly virus-tolerant. Lilies must persist and grow well despite infection if they are to survive in gardens for any time.

6. Lilies must also possess resistance to fungal disease, especially basal rot caused by *Fusarium* and *Cylindrocarpon*. In addition, a remarkable resistance to *Botrytis* blight has been observed in some species and hybrids, such as *Lilium lankongense*. Reports indicate that Dutch hybridizers are producing lilies with more resistance to basal rot, an encouraging development.

7. A selection must be adaptable to commercial handling, storage, and shipping. Bulbs with less susceptibility to mechanical damage and decay are to be preferred.

8. Varieties destined for cut-flower and pot-plant growing must be adaptable to year-round forcing. They must be able to grow satisfactorily under stress and low light. Both the cut flower stems and the potted plants must store and ship well. Vase life is also critical.

9. Meticulous records must be kept of all crosses, clonal selections, field and greenhouse trials, and other phases. All material must be carefully labeled.

CHAPTER 15

Lilies Around the World

Lilies are grown commercially in several centers: North America, Australia, New Zealand, the Netherlands, South Africa, and several smaller countries in Europe and South America.

North America

The western United States has been the center of lily growing in North America since the middle of the twentieth century. The coastal region of southern Oregon and northern California has been an important center for growing Easter lilies (*Lilium longiflorum*) since the end of World War II. Later years witnessed an increase in the planting of other lily varieties there, particularly Orientals, which seem to prefer the cooler growing conditions of this coastal region.

Oregon Bulb Farms commenced commercial growing of lilies in the early 1950s; the bulk of its crops over the following 35 years were grown in the northern Willamette Valley, just south of Portland, Oregon. Crops were also grown near Sandy, 20 miles east of Portland in the foothills of the Cascade Mountains. In its final years of operation, this company ventured into widely scattered locales in western Washington, including fields near Woodland, Mossyrock, and Mount Vernon. The soils in these areas varied from clay loam to very sandy loam and their pH ranged from 5 to 7. The soils also varied dramatically in humus content. Despite these variables, excellent crops of lily bulbs were produced at all sites.

There are, however, certain disadvantages to growing lilies in western Oregon and Washington in the area west of the Cascade range known as the Maritime Northwest. Spring rains can play havoc with plantings, particularly if the soil remains saturated until mid-May or even early June. Many lilies are close to flowering stage then, and the growing season is drastically reduced for these late-planted bulbs.

The rains of western Oregon also dictate an end to harvesting by the third week of October in a typical year. At that time soils become so saturated that diggers and other heavy equipment cannot move through the fields. Ideally, a grower should be able to harvest lilies through late November.

To solve these problems and increase production, Oregon Bulb Farms moved part of its growing operation to the Yakima Valley of eastern Washington in the early 1970s. This venture was quite successful. Bulbs could be planted at ideal times in spring, and harvest could continue through early December when necessary. *Botrytis* blight, the foliar disease that plagues lilies in the maritime region during periods of wet, muggy weather, also seemed to be absent in the semiarid climate of the Yakima Valley. The cost of spraying to control this disease was virtually eliminated.

Large commercial crops of lilies have been grown very successfully in the Columbia Basin of northeastern Oregon. If adequate water supplies continue to be available and diseases are controlled, this venture should flourish.

New Zealand

The island nation of New Zealand has a mild temperate climate; the prevailing maritime influence creates rapid weather changes, frequent rains, and a narrow range of temperature variation between summer and winter. Combined with abundant sunshine—at least 2000 hours a year in most places—these conditions are ideal for growing many kinds of plants, including most lilies.

Lilies were sold by nurseries here as early as 1851. British settlers imported many favorite plants for the colonial community. In 1882 Nairn and Sons were offering 11 varieties of lilies; 24 years later the number of lilies offered had doubled to 23 varieties. Interest in lily growing as a hobby increased, and the New Zealand Lily Society was formed in 1932; it was the first lily society in the world. Another group, the Auckland Lily Society, was established in 1953.

Perhaps the foremost New Zealand lily hybridizer was J. S. Yeates of Palmerston North. A botanist by profession, he was given the Oriental lily 'Crimson Queen' by a nurseryman in the 1930s and embarked on a hybridizing program using this and other Orientals. The famous clone 'Journey's End', important in many breeding programs, came from his work. Yeates also bred the earliest Oriental lilies of dwarf stature, leading to the Little Rascals strain.

Leslie Jury of New Plymouth, another noted hybridizer, created a beautiful garden of rhododendrons, camellias, native plants, and lilies in an abandoned quarry. He began hybridizing Oriental lilies in 1949, eventually developing the Parkmannii hybrids and Samson strain. He distributed seed to growers around the world so they could carry on his work, broadening the color range and creating Orientals that would flourish in areas where *Lilium auratum* had been considered difficult.

Other important lily breeders of New Zealand include L. Tuffery, creator of the Zealandia hybrids strain of Oriental lilies; Don J. Ross, whose 'Marlynn Ross' was extensively used in breeding upright Asiatic hybrids; Dick Barry of Auckland, who concentrated on yellow trumpet lilies; and Athol Smith of Kaiapoi, a great grower and exhibitor of trumpets.

New Zealand's largest producer of lilies in the mid-twentieth century was Harrison's Nurseries, founded by R. E. Harrison. Today the country's leading commercial producer of lilies is Lilies International, in Levin. Blessed with 100 centimeters (40 inches) of rainfall annually and a silt loam soil, Lilies International grows Oriental, trumpet, and Asiatic lilies using modern mechanized methods and careful hygiene. It sells prepackaged bulbs to home gardeners and supplies cut-flower growers all over the world, 12 months a year. The company was founded in the 1960s by William F. Doreen, who had been a student of Yeates in Wellington and obtained his first stocks there. The nursery also acquired the entire stock of Jury's *Lilium auratum* × *L. speciosum* hybrids, which had been grown virus-free; over the years several fine clones were selected from this group.

Lilies International began a large-scale breeding program in the early 1970s, which continues today, concentrating on Oriental lilies. Two of their noted introductions are 'Casa Blanca' (synonym 'Snowdrift'), an outfacing pure white once described by Harold F. Comber as the best white *Lilium auratum* hybrid he had seen; and 'Black Knight', a semi-dwarf Oriental lily, about 40 centimeters (15 inches) tall, with mahogany red, white-margined flowers in proportion to the plant's height. Several good dwarf forms have been produced using 'Black Knight'.

The company's current breeding program is concentrated on improving the upright-flowered Orientals so popular in the cut-flower trade. 'Stargazer' was crossed with plants that featured taller stems, good leaf color, strong root systems, and resistance to *Botrytis*. Standout clones have included 'Ballet Improved', with a touch of pink on the midrib of the petal; 'Candy Floss', with huge flowers of delicate pink; and 'Celebration', a rich red. A lily selected by Dutch cut-flower growers was distinguished by having little fragrance, a desirable quality to customers who feel the usual Oriental perfume is overpowering in a small room.

Australia

Lilies grow very well in the southern half of Australia, where winter temperatures fall below 10°C (50°F) at night for at least two months. In the tropical or dry north of the continent, they succeed only in isolated microclimates. The finest lily-growing areas are the Dandenong Ranges, Mount Madecon, and Gippsland in Victoria, where the rich volcanic soil is amended with leaf litter from deciduous trees and eucalypts. The ground is usually sloping, often with a rocky substrate to improve drainage. Other regions where lilies thrive include parts of Adelaide and the Lofty Ranges, providing soil and water alkalinity can be counteracted; this is often done with a mulch of pine bark. In New South Wales lilies are grown around Sydney (where they need afternoon shade), along the Great Dividing Range, and in the Blue Mountains. In Tasmania lilies do well in the cool inland hills, but not in the coastal areas.

In the tropical north lilies are almost impossible to grow. The bulbs must be lifted and artificially cooled to provide the cold period they require, and the high summer rainfall induces fungus diseases, such as *Fusarium*. In Western Australia, the long, hot, dry summers are not to the liking of lilies, and what water can be provided is often alkaline. Gardeners determined to grow lilies need to work hard, improving the soil with compost and applying thick mulches. One keen gardener on the edge of the Simpson Desert was able to succeed with trumpet lilies by growing them in the shade under 45 centimeters (18 inches) of mulch.

Hybrid Asiatic, trumpet, and Oriental lilies are all popular in Australia. A few species are also grown, particularly *Lilium lancifolium,* the tiger lily. *Lilium formosanum* has escaped from gardens and become naturalized so extensively that it is now classed as a noxious weed in New South Wales.

During the 1950s and 1960s, Australia and New Zealand were in the forefront of lily breeding and growing, but Dutch varieties now dominate the market. The Dutch hybrids, however, are not always well suited to the Australian climate, and enthusiasts understand the need to preserve such vigorous older, southern-bred clones as Roy Wallace's 'Jillian Wallace', or Eric Genat's 'Apricot Belle', 'Christabel', 'Mimosa Star', 'Sungold', and 'Wildfire'. Eric's son Peter is carrying on the family lily business and producing new varieties.

As cut flowers, lilies enjoy great popularity in Australia. Thousands of Dutch-grown bulbs are imported every month for year-round forcing. Many are cropped three times before being discarded. Some also are resold to home gardeners. Because many of the cut-flower varieties are patented, they may not be propagated in Australia. Perhaps as a result, tissue culture has not yet become a widespread technique here. Instead, most growers rely on division and scaling to increase their stocks.

The Australian Lilium Society (enthusiasts here use the word *lilium* instead of *lily*) was formed in 1957 by a band of dedicated growers, including Robert Withers and Gordon Chandler, both of whom are still active in the society. The society meets monthly and holds annual shows, as well as running a seed exchange and a library. Members also receive a bulletin. Chandler, although nearly 90 years old, gives frequent lectures and continues to hybridize. His introductions include two selections of *Lilium speciosum*—'Calanthe's Favourite' and 'Claire of Calanthe'—the three Oriental lilies—'Cymbeline', the popular, hardy 'Electra', and 'Opaline'.

The Netherlands

In the Netherlands, the land of flowers, the production of lilies is the fourth most important segment of that industry, exceeded only by roses, chrysanthemums, and tulips. Dutch lily growing is devoted almost entirely to the production of bulbs for cut flowers, many of which are exported all over the world. There are also many greenhouse cut-flower producers in the country; in 1995 a total of 317,906,235 stems of lilies was sold at Dutch flower auctions, for a total revenue of about $176 million.

Asiatic Lilies

Before 1960, the lily varieties grown in the Netherlands consisted mainly of a few clones of *Lilium* ×*hollandicum* such as 'Fire King' and 'Orange Triumph', as well as clones of *L. longiflorum* and *L. speciosum.*

The introduction of 'Enchantment' from Oregon Bulb Farms in 1960 revolutionized the Asiatic lily cut-flower industry in the Netherlands; acreage devoted to this variety reached approximately 300 hectares (750 acres) in the mid-1970s. Fifteen years later, the beautiful bright yellow 'Connecticut King' was introduced, giving the industry a second boost and reaching 300 hectares (750 acres) by the mid-1980s. During the mid-1970s several varieties in the new pastel color range were introduced from Oregon Bulb Farms, including salmon 'Chinook', rose-pink 'Scout', and cream-white 'Sterling Star' (Plate 92).

Plate 92. *Lilium* 'Sterling Star', introduced to the Netherlands from the United States in the 1970s. Photo by Herman v. Wall.

Table 15-1 shows how Dutch lily production has increased since 1960. The land devoted to lilies constituted only 1 percent of total flowerbulb acreage in 1960, but by 1996 it had risen to more than 16 percent.

Several Dutch companies have been busy developing new varieties of Asiatics, mostly since the early 1970s. The earliest of these growers were

Table 15-1. Land devoted to lily bulb production in the Netherlands, in hectares (2.5 hectares = 1 acre).

YEAR	ALL BULBS (hectares)	LILY BULBS (hectares)	LILIES (percent)
1960	10,242	102	1.0
1970	12,228	227	1.9
1980	14,307	1,119	7.8
1990	15,293	2,574	16.2
1996	18,356	3,055	16.6

Laan Brothers and De Jong Lilies, followed by Vletter and den Haan, Bischoff Tulleken, Hoffgaarde B.V., Sande B.V., and several others. Special attention has been paid to breeding varieties suitable for low light conditions in greenhouses, and those with clear colors and larger flowers. Many breeders, such as Bischoff Tulleken, are also working extensively with tetraploids and pot lily varieties.

A fascinating new color pattern has been introduced to the Dutch trade via the clone 'Tango Nocturno', bred by Victor Orekov in Latvia. This pattern, which has been called "spreckles," consists of dark spotting or small blotches that are densest toward the center of the flower (Plate 93). It is readily inherited and beautiful hybrids have been obtained by crossing it with both Asiatics and *Lilium longiflorum* × Asiatic hybrids.

Table 15-2 lists the leading Asiatic lily varieties grown in the Netherlands in 1996.

Oriental Lilies

The second most important group of lilies in the Netherlands are the Orientals. Their production was launched with the introduction of the upright crimson 'Stargazer' in the early 1970s. Hybridized by Leslie Woodriff, 'Stargazer' was originally grown at Sun Valley Bulb Farms in California and sold by them to several Dutch companies. Its rapid increase was due to tissue culture: perhaps every laboratory in the Netherlands was propagating this clone during its early years. In 1996 nearly 400 hectares (1000 acres) of 'Stargazer' were being grown in the Netherlands, by far the most land devoted to any single lily variety.

Plate 93. A hybrid with the 'spreckles' pattern introduced to the Dutch trade via *Lilium* 'Tango Nocturno', bred by Latvian Victor Orekov. Photo by Bischoff Tulleken.

Table 15-2. Leading hybrid lilies produced in the Netherlands in 1996.

Asiatics
'Adelina', bright yellow with gold blotch
'America', purplish-red
'Avignon', an orange-red tetraploid
'Chianti', strong pink
'Compass', soft orange
'Cordelia', bright yellow with gold
    blotch
'Dreamland', yellow with gold blotch
'Gibraltar', bicolor
'Gran Paradiso', orange-red tetraploid
'Gran Sasso', vivid orange
'Hilde', bright yellow
'Jolanda', red-orange
'Mona', bright yellow
'Monte Negro', blood-red
'Montreaux', rose
'Nova Cento', vivid yellow tetraploid
'Pollyanna', bright yellow with gold
    blotch
'Prato', reddish-orange

'Sancerre', pure white
'Sole Mio', bright yellow
'Vivaldi', purple-pink
'Yellow Giant', yellow with gold blotch

Upright Orientals
Acapulco', rose pink
'Berlin', purple-pink
'Con Amore', rose-pink
'Dame Blanche', pure white
'Le Rève', soft pink
'Marco Polo', soft pink
'Mediterranee', purple-pink
'Merostar', deep crimson
'Muscadet', white with pink marks
'Pesaro', purple-pink
'Siberia', pure white
'Stargazer', dark crimson
'White Stargazer', white
'Woodriff's Memory', soft pink

Several other Oriental varieties were introduced from Sun Valley in the early 1970s, with 'Le Rêve' (synonym 'Joy'), an early flowering soft pink, being the most useful and best known. In 1996, there were 47 hectares (118 acres) devoted to 'Le Rêve'.

Other Dutch companies became very active in Oriental hybridizing following these introductions. The leading introductions eventually came from the firms of Vletter and den Haan and Bischoff Tulleken. Both used 'Stargazer' and 'Le Rêve' extensively in their programs. Table 15-2 lists the leading upright Oriental lilies in Dutch production at present.

Although upright Orientals dominate in the Netherlands, the outfacing pure white 'Casa Blanca' has also been grown in large numbers. It is very popular in wedding arrangements. Other exceptions to the general trend are 'Mona Lisa' and several other shorter Oriental lilies introduced by the talented breeder Johann Mak.

Lilium longiflorum × Asiatic Hybrids

Another important group is the *Lilium longiflorum* × Asiatic hybrids or L.A. hybrids. Breeding of these was begun in the Netherlands in 1977 by Peter Schenk of Bischoff Tulleken, who was inspired by slides of a hybrid between *L. longiflorum* and the trumpet lily 'Damson', produced by Peter Ascher at the University of Minnesota. This lily resembled a pink *L. longiflorum*. He had also seen slides of crosses made in Japan between *L. longiflorum* and *L. auratum,* and at Sun Valley between *L. longiflorum* and *L. centifolium* 'Black Dragon'.

In 1977 Schenk made several crosses between *Lilium longiflorum* and Asiatic hybrids. He was careful in his choice of *L. longiflorum* clones, using 'Indian Summer', which was not susceptible to "second growth" (premature sprouting) as many varieties of *L. longiflorum* are. He employed the amputated style and embryo culture techniques to obtain these hybrids. Successful crosses occurred with 'Aristo', 'Connecticut King', 'Sterling Star' (producing 'Longistar'), and an unnamed pink Asiatic with small flowers and narrow leaves.

The cross with 'Aristo' produced one clone with very fertile pollen, which was used to backcross on several Asiatics. The 'Aristo' hybrids are typified by early flowering, pubescent buds, large flowers, and a rather low bud count; the colors are mostly salmon-creme or soft orange. The clones introduced include 'Centurion', 'Donau', 'Modern Style', 'Party Time', 'Salmon Classic', 'San Jose', and 'Swing'.

Another successful group of seedlings was derived from the cross with the unnamed pink Asiatic clone. These were later-flowering, with hairless buds, and somewhat smaller flowers in pink shades and pink bicolors. Named clones include 'Don Quichotte' (Plate 94), 'Money-maker', 'Royal Club', and 'Showbiz' (Plate 95).

In the 1980s L.A. hybrids from Sun Valley were introduced in the Netherlands and incorporated in several breeding programs. In the early 1990s many more combinations were tried, resulting in a broader color range in the L.A. hybrids. The brighter colors were obtained by breeding back to Asiatics. Another breeding line, pursued by the government-sponsored Centre for Plant Breeding at Wageningen, crossed *Lilium longiflorum* with 'Mont Blanc' and 'Apollo'.

Orienpet Lilies
Several Dutch hybridizers are now working extensively with the Orienpet group, hybrids of trumpet and Oriental lilies. Peter Schenk has been active in this work. The hope is to produce upright lilies for the cut-flower trade in new colors including yellow, peach, and orange.

Plate 94. *Lilium* 'Don Quichotte', an L.A. hybrid from Dutch hybridizer Peter Schenk. Photo by Jaap Westland.

Plate 95. *Lilium* 'Showbiz', an L.A. hybrid from Dutch hybridizer Peter Schenk. Photo by Jaap Westland.

Pot Lilies

The breeding of pot lilies in the Netherlands is done mainly at Bischoff Tulleken, where several attractive Asiatic hybrids, including 'Horizon', have been produced. Bischoff Tulleken has also introduced several Oriental pot lilies from the Little Rascal group; some of the most attractive are in the clear pink range. There are also several L.A. hybrids being produced for pot culture.

An important resource is the Centre for Plant Breeding (also known as the IVT) in Wageningen, where breeding and research go on under the direction of Jaap van Tuyl. Eleven commercial firms cooperated in the lily-breeding program. Breeding for resistance to *Fusarium* has been a special concern, as well as the production of hybrids suitable for forcing under low light conditions. From the commercial standpoint, the most important work has been done in the last half of the twentieth century in crossing Oriental with Asiatic hybrids.

The Centre has also produced several fascinating interspecific hybrids, using the cut style method in combination with embryo culture, along with other advanced techniques such as ovary culture. These include crosses of *Lilium longiflorum* with *L.canadense, L.candidum, L.concolor, L. dauricum, L. henryi, L. martagon, L. rubellum,* and Asiatic and Oriental hybrids. Another very interesting cross is between *L. henryi* and *L.candidum.* These distant hybrids are nearly all sterile in their diploid form, but tetraploids produced from them show increased fertility and have been backcrossed on Asiatic and Oriental hybrids. Most of the tetraploids were induced using oryzalin.

Lily Patents

Dutch lily breeders participate in a system similar to copyright or patent protection known as *kwekersrechts* (breeders' rights). Applications are made to the Centre in Wageningen, where bulbs submitted by breeders are grown and evaluated to determine whether the clone constitutes a truly distinct new variety. Once approved, a clone is protected for years, during which growers must pay royalties on its production to the breeder.

An examination of the history of applications for *kwekersrechts* shows the fluctuating interests of the Dutch lily industry. Applications for Asiatic hybrids ranged from 15 in 1984 to 69 in 1988, but dropped to 29 in 1995. Orientals had 6 applications in 1984, rising to a high of 60 in 1991, then dropping to 38 in 1996. *Lilium longiflorum* clones stayed steady at 3 to 5 per year. Beginning in 1992, there has been an annual increase in L.A. hybrids submitted, with 14 under review in 1996.

CHAPTER 16

Commercial Bulb Production

The lily hobbyist and home gardener may be curious to know how the bulbs are produced and delivered to them. Understanding the commercial growing process can be useful in deciding which suppliers to patronize and when to plant. Some lily farms hold open days when the public can visit during flowering season.

Home gardeners should be aware that the chemicals used in commercial lily growing are handled carefully by professionals using industrial equipment and protective clothing. Most are dangerous, and an applicator's license may be required. Hobbyists are advised to consult their local extension agents before using most of the products mentioned in this chapter, including herbicides, soil fumigants, fungicides, and insecticides.

Site and Soil

Much skill is involved in selecting the fields for lily planting; land contours, soil type, drainage, and crop history are important factors to be considered. In North America's northern Willamette Valley, lily growers avoided fields with loam soils too heavy in clay, which would further hinder spring planting and fall harvest.

A three-year cycle of crop rotation was practiced for many years in the northern Willamette Valley. The first year the field was planted to wheat, followed by a cover crop (usually perennial ryegrass), and finally by lilies. In other areas, such as western Oregon, crops of lilies followed pasture. In eastern Oregon and Washington, crops of lilies frequently followed sweet corn. Although this practice has been discontinued by many growers, it is highly beneficial.

Land is prepared for lily planting during summer, when soil temperatures are high. A cover crop of ryegrass is tall then and must be flattened by disking. This is followed by deep plowing and further cultivation to produce a good tilth.

The field is then fumigated, a procedure that kills or drastically reduces insect pests, disease-causing organisms, and weeds. Nematodes and symphylids were serious pests in the northern Willamette Valley, and these ground-dwelling organisms succumb to fumigation. *Fusarium,* which causes basal rot, and other parasitic fungi are also killed or reduced. Perennial weeds are a serious problem in lily fields, and all are killed in effective soil treatment; a high percentage of weed seeds is also eliminated.

Chloropicrin (e.g., Telone) was used successfully for many years. This chemical is not as thorough as methyl bromide, and no tarp cover is used with it. Methyl bromide has been used in commercial fields, particularly in areas such as seedbeds where very valuable crops are to be planted. This chemical offers the most thorough control of all organisms, including weeds. Several weed seeds have an unusually thick, impenetrable seed coat and are difficult to kill even with methyl bromide; varieties of vetch and clover thus frequently are seen growing profusely in fumigated fields.

Planting Time and Techniques

Lily bulbs are planted in both fall and spring. The soil must be well prepared, with just the right moisture content. When too much water is present, the structure of a soil, especially a heavy one, can break down and become unsuitable for plant growth. Commercial planting is carried out with Dutch planting machinery, simple in design but very efficient. The density and depth of planting depend on the size of the bulbs and whether they are to remain in place for one or two growing seasons. The bulbs to be planted must be clean. They are dipped in a fungicide to control pathogens such as *Fusarium.*

Fall planting has several distinct advantages over spring planting.

Lily bulbs planted then form basal or contractile roots almost immediately when the soil temperature and moisture level are satisfactory. The advantages of fall planting diminish by late October or early November in most regions; by this time the soil temperature is likely to have dropped so low that basal roots will not form.

Spring planting times vary with climate and soil conditions. The most important difference between fall and spring planting is that in the latter, the bulbs have been in cold storage during the winter months, where they have been conditioned to sprout and grow. Growers have to be aware that a very early spell of good weather (perhaps in early February) can be followed by weeks of inclement weather. In such an event planting too early can have disastrous results; bulbs planted under these conditions deteriorate rapidly.

Planting Material

The material that goes into the field may consist of bulb scales, small bulblets, or larger bulbs. Different techniques are preferred for the various classes of lilies.

Asiatic Lily Crops

To produce Asiatics, scales are incubated and kept in cold storage (see Chapter 3); planted in spring, they are usually allowed to remain down for two growing seasons. They may, however, be lifted late in the season; the bulbs are graded into large and small sizes, stored over winter, and replanted the following spring. The costs involved in the latter method are considerable.

Small stem bulblets produced by Asiatic lilies are usually planted in the fall and left down for one season. These can produce a good percentage of saleable-size bulbs, depending on the variety and growing conditions. Many of these bulblets, however, require two seasons to reach commercial size. This method has become less popular and is being replaced by scale planting.

Large bulbs of Asiatics (6/8, 8/10, or 10/12 centimeters in diameter) may be planted in the fall or the spring and left for one growing season. Fall planting is always preferable.

Trumpet and Aurelian Lily Crops

Seedling bulblets of trumpets and Aurelians are planted in spring after a year in a greenhouse or outdoor seedbed. The bulblets are generally separated into large and small sizes, with the larger ones being planted for one season and the very small ones for two. Both clones and larger seedling bulbs may be used to produce scales, which are incubated and placed in cool storage before planting in spring. These are allowed to remain down for two growing seasons. The large bulbs (6/8 through 12/14 centimeters) are planted in the fall or spring and allowed to remain down for one growing season.

Oriental Lily Crops

Seedling bulblets of Oriental lilies are planted in spring following a year in the greenhouse. They remain down for two growing seasons. Incubated and cold-stored scales from both clones and large seedling bulbs are planted in spring and left down for two seasons. Large bulbs (6/8 through 12/14 centimeters) are planted in fall or spring, remaining down for one season.

Residues from Scaling and Seedling Production

Planting-size bulbs are saved from the stocks originating from scaling and seed production after the commercial-sized bulbs are removed. These are labeled F.R.Sc. (first residue scales) and F.R.Sd. (first residue seedlings), respectively. Planting-size bulbs saved when these are later harvested become second residue, followed by third residue and so on. Only in exceptional circumstances—when very few bulbs of a clone are available, or if the clone is exceptionally strong—would third residue stocks be retained; some deterioration of the stock usually occurs by that stage because of a buildup of disease organisms. To maintain quality, it is imperative that clones be scaled and seedling strains raised from seed on a regular basis. Conscientious growers concerned with quality will label the origin of all stocks carefully.

Fertilizers

Before applying fertilizers, a grower must take a soil sample for analysis, because soils vary enormously in their requirements. Many agricultural suppliers will mix fertilizers according to an individual grower's needs. In most areas, a balanced fertilizer should be applied in early spring at an average rate of 600 to 725 kilograms per hectare (500 to 600 pounds per acre). It is unwise to use very high levels of nitrogen fertilizer in lily plantings. This nutrient can induce soft bulbs that are highly susceptible to both disease and mechanical damage during harvest.

Weed Control

Weeds in lily crops are controlled effectively by two classes of agricultural chemicals, pre-emergence and post-emergence herbicides. Pre-emergence products can be applied at any time when plants are dormant; the best time is usually just before growth emerges in spring. There are several products available, including paraquat and glyphosate (e.g., Round-Up), if perennial weeds are present. Post-emergence herbicides can be applied after shoots emerge. Their purpose is to kill germinating weeds. Several of these products can be applied throughout the growing season. Availability changes frequently, so it is wise to check with a local extension agent before taking action.

Irrigation

It is critical to maintain adequate moisture levels in lily plantings during the active growing season. Lily varieties differ in their water requirements, depending on the climates in which their ancestral stocks evolved. Growers avoid planting early blooming and late-blooming varieties in the same area; Asiatics, trumpets and Aurelians, and Orientals are segregated according to their different growth patterns and water requirements.

All lilies require adequate moisture before flowering and for two to four weeks following it. Thereafter it is best to decrease moisture gradually, a pattern that occurs naturally in most climates.

Many growers continue to irrigate late in the season, believing that this practice will result in a larger crop. This is questionable; greater emphasis needs to be placed on bulb quality than on bulb size, with special attention to freedom from disease, particularly *Fusarium* basal rot. Late watering in hot temperatures can encourage disease.

Plate 96. A field of *Lilium auratum* var. *platyphyllum* at Oregon Bulb Farms

Pests and Diseases

The commercial grower must establish a regular program to control diseases and pests throughout the growing season. *Botrytis* blight and aphids are by far the most important targets. Details of the control of specific pests and pathogens are given in Chapters 5 and 6.

Summer Care

The crops are inspected on a regular basis while in growth, both for quality and to ensure that they are true to name. When a "rogue" appears, it must be removed immediately. A close watch for virus symptoms is equally important. Badly infected plants must be removed and destroyed as early as possible. In most plantings, buds and flowers are removed either mechanically or by hand. Most growers believe this increases bulb yields because the plant's energy is not diverted into seed production. Weeds that escape herbicide control must be eradicated continually. Summer-growing weeds such as pigweed can be troublesome late in the season.

Harvest

Lily bulbs destined for the garden trade are harvested while the tops are still green and the plants are still in active growth, usually beginning in early August. It would be better for the lilies to wait until they are dormant, but at least six weeks is required for processing, shipping, and sale, and the bulbs must reach customers in time to be planted before winter's hard frosts arrive. The plant's respiration rate is high, and the bulbs are very susceptible to damage at this time. Great care must be taken to avoid bruising and other mechanical injury. In large mechanical harvesters, a cushion of soil can protect the bulbs as they pass through the machine. Bulbs must be transported slowly and carefully; bouncing is prohibited! Bulbs harvested late, after the tops have died back, are much less susceptible to damage than those harvested early.

The tops of stems are removed using a sharp mower at soil level. The harvesting machinery must dig deep enough to loosen all basal roots, the presence of which is critical for a high-quality lily bulb. The dug bulbs are transferred by the harvester into large bins called "totes." They are taken quickly to storage barns, where they are stacked in cold rooms at a temperature of 4°C (40°F) for a minimum of three days. This treatment lowers the bulb's metabolic rate and renders it less susceptible to bruising during processing.

Bulbs destined for the forcing trade are harvested later. The stage of morphological and physiological development that has been reached is crucial to how well the bulbs will store after processing and packing. Decreasing day length and light intensity, as well as cooling air and soil temperatures, induce the bulb to enter its resting stage. These factors eventually trigger the cessation of top growth and the plants turn yellow or brown. This stage of senescence must be reached before forcing bulbs are harvested.

Tests of lilies hybridized for the forcing trade were carried out at Oregon Bulb Farms for many years. The tests were established from bulbs harvested from mid-September through the end of October in most seasons; later harvesting was impossible owing to the onset of fall rains, which prevented digging by the last week in October. All but the latest-harvested lilies still had green tops when dug. The results from these forcing trials were quite variable, depending on the variety, season, and harvest date. The tests thoroughly convinced us that western Oregon was not the right climate in which to grow lilies for the forcing trade. Lily bulbs require an optimal growing season with a late harvest to give a strong, dependable crop as cut flowers.

The late harvesting of forcing varieties in the Netherlands has produced bulbs that perform well under forcing conditions. They consistently produce crops superior to those harvested in either North America or South Africa. In warmer climates, such as the western United States, South Africa, and southern France, aphid populations are higher and thus virus is more difficult to control.

Processing

Lily bulbs bruise just as easily as apples if they are dropped or handled carelessly. Unlike some other bulbs, such as tulips, hyacinths, and daffodils, they do not possess protective skins (tunics). Careful handling is therefore imperative with early harvested lilies. Several days of storage at cool temperature reduce the risk somewhat. Any severe damage to the tissues during processing is likely to result in decay.

Many growers wash their bulbs before packing them, although this is seldom necessary if they have been grown in sandy soil. The removal of soil by washing also eliminates certain pathogens and other organisms carried in the soil, reducing potential problems during storage. The bulbs are often dipped in a fungicide solution to control *Fusarium* and other diseases. TBZ (e.g., Mertect) at a concentration of 700 ppm and a temperature of 21° to 27°C (70° to 80°F) for 20 minutes is very effective.

Bulbs that have been bruised or scratched can be exposed to air at normal temperatures for a few days before they are packed, especially if they have been washed. This helps the damaged areas to suberize, or form thin, protective wound tissue. Such bulbs must never be packed in a moist medium, which will exacerbate rotting. Depending on the temperature and humidity, the bulbs require two or more days to dry before packing.

Packing

The critical factors in bulb storage are temperature and aeration. Bulbs must never be packed in airtight containers. Lilies harvested early for the garden trade are still rapidly respiring, and they will soon generate excessive heat if packed in airtight boxes or bags, resulting in the degeneration of the bulbs until they are a rotten mass. The correct procedure is to cool the bulbs before processing and to maintain cool temperatures afterwards. The bulbs are packed in a dry medium, using large trays with plastic liners. All these containers have small holes to ensure good ventilation. The packing medium must be coarse enough to permit good aeration, especially when bulbs are packed in large boxes and trays. Coarse sphagnum peat and wood shavings are both ideal. To ensure satisfactory short-term and long-term storage, bulbs for the forcing trade are usually packed in boxes with plastic liners using moist spaghum peat.

Plate 97. A field of Western American hybrids, showing *Lilium* San Gabriel strain (foreground) and *L.* 'Nightingale' (background). Photo by Herman v. Wall.

Storing

Bulbs destined for the garden trade are stored at 4°C (40°F) through mid-February. This delays sprouting, which can cause problems when bulbs are delivered in spring, especially if they are sold in heated environments such as supermarkets and indoor garden stores. To further retard sprouting, the cold room temperature must be lowered to 1°C (34°F) after mid-February and kept there until the bulbs are shipped. It is important to remember that tray temperatures can increase rapidly to far above the cold-room temperature because of accelerated respiration in the bulbs. This is true with earlier-harvested bulbs.

Lily bulbs can be stored for a considerable period without freezing, the duration depending on variety, harvest date, and storage temperature. Bulbs harvested in mid-September through October at Oregon Bulb Farms could be stored at 1°C (34°F) through mid-February without problems, using dry sphagnum peat as a packing medium and plastic liners.

Bulbs for the forcing trade are stored at a low temperature (around 1°C or 34°F). In late January the storage temperature is dropped below freezing. The precise temperature depends on the type of bulb: Asiatic varieties are stored at –2°C (28°F), while Oriental varieties and hybrids of *Lilium longiflorum* are stored at –1.5°C (29°F).

Bulbs of most Asiatic varieties can then be stored for six months without any reduction in quality, and for up to one year, with a gradual reduction in quality. Bulbs stored for longer periods develop more rapidly when forced; the plants are shorter and have a lower bud count. Orientals and *Lilium longiflorum* hybrids usually cannot be stored for such a long period. Bulbs stored past August experience a gradual decrease in quality, depending on the conditions and variety; there is a risk that storage problems such as premature shoot formation and frost damage will occur.

The cold rooms require adequate insulation to maintain cold temperatures, and fans to ensure good air circulation. It is very important to maintain a uniform temperature throughout the cold-storage area, and air movement is critical to achieving this. Sufficient space must also be allowed between the stacks and boxes to permit good air circulation throughout the area, avoiding pockets of stagnant air. Minor differences in temperature can cause frost damage or induce shoots to develop.

Lily bulbs cannot be refrozen after thawing, or damage is likely. The amount of damage depends on the variety, time of year, and time out of storage.

To succeed, the lily forcer must obtain bulbs of the highest quality. This is a critical point. A good relationship between grower and wholesaler does much to ensure consistent quality. The wholesaler must pay special attention to delivering bulbs from the most reliable growers.

CHAPTER 17

Commercial Cut Flower and Pot Lily Production

The quantity of lilies grown for cut flowers and pot plants increased dramatically during the 1980s and 1990s. The plants may be grown in greenhouses of various types, and outdoors, with or without overhead protection. Asiatic and Oriental varieties have been used extensively over many years, with *Lilium longiflorum* (Easter lily) hybrids becoming more popular. Tables 17-1 and 17-2 list lilies suitable for cut flowers and pot plants. Since the varieties may change dramatically from year to year as newer forms are developed, expert advice should be sought before purchasing bulbs. Growers requiring further information can find it in the very helpful publication *The Lily as a Cutflower and Pot Plant,* published by the International Flower Bulb Center, Parklaan 5, P. O. Box 172, 2180 AD Hillegom, The Netherlands.

The key to success in growing cut flowers or pot plants is the quality of the bulbs with which one begins. The bud count of a specific variety cannot be guaranteed if the bulb is inferior. The methods of growing and storage discussed later in this chapter are the means by which this quality can be produced.

Lily hybridizers, especially in the Netherlands, have been very active since the 1970s in searching out superior varieties suited to the cut-flower industry. The characteristics considered most important in cutting varieties include the following:

- Sturdy stems, of upright habit and thus easy to pack.
- Shorter, not too dense foliage that permits closer planting, increasing returns and preventing disease.

- High bud count, essential in permitting the forcing of smaller bulbs; an Asiatic bulb 10 to 12 centimeters (4 to 5 inches) in circumference should give 4 to 6 flowers, and an Oriental bulb 12 to 14 centimeters (5 to 6 inches) in circumference, 4 to 5 flowers. Prolonged storage leads to a reduction in bud count.
- Early flowering, which reduces the time required for forcing.
- Buds that color well before opening, adding visual appeal for the purchaser.
- Clear and attractive color; unspotted flowers seem to be preferred to spotted ones.
- Virus tolerance, in plants that grow satisfactorily despite infection and never show severe visible symptoms such as foliar mottling, distortion, and stunting.
- Resistance to other diseases, such as *Fusarium* (basal rot).
- Ability to maintain quality after long periods of storage.
- Flowers with good keeping quality or "vase life."
- Lack of susceptibility to leaf scorch and premature bud drop.
- Good firm bulbs with well-formed basal roots, which are less susceptible to molds in storage than are softer bulbs.
- Ability to grow well under low light conditions.

Site and Soil

Lilies can be grown in a wide variety of soils. It is important that growers cultivate lilies in soil that has a good structure throughout, especially in the top few inches. Drainage must be excellent. Heavy loam and clay soils are less suitable but can certainly be used if well-decayed, coarse organic material is incorporated to improve soil structure and increase aeration to a depth of 30 centimeters (12 inches). A neutral pH is considered ideal; in alkaline soils, peat products can be worked in to reduce the pH.

Lilies can be damaged by salt and chlorine. If levels of these substances in the soil are too high, the soil must be thoroughly flooded to leach them out before planting.

Soil fumigation is advised before planting lilies outdoors if weeds, diseases, or pests have been a problem. Under greenhouse conditions, steam sterilization is most often used to control such diseases as *Fusar-*

ium and *Pythium* as well as weeds. Four crops of lilies can be raised over a year in greenhouse beds before steaming is carried out, usually on an annual basis. The steaming is more effective when done in summer, when soil temperatures are already high. If problems arise, such as *Fusarium* from infected bulbs, steaming should always be done before planting the next crop.

In steaming, a large tarp is spread over the area to be treated. The steam is injected until a temperature of 71° to 76°C (160° to 170°F) is maintained for 30 minutes to a depth of 25 centimeters (10 inches). The entire process requires eight to nine hours because it takes this long for the soil to reach the required temperature.

Field and Greenhouse Cultivation

The outdoor cultivation of lilies for the florist trade is possible only in regions where the weather remains favorable throughout the growing period. Growers must be aware of the risks involved in outdoor culture, including strong winds, hail, frost, and *Botrytis* infection. An excellent, well-drained, fertile soil, a good irrigation system, and shade and wind screens are all essential. The varieties selected need to be the strongest available; always include those that have been found to be suitable for outdoor growing.

Greenhouses for forcing lilies must have good, reliable ventilation and heating systems. Shading is essential to control climate during warm spells. This can be provided with shade curtains or whitewash (which is washed off in the fall).

Planting in Beds

Bulbs that have not been frozen (new crop, in December, January, and February) should be planted immediately following their removal from cold storage. Frozen bulbs must be gently defrosted (never in the sun) at a temperature of 10° to 15°C (50° to 59°F), with the plastic liners opened up. Prevent the bulbs from drying out by planting a small number at a time. If possible, plant them directly from the box. Dried-out bulb scales and basal roots result in a loss of quality. During warm weather, plant only in the morning and evening.

Planting density depends on the type of soil, time of year, variety, and bulb size. Density can be greater during the summer months when light conditions are excellent. The bulbs are planted with 7 to 13 centimeters (3 to 5 inches) of soil on top of them. Deeper planting is recommended during the warmer months.

Planting tests are advised early in the year to establish the quality of the stocks of all varieties. Plant one tray of each stock or field number early for this purpose. When the test results have been evaluated, the better stocks should be retained for late planting. For example, one might have stocks of a single clone from three sources, each identified by a separate "field number." It is important to determine whether the quality of these stocks is consistent; if one is inferior, it should be planted early because it will not store as well as the better ones.

During the first two to three weeks after planting, a lily bulb depends on basal roots for its uptake of water. It is therefore important that bulbs have strong, disease-free, healthy roots when planted. The stem roots develop on the underground portion of the stem directly above the bulb; these provide water and nutrient intake, and their satisfactory development is essential for high-quality lily stems.

Growing Lilies in Trays

Lilies grown in trays can be brought directly into the greenhouse following planting, or they may be given a rooting period in a cool storage room first. Many growers prefer the latter procedure for Oriental varieties, finding the cool rooting period highly beneficial in producing higher-quality stems. The rooting period also reduces the time required for forcing in the greenhouse.

After being defrosted, the bulbs are planted in the trays—large plastic containers about 30 centimeters (12 inches) deep—placing 1 centimeter (0.5 inch) of soil under the bulbs and 8 centimeters (3 inches) on top. The bulbs must never be allowed to dry out; in addition, they should be protected from direct sun so that the soil does not heat up too much.

The length of the rooting period in the cool storage room depends on how long the bulbs were in freezer storage: the longer the frozen storage, the less time is required in the rooting area. This is because the longer the bulbs have been in cold storage, the faster the sprouts will develop: sprout development thus controls the duration in the rooting room. Early in the year the bulbs require approximately four weeks at 9°C (48°F) for adequate development, and later in the year, approximately two weeks. Oriental lilies have shoots about 5 to 8 centimeters (2 to 3 inches) long when they are ready to take to the greenhouse.

The move from frozen storage to the rooting area must be a gradual transition. The bulbs must be gently defrosted and never exposed to high temperatures or dry conditions. The loose planting medium must never be allowed to dry out or become warm. The trays are watered thoroughly immediately following planting and placed in the rooting area quickly. A uniform temperature must be maintained constantly in the rooting area. Again, this requires adequate air circulation to prevent pockets of warm or cold air developing.

Various soil mixes have been used for lilies forced in trays. A clean, loose, free-draining mixture of peat and barkdust proved ideal at Oregon Flowers in Aurora, Oregon, where top-quality forcing varieties are grown.

Fertilizers

It must always be remembered that a high-quality, well-grown bulb is an excellent food reservoir in itself. For this reason, overfertilizing must be avoided when forcing lilies.

Taking a soil sample is strongly recommended before lilies are planted in forcing beds. A good balance can then be ensured by applying only the nutrients that are required. Excessive applications of nitrogen are discouraged because they produce weak stems and soft leaves.

A foliar feed just before the bud-visible stage is very beneficial in producing a good dark green color in the foliage. This application should be a well-balanced fertilizer containing micronutrients. Foliar fertilizers must stay on the foliage for a certain period to be absorbed; the concentration is so low that there is no danger of burning.

If other types of fertilizers are applied through the irrigation system, the crop must be washed off thoroughly with plain water after application.

Lilies are easily damaged by fluorine, which causes a different type of leaf scorch, particularly in acid soils. In this case, all the leaves develop brown tips and margins. Fertilizers containing fluoride, such as superphosphate and triple superphosphate, should not be used. The soil pH can also be increased by the addition of dolomite lime.

It is often advised that the grower enrich the atmosphere in the greenhouse with carbon dioxide (CO_2) because of its beneficial effect on the growth and flowering of lilies. The crop becomes sturdier and darker green in color, and there is less risk of bud drop. The application must be carefully regulated.

Irrigation

The medium into which the bulbs are planted, whether they are grown in trays or in the ground, must be thoroughly moistened immediately after planting. An overhead irrigation system is preferred to provide even distribution of water and wash off the crop. Water thoroughly at all times and always watch for dry spots. An added advantage of overhead irrigation is its cooling effect.

Too much moisture must be avoided during the early stage of crop development when stem roots are still developing and the water uptake by the plants is low. Excessive moisture affects the oxygen supply to the roots, hampering their development and function. This is a problem in heavier soils.

The best time to water is early in the morning, allowing the crop to dry out before evening. If necessary, manage heat and ventilation to dry out the foliage and decrease the risk of *Botrytis* blight.

Temperature and Light

It is strongly advised that lilies be forced at cool temperatures to ensure sturdier stems and prime quality. Extremes of temperature must be avoided at all costs. For Asiatic varieties, a range of 14° to 17°C (58° to 62°F) is ideal; for Orientals and *Lilium longiflorum* hybrids, 17° to 19°C (62° to 66°F). A superior crop is also obtained if soil temperatures are kept as cool as possible always. Shading is the primary means of accomplishing this, along with adequate watering.

Plants are most susceptible to scorch, a type of physical damage, just as the buds become visible. It appears as white blotches on the leaves that are exposed to the most light at the buds-visible stage. Rapid changes in light and temperature conditions when the crop is reaching this stage always cause problems in certain varieties. A long cloudy period followed by sudden bright sunshine at the critical growth stage is a particular headache. Every effort must be made to reduce the temperature and increase humidity by modifying ventilation, shading, and irrigation. Certain varieties are very susceptible, such as 'Stargazer' and 'Sterling Star' (Plate 98).

Several varieties, including some Asiatic hybrids, are susceptible to bud drop. The small buds simply drop off when they are about 1 centimeter (0.5 inch) long. This is a problem during the winter months, because it is caused by poor light conditions. It is therefore essential to have a greenhouse with good light penetration during periods of dull weather. Poor light not only increases the risk of bud drop but also induces an overall deterioration in quality, with weak stems and soft foliage.

This situation can be avoided largely by providing artificial lighting. Various lighting systems are available, and professional advice is recommended before choosing and installing them. Oregon Flowers uses 400-watt high-pressure sodium lights, with one light covering 10 square meters (12 square yards). The lights function for 16 hours a day, with an 8-hour rest period every 24 hours, during the season of low natural light.

Incandescent lighting is also used by some growers to increase daylength. This keeps the lilies growing longer and speeds up the development of the crop.

Pests and Diseases

The foliar disease most prevalent in forcing conditions is *Botrytis* blight. This can usually be controlled effectively in the greenhouse by good cultural practices, correct planting density, careful watering, and good ventilation. In outdoor plantings the disease must be controlled by regular spraying with a suitable fungicide that does not leave an ugly residue on the leaves.

Aphids must be controlled always, either by spraying with a suitable insecticide or, in greenhouses, by fumigation.

Plate 98. Asiatic hybrids in the field

Harvest

The stems are cut just as the first buds begin to color. The stems must never be allowed to dry out. The foliage is removed from the bottom 10 centimeters (4 inches) of the stems. The stems are graded and bunched and placed in plastic sleeves. They are set in containers with a little water and stored at 2° to 3°C (about 36°F) before packing and shipping. Vase life can be improved by adding a pretreatment agent to the water. The foliage must always be completely dry before the stems are cut and packed. Any moisture present will cause enormous problems.

Table 17-1. Hybrid lilies for cut flowers.

Asiatics	Longiflorum x Asiatic Hybrids
'Alaska', white	'Centurion', salmon orange
'Avignon', orange-red	'Dynamico', deep pink
'Chianti', light pink	'Moneymaker', deep pink
'Connecticut King', yellow	'Royal Dream', white
'Elite', orange	'Royal Fantasy', cream
'Enchantment', orange	'Royal Victory', cream
'Geneva', cream-and-blush	'Salmon Queen', salmon-orange
'Gran Paradiso', orange-red	
'Joanna' (synonym 'Yellow Giant'),	**Upright Orientals**
yellow 'Milano', red	'Acapulco', rose-pink
'Monte Negro', dark red	'Le Rève', soft pink
'Montreaux', pink	'Marco Polo', clear pink
'Pollyanna', yellow	'Siberia', white[1]
'Trendsetter', light orange	'Stargazer', crimson
	'White Stargazer', white
	'Woodriff's Memory', soft rose
	Outfacing Oriental
	'Casablanca', white, unspotted[2]

[1] 'Siberia' is very amenable to absorbing various dyes, so presumably one could have a blue Oriental lily, appalling as the idea may seem.

[2] 'Casablanca' is very popular for weddings.

Lilies as Pot Plants

The characteristics desired in a pot lily are almost identical with those important in cut-flower varieties; the one exception is plant habit (Plate 99). Harvest dates, packing, and storage procedures, however, are identical.

The ideal plant habit for a pot lily is a height of 30 to 45 centimeters (12 to 18 inches), with full, attractive foliage. Varieties that have a tendency to lose their lower leaves should be avoided.

Several years ago taller lilies were used as pot subjects. Their height was reduced by growth inhibitors such as ancymidol (e.g., A-Rest). The chemical was applied by watering it into the pots, spraying the foliage, or immersing the bulbs in it before planting. Results were quite varied, depending on variety, season, temperature, soil, and light conditions. Tests over a period of years at Oregon Bulb Farms demonstrated that soil drenches applied to the pots were the most dependable means of application. The chemical was applied when the shoots were about 2.5 centimeters (1 inch) tall and again one week later. The cultivation of pot lilies is now much less complicated because there are many genetically short lilies in a wide variety of colors.

A light, open medium with good moisture retention and a near-neutral pH (6.0 to 6.7) are recommended for pot lilies. A mixture of well-decayed barkdust, sphagnum peat, and pumice was used at Oregon Bulb Farms quite successfully. The plants will, however, grow satisfactorily in a wide variety of soil mixes.

Different bulb and container sizes are used for pot cultivation. De-

Plate 99. *Lilium* 'Connecticut Lemonglow'   Plate 100. *Lilium* 'Golden Pixie'

pending on bud count and foliage volume, from one to five bulbs may be planted in each pot. Size and number of bulbs must be calculated to produce a required minimum number of buds per pot.

The bulbs are planted at the bottom of the pot, with 1 centimeter (0.5 inch) of soil below them. If more than one bulb is in a pot, the bulb noses must face the outside of the pot. The bulbs are covered with about 8 centimeters (3 inches) of medium, which is then firmed lightly. One to two centimeters (0.5 to 1 inch) must be left between the top of the soil and the top of the pot to allow for watering.

The satisfactory production of stem roots is just as important for pot lilies as for cut-flower lilies. Adequate moisture must be available always, with overwatering avoided at the early stages of development.

The procedures for cultivating pot lilies are virtually identical to those recommended for cut-flower production: cool temperatures, adequate light, good ventilation, and sufficient space for the plant to develop attractively. If the pots are too crowded on the benches, this frequently leads to yellowing of the lower leaves, a very undesirable condition.

Pot lilies are marketed when the lower buds show sufficient color. It is unacceptable to dispatch lilies at an earlier stage of development because of their increased susceptibility to lack of light then. The pots are watered thoroughly and placed in attractive sleeves before sale.

Lilies that have been prepared for marketing can be placed in cool storage (5°C or 41°F for Orientals, 3°C or 38°F for Asiatics) for a short time. Although these lower temperatures do not stop flower development, they can cause poor opening of the first flowers and damage to the very young upper buds when plants are stored too long.

Table 17-2. Hybrid lilies for pot flowers.

Asiatics	Orientals
'Buff Pixie', salmon-orange	'Chameur', red-pink
'Butter Pixie', golden-yellow	'Little Girl', pink-and-ivory
'Dandy', soft pink	'Little Joy', purple-and-white
'Horizon', orange	'Miss Rio', pink
'Lemon Pixie', bright yellow	'Mr. Ed', white
'Orange Pixie', bright orange	'Mr. Ruud', white with gold band
'White Pixie', white	'Mr. Sam', crimson with white margins
	'Mona Lisa', pink
	'Stargazer', crimson[1]

[1] 'Stargazer' may require dwarfing compounds to stay sufficiently short.

CHAPTER 18

Personalities of the Lily World

I met Jan de Graaff of Oregon Bulb Farms in Edinburgh, Scotland, in 1960, when I was working at the Edinburgh Botanic Garden. He persuaded me to join his team in Oregon; his enthusiasm for the work going on there must have been infectious. I came to Oregon in May 1961 and began to work under the direction of Harold F. Comber and Earl Hornback, who became my mentors in the early years.

I was awed by the vast range of lily species and hybrids that had been assembled at Oregon Bulb Farms. I was equally amazed at the number of hybridizers involved in the creation of those early lilies. They received the Stenographer Asiatic hybrids from Isabella Preston; an outstanding group from George Slate (who had worked along similar lines to Preston's); several strong hybrid clones from Frank Leith Skinner, including *Lilium* ×*scottiae*; and finally, the beautiful pastel Asiatic hybrids developed by Cecil Patterson. A few years later we received several interesting hybrids from Bert Porter, and others from Carl Feldmaier in Germany, including 'Schellenbaum' and 'Schuetzenlisl'.

The work with tetraploid Asiatic lilies 20 years later was enhanced by gifts of pollen and bulbs from many friends, including Peter Schenk and Jaap Spaans in the Netherlands, and Arthur Evans, Dorothy Schaefer, and Dick Thomas in North America.

The beautiful group of Madonna lilies named the Cascade strain was made possible through many years of patient selection by George Slate.

The trumpet lily hybrid strains produced at Oregon Bulb Farms arose out of the work of several hybridizers, especially Carlton Yerex and LeVern Freimann, true pioneers in this field. The development of tetraploid trumpet hybrid forms was due entirely to more than 30 years of excellent and patient work by Robert Griesbach.

Our early Oriental hybrids originated mostly from New Zealand and the work of such hybridizers as Leslie Jury, Len Tullery, and Roy Wallace. The earlier hybrids from *Lilium japonicum* were the work of Norma Pfeiffer. The beautiful, pearl-white 'Allegra' (Plate 101) from Samuel Emsweller was used for many years and is still valued by many hybridizers of Oriental lilies. Several strong clones from J. S. Yeates in New Zealand added enormously to the value of the Oriental lilies. The miniature Little Rascals strain also came originally from Yeates. Leslie Woodriff's 'Stargazer' was used extensively to breed upright forms in later years.

The unique and unusual hybrids produced more from distant crosses were due entirely to the skilled embryo culture work carried out by Judith Freeman. This work covered many groups: Asiatic species, rare Oriental species, and the Orienpets, including the tetraploid form of 'Black Beauty'.

The enormous advances in lily hybridizing since the 1960s have been due to a host of contributors. I hope we can always give them the credit

Plate 101. *Lilium* 'Allegra', from Samuel Emsweller. Photo by Herman v. Wall.

they deserve. The sharing of knowledge and material is essential if we are to make true advances in the future. What I have achieved has indeed been made possible through the generosity of friends all over the world. In this chapter, therefore, I would like to introduce the reader to some of the most prominent lily hybridizers and their work.

Ruth P. H. Clas

Ruth Clas (1909–1979) spent her entire life in the Albany, New York, area. She became interested in lilies when she encountered a magnificent form of *Lilium auratum* in 1932.

Clas's hybridizing work was characterized by unique insight, curiosity, disciplined experimentation, and generosity. She bred lilies using a wide range of species and hybrids. The species involved were *Lilium amabile, L. bulbiferum, L. callosum, L. dauricum, L. leichtlinii* var. *maximowiczii, L. pumilum,* and *L. lancifolium.* Her work with hybrids yielded the following: 'Black Cherry', 'Dolly', and 'Mame' (all 'Edith Cecilia' × 'Byam's Ruby'); 'Fisheyes' ('Edith Cecilia' × 'Fireflame'); 'Maxiclas', a very fertile and useful hybrid from her work combining *L. amabile, L. callosum,* and *L. leichtlinii* var. *maximowiczii;* 'Pussycat' ('Pink Tiger' × 'Dolly'), a beautiful and fascinating lily; 'Scamp' (*L. pumilum* × 'Golden Chalice'), a charming, early, fragrant miniature that was used intensively in producing early and miniature Asiatic hybrids; and 'Top Clas' (from her many crosses with 'Orchid Queen'), named in her honor and introduced by Oregon Bulb Farms. Her hybrids are particularly valuable for further breeding because of the thought that went into the parentage and the meticulous care with which she protected her pollinations. One of her criteria was that evidence of both parents should be obvious in the offspring of any true cross.

On Easter Sunday of 1965, Clas pollinated *Lilium alexandrae,* which she had flowered on her windowsill, with stored pollen of *L. speciosum.* Only one seedling developed, and it eventually produced the plant named 'Easter Bunny'. This was the first important hybrid of *L. alexandrae,* and Clas was among the first to recognize the importance of this species for hybridizing.

For many years Clas carried out extensive work delineating the factors involved in seed germination for a wide range of lily species. Her meticulous, thoroughly researched, highly scientific work in this field surpassed the requirements of any Ph.D. thesis; sadly, however, this outstanding work was never published. She looked for truth supported by documentary and observational evidence. The love she held for lilies and learning more about them overflowed into her correspondence and all her work with them. Those who knew her cannot fail to carry some of her interest, love, and disciplined inquiry into their work with lilies.

Harold F. Comber

Harold Comber (1897–1969) was born in Staplefield, Sussex, England. His father, James Comber, was head gardener at a beautiful estate called Nymans, where Harold was exposed to plants at a very early age. As a teenager, Harold worked for Henry John Elwes, author of a monograph on the genus *Lilium*. Elwes was undoubtedly responsible for Comber's lifelong interest in lily species, which culminated in his publication of "A New Classification of the Genus *Lilium*" in the 1949 *Lily Year Book* of the Royal Horticultural Society. Elwes urged Comber to study at the Royal Botanic Garden in Edinburgh, where he was an outstanding student for three years.

Following his tour in Edinburgh, Comber spent two years in the Andes of Argentina and Chile, collecting many new plants for introduction to British gardens. His discoveries are commemorated in the name of the genus *Combera*, alpine plants in the family Solanaceae. After Comber's return from South America, he went on a plant-collecting trip to Tasmania, where he gathered seed of 147 species. After a second trip to South America, he accepted a position as nursery manager at Burnham Lily Nursery in Buckinghamshire, operated by W. A. Constable. He was successful in growing a wide variety of lily species, even those that were very difficult in cultivation. He was also involved in making many crosses, including *Lilium* ×*intermedium* (*L. concolor* var. *pulchellum* × *L. pumilum*). The hard-cover catalogs from Constable's nursery in the pre–World War II years are beautifully illustrated with black-and-white photographs, most of them taken by Comber, who was a talented photographer. In 1949 two of his magnificent Aurelian clones, 'Mary' and 'Susan', received awards of merit from the Royal Horticultural Society.

In 1952 Comber accepted Jan de Graaff's invitation to join the staff at Oregon Bulb Farms. For the next 10 years he held primary responsibility for hybridizing, propagation, and selection of lilies, working closely with manager Earl Hornback. The enduring contribution Comber made at Oregon Bulb Farms has perhaps not been adequately recognized. He established an excellent system of records for crosses made and for clonal selections. He also initiated efficient and reliable methods of seed production, cleaning, recording, and storage. His far-reaching and meticulous work in producing high-quality, true-breeding first-generation seedling strains in trumpet, Aurelian, and Oriental lilies laid the foundations for material that is still produced and enjoyed today. The great value of producing disease-free stocks of these fine strains annually from seed is only now becoming fully appreciated. The H. F. Comber Award is presented annually at the International Show of the North American Lily Society for the best species exhibited.

Comber's sound, practical ideas about selecting and thoroughly testing new varieties have also stood the test of time. Would that they were more widely employed worldwide! That would spare the innocent lily enthusiasts and growers many unpleasant experiences with undistinguished and inadequate cultivars. Harold was a plantsman of unparalleled knowledge. He was also a giant in the world of lilies, and a true friend to all who shared his interest.

Warren Kenneth Crutcher

Ken Crutcher was born in Oregon in 1927 and started working at Oregon Bulb Farms at the tender age of fourteen. He worked with Jan de Graaff and the pioneer hybridizers John Heyer and Earl Hornback. He was also involved in designing and building machinery, cold rooms, treating tanks, and grading equipment. He was in charge of processing and grading for many years before becoming production manager in 1968.

Four years later Crutcher left Oregon Bulb Farms to pursue other interests. He returned to lilies in 1985, however, and used his vast knowledge and skills to establish his breeding and production business. The focus of his breeding work has been Asiatics and Orientals, using the strongest and most disease-resistant parents.

Among Crutcher's Asiatic introductions are 'Eyecatcher' and 'Rawhide', both brushmarks; 'Peach Sunrise', rose-pink; 'Sunny Day', clear yellow; and 'Top Honor', rose-pink. His Oriental introductions include several strains as well as clones: Celebration, a group of beautiful reds resembling the old Jamboree strain; 'Debutante', rose-pink; Golden Discovery strain; 'Intense'; Pink Sensation strain; 'Sonic'; and Snowdrift strain ('Allegra' × 'Casa Blanca').

Crutcher's interest and love of lilies extends well over 50 years and shows no sign of fading. His contributions have been of great value.

Samuel L. Emsweller

Samuel Emsweller (1898–1966) was the director of the Ornamental Plants Research Section of the U.S. Department of Agriculture station at Beltsville, Maryland, from 1935 until his death. He was intensely interested in the genus *Lilium* and knew the problems of lily growing, hybridizing, and propagation from first-hand experience. He was one of the first to verify by cytological techniques (study of cell structures) the parentage of several hybrid lilies, including the famous 'Black Beauty'. He also created tetraploid lilies in the 1950s, of which perhaps the best known are 'Brandywine', 'Mega', and 'Mountaineer'. His tetraploid forms of *Lilium longiflorum* that were produced in the 1950s are still grown.

The Oriental hybrids produced by Emsweller were outstanding for their disease resistance and virus tolerance: 'Advance', 'Allegra', 'Aurora', and the Potomac hybrid strain. 'Allegra' is perhaps the best known, having been used extensively in hybridizing and still growing profusely and strongly despite being more than 50 years old.

Emsweller's extensive research on lily hybridizing, propagation, pests, diseases, and nutrition is well documented. An interesting account of *Lilium wallichianum* var. *neilgherrense* showing bulbils was published in the 1963 *Yearbook of the North American Lily Society*, and a bibliography of his many excellent articles on lilies appears in the 1966 *Yearbook of the North American Lily Society*.

Many honors were bestowed on Emsweller. Those pertaining to lilies included the E. H. Wilson Award from the North American Lily Society in 1968, and the Lyttel Lily Cup from the Royal Horticultural Society in 1960. Those who knew him were happy that he lived to know that his outstanding work with lilies received honors and acclaim in many lands.

Carl Feldmaier

Carl Feldmaier (d. 1985) of Pfarrkirchen, Germany, was an architect by profession, as well as a fine artist and horticulturist. He worked extensively with many groups of lilies, including Asiatics, martagons, and Aurelians. His finest hybrids were in the Asiatic group. Among his introductions are 'Feuer und Rausch' (Fire and Smoke), 'Hesperos' (Evening Star), 'Roter Prinz' (Red Prince), 'Schellenbaum' (Tree of Bells), 'Schuetzenlisl' (a little girl mascot of a hunting club), and 'Sonnentiger' (Sun Tiger).

Feldmaier held lasting garden-worthiness to be the highest criterion, and all his lilies are robust garden plants. He often mourned the loss of a fiery red trumpet he once produced, writing, "It seems that the inner tissue of the flower contained deep golden yellow carotinoid pigments, whereas the epidermal cells carried magenta anthocyanin pigment; this worked like a red glass above a yellow one and created a fiery red appearance."

Die neuen Lilien (The New Lilies), Feldmaier's excellent book, was published in 1967. A revised edition written with Judith Freeman was published in German in 1982 under the title *Die Lilien*. The latter included excellent chapters on embryo culture, tissue culture, and hybridizing advances.

A quiet, dignified man, Feldmaier had a character hard to find in today's superficial, fast-living society. He generously passed his knowledge on to others, and his contribution to the world of lilies is monumental.

Judith Freeman

Born and reared in North Carolina, Judith Freeman became interested in lilies before she reached her teens after finding a copy of Jan de Graaff's *The New Book of Lilies* (1951) in her local library. Her early work in lily hybridizing and her earlier publications appeared under her former married name, Judith McRae.

Freeman joined the staff at Oregon Bulb Farms in 1971 as a geneticist. Her work there involved many aspects of hybridizing, with special emphasis on chromosome and pollen studies and embryo culture. Her intensive research into previous achievements in embryo culture did much toward eventually establishing her as the foremost authority in that area. She produced superb and unique hybrids from *Lilium alexandrae* crossed with *L. speciosum* and many other Oriental lilies; crosses with *L. longiflorum* and Asiatic hybrids; Orienpet hybrids; *L. lankongense* crossed with Asiatics; *L. pumilum* crosses; and many others. For several years she also directed the tissue culture laboratory at Oregon Bulb Farms, becoming a leading authority in this field as well.

From 1979 to 1981 Freeman worked with Carl Feldmaier on the revision of his monumental work *Die neuen Lilien* (The New Lilies), contributing new sections on hybrids, embryo and tissue culture, and commercial lily production. Their joint work was published in Germany in 1982 under the title *Die Lilien*. From 1974 to 1981 she served as editor of the *Yearbook of the North American Lily Society*. Over the years she has also published an excellent series of articles in these yearbooks.

With Leonard Marshall, Freeman founded Columbia-Platte Lilies in 1979. Their hybridizing program aimed to broaden the range of garden lilies, then dominated by forcing-type Asiatic lilies, by introducing new species into the lines. The introductions include the Chippendale and Rosepoint Lace strains (second-generation hybrids from the *Lilium lankongense* hybrids known as Southern Belles), 'Summit' (*L. callosum* var. *flaviflorum* × Asiatic), 'Tiger Babies', 'Tinkerbelle' (*L. cernuum* hybrid), 'Elf' (*L. cernuum* hybrid; Plate 102), and 'Viva' (*L. pumilum* × *L. leichtlinii* var. *maximowiczii* 'Unicolor'). Freeman now offers a wide spectrum of lilies in the catalog of her nursery, The Lily Garden.

Freeman received the Slate-MacDaniels Award in 1984 for her outstanding contributions to the North American Lily Society. In 1995 she received the E. H. Wilson Award for outstanding contributions to the world of lilies. Both awards were richly deserved.

LeVern N. Freimann

LeVern Freimann, now retired from horticulture, has lived in Bellingham, Washington, for many years. His interest in lilies dates back to 1929, when he acquired a specimen of *Lilium sulphureum*. His article "Lilies as an Avocation," in the 1943 *Yearbook of the North American*

Plate 102. *Lilium* 'Elf', from Judith Freeman. Photo by Judith L. Freeman.

Lily Society, gives an account of his early work, and the early years of his work with the golden regal lilies are reported in the 1954 *Yearbook of the North American Lily Society.* His authoritative articles discuss the inheritance of both yellow and pink colors in trumpet lilies.

Freimann worked with both *Lilium ×aurelianense* and 'T. A. Havemeyer'. Many of his excellent trumpet and Aurelian hybrids were introduced and used in breeding at Oregon Bulb Farms.

He was a true pioneer and corresponded with lily enthusiasts in many parts of the world. His dream was to produce Oriental varieties that would thrive in a wide range of climates and soil conditions. He believed he had found the key to his dream with the arrival of Leslie Woodriff's 'Black Beauty', though it was completely sterile in its diploid form. Freimann produced a tetraploid form of 'Black Beauty' by soaking the broken scale bases in a mass of *Colchicum* bulbs reduced to pulp in a kitchen blender—a primitive form of the colchicine treatment now used to induce tetraploidy. He then crossed this form with several clones, including 'Thunderbolt' (an aneuploid), to produce strong, beautiful hybrids such as 'Scheherazade' (Plate 103) and 'Vern's Beauty'. He also acquired a tetraploid form of 'Journey's End' from his friend J. S. Yeates in New Zealand, which he crossed with his tetraploid form of 'Black Beauty' to produce a host of beautiful seedlings. The clones 'Catherine Walton' and 'Scarlet Delight' were among those introduced.

Among tetraploid Asiatic hybrids, 'Apricot Supreme' is the best known of the ones with which Freimann created. He produced some beautiful seedlings from this clone. Others followed in his footsteps to breed spectacular Asiatic hybrids from his lines.

Freimann believed in keeping careful records and stressed this constantly. He wrote in the 1956 *Yearbook of the North American Lily Society:*

> There is a considerable pleasure in knowing the history of every plant, thereby being able to check the ancestry of each individual for several years. By keeping records it is possible to predict what the future generations will bring, especially in recessive characters.

He also believed in the age-old tradition of plant trading among friends and acquaintances. For the good of lilies, may we all follow the example of this fine gentleman. He received the E. H. Wilson Award from the North American Lily Society in 1975 for his outstanding contributions to the genus *Lilium* over many years.

Plate 103. *Lilium* 'Scheherazade'. Photo by Judith L. Freeman.

Jan de Graaff

Jan de Graaff (1903–1989) was born in Leiden, Netherlands, and studied horticulture in England. He was in the diplomatic service before joining his family's business. In 1928 he came to the United States on behalf of his firm, eventually purchasing Oregon Bulb Farms in 1934. The company first produced the traditional line of Dutch bulbs, starting with 48 hectares (120 acres) of daffodils and 12 hectares (30 acres) of Dutch iris. De Graaff and his staff were active in breeding varieties of both. By the late 1950s, the firm had come to devote its entire acreage to the cultivation of lilies.

A man of many talents, de Graaff was an excellent promoter, manager, and salesman, who knew exactly how a successful company should be run. He was also a fine, prolific writer who believed that knowledge should be shared. He wrote, "I see no danger in making the knowledge we have acquired available to other growers, amateur or professional. The more competition, the better for all of us, for inevitably, new sources of supply will open up new markets."

The lily varieties hybridized at Oregon Bulb Farms are legion. Perhaps the best known from de Graaff's era are the Mid-Century hybrids and several strains of trumpet and Oriental lilies.

De Graaff published several books, including *The Complete Book of Lilies* (1961), as well as excellent articles for the general public in *Life* magazine, the *Saturday Evening Post,* and *Reader's Digest.* He received many awards, including the Veitch Memorial Medal from the Royal Horticultural Society in 1967, and the E. H. Wilson Award from the North American Lily Society in 1966. A series of tributes to him appeared in the 1989 *Yearbook of the North American Lily Society.*

All who love, enjoy, and appreciate lilies owe Jan de Graaff an enormous debt. He was the one who advanced and stimulated the interests of others and, with their help, made the beauty of the lily universally accessible. May we all be blessed with such a legacy! The creations he inspired made many lives richer and brought a unique beauty to a world too often engulfed by the opposite. For this we offer our heartfelt gratitude.

Robert A. Griesbach

Robert Griesbach began his work with lilies in 1960. His first attempts at doubling the chromosome number in a Chinese trumpet lily involved treating germinating seeds and seedlings with colchicine. In an experiment with 180 seedlings of *Lilium regale,* he obtained three plants that were completely tetraploid yet quite fertile.

Griesbach carried out successful scale treatments, again using colchicine, with Chinese trumpet hybrids in the 1960s, using the Golden Clarion strain and 'Bright Star'. The tetraploid forms he obtained from these cultivars contributed heavily to his breeding program, which had previously been based on tetraploid forms of *Lilium regale* and *L. leucanthum* var. *centifolium* produced by seedling treatment. In later years, Griesbach produced tetraploid forms of the beautiful and indestructible 'White Henryi' through colchicine scale treatment.

After obtaining the tetraploid forms of 'Mega' and 'Mountaineer' from Samuel Emsweller in 1961, Griesbach became interested in converting Asiatic lilies to their tetraploid forms. Among those he converted are 'Connecticut King', 'Connecticut Yankee', Fiesta hybrids, 'Lime Ice', 'Magic Cream', 'Maureen', 'Nutmegger', Pastel hybrids, 'Pipestone Giant', 'Sterling Star', and 'Top Clas'. He also produced the tetraploid form of 'Black Beauty' also by treating the scales with colchicine. He crossed it both ways to his tetraploid 'White Henryi'. The clone 'Leslie Woodriff' was named from the original five seedlings that resulted from crossing tetraploid 'Black Beauty' with tetraploid 'White Henryi'. All these hybrids were moderately fertile, as were those from the reciprocal cross. Griesbach produced many remarkable new colors and patterns by deriving second and third generations from these lines.

The lily world has been greatly enriched by Griesbach's remarkable work with tetraploids. The tetraploid trumpet hybrids have been introduced by Wayside Gardens under the name American Classics; five strains are named after our national parks (Plate 104). The clone 'Leslie Woodriff' is well known and climbing steadily to the top of the North American Lily Society's lily popularity poll; other beautiful clones have been propagated, including clear reds with gold margins. Griesbach's magnificent work, gratifyingly, is being continued by him and others.

Plate 104. *Lilium* Yosemite strain, from Robert Griesbach

Earl N. Hornback

Earl Hornback (1912–1966) was born in Centralia, Washington; he joined the staff of Oregon Bulb Farms in 1930. In the early years he was involved in hybridizing and growing of superior daffodils. Later he worked closely with Harold Comber to create superior clones and strains of lilies, a subject on which his knowledge was unparalleled.

Hornback was one of those rare individuals whose knowledge and stature grew as the job he was engaged in increased in importance. He was ruthless in destroying any plants that did not meet his high standards. His knowledge of lilies extended into every area, including hybridizing and genetics, propagation, growing, harvesting, processing, packing, storage, and shipping. He read extensively and constantly searched for new and superior handling methods. He also designed machines for planting, harvesting, processing, and packing lily bulbs. In the foreword of the 1966 *Yearbook of the North American Lily Society*, he wrote:

> In mass production, we look forward to steady progress in better growing and handling methods and to further improvements in the machinery used in planting, harvesting, grading, and packaging. This will ensure an ample supply of lily bulbs of fine quality and lead to their ever-increasing popularity.

A skilled photographer, Hornback produced a film in 1965 that is a classic, showing every aspect of the lily industry. Many articles by Hornback appeared in the yearbooks of the North American Lily Society and Royal Horticultural Society. They covered such topics as genetics, hybridizing, propagation, and growing. The Earl N. Hornback Award is given annually by the North American Lily Society to the seedling showing the greatest advance in hybridizing.

Hornback was not satisfied with any result unless he knew how and why it had been obtained. He had to understand the workings of nature's miracles. His discipline, courage, honesty, and faith in the future stand out in my memory. The world is a better place because he saw opportunities and made them reality.

Chris North

Chris North worked with lilies at the Scottish Horticultural Research Institute in Invergowrie, Scotland, from 1966 to the mid-1970s. He was a true pioneer in the use of embryo culture to obtain unusual lily hybrids from distantly related species and hybrids. His remarkable results inspired others to follow in his footsteps.

In an excellent article, "New Lily Hybrids with the Aid of Embryo Culture," published in the 1970 yearbook of the Royal Horticultural Society, North wrote that if there were no barriers to hybridization between the approximately 90 *Lilium* species, it should be possible to obtain more than 3000 different paired species combinations. Yet, by the early 1960s, only about 50 combinations had been produced. North worked to increase their number, focusing on the Euro-Caucasian group of lilies and a wide range of Asiatic species and hybrids.

Many of the Euro-Caucasian group had grown strongly in North European gardens for many years with *Lilium* ×*testaceum* being the only known hybrid. Using embryo culture, North crossed *L. pyrenaicum* with *L. chalcedonicum, L. ciliatum, L. monadelphum, L. pyrenaicum* subsp. *ponticum, L. pyrenaicum* subsp. *carniolicum* var. *jankae,* and *L. szovitsianum* to produce exotic hybrids. He also crossed *L. szovitsianum* with *L. candidum* and *L. chalcedonicum.* He created other exotic hybrids. Of the Asiatic species, North used *L. bulbiferum* var. *croceum, L. davidii, L. lankongense, L. tigrinum* var. *flaviflorum,* and *L. wilsonii* var. *flavum.* He also used Asiatic hybrids, including the three Mid-Century clones, 'Cinnabar', 'Destiny', and 'Enchantment' and several hybrids with strong influence of *L. davidii* in their ancestry, such as 'Amber Gold', 'Black Butterfly', 'Delicious', 'Edith Cecilia', 'Red Fortune', and 'Viking'. North put great emphasis on virus-tolerance in this Asiatic parental selections.

The two most important hybrids produced by North were 'Adonis' (*Lilium lankongense* × *L.* 'Edith Cecilia') and 'Ariadne' *L. lankongense* × *L. davidii* 'Maxwill'). The latter has been a strong, reliable clone in Oregon for more than 20 years, winning many awards. The triploid hybrids of *L. lankongense* were crossed to Asiatic hybrids again using embryo culture. 'Eros' (clear pink), 'Pan' (soft cream), and 'Theseus' (dark red) were among those introduced. The beautiful clones 'Iona' (yellow-orange) and 'Invergowrie' (red-purple) were crosses between *L. lankongense* and Asiatic hybrids. The "North Family" group of beautiful hybrids resulted from crossing (*L. lankongense* × *L. davidii*) with Asiatic hybrids. It includes 'Angela North' (dark red; Plate 105), 'Barbara North' (medium pink), 'Bronwen North' (pale mauve-pink), 'Eileen North' (deep rose-pink), 'Hannah North' (pale yellow), 'Helen North' (red-mauve), 'Karen North' (orange-pink), 'Marie North' (pale mauve-pink), 'Peggy North' (orange), and 'Rosemary North' (orange). All are triploids with a distinct fragrance and with varying degrees of speckles patterns on the flower.

Plate 105. *Lilium* 'Angela North', from Chris North. Photo by Willard Hoffman.

The lily world owes much to Chris North for the wealth of unique and beautiful lilies he and his team produced. In 1977 the Royal Horticultural Society awarded North the Lyttel Lily Cup.

Cecil F. Patterson

Cecil Patterson (1892–1961) was professor and head of the department of horticulture at the University of Saskatchewan in Saskatoon. His work with lilies started in 1934; his goal was to develop pink and white lilies that would be hardy under ordinary garden conditions in the prairies of northwestern Canada.

His most successful cross was between *Lilium davidii* var. *willmottiae* and *L. cernuum,* which led to a host of pastel-flowered hybrids. These included 'Apricot Glow', 'Burnished Rose', 'Edith Cecilia', 'Lemon Queen', 'Orchid Queen', 'Rose Dawn', 'White Gold', and 'White Princess'. Most of the Patterson hybrids were aneuploids and thus quite infertile. 'Edith Cecilia' and 'Lemon Queen' were most fertile and were used extensively at Oregon Bulb Farms to produce the beautiful Harlequin hybrids, and eventually upright Asiatics in a wide pastel range.

The lily world was greatly enriched by the work of this dedicated

Canadian scientist. It is safe to say that most of the fine pastel-colored Asiatics now in commerce are derived from his original cross, especially from 'Edith Cecilia'.

Norma E. Pfeiffer

Norma Pfeiffer (1889–1989) held a doctorate in biology and worked at the Boyce Thompson Institute of Plant Research at Yonkers, New York, now part of Cornell University. A fellowship had been established there to further knowledge of lily diseases, and a fine collection of species and hybrids had been assembled. It was suggested to Pfeiffer that this collection provided an excellent opportunity for hybridizing work.

Pfeiffer made extensive crosses with Asiatics, martagon hybrids, trumpets, and Orientals. Her seedlings were given to commercial growers, who propagated, named, and sold them. The only lilies she herself named and registered were the Terrace City hybrids, a strain that resulted from a cross between *Lilium martagon* var. *album* and *L. hansonii*. She considered her greatest contribution to lilies to be the work she did in crossing *L. auratum* var. *platyphyllum* and *L. speciosum* with *L. japonicum* and *L. rubellum*. This fine material was used at Oregon Bulb Farms to produce the Imperial Pink, Pink Glory, and Celebrity strains. Other subjects Pfeiffer researched included pollen storage, propagation, forcing, fasciation, and dormancy.

Perhaps the most outstanding series of articles ever published in the *Yearbook of the North American Lily Society* was Pfeiffer's "Great Names in Lilies," which appeared between 1961 and 1979. Her thorough research made this series great. In all, she wrote more than 50 articles for the Society's yearbooks and quarterly bulletins. She received the E. H. Wilson Award in 1962.

A. J. Porter

A. J. "Bert" Porter was born in Guilford, Surrey, England, in 1907 and came with his parents to Canada when he was six years old. His love for lilies began at a very early age. He was the founder of Honeywood Nursery near Parkside, Saskatchewan, where he bred hardy plants for the Canadian prairie provinces. He worked closely with other hybridizers, including Frank Leith Skinner and Percy Wright.

Porter introduced a host of hardy, strong, dependable lilies over the years, including 'Earlibird', 'Girls Only', 'Orange Light', 'Pink Champagne', 'Red Carpet', 'Redland' (synonym 'Warrior'), and 'Rusty'. 'Red Carpet' was the first outstanding lily of miniature habit and was used extensively at Oregon Bulb Farms and elsewhere in breeding lilies for pot culture and border planting.

Porter has written many articles over the years, many of them published in the *Yearbook of the North American Lily Society*. They deal with hybridizing, propagation, and hardiness in lilies. He was presented with the E. H. Wilson Award in 1977.

Isabella Preston

Isabella Preston (1881–1965) was born in Lancaster, England, and came to Ontario, Canada, in 1912. Eight years later she joined the staff of the division of horticulture at the Central Experimental Farm near Ottawa.

In July 1916 Preston crossed *Lilium sargentiae* with *L. regale* to produce several beautiful seedlings; one was named 'George C. Creelman'. Many of the fine trumpet lily clones and seedling strains today are descendants of this lily and its sister seedlings. The Stenographer series, named for the secretaries at the experimental farm, was Preston's greatest achievement in lily breeding. These resulted from a 1929 cross between *Lilium davidii* var. *willmottiae* and a *L.* ×*elegans* × *L. dauricum* seedling. The Preston hybrids were used extensively in the breeding program at Oregon Bulb Farms. Several of the original Stenographer lilies, and perhaps others, are still being grown commercially by Barrie Strohman in Manitoba.

A list of Preston's hybrids and the articles she published appears in the 1966 *Yearbook of the North American Lily Society*. She received many honors, including the E. H. Wilson Award in 1961. The Isabella Preston Trophy is now awarded by the North American Lily Society for the best lily in show at their annual international shows. The Royal Horticultural Society bestowed on her the Veitch Memorial Medal in 1938, and the Lyttel Lily Cup in 1950. Beyond the world of lilies, she is also remembered for her work in hybridizing lilacs; the series of vigorous hybrids she developed in the 1920s is known as *Syringa* ×*prestoniae*.

Charles Robinson

Charles "Robbie" Robinson was born in Lancashire, England, in 1908. After studying at the Lancaster Agricultural College, John Innes Horticultural Research Institute in Surrey, and the Royal Botanic Gardens at Kew, he entered the British Ministry of Agriculture as a field officer, serving in England and Kenya. He immigrated to Canada in 1946. A professional botanist, he has been studying lilies since 1928; after retirement, he transferred his knowledge and skills into the development of new lilies.

In 1970 Robinson received premier recognition, the Earl N. Hornback Award, for an outstanding seedling, a cross between *Lilium candidum* var. *salonikae* and *L. monadelphum* that was later named 'June Fragrance'. This interesting hybrid produced many fascinating new forms when crossed with Asiatic hybrids; in most cases embryo culture was used to obtain them.

For many years Robinson engaged in a program to create new color variations in the Asiatic group and to introduce new species into those breeding lines. He worked with *Lilium amabile, L. callosum, L. cernuum,* and *L. pumilum.* He also worked to improve flower texture, to produce fragrance in Asiatics, and to increase hardiness and bud count. His work with *L. pumilum* and the varieties of this species was truly outstanding, with many magnificent hybrids produced. 'Fiery Sunset', introduced in 1980, is perhaps the best known. His excellent article on the species and its hybrids appeared in the 1977 *Yearbook of the North American Lily Society.*

Robinson looked for unusual traits in his hybrids and used the best Connecticut hybrids for breeding. Lilies with orange-red bars and with blotches and ribs fascinated him. Named hybrids he originated included 'Diplomat', 'Statesman', and 'Torchbearer'. He was generous in releasing his hybrids to other breeders; the *Lilium pumilum* hybrids were used extensively at Oregon Bulb Farms and by Columbia-Platte Lilies.

Besides his breeding achievements, Robinson's contributions to the lily world must include his well-researched articles, which appeared in the yearbooks of the North American Lily Society and the Royal Horticultural Society. "Color Pigments of Lily Flowers," published in the

1976 *Yearbook of the North American Lily Society,* is required reading for anyone interested in hybridizing. The value of his writing prompted the Ontario Regional Lily Society to reprint his articles as a booklet in 1979.

Robinson received the E. H. Wilson Award in 1983, an award he richly deserved.

Dorothy B. Schaefer

Dorothy Schaefer is an Iowan by birth and by choice. After growing up in Des Moines and graduating from Drake University, she worked for the federal government until her retirement in 1982. In 1976 she moved from Des Moines to an acre of rich farmland 10 miles west, where she built a home and established her garden. Her perennial borders of lilies, irises, delphiniums, peonies, and other showy flowers are a blaze of color from early spring until fall. Her intense interest in lilies is evident in the hundreds of seedlings growing in separate beds near the house.

Schaefer became a member of the North American Lily Society in 1974; she was elected secretary of the Society in 1980 and took over the duties of executive secretary-treasurer in 1981. Her work in this capacity was truly outstanding. She has traveled extensively in Europe, South America, Asia, and the South Pacific, and she corresponds with friends all over the world. She has become a true ambassador for lilies in this respect, keeping in touch with lily friends worldwide; who can estimate the impact of this fine correspondent?

To communicate the beauty of lilies has always been her goal. This has been very evident in the seed exchange, for which she served as chairperson several times, carrying out the tasks in her own highly efficient manner.

During the summer months Dorothy Schaefer can be found in her garden, carefully and intelligently pollinating a wide variety of lilies. Her work with Asiatic tetraploids was exceptional, and many hybridizers are eternally grateful for the seed she produced in a wide color range. She also did remarkable work with tetraploid trumpets and their hybrids. She obtained material from the fine work of Robert Griesbach, produced plenty of seed, and generously distributed the fruits of her labors over many years.

Dorothy Schaefer received the Slate-MacDaniels Award in 1984 for an unparalleled contribution to the world of lilies.

Peter Schenk

Peter Schenk lives in the coastal community of Medemblik in the Netherlands. He spent a year in the work-study program at Oregon Bulb Farms, starting in May 1967. Upon graduation, Schenk worked for the Dutch government and was deeply involved in the flower forcing industry, advising growers on methods of handling a wide range of new lilies that were then coming on the market. He eventually joined the firm of Bischoff Tulleken.

Schenk is a hybridizer of international renown; his research and experiments have extended to the use of tissue culture and embryo culture, both critical to his work. Although he has dealt with all groups of lilies, he is best known for his Asiatic hybrids, notably 'Compass', 'Gran Sasso', and 'Parisienne'. His work with tetraploids has produced many spectacular clones. He has also bred Asiatic pot lilies; 'Horizon' is particularly well known.

The outstanding crosses between *Lilium longiflorum* and Asiatic hybrids at Bischoff Tulleken are a reflection of Schenk's skills. His clone 'Longistar' has figured largely in this work, as has its tetraploid form. 'Moneymaker' is a standout among the L.A. hybrids. He has also produced many fine upright Oriental lilies in a wide range of colors, including the pure white clones 'Jan de Graaff' and 'White Stargazer'. His contributions in pot Orientals have also been notable. As a result of his work with Orienpets over many years, he produced several clones of unique color or form. His basic goal is to produce strong upright hybrids in colors that will increase the color range of upright Orienpets.

Schenk generously shares his findings with growers and hybridizers around the world. He is equally generous in sharing pollen and bulbs with those who express interest. His articles in the yearbooks of the North American Lily Society keep all informed of activities in the Netherlands.

The leading lily judge in his country, Schenk is also a longtime member of the committee for breeders' rights, which deals with plant patent protection. He has traveled and lectured worldwide, encouraging people to do their own growing and hybridizing.

Schenk was given the E. H. Wilson Award by the North American Lily Society in 1991, as a true friend of the Society and the foremost lily authority of the Netherlands. No one could have been more deserving.

Frank Leith Skinner

Frank Skinner (1882–1967) was born in Rosehearty, Aberdeenshire, Scotland, and moved to Canada at the age of eighteen. He eventually established a nursery near Dropmore, Manitoba, where he soon began breeding plants in the hope of increasing the number of hardy subjects for use in the prairie provinces. He brought many plants from the colder regions of the world to Dropmore to be tested and used in his breeding work.

Skinner's work with lilies was extensive, and he introduced a host of varieties from the early 1930s on. They included 'Black Prince' (*Lilium martagon* × *L. hansonii* F2), 'Dunkirk' (dark red Asiatic), 'Glacier' (*L. martagon* var. *album* hybrid), 'Helen Carol' (yellow *L. maculatum* hybrid), 'Lady Lou' (*L. davidii* hybrid), 'Lemon Lady' (*L. davidii* hybrid), 'Margaret Johnson' (*L. tigrinum* × *L. maculatum,* with a remarkable resemblance to 'Enchantment'), 'Maxwill' (a form of *L. davidii* he originally thought to be a hybrid), *Lilium ×scottiae* (*L. davidii* var. *willmottiae* × *L. ×elegans* 'Mahogany'), and 'The Duchess' (*L. amabile* var. *luteum* × *L. ×elegans* 'Yellow Purity').

Skinner received many honors for his plant-breeding achievements, including the Order of the British Empire and the E. H. Wilson Award from the North American Lily Society in 1964. He was a great pioneer in the realm of lily hybridizing.

George L. Slate

George Slate (1899–1976) was professor of pomology and viticulture at the New York State Agricultural Experiment Station in Geneva, New York. He retired in 1969 after 47 years of dedicated service to all phases of horticulture.

Slate became interested in lilies after receiving a collection of lily bulbs from his father-in-law, the great plant collector E. H. Wilson.

Slate's book *Lilies for American Gardens,* published in 1939, was a model of its kind. The history of the lily, especially about American species, was covered in greater detail than in any other book.

Because of his knowledge of the historical background of lilies and his close acquaintance with hybridizers over many years, Slate was one of the few real experts in the lily world. He was editor of the North American Lily Society yearbooks from 1947 until 1973. He was quite interested in lily diseases and pests, and his authoritative *Lily Disease Handbook* aided growers for many years. He was a prolific writer, contributing articles to the yearbooks of the North American Lily Society and Royal Horticultural Society.

The contributions made by Slate to lily hybridizing were enormous. The Cascade strain of *Lilium candidum* involved more than 30 years of careful selection for strength, flower size and placement, and disease resistance. His hybrids involving *L. martagon,* its varieties *album* and *cattaniae,* and *L. hansonii* included spectacular colors such as bright yellows and golds. His early Asiatic hybrids employed *L. ×elegans* 'Mahogany' crossed with *L. davidii* hybrids, which led to the clones 'Paprika' and 'Tabasco' grown for many years at Oregon Bulb Farms. The Aurelian hybrids also interested Slate, who sent many beautiful clones to Oregon Bulb Farms. He was concerned with introducing *L. regale* into the Aurelian lines. His Potomac hybrids from *L. speciosum* were remarkably strong and were used for many years to produce outstanding strains in Oregon.

Slate was generous in releasing his hybrids, taking no thought for compensation other than the knowledge that they were being used and growing in his friends' gardens. He often remarked that success in plant breeding depended mostly on choosing the right parents, and he had a knack for doing just that. His perception and knowledge, combined with a great sense of humor, made him a favorite with all who were privileged to know him. He was a giant in the world of lilies. The countless awards given to him included the E. H. Wilson Award in 1960.

David Stone and F. Henry Payne

David Stone (1919–1978) was in the heating and plumbing business, but it was his dream to retire and pursue horticulture as both hobby and vocation. Unfortunately, he died quite young. Stone was recognized nationally for his knowledge of hybridizing, a subject on which he lectured throughout the country. He was one of several New Englanders who inherited the Ralph Warner line of lilies. His main idea was to produce Asiatic lilies without spots. For this he crossed 'Gold Urn', an unspotted marigold orange, with *Lilium lancifolium* var. *flaviflorum* to produce the well-known 'Connecticut Yankee' and 'Nutmegger', the forerunners of other famous Connecticut hybrids.

Stone continued his breeding work in partnership with F. Henry Payne, a skilled horticulturist and hybridizer. They worked with every spotless lily available and introduced several true species into their program, including *Lilium wilsonii* var. *flavum*. They experimented with the ways varied growing conditions affected vitality and disease resistance. Many of their hybrids were purchased by Jan de Graaff in the mid-1960s. The vigor and disease resistance of these plants were without equal, and they were an enormous boost to the lily industry in both North America and the Netherlands.

'Connecticut King' was, in my opinion, the finest, most disease-resistant Asiatic hybrid clone ever produced. Its impact on lily hybridizing has been greater than that of any other Asiatic clone; it is proving equally useful in its tetraploid form. It is still grown extensively as a cut flower in the Netherlands. 'Sunray', a shorter upright yellow with gold markings, is also grown in the Netherlands for cutting. It is an excellent garden lily and was used to hybridize some of the orange and yellow pot lilies. The beautiful outfacing golden yellow 'Connecticut Lemonglow' (Plate 106) and the shorter 'Keystone' were superb garden lilies used to breed shorter Asiatic lilies with good foliage. 'Connecticut Beauty' (synonym 'Medallion'), a soft yellow with huge flowers, was a fine lily for both garden planting and cut-flower production. 'Connecticut Queen' and 'Connecticut Red' were two more fine hybrids used in breeding at Oregon Bulb Farms. The Yellow Blaze strain from Stone and Payne includes perhaps the most indestructible of all their lilies. Hybrids between 'Nutmegger' and *Lilium wilsonii* var. *flavum*, they simply grow like weeds; they are also appreciated for their late flowering.

The lily world will forever be grateful for the enormous contributions made by David Stone and F. Henry Payne. Payne received the

E. H. Wilson Award for his outstanding contribution to the world of lilies in 1976.

Plate 106. *Lilium* 'Connecticut Lemonglow', from David Stone and F. Henry Payne

Harve and Ruth Strahm

An opportunity to grow Easter lilies (*Lilium longiflorum*) commercially lured Harve and Ruth Strahm and their family to the southern Oregon coast in 1959. They settled in Harbor near Brookings, just south of the Chetco River. Upon meeting the neighboring lily grower and hybridizer Leslie Woodriff and discovering his magnificent Oriental hybrid lilies, they conceived a strong desire to branch out and grow these beautiful flowers. Ruth eventually went to work for the Woodriffs; at the end of her second year of employment there, she asked for and received tiny seedling bulblets in payment for her time.

The Strahms grew Orientals in a wide range of colors and habits, including forms suitable for garden planting, cut flowers (upright forms), and pot plants. Visitors to their nursery recognized their good eyes for beauty and form. Among the Strahms' outstanding introductions were 'Allura', 'Fanfare', 'Fantango', 'Harbor Star', 'Rosalie', 'White Frills', and 'White Ice'. 'Sans Souci' is perhaps their best known, having been grown for many years as a pot subject. The profusely illustrated catalog issued by the Strahms encouraged many to grow and love Oriental lilies.

The North American Lily Society presented them with the E. H. Wilson Award in 1987, an award richly deserved.

James C. Taylor

James Taylor (1898–1976) was appointed in 1936 to the staff of what is now the department of horticultural science at Ontario Agricultural College, a division of the University of Guelph. He proved himself a dedicated teacher, an unusually capable plantsman, and a hybridizer well respected in the world of lilies. He was a Scot whose horticultural training was in the British tradition, gained at private gardens, at the John Innes Horticultural Institute, and at the Royal Botanic Gardens, Kew. His interest in lilies began at Kew and was reinforced when he set foot in Canada in 1935, when he began working with E. Frank Palmer.

Taylor eventually introduced a range of fascinating hybrids including 'Cardinal' (*Lilium lancifolium* × *L. amabile*), 'Goldcrest' (Asiatic hybrid × *L. pumilum* 'Golden Gleam'), 'Meadowlark' (involving Stenographer hybrids, *L.* ×*hollandicum,* and *L. lancifolium*), 'Redstart' (*L.* ×*hollandicum* × *L. lancifolium*), 'Skylark' (*L. lancifolium* hybrid), and 'Waxwing' (Asiatic hybrid × *L. amabile*). Many of his hybrids were used in breeding in the early years of Oregon Bulb Farms. 'Goldcrest' proved virtually indestructible; it had a tendency to produce unreduced gametes, resulting in occasional triploid and tetraploid offspring. Taylor would have been proud to see so many strong, disease-resistant lilies descended from his crosses.

Julius Wadekamper

A teacher by profession, Julius Wadekamper earned a master's degree in horticulture at the University of Minnesota. His interest in lilies and their culture began in his teens, but it was not until he returned from a teaching post in Brazil that he began to hybridize lilies. He has introduced 'Bully', 'Chiquita', 'Dr. Yu', 'King Midas', 'Orange Ray', 'Seashell', 'Snowlark', 'White Prince', and 'Winnie'. The beautiful clone 'Miss Alice' (synonym 'Senhora Alice') is named in honor of his mother.

Wadekamper is working to develop early and late-blooming lilies to extend the season. His special interest is brushmarks. 'Pumpkin Pie' and 'Willowwood' are two of his early introductions in that series. A later introduction, 'Purple Reign' (white with intense brushmarks), is truly spectacular.

One of Wadekamper's most important contributions was his introduction and marketing of new lilies hybridized by more than 50 individuals and institutions in both North American and Europe. Through his company, Borbeleta Gardens, he made possible the worldwide distribution of such fine lilies as 'Czardas', 'Earl of Rochester', 'Gold Lode', 'King Pete', 'Leslie Woodriff', 'Paul Bunyan', and many others.

Wadekamper's unsurpassed record of service to the North American Lily Society has included serving as director, vice president, president, chairperson of judges' training, chairperson of the seed exchange, and chairperson of the research committee. For his outstanding contributions, he received the E. H. Wilson Award in 1984.

Leslie Woodriff

Leslie Woodriff (1910–1997) was born in Quanah, Texas. In the mid-1940s he, his wife, Ruth, and their family moved to the small community of Harbor on the southern Oregon coast. They established Fairyland Lily and Begonia Gardens, continuing in that location until the 1970s, when they moved to McKinleyville, California.

The material used by the Woodriffs to achieve their hybridizing goals may have seemed unconventional, even unorthodox, to many; incompatibility barriers did not exist, as far as Leslie and his helpers were concerned. Their use of large quantities of mixed pollen may have held the key to their success; this surprising method did bring results.

One of the Woodriffs' most remarkable achievements was 'Black Beauty'. The tetraploid form of this remarkable hybrid was used by Griesbach in breeding the clone 'Leslie Woodriff', and by LeVern Freimann to produce 'Scarlet Delight'. Other Woodriff introductions include 'Pink Tiger' (*L. regale* hybrid × *L. lancifolium* hybrid), 'Oriental Charm' (*L. speciosum* var. *rubrum* × *L. nepalense*), and 'Ruth Woodriff' (*L. nobilissimum* × *L.* ×*parkmannii*). The North American Lily Society's Hall of Fame lists not only 'Black Beauty', but also Woodriff's outstanding Aurelian hybrids 'Gold Eagle' and 'White Henryi'.

Leslie was one of the first to use the earlier-flowering species *Lilium japonicum* and *L. rubellum* in Oriental hybridizing. His dream was to flower these lilies in 70 to 80 days from planting in the greenhouse, as Asiatic hybrids do. This program resulted in the strains Atomic Hybrids, Exotics, and Little Fairies. The upright Orientals, however, are the group that brought Woodriff international recognition. 'Stargazer' has achieved by far the greatest acreage devoted to any commercial lily. The beautiful clear pink 'Le Rêve' is also well known, and the beautiful clear pink upright 'Woodriff's Memory' was named in honor of the man who made it all possible.

An account of the Woodriff family's work can be found in the 1991 *Yearbook of the North American Lily Society*. Leslie has received several awards. The Dutch Lily Growers presented him with the coveted Dix Award in 1991, recognizing his vast achievements in lily hybridizing. The North American Lily Society gave him the E. H. Wilson Award in 1978. To these were added honors from the New Zealand Lily Society and the Oregon Federation of Garden Clubs. "We have opened a few doors," Leslie Woodriff has often said; and indeed he and his family have. Through these doors Oriental cut-flower lilies have been made available to countless millions of homes, and indestructible plants to thousands of gardens.

J. S. Yeates

J. S. Yeates (1900–1986) was appointed to the staff of Massey Agricultural College near Palmerston North, New Zealand, in 1928, after distinguishing himself as a scholar and researcher. At the time of his death he was the oldest surviving member of the original staff of the college, now known as Massey University.

Yeates earned an international reputation for his contributions to both rhododendron and lily breeding, the results of which can be seen in many parts of the world. His work with lilies concentrated mainly on the *Lilium ×parkmannii* (Oriental) group, although he also dealt with trumpet lilies and their hybrids. He introduced several Oriental clones, including 'Elizabeth' (perhaps the most disease-resistant and virus-tolerant Oriental lily), 'Kimbolton Pink', 'Red Ruby', 'Red Trump', and 'Snowdrift'. The best known, however, is 'Journey's End', grown extensively for forcing in both North America and Europe. Oriental clones from Yeates's work were used in the hybridizing program at Oregon Bulb Farms for many years.

Yeates is known as the originator of the genetic dwarf Oriental lilies. The first of these resulted from inbreeding normal forms of *Lilium auratum* to produce Tom Thumb. This in turn was crossed to other Oriental hybrids, resulting in dwarf lilies in a wide color range. Selected clones included 'Little Gem', 'Little Jane', 'Little Lavender', 'Little Pink', 'Little Robin', and 'Little Tom'. Yeates generously sent clones and seed to Oregon Bulb Farms, where the seedlings were later introduced as the Little Rascals strain (Plate 107).

Plate 107. *Lilium* Little Rascal strain, from J. S. Yeates. Photo by Herman v. Wall.

In hybridizing trumpet lilies, Yeates looked for the classical trumpet shape, good texture, and superior flower placement. His clone 'Penelope' was outstanding in all these respects. In later years Yeates worked with tetraploids, converting his clone 'Journey's End' to this form with colchicine.

Yeates received many awards, including the Lyttel Lily Cup from the Royal Horticultural Society in 1969. He was also named a Member of the British Empire, a royal honor, in 1977. He received the Victoria Memorial gold medal for advancement and achievement in the science of practical horticulture. The lily world is much indebted to this fine man.

Carlton R. Yerex

Carlton Yerex (d. 1981) started a nursery devoted mainly to lilies in the early 1930s. He developed sizable stocks of species and hybrids that were more disease-resistant than any others in the Pacific Northwest. After several moves, he installed his plantings near Sherwood, Oregon.

Yerex became acquainted with Edouard Debras, who in 1925 had succeeded in crossing *Lilium sargentiae* with *L. henryi* to produce *L. ×aurelianense*. They exchanged stock, and Yerex used *L. ×aurelianense* extensively in his hybridizing. When Yerex realized that he had produced a group of outstanding plants, he decided to call them Aurelian hybrids, a name later appropriated by others to cover a multitude of strains and clones from crosses between *L. henryi* and Chinese trumpet species unrelated to Yerex's original stock. Among the many clones and strains introduced by Yerex are 'Bright Cloud', 'Eventide', 'Moonlight Sonata', 'Shenandoah', 'Ta Ming', and 'Whirlybird'. Much of his excellent material was both introduced and used in hybridizing by Oregon Bulb Farms.

Yerex was a quiet, gentle man of unusual warmth and depth, and a faithful steward of the gifts given to him. His work with lilies will live down through the generations of trumpet and Aurelian hybrids. He was an unselfish lover of beauty and a scholarly seeker of truth. He received the E. H. Wilson Award from the North American Lily Society in 1975.

Glossary

alternate: of leaves, placed singly at intervals along the stem, rather than in pairs or whorls.

aneuploid: a plant with an abnormal number of chromosomes in its cells.

anther: the pollen-bearing part of the stamen.

apomixis: reproduction from cells other than ovules, in which the normal sexual reproduction is replaced by an asexual type and seed is produced without pollination; adjectival form, **apomictic**.

asexual propagation: propagation by vegetative means, such as stem bulbils, underground stem bulblets, scales, or tissue culture.

auxin: a plant growth hormone.

basal plate: lower part of the bulb, where the scales originate.

basal roots: roots that arise from the basal plate to anchor and sustain the bulb following planting.

botrytis: a fungal disease that attacks the foliage of lilies and is especially prevalent during warm, humid conditions in spring.

bulbil: small bulb borne above ground in the axil of the leaf on some lilies, such as *Lilium tigrinum* and its hybrids.

bulblet: small bulb formed on the underground part of the stem, just above the main bulb.

capsule: the seedpod containing the seed following fertilization.

carotinoids: yellow and orange pigments that color the flowers of some lilies.

chaff: light matter in the capsule that contains no endosperm or embryo; nonviable seed which should be separated from normal seed before sowing.

chromosome: rod- or loop-shaped body into which the chromatin of the cell nucleus forms during cell division and in which the genes are located. Lilies (except polyploids) have 24 chromosomes; the chromosomes of each species differ such that their presence can identify hybrids from unusual crosses.

clone: genetically identical plants derived from a single individual through constant asexual propagation.

concentric: of bulbs, having a common center, with new scales forming within the parent bulb in order around the plate.

contractile: of basal roots that can contract and pull the bulb deeper in the soil.

cotyledon: first leaf emerging from epigeal or quick-germinating seed, appearing as a loop or "hairpin" and then straightening into a grasslike leaf, often carrying the seed coat on the tip.

cross: the process of transferring the pollen of one lily to the stigma of another.

cultivar: a genetically unique plant selected and maintained in cultivation, given a cultivar name written capitalized within single quotes.

desiccated: dried out, water-deficient or liquid-deficient; can sometimes be restored with soaking.

dehisce: of plant parts, to separate from the rest of the plant at maturity; in lilies, used in regard to pollen and seedpods (capsules).

embryo: the earliest stage in the development of an organism; the rudimentary plant within the seed, appearing as a rod-shaped mass in the endosperm of the lily seed, often visible against light.

embryo culture, embryo rescue: technique used to raise hybrids of distantly-related lilies when the seed's endosperm does not develop normally; the embryos are excised before ripening and cultured in suitable media in test tubes.

endosperm: the nutritive substance within the embryo sac of the ovule, a food supply in which the embryo is embedded.

epigeal germination: rapid germination pattern in which the seed produces a cotyledon above ground, followed by true leaves.

fertile: capable of producing viable seeds or pollen; able to reproduce when crossed with either closely or distantly related individuals.

fertilization: the fusion of the contents of the pollen grain with those of the ovule, resulting in the initiation of a viable seed.

filament: the stalk or support of the anther.

flocculation: aggregation; forming small masses; used about soil properties.

fusarium: a soil-borne fungal disease that attacks bulbs and roots.

gene: the unit of inheritance, carried on a chromosome and passed from generation to generation.

generation: in hybrids, F_1 denotes the first generation of seedlings obtained from a cross; the F_2 generation arises from crossing seedlings of the F_1 generation.

genus (plural, **genera**): a group of closely related species; lilies, for example, belong to the genus *Lilium* within the family Liliaceae.

grex: see **strain.**

hardening off: a process of acclimatizing plants to cooler temperatures and stronger light.

homozygous: of clones that are true-breeding (that is, have dominant genes) for a particular characteristic, such as color of flower.

hybrid: a plant produced from a cross between two different species, a species and a hybrid, or two hybrids.

hypogeal germination: a slow germination pattern in which seed produces only a tiny bulb and no above-ground cotyledon the first season, requiring a period of cold before producing true leaves.

inflorescence: the pattern of arrangement of the flowers on a stem; in lilies, usually a raceme or umbel.

mule: of hybrids such as 'Black Beauty' that are sterile, having no fertile pollen or ovules.

mutation: also called "sporting," a spontaneous, genetically transmissible variation in a plant, the result of modifications in the genes.

nectary, nectary furrow: a gland that secretes nectar; the nectar-producing groove on the perianth segment; in lilies, often of contrasting color, resulting in a star-shaped central pattern.

outfacing: of flowers, held so that they face out in all directions from the main stem.

ovary: the base of the pistil, in which the ovules are contained; a single lily ovary may contain as many as 2000 ovules.

ovule: the structure which, after being fertilized by pollen, becomes a seed.

papillae: tiny whisker-like projections surrounding the nectaries in certain lilies, such as *Lilium speciosum* and *L. henryi*.

pasteurized: of soil that is heat-sterilized before planting.

pathogen: a disease-causing organism.

pedicel: the small stalk that joins each flower to the main stem.

pendent: of flowers, hanging down from their stalks or pedicels, as in *Lilium martagon, L. pardalinum,* and their hybrids.

perianth: the envelope of a flower, especially one in which the petals and sepals are so alike as to be indistinguishable, as in lilies, composed of three petals and three sepals.

petiole: the stem or slender stalk of a leaf, pronounced in such lily species as *Lilium auratum* and *L. amabile*.

pistil: the central female part of the flower, composed of the ovary, style, and stigma.

pollen: powdery grains produced on the anthers following their dehiscence; contains the male reproductive material.

pollen parent: the plant that provides the pollen used in a cross.

pollinate: to transfer pollen from the anthers of one flower to the stigma of another.

polyploid: having more than the normal multiple of chromosomes for the species. Lilies are normally **diploid**, with 24 chromosomes (2×12); they may also be **triploid** $(3 \times 12 = 36)$ or **tetraploid** $(4 \times 12 = 48)$. Polyploidy may occur naturally but is usually induced by colchicine treatment; polyploid plants are larger and more substantial than diploid counterparts in all respects.

propagate: to multiply plants, either by vegetative means or by sowing seed.

pubescence: soft, fine hairs or down on the surfaces of plant parts; in lilies, occurs on some leaves, stems, and buds, most heavily on buds.

raceme: a simple inflorescence with pedicels spaced fairly evenly, one above another, to the top of the stem.

reciprocal cross: a cross in which the pollen parent becomes the seed parent, and the seed parent becomes the pollen parent.

reflexed: of flowers, in which the petals recurve sharply, as in *Lilium martagon* and most North American species.

rhizome: a perennial, stout, horizontally branching rootstock; in rhizomatous lilies, new bulbs are produced as extensions of this rhizome; examples are *Lilium pardalinum* and *L. canadense.*

rogue: a plant that does not conform to the variety planted.

scales: fleshy, modified leaves which form the lily bulb; used extensively in propagation.

seed parent: in a cross, the parent that produces the seed.

seedling: a small plant grown from seed, distinguished from one produced vegetatively; also, an unnamed mature plant raised from seed.

segment: one of the six parts of the lily perianth.

selfing: pollinating the stigma with pollen from the anthers of the same plant or clone; ineffective in lilies, which are self-sterile.

self-sterile: of a plant, incapable of being fertilized by pollen taken from the same plant or a genetically identical one.

senesce: to dry up and turn brown.

singulation: the process of separating clumps of bulbs that have been tissue cultured.

species: a naturally occurring group of plants which breed true among themselves, with minor variations; the second word in the italicized botanical name of a plant.

stamen: the pollen-bearing organ of a flower, consisting of the filament and the anther.

stem bulblets: small bulbs growing underground on the stem between the bulb and ground level.

stem roots: roots emerging from the stem underground between the bulb and ground level; present in most lilies, they support and nourish the plant.

sterile: incapable of reproducing, either as a seed or a pollen parent; lilies may be seed-sterile, pollen-sterile, both, or neither.

stigma: structure on the end of the pistil which receives the pollen; often bathed with a sticky substance, stigmatic fluid, when receptive.

stoloniferous: of bulbs, producing new bulbs on the ends of long rhizomes called **stolons**; examples are *Lilium superbum, L. grayi,* and *L. michiganense.*

stoloniform: of lilies, having stems that creep horizontally underground before emerging; one or more small to full-sized bulbs may form along the stem before it emerges; examples are *Lilium lankongense* and *L. nepalense*.

stomate: a minute orifice or pore in the epidermis of plant tissue, especially leaves and stems, which opens and closes to regulate the passage of air and water vapor.

strain: a group of genetically related lilies that strongly resemble one another, primarily in color and flowering season; derived from repeated crosses of similar parents which consistently produce uniform seedling populations.

style: the stalk of the ovary, bearing the stigma at its apex.

subculture: to divide a culture into multiple new cultures, as in tissue culture.

substance: the thickness of the perianth tissue; lilies with good substance generally are longer-lasting and therefore more desirable.

TBZ: thiabendazole, a fungicide.

tepal: a perianth segment.

transfer chamber: a glass-topped box with or without a germicidal ultraviolet light that is used to provide a sterile environment for tissue culture.

umbel: type of inflorescence in which several nearly equal flower stalks radiate from a small area at the top of the main stem, like the spokes of an umbrella or a wheel.

variety: in botany, a subdivision of a species displaying one or more distinct characteristics, such as *Lilium amabile* var. *luteum*; in horticulture, often used incorrectly as a synonym for **cultivar**.

vegetative propagation: multiplying a plant by a means other than seed; in lilies, by bulbils, bulblets, scales, or tissue culture.

vernalization: cold storage for a given period, differs for lily divisions.

viable: usually of seed, capable of living and developing normally into a seedling.

viruliferous: virus-bearing.

virus: a microscopic disease-producing organism which invades cells and alters their genetic composition; in lilies, spread primarily by aphids.

whorl: a ring of leaves attached at the same level on the stem; typical of *Lilium martagon* and most American species.

Bibliography

de Graaff, Jan. 1951. *The New Book of Lilies.* New York: M. Barrows & Company.

de Graaff, Jan, and Edward Hyams. 1967. *Lilies.* London: Funk & Wagnalls.

Feldmaier, Carl. 1970. *Die neuen Lilien.* Stuttgart: Verlag Eugen Ulmer; trans. as *Lilies.* Batsford.

Feldmaier, Carl, and Judith F. McRae. 1982. *Lilien.* Stuttgart: Verlag Eugen Ulmer.

Fox, Derek. 1985. *Growing Lilies.* London: Croom Helm.

Haw, Stephen G. 1986. *The Lilies of China.* Portland, Oregon: Timber Press.

Hornback, Earl. 1962. "Color Distribution in Trumpet Lilies." *Lily Year Book* of the Royal Horticultural Society.

Kyte, Lydiane, and John Kleyn. 1996. *Plants from Test Tubes: An Introduction to Micropropagation.* 3rd ed. Portland, Oregon: Timber Press.

Matthews, Victoria. 1984. "*Lilium pyrenaicum*: A complex species," *Kew Magazine* 1984 (part 1): 36–43.

Munz, Philip A., and David D. Keck. 1968. *A California Flora.* 4th ed. Berkeley: University of California Press.

North American Lily Society. 1948–. *The Lily Yearbook.* Published annually by the Society.

Royal Horticultural Society. 1973–. *Lilies and Other Liliaceae.* Published annually to biannually. London: RHS.

Royal Horticultural Society. 1992. *The New Royal Horticulture Society Dictionary of Gardening.* London: Macmillan.

Royal Horticultural Society Lily Committee. 1972. *Lilies and Allied Plants.* London: RHS.

Royal Horticultural Society Lily Group. 1981, 1982. *Bulletin.* London: RHS.

Royal Horticultural Society Lily Group. 1985. *Lilies and Related Plants, 1984/85.* London: RHS.

Slate, George L. *Lilies for American Gardens.* New York and London: Penguin.

Synge, P. M. 1980. *Lilies.* London: Batsford.

Wilson, E. H. 1925. *The Lilies of Eastern Asia.* London: Dulau.

Woodcock, H. B. D., and W. T. Stearn. 1950. *Lilies of the World: Their Cultivation and Classification.* London: Country Life.

Index of Plant Names